AIRLINER PERFORMANCE

INSIGHTS FOR AVIATION BUSINESS PROFESSIONALS

A COMPREHENSIVE TEXTBOOK

SHANNON ACKERT

Aircraft Monitor

Paperback ISBN: ISBN 979-8-9924958-0-5
Ebook ISBN 979-8-9924958-1-2

Cover design by Jess LaGreca, Mayfly book design

Library of Congress Control Number: 2025902077
First Printing: 2025

Table of Contents

List of Figures

List of Tables

Preface

Over my career in the aircraft leasing industry, I have developed a deep understanding of asset-oriented investing, particularly in identifying the characteristics that make an aircraft resilient and valuable. The most sought-after aircraft consistently maintain high residual values, driven by market dominance, a broad customer base, and widespread global operations. Their ability to transition seamlessly between operators in active, liquid markets further enhances asset flexibility and appeal.

Despite this, aircraft financing is often treated separately from performance analysis, prioritizing traditional valuation metrics over a comprehensive understanding of how an aircraft's capabilities influence its operational success. This book addresses that gap by focusing exclusively on the technical and performance attributes that define an aircraft's efficiency and capability.

Organized into two parts, this textbook provides a deep dive into the key aspects of aircraft performance:

- **Part 1: Aircraft Characteristics**—Covers foundational topics such as aircraft weights, capacities (cabin, fuel, and cargo), payload capabilities, and engine attributes.
- **Part 2: Aircraft Performance**—Builds on these foundations, addressing study-flight rules, airport characteristics, performance analysis, and strategies for enhancing performance.

Each section integrates industry perspectives, real-world applications, and examples to bridge theory and practice. To deepen understanding, two case studies are included per chapter, providing practical insights into key concepts. Practical exercises, diagrams, and key takeaways further reinforce learning, while a glossary clarifies technical terms for enhanced comprehension.

Designed for professionals and students, this book provides a clear and structured introduction to aircraft performance, equipping readers with the knowledge to navigate the complexities of aircraft characteristics and their impact on operations and efficiency.

Shannon Ackert
March, 2025

Section 1

Aircraft Characteristics

Chapter 1

Aircraft Weights

This Chapter is About:

This chapter examines aircraft weights and their impact on performance. We begin by exploring different **weight groups**, including empty weight, zero-fuel weight (ZFW), taxi weight, takeoff weight (TOW), and landing weight. Proper management of these weights is essential to optimizing fuel consumption, maximizing payload, extending range, and ensuring compliance with safety and regulatory limits. These factors collectively enhance operational flexibility and play a critical role in benchmarking an airliner's performance and efficiency.

After our deep dive into weight groups, we shift our focus to **gross weights**, which represent the total weight of the aircraft at any point during its operation, including passengers, cargo, and fuel. This weight changes primarily due to fuel consumption during flight and directly impacts the aircraft's balance, performance, and fuel efficiency.

Our next section covers aircraft limit weights, which are critical for safe and effective operation. We examine two categories: **structural limit weights** and **certified limit weights**. Structural limit weights, such as Maximum Design Takeoff Weight (MDTOW), represent the highest weight an aircraft can safely manage based on its design and structural capability. These limits are determined by the aircraft's **build specifications** and must comply with **regulatory requirements**, ensuring the airframe operates within safe margins and the center of gravity (CG) envelope is maintained without overstressing the structure.

Certified limit weights are the maximum allowable weights that can be **legally used**, as listed in the Aircraft Flight Manual (AFM), and set by regulatory authorities for operating an aircraft. These limits are selected by the operator based on operational needs and are often set lower than the structural limit weights. Operators may choose to set certified limits below the structural capabilities to reduce purchase costs and lower associated fees like landing and navigation charges. These limits consider operation type (passenger or cargo) and route network, ensuring that the aircraft operates within safe, efficient, and regulatory-approved parameters.

We then explore weight efficiency, focusing on **structural efficiency** and **payload efficiency**. These metrics evaluate how effectively an aircraft's structural design supports its payload, which includes passengers, cargo, and fuel. A detailed examination of these metrics provides insights into how aircraft design and construction are optimized to balance weight, maximize payload capacity, and meet performance requirements efficiently.

By the end of this chapter, you will have a solid understanding of aircraft weight groups, limit weights, and structural efficiency, enhancing your ability to assess different aircraft types' performance.

1.1 Weight Groups

Weight is a critical factor in evaluating an aircraft's performance capabilities and structural integrity. To effectively benchmark airliners, it is essential to understand the different weight elements that comprise an aircraft's overall weight profile. These elements form the foundation of various weight groups, each playing a vital role in the aircraft's design, certification, and operational limits.

The following are key components of an aircraft's weight profile:

- **Weight Elements:** Weight elements refer to the key components that contribute to the total aircraft weight, categorized systematically to define operational and regulatory weight limits. These elements include airframe structure, propulsion systems, onboard equipment, payload (passengers, baggage, cargo), and fuel (trip fuel, reserve fuel).
- **Weight Groups:** These broader categories combine various weight elements and define an aircraft's operational boundaries. Key weight groups include the **Operating Empty Weight (OEW), Zero-Fuel Weight (ZFW)**, **Landing Weight**, **Takeoff Weight (TOW)**, and **Taxi Weight**. These groups are essential for determining an aircraft's payload capacity, range, and compliance with safety standards.

Aviation regulatory bodies, such as the **FAA** and **EASA**, use these weight groups to set operational parameters during certification. These parameters include **Maximum Taxi Weight (MTW)**, **Maximum Takeoff Weight (MTOW)**, **Maximum Zero-Fuel Weight (MZFW)**, and **Maximum Landing Weight (MLW)**. Together, these limits define an aircraft's safe operational boundaries and directly influence its payload capacity and range.

As shown in **Figure 1-1**, the different weight elements of an aircraft form the foundation for organized weight groups, each representing a distinct operational configuration. These groups, which include components like fuel, passenger, and cargo weights, are critical in shaping an aircraft's performance characteristics, such as range, payload capacity, and fuel efficiency. For example, an aircraft with a lower **Zero-Fuel Weight (ZFW)** can carry more fuel, extending its range, while one with a higher **Landing Weight (LW)** may be optimized for shorter routes with higher payloads. These variations in weight configurations significantly impact an aircraft's operational profile, highlighting the importance of understanding these distinctions when benchmarking aircraft performance.

Figure 1-1. Aircraft weight elements and groups

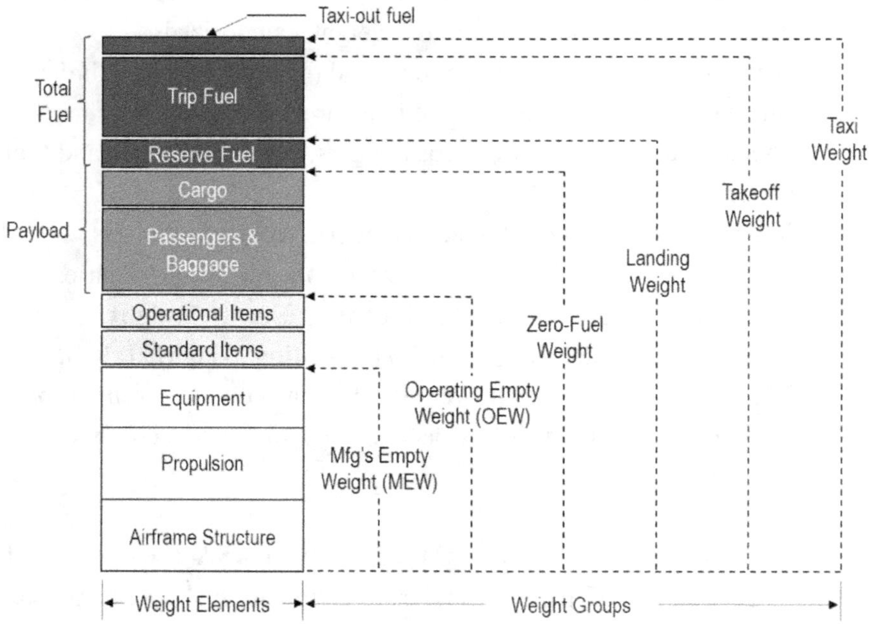

Source: Author's analysis.

1.1.1 Manufacturing Empty Weight (MEW)

The **Manufacturing Empty Weight (MEW)**, also called **Basic Empty Weight (BEW)**, represents the weight of an aircraft in its most fundamental form as it comes off the production line. This weight includes the airframe, engines, and installed systems but excludes operational fluids (e.g., fuel and oil), crew, their baggage, passengers, cargo, and any mission-specific equipment or modifications.

MEW is a relatively constant weight figure, serving as a baseline for understanding an aircraft's structural design. It excludes additional elements added for specific operations, providing a consistent reference point for aligning structural components with performance specifications. In contrast, **Operating Empty Weight (OEW)**, which includes standard and operational items, can vary due to changes such as interior modifications or equipment updates.

The MEW encompasses essential structural and propulsion elements that define an aircraft's baseline configuration:

- **Airframe Structure:** This comprises the fuselage, wings, landing gear, tail group, and other essential structural elements.
- **Propulsion System:** Encompasses the engines, cowlings, quick-exchange components (QEC), and thrust reversers, which assist in slowing the aircraft after landing.
- **Equipment:** Includes the auxiliary power unit (APU), seats, galleys, emergency equipment, communication and navigation hardware, furnishings, wheels, and tires.

As illustrated in **Figure 1-2**, these components collectively define the MEW of an aircraft. Understanding MEW provides a foundational reference for evaluating an aircraft's structural design and its alignment with intended performance capabilities.

Figure 1-2. MEW Components

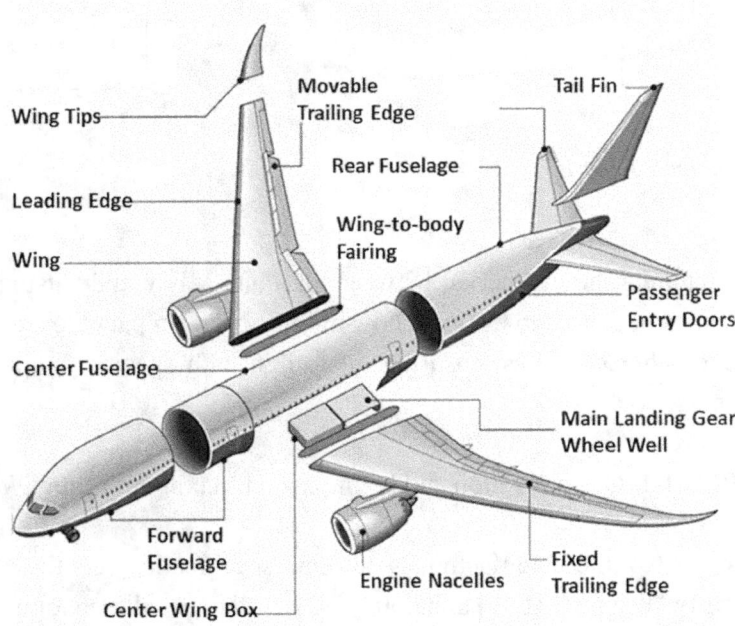

Source: Supply Chain Management Blog [1], with modifications by the author

Baseline MEW vs. Operator (Customized) MEW

Baseline MEW refers to the weight of an aircraft built to the manufacturer's standard specifications, without any customer-specific modifications. This baseline serves as a reference point, allowing customers and operators to tailor the aircraft to meet their unique operational needs. The resulting **Customized MEW**, which incorporates these modifications, is documented in a **Detailed Specification Document** unique to each aircraft. This document provides a comprehensive record of the aircraft's configuration post-customization, detailing any changes made from the baseline (see **Figure 1-3**).

Figure 1-3. Baseline vs. detail specification

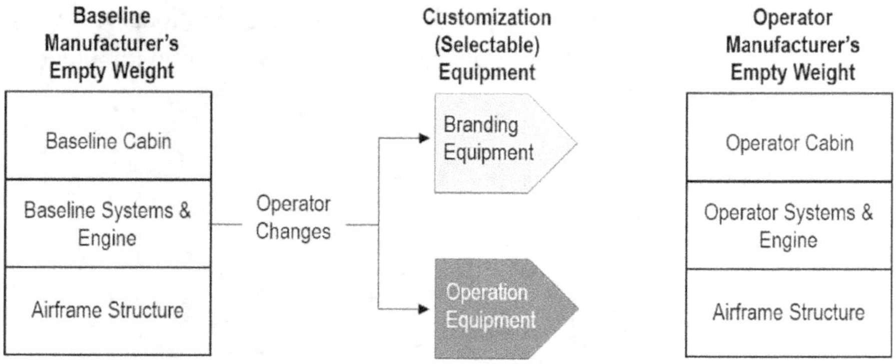

Baseline Manufacturer's Empty Weight	Customization (Selectable) Equipment	Operator Manufacturer's Empty Weight
Baseline Cabin	Branding Equipment	Operator Cabin
Baseline Systems & Engine — Operator Changes		Operator Systems & Engine
Airframe Structure	Operation Equipment	Airframe Structure

Source: Author's analysis

Understanding the distinction between Baseline MEW and Customized MEW enables operators to evaluate how modifications impact the aircraft's performance characteristics, ensuring they align with specific operational requirements.

EXAMPLE 1-1. Customization and Its Impact on Maximum Empty Weight (MEW)

In **Figure 1-4**, the manufacturer's baseline specification sets the **Maximum Empty Weight (MEW)** at 88,500 lbs., based on an all-economy, 189-seat layout with steel brakes. The operator, however, makes several configuration changes: a dual-class 178-seat interior, carbon brakes replacing steel, and an in-flight entertainment system. These modifications increase the MEW from 88,500 lbs. to a revised 90,000 lbs.

Figure 1-4. Adjustment from baseline to operator MEW

Baseline Manufacturer's Empty Weight (MEW)		88,500 lb
Baseline Specification		
189Y Seats: Interior 24,000 lb-thrust Engines 154,200 MTOW Steel Brakes	4,725 lb	
Operator Specification		
Interior change to 178 seats (12 BC / 166 Y)	4,925 lb	200 lb
26,000 lb-thrust Engine		
174,200 lb MTOW (paper change)		
Carbon Brakes		(700 lb)
In-Flight Entertainment System (11.2 lb/seat)		2,000 lb
Operator Manufacturer's Empty Weight (MEW)		90,000 lb

Source: Author's analysis

These modifications demonstrate how operator-specific changes can influence MEW. Key examples include:

- **Interior Configuration:** Switching from an all-economy to a dual-class interior layout increases weight due to variations in seating arrangements and additional cabin amenities.
- **Brake System:** Replacing steel brakes with carbon brakes results in weight savings, as carbon brakes are significantly lighter.
- **In-Flight Entertainment:** Adding an in-flight entertainment system increases weight due to the additional equipment and wiring.

Understanding the impact of these changes on MEW is essential for operators to effectively plan and manage the aircraft's performance capabilities.

This example underscores the significance of **Customized MEW** in benchmarking airliners, as such variations can have a substantial effect on performance metrics.

Industry Perspective 1-1. *Flyaway Price Determination*

*The **flyaway price** is a critical figure in aircraft acquisition and finance, reflecting an aircraft's configuration, operational readiness, and **Manufacturer's Empty Weight (MEW)**. As illustrated in **Figure 1-5**, the process begins with the manufacturer's baseline price, which includes the basic airframe and standard features such as seating and avionics. This baseline price represents the aircraft in its initial operational state.*

Figure 1-5. Flyaway price breakdown

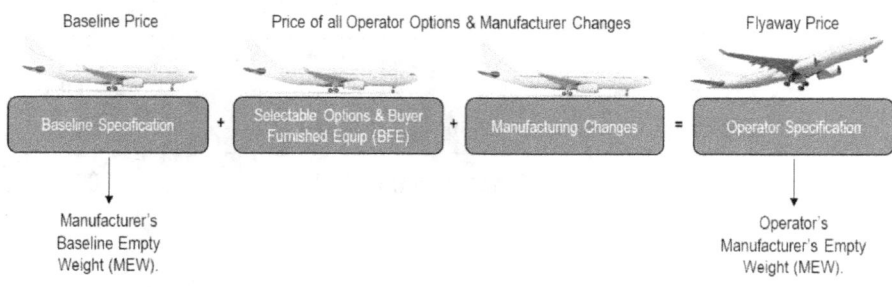

Source: Author's analysis

*The next step is the **customization phase**, where customers select features tailored to their specific operational needs and mission profiles. These choices—such as additional features or **buyer-furnished equipment (BFE)**—directly affect the MEW, influencing fuel efficiency, payload capacity, and overall performance. Manufacturers may also provide upgrades or enhancements, occasionally at no extra cost, to incorporate technological advancements or meet regulatory requirements. Whether customer-driven or manufacturer-provided, these modifications shape the final MEW and enhance the aircraft's capabilities.*

*The **flyaway price** combines the manufacturer's baseline price, customer-selected options, BFE, and manufacturer upgrades. It represents an* *aircraft optimized for specific operational strategies and market demands, offering valuable insights into the financial and operational implications of aircraft acquisition.*

1.1.2 Operating Empty Weight (OEW)

Operating Empty Weight (OEW) is the total weight of an aircraft ready for flight, excluding variable loads such as passengers, baggage, cargo, and usable fuel. It includes the aircraft's **Manufacturer's Empty Weight (MEW)**, non-fuel fluids, onboard supplies, flight crew provisions, and other standard operating items required for flight.

OEW serves as a stable reference point in flight planning and operations, as it remains largely consistent across flights, independent of variable payload and fuel loads. However, it is important to note that OEW is not fixed—it can vary between operators based on factors such as interior configurations, modifications, and optional equipment. For instance, an airline might choose to install extra seats or premium cabin amenities, which could increase OEW and affect operational calculations. See "Factors Influencing OEW" for more details on how these elements impact weight.

Upon delivery, manufacturers provide operators with OEW and center of gravity (CG) data, both of which are critical for payload capacity calculations, fuel consumption projections, and performance guarantees. This baseline information enables operators to effectively plan operations and benchmark aircraft performance, setting the stage for understanding concepts like Useful Load and Maximum Structural Payload in later sections.

OEW is calculated using the following formula:

$$OEW = MEW + SI + OI \quad \text{(Eq. 1-1)}$$

Where:

- **Standard Items (SI):** Uniform equipment and fluids across all aircraft of the same type, such as emergency oxygen, engine oil, and toilet fluids.
- **Operational Items (OI):** Specific to the airline or operator, these can vary between aircraft. Examples include crew and their

baggage, passenger food and beverages, navigation equipment, and mission-specific items like spare parts or life rafts.

Understanding **OEW** is essential in benchmarking airliners, as it provides a consistent reference point for comparing performance across different models. OEW influences key operational calculations, including maximum payload, fuel requirements, and range. Since OEW contributes to the aircraft's total weight, a higher OEW increases takeoff weight, leading to higher fuel consumption for a given mission. Thus, OEW is a critical factor in evaluating an aircraft's performance and operational efficiency.

Building on the importance of OEW, **Useful Load** represents the total weight an aircraft can carry beyond its OEW, including payload (passengers and cargo) and usable fuel. It is calculated by subtracting OEW from the **Maximum Takeoff Weight (MTOW)**. A lower OEW increases the Useful Load, allowing greater flexibility in weight allocation between payload and fuel, which enhances mission capabilities and operational efficiency.

EXAMPLE 1-2. Calculating Operator's Empty Weight (OEW) from Manufacturing Empty Weight (MEW)

Figure 1-6 illustrates the process of adjusting the Manufacturer's Empty Weight (MEW) to calculate the Operator's Empty Weight (OEW). In this example, the MEW is 90,000 lbs. To determine the OEW, two allowances are added: 1,460 lbs. for Standard Items (SI) and 3,640 lbs. for Operator's Items (OI). The resulting OEW is 95,000 lbs.

This method provides operators with a practical approach for calculating OEW, which is crucial for precise flight planning and performance analysis. OEW serves as a consistent basis for benchmarking aircraft by enabling comparisons of performance metrics across models, such as fuel requirements and payload capacity.

Figure 1-6. Adjustment from MEW to OEW

Operator's Manufacturer's Empty Weight (MEW)		90,000 lb
Standard Items Allowance		1,460 lb
Unusable Fuel	130 lb	
Oil	250 lb	
Oxygen Equipment	30 lb	
Miscellaneous Equipment	30 lb	
Galley Structure & Fixed Inserts	1,020 lb	
Operational Items Allowance		3,540 lb
Crew and Crew Baggage	1,320 lb	
Catering Allowance	1,120 lb	
Passenger Service Equipment (178)	355 lb	
Potable Water – 40 USG	345 lb	
Water Tank Disinfectant	5 lb	
Emergency Equipment	395 lb	
Operator's Empty Weight (OEW)		95,000 lb

Source: Author's analysis

Calculation:

OEW = MEW + SI + OI = 90,000 lbs. + 1,460 lbs. + 3,640 lbs. = 95,000 lbs.

This calculation enables operators to accurately determine OEW, a key factor in optimizing aircraft operations and ensuring compliance with weight limitations. By understanding OEW, aviation professionals can make informed decisions about aircraft performance and operational planning.

Industry Perspective 1-2. *Classifying Operational Items*

The classification of Operational Items (OI) in Operating Empty Weight (OEW) calculations is often ambiguous due to the lack of specific guidance from regulatory authorities such as the FAA and EU-OPS. Establishing clear standards would help minimize inconsistencies in OEW calculations across airlines.

*For example, airlines differ in how they classify potable water. Some consider it a **Standard Item (SI)**, including it as a fixed part of OEW, while others treat it as an **Operational Item (OI)**, excluding it because its quantity can vary depending on flight requirements. These differing approaches can significantly affect fuel planning and payload capacity.*

Understanding these discrepancies is critical for benchmarking, as variations in OEW classification influence aircraft performance comparisons across airlines and models. Consistency in classifying Operational Items is essential for ensuring accurate and reliable OEW assessments.

Factors Influencing OEW

An aircraft's **Operating Empty Weight (OEW)** can fluctuate over its service life due to various factors, each affecting performance characteristics differently. The following are key contributors to these fluctuations:

- **Upgrades, Modifications, & Interior Configuration:** Technological upgrades, performance enhancements, and cabin reconfigurations can directly alter OEW. Examples include installing new systems for passenger comfort, adjusting cabin layouts, or changing the number of seats. Such modifications affect key performance metrics; for instance, an increase in OEW reduces the weight available for payload, impacting calculations like Maximum Structural Payload (MSP) (discussed in Chapter 3, Payload Capacities).
- **Maintenance and Repairs:** OEW can change due to maintenance activities, part replacements, or repairs. Depending on the nature of these updates, OEW may increase or decrease, altering performance characteristics.
- **Regulatory Changes:** Compliance with new aviation regulations may require additional equipment or system modifications, leading to increased OEW. For example, safety features mandated by regulatory bodies like **EASA** or the **FAA** can add weight.
- **Environmental and Material Accumulation**: Over time, exposure to environmental elements and material build-up, such as dirt, contaminants, or moisture retention in cabin insulation, can gradually increase OEW, impacting performance.

While OEW generally remains stable, operators must monitor changes arising from modifications, maintenance, and environmental factors. Regulatory bodies require periodic aircraft weighing (typically every 3–4 years) to ensure OEW accuracy. Consistent monitoring is essential for maintaining reliable OEW data, critical for both performance optimization and regulatory compliance.

1.1.3 Zero-Fuel Weight (ZFW)

Zero-Fuel Weight (ZFW) is a key metric in flight planning and performance analysis, representing the total weight of the aircraft excluding usable fuel. ZFW comprises the **Operating Empty Weight (OEW)**—which includes the aircraft's basic weight, crew, and fixed equipment—and the **payload**, consisting of passengers, baggage, and cargo. The formula for ZFW is as follows:

$$ZFW = OEW + Payload = OEW + W\_\ passengers + W\_baggage + W\_cargo \quad (Eq.\ 1\text{-}2)$$

This equation illustrates the direct relationship between OEW and ZFW. Even small increases in OEW—due to additional equipment, cabin modifications, or operator-specific configurations—can reduce payload capacity, limiting the available weight for passengers, cargo, or fuel.

EXAMPLE 1-3. Determining Zero-Fuel Weight (ZFW) from Operator's Empty Weight (OEW)

As shown in **Figure 1-7**, ZFW is calculated starting with an OEW of **95,000 lbs.** Adding a payload of **42,160 lbs.** (including passengers, baggage, and cargo) results in a ZFW of **137,160 lbs.**

Figure 1-7. Adjustment from OEW to ZFW

Operator's Empty Weight (OEW)		**95,000 lb**
Payload		**42,160 lb**
Passengers * (178)	32,040 lb	
Baggage *	7,120 lb	
Cargo	3,000 lb	
Zero Fuel Weight (ZFW)		**137,160 lb**

*The following average passenger and baggage weight is assumed:
Passenger = 180 lb (82 kg)
Baggage = 40 lb (18 kg)*

Source: Author's analysis

The example demonstrates how Operating Empty Weight (OEW) and payload combine to determine Zero-Fuel Weight (ZFW). Key takeaways include:

- The contribution of passengers, baggage, and cargo to the overall payload emphasizes the importance of optimizing each component to stay within ZFW limits.
- ZFW as a baseline: Because ZFW remains constant during flight, it directly influences how much fuel can be added without exceeding the Maximum Takeoff Weight (MTOW), impacting range and operational flexibility.
- Adjusting passenger and baggage assumptions (e.g., average weights) could alter the payload distribution, influencing ZFW and overall operational efficiency.

Operational Impact of Zero-Fuel Weight (ZFW)

Zero-Fuel Weight (ZFW) plays an essential role in flight planning and operational performance. Since ZFW remains unchanged throughout the flight, it provides a critical baseline for determining the allowable fuel load while staying within the Maximum Takeoff Weight (MTOW).

A higher ZFW, often driven by increased OEW due to additional passenger amenities, cabin modifications, or heavier operational equipment, reduces the available fuel weight within MTOW limits, directly impacting the aircraft's range. For instance, an aircraft with a heavier cabin or added equipment may require payload or fuel reductions on long-haul routes to comply with weight restrictions and achieve the necessary range.

Thus, managing ZFW is essential for optimizing range and operational flexibility, particularly on fuel-sensitive routes. Maintaining a careful balance between payload, ZFW, and MTOW ensures operational efficiency and supports the airline's ability to meet performance and profitability targets.

1.1.4 Takeoff Weight (TOW)

Takeoff Weight (TOW) is the total weight of an aircraft at the start of its takeoff roll or brake release. It includes the aircraft's weight, fuel, passengers, cargo, and any additional items loaded for the flight. Fuel weight, a significant component, varies based on factors such as the flight profile, weather conditions, alternate airport needs, and specific airline policies.

TOW is calculated by adding the Zero-Fuel Weight (ZFW) to the fuel onboard for the flight. The total fuel weight includes **taxi fuel**, **trip fuel**, and **reserve fuel**. The formula for TOW is expressed as:

$$TOW = ZFW + \text{Fuel at takeoff} \quad \text{(Eq. 1-3)}$$

Where:

$$\text{Fuel at takeoff} = \text{Total Fuel} - \text{Taxi-out Fuel}$$
$$\text{Total Fuel} = \text{Trip Fuel} + \text{Reserve Fuel} + \text{Taxi-out Fuel}$$

Therefore, an alternate equation for TOW is:

$$TOW = ZFW + \text{Trip Fuel} + \text{Reserve Fuel} - \text{Taxi-out Fuel} \quad \text{(Eq. 1-4)}$$

EXAMPLE 1-4. Deriving TOW from ZFW and Takeoff Fuel

Figure 1-8 illustrates the adjustment from Zero-Fuel Weight (ZFW) to Takeoff Weight (TOW). Starting with a ZFW of 137,160 lbs., the Takeoff

Fuel is calculated as 20,000 lbs. by subtracting Taxi-out Fuel from Total Fuel. This adjustment prevents double counting in the calculations. The resulting Takeoff Weight (TOW) is 157,160 lbs.

Figure 1-8. Adjustment from ZFW to TOW

Zero Fuel Weight (ZFW)			137,160 lb
Takeoff Fuel			**20,000 lb**
Total Fuel		20,500 lb	
Taxi-out Fuel	500 lb		
Trip Fuel (1,000 nm)	14,000 lb		
Reserve Fuel	6,000 lb		
Taxi-out Fuel		(500 lb)	
Takeoff Weight (TOW)			**157,160 lb**

Source: Author's analysis

Operational Impact of Takeoff Weight (TOW)

Takeoff Weight (TOW) is a critical factor in an aircraft's operational performance, influencing takeoff, climb, payload capacity, and structural stress. The following are key areas where TOW plays a significant role:

1. **Takeoff and Climb**
   » **Takeoff Roll**: A higher TOW requires a longer runway to reach liftoff speed due to slower acceleration. This is especially critical at airports with shorter runways or in challenging conditions like high altitudes or hot weather.
   » **Climb Efficiency**: Increased TOW reduces climb performance, requiring more thrust and resulting in a shallower climb angle. This affects fuel efficiency, increases time to cruising altitude, and may impact obstacle clearance and noise levels near airports.
2. **Operational Constraints**
   » **Payload Versus Range Tradeoff**: At maximum TOW, airlines must balance fuel and payload. Carrying more payload reduces

fuel capacity, limiting range, while maximizing fuel limits payload capacity but extends range.

» **Runway Constraints**: Higher TOW may restrict operations to airports with longer runways, influencing route planning and airport selection.

3. **Maintenance and Safety Considerations**

» **Engine Wear**: Higher TOW increases engine strain, requiring greater thrust during takeoff and climb, accelerating wear and raising maintenance requirements.

» **Structural Stress**: Elevated TOW places additional pressure on the aircraft's structure, particularly the wings and landing gear, potentially reducing their lifespan and necessitating closer monitoring for fatigue.

EXAMPLE 1-5. Payload Versus Range Tradeoff for the A320CEO

The **A320CEO** has a Maximum Takeoff Weight (MTOW) of 77 tonnes and a typical Operating Empty Weight (OEW) of approximately 42 tonnes. This leaves 35 tonnes available for Useful Load, which includes both payload (passengers, baggage, and cargo) and fuel.

1. **Scenario 1: Short-Haul Route with High Payload**

» **Payload:** 20 tonnes (e.g., full passenger load with baggage and some cargo).

» **Fuel Weight:** 15 tonnes (sufficient for a short-haul flight of ~1,500 nm).

» **Range:** The aircraft can operate this shorter route with a heavier payload, maximizing revenue from passengers and cargo.

2. **Scenario 2: Long-Haul Route with Maximum Range**

» **Payload:** 10 tonnes (e.g., reduced passenger load with minimal cargo).

» **Fuel Weight:** 25 tonnes (to achieve a maximum range of ~3,300 nm).

» **Range:** By reducing payload, the aircraft can carry enough fuel to complete a longer flight, such as connecting secondary hubs across continents.

1.1.5 Taxi Weight (TW)

Taxi Weight (TW) is the total weight of an aircraft as it begins to taxi from the terminal to the runway for takeoff. This weight includes the aircraft itself, passengers, cargo, operational items, and all onboard fuel, including the fuel that will be consumed during taxiing.

During taxiing, the aircraft burns a portion of its fuel, reducing its weight by the time it reaches the runway. Taxi Weight accounts for this fuel consumption by including Taxi Fuel in the initial weight calculation. The formula for calculating Taxi Weight is:

$$TW = ZFW + Total\ Fuel \quad (Eq.\ 1\text{-}5)$$

Where: Total Fuel = Trip Fuel + Reserve Fuel + Taxi Fuel

Alternatively, the equation can be expressed as:

$$TW = OEW + Payload + Total\ Fuel \quad (Eq.\ 1\text{-}6)$$

EXAMPLE 1-6. Deriving TW from ZFW and Total Fuel

Figure 1-9 illustrates how to adjust the Zero-Fuel Weight (ZFW) to determine the Taxi Weight (TW). Starting with a ZFW of 137,160 lbs., we add the Total Fuel weight of 20,500 lbs. After adding this fuel weight to the ZFW, the resulting Taxi Weight (TW) is 157,660 lbs.

Figure 1-9. Adjustment from ZFW to TW

Takeoff Weight (TOW)	**157,160 lb**
Taxi-out Fuel	500 lb
Taxi Weight (TW)	**157,660 lb**

Source: Author's analysis

1.1.6 Landing Weight (LW)

Landing Weight (LW) is the weight of an aircraft at the moment it touches down on the runway. It is derived from the Zero-Fuel Weight (ZFW) and the fuel remaining onboard at landing, which includes reserve fuel and any additional unburned fuel.

Landing Weight comprises two primary components:

1. **Zero-Fuel Weight (ZFW)**: The sum of the Operating Empty Weight (OEW) and the payload.
2. **Fuel Onboard at Landing:**
   » **Reserve Fuel:** Mandated by aviation regulations to account for unforeseen circumstances like delays or diversions, serving as a safety buffer.
   » **Additional Fuel Not Used:** Any extra fuel beyond the trip and reserve requirements, providing flexibility in managing unexpected situations.

The formula for calculating Landing Weight is:

$$LW = ZFW + \text{Fuel on Board at Landing} \quad \text{(Eq. 1-7)}$$

or more explicitly:

$$LW = OEW + \text{Payload} + \text{Weight of Reserve Fuel}$$
$$+ \text{Additional Fuel Not Used} \quad \text{(Eq. 1-8)}$$

In an ideal scenario where all trip fuel is consumed, leaving only reserve fuel at landing:

$$LW = ZFW + \text{Weight of Reserve Fuel} \quad \text{(Eq. 1-9)}$$

This assumes optimal fuel consumption, emphasizing reserve fuel as a critical safety margin. Factors such as weather, air traffic, or operational adjustments may cause deviations, making it essential to understand this relationship for effective fuel management and operational planning.

EXAMPLE 1-7. Deriving LW From ZFW & Reserve Fuel

To determine Landing Weight (LW), assume a ZFW of 137,160 lbs. and reserve fuel of 6,000 lbs. If all trip fuel is consumed, the Landing Weight (LW) would be:

LW = 137,160 lbs. + 6,000 lbs. = 143,160 lbs. This is detailed in **Figure 1-10**.

Figure 1-10. Adjustment from ZFW to LW

Zero Fuel Weight (ZFW)	137,160 lb
Reserve Fuel	6,000 lb
Landing Weight (LW))	143,160 lb

Source: Author's analysis

Operational Impact of Landing Weight (LW)

Landing Weight (LW) has a direct impact on aircraft performance during landing. Key considerations include:

- **Landing Roll and Deceleration**: Higher LW increases momentum, requiring longer distances to decelerate and stop. Runways must be long enough to safely accommodate the increased weight.
- **Structural Loads**: Elevated LW places more stress on the aircraft structure, particularly the landing gear and wings, potentially necessitating more frequent maintenance checks to ensure structural integrity.
- **Brake Energy Limits**: Heavier landing weights require greater energy absorption by the braking system, increasing the risk of overheating or brake failure. This accelerates brake wear and tear, impacting operational safety and requiring close monitoring.

1.2 Gross Weights

Gross Weight refers to the total weight of an aircraft at any given point during its operation. This includes the aircraft's empty weight, passengers, cargo, fuel, and other onboard loads. Unlike Zero-Fuel Weight (ZFW)—which remains constant throughout the flight—Gross Weight changes dynamically due to fuel consumption. Gross Weight is subject to certified weight limits, such as Maximum Taxi Weight (MTW), Maximum Takeoff Weight (MTOW), and Maximum Landing Weight (MLW), which define structural thresholds for safe operation (see **Section 1.4**). A thorough understanding of Gross Weight dynamics and its variation across flight phases is fundamental for efficient flight planning, operational range, and payload optimization.

Effective Gross Weight Management

Airlines focus on weight optimization strategies that indirectly impact Gross Weight. For example:

- Some carriers reduce **Operating Empty Weight (OEW)** by installing lightweight seating and galley equipment, allowing more payload or fuel flexibility without exceeding weight limits.
- Airlines monitor potable water consumption trends and adjust onboard water loads to reduce unnecessary weight, directly impacting Gross Weight at departure.

Weight Variation Across Mission Profile Phases

Understanding Gross Weight dynamics across each stage of a flight is essential for effective weight management. **Figure 1-11, Mission Profile Phases**, illustrates the specific weight and fuel changes at each flight phase, helping operators monitor weight fluctuations throughout the journey.

During the mission profile, Gross Weight evolves as fuel is consumed. Each phase of the flight—taxi, takeoff, climb, cruise, descent, and landing—presents unique weight considerations that influence aircraft performance and operational decisions. Key highlights include:

- **Taxi**: Taxi Weight (TW) represents the aircraft's weight after engine start, incorporating payload, fuel, and operational fluids, but excluding the fuel burned during taxi-out.
- **Takeoff**: Takeoff Weight (TOW) includes Zero-Fuel Weight (ZFW), required Trip Fuel, and any contingency fuel. It represents the maximum weight at which the aircraft can safely lift off.
- **Climb**: Fuel is consumed at an accelerated rate due to the higher power output needed for liftoff and altitude gain, leading to a significant reduction in Gross Weight.
- **Cruise**: At stable altitude, fuel consumption moderates, resulting in a gradual decrease in Gross Weight that improves aerodynamic efficiency and reduces fuel burn.
- **Descent and Landing**: Fuel burn decreases as engine power requirements are lower. Landing Weight (LW) accounts for the remaining fuel and is a critical factor for safe touchdown. If actual Landing Weight exceeds the Maximum Landing Weight (MLW), operational adjustments such as fuel burn-off or fuel jettison (for aircraft equipped with fuel dump systems) may be required to comply with landing limitations.

Figure 1-11. Mission profile phases

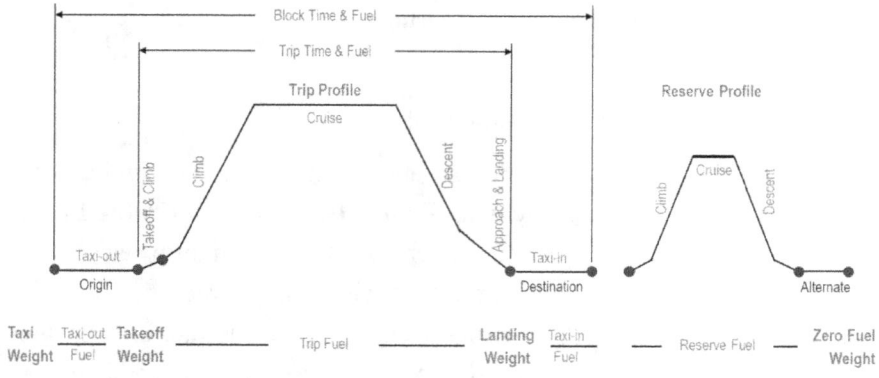

Source: Author's analysis

These phase-specific weight metrics are essential for maintaining an optimal balance of payload, operational efficiency, and safety throughout the flight.

Fuel Management's Role in Gross Weight Dynamics

Fuel components impacting Gross Weight include:

1. **Block Fuel** – The total fuel onboard at departure, covering **taxi, trip, alternate, reserve, and contingency fuel**.
2. **Trip Fuel** – The fuel required **from takeoff to landing**, excluding reserves and alternate fuel.

Effective fuel management directly impacts operational range, payload capacity, and weight distribution, ensuring alignment with mission requirements.

Integrating Gross Weight and Mission Phase Insights

The interplay between Gross Weight dynamics and flight phases is a cornerstone of flight planning. Heavier weights allow for greater payload and revenue but increase drag, fuel consumption, and operational costs—especially during takeoff and climb. By carefully monitoring weight fluctuations, operators can optimize flight efficiency, manage costs, and maintain compliance with safety margins.

EXAMPLE 1-8. Estimating an Aircraft's Pre-Departure Gross Weights
Flight planning requires accurate estimation of an aircraft's total weight before departure to ensure safe and efficient operations. **Figure 1-12** illustrates the calculation process for determining key gross weights prior to a flight. In this scenario:

- **Operating Empty Weight (OEW):** 125,000 lbs.
- **Payload (passengers, baggage, and cargo):** 57,000 lbs.
- **Trip Fuel:** 20,000 lbs.
- **Reserve Fuel:** 10,000 lbs.
- **Taxi-out Fuel:** 1,000 lbs.

Figure 1-12. Gross weight build-up

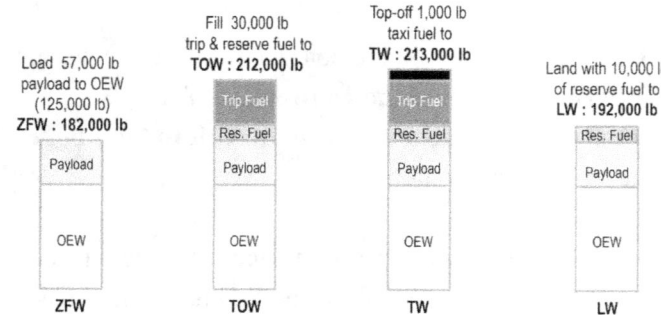

Source: Author's analysis

Gross Weight Build-up Calculations

1. **Zero-Fuel Weight (ZFW):** Calculated as OEW + Payload. ZFW = 125,000 lbs. + 57,000 lbs. = 182,000 lbs.
2. **Takeoff Weight (TOW):** Includes ZFW + Trip Fuel and Reserve Fuel. TOW = 182,000 lbs. + 20,000 lbs. + 10,000 lbs. = 212,000 lbs.
3. **Block Fuel:** Total fuel onboard at departure, including Taxi-out Fuel, Trip Fuel, and Reserve Fuel. Block Fuel = 1,000 lbs. + 20,000 lbs. + 10,000 lbs. = 31,000 lbs.
4. **Taxi Weight (TW):** Calculated as TOW + Taxi-out Fuel. TW = 212,000 lbs. + 1,000 lbs. = 213,000 lbs.
5. **Landing Weight (LW):** Estimated weight upon arrival, calculated as ZFW + Reserve Fuel (assuming no reserve fuel is used). LW = 182,000 lbs. + 10,000 lbs. = 192,000 lbs.

1.3 Structural Limit Weights

Structural Limit Weights, or **Structural Design Weights**, are fundamental to an aircraft's safe operation. Similar to load limits on bridges, these weights define the maximum safe operating thresholds for an aircraft under various conditions. Determined through rigorous testing and analysis, they are a critical component of the aircraft certification process. Adhering to these limits is essential to maintaining structural integrity and ensuring compliance with safety and regulatory standards.

These Structural Limit Weights represent the maximum allowable weights for specific phases of an aircraft's operation and include:

- Maximum Design Taxi Weight (MDTW)
- Maximum Design Takeoff Weight (MDTOW)
- Maximum Design Zero-Fuel Weight (MDZFW)
- Maximum Design Landing Weight (MDLW)

Each of these weights establishes specific operational boundaries, ensuring the aircraft operates safely under various conditions. **Table 1-1** illustrates these critical parameters using the design weights for the Boeing 787-9.

Table 1-1. 787-9 maximum design weights

Structural Design Weight	Weight **lb** (kg)
Maximum Design Taxi Weight	**563,000** (255,372)
Maximum Design Takeoff Weight	**561,500** (254,692)
Maximum Design Landing Weight	**425,000** (192,776)
Maximum Design Zero-Fuel Weight	**400,000** (181,436)

Source: Boeing "787 Airplane Characteristics for Airport Planning" document [2]

In the following sections, we will explore each of these Structural Limit Weights in detail, highlighting their significance in aircraft design and operational performance. Understanding these limits is essential for benchmarking airliners and comparing capabilities across models and manufacturers. By analyzing these parameters, operators and manufacturers gain valuable insights into how design choices impact an aircraft's payload capacity, range, and overall performance.

1.3.1 Maximum Design Zero-Fuel Weight (MDZFW)

The **Maximum Design Zero-Fuel Weight (MDZFW)** is the highest weight an aircraft can carry without usable fuel onboard, meaning any weight above the MDZFW must consist solely of fuel. This limit is determined based on the aircraft's structural strength and airworthiness requirements and is critical for ensuring safe operations.

Structural Significance of MDZFW

The MDZFW is fundamental to maintaining structural integrity, particularly in managing wing stress. This weight limit ensures the aircraft can safely support its payload, which is primarily concentrated in the fuselage. Since the fuselage does not contribute to lift, the wings must generate sufficient lift to support the entire aircraft. This creates a bending moment around the wing root (the point where the wing meets the fuselage), which is most pronounced when the wing fuel tanks are low.

As shown in **Figure 1-13**, fuel stored in the wings typically helps balance the aircraft, reducing structural stress. At MDZFW, with minimal fuel in the tanks, the wings must be designed to safely handle increased stress, highlighting the critical role of MDZFW in structural design.

Figure 1-13: MDZFW limitation

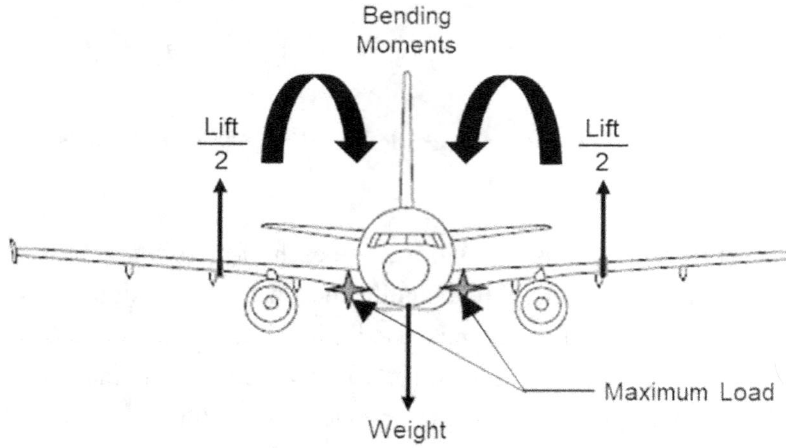

Source: Airbus. "Getting to Grips with Weight & Balance" [3]

Operational Impact of MDZFW

Adhering to the MDZFW is essential to prevent overstress on the wings and overall structure, which could compromise airworthiness. Managing MDZFW is critical during both the design and operational phases, as it directly impacts the durability and strength of key structural components.

Proper planning of payload configurations and fuel distribution is necessary to maintain structural integrity, particularly during flight phases when fuel levels are low, and the wings bear increased loads. For example, operators must carefully balance passenger and cargo weight in the fuselage with fuel in the wings to prevent excessive stress. This underscores the importance of structural limit weights in ensuring safe and efficient operations.

To further understand MDZFW's implications, it is important to examine how it relates to the weight an aircraft can safely carry beyond its Operating Empty Weight (OEW), referred to as Maximum Structural Payload (MSP).

Maximum Structural Payload

The **Maximum Structural Payload (MSP)** is the combined weight of passengers, baggage, and cargo that an aircraft can safely carry, excluding fuel. Understanding MSP is essential for analyzing the Maximum Design Zero-Fuel Weight (MDZFW), a critical limit that specifies the maximum weight the aircraft can safely bear without fuel.

The relationship between MDZFW and MSP is expressed as:

$$\text{MDZFW} = \text{OEW} + \text{Maximum Structural Payload} \quad \text{(Eq. 1-10)}$$

This equation highlights that the MDZFW ensures the combined weight of the aircraft's Operating Empty Weight (OEW) and MSP remains within the design's structural constraints. Understanding and adhering to this limit is essential for safe flight operations and regulatory compliance.

This concept will be further explored in **Chapter 3: Payload Capacities**, where the operational implications of payload management will be discussed in greater detail.

1.3.2 Maximum Design Taxi Weight (MDTW)

The **Maximum Design Taxi Weight (MDTW)** is the highest allowable weight for an aircraft during ground operations. This limit is crucial for maintaining the structural integrity of the landing gear, which must withstand the stresses and dynamic loads encountered during taxiing. These loads include stresses from braking, turning, and rolling over uneven surfaces, all of which are critical considerations in the design of the landing gear.

Although some fuel is burned during taxiing, this generally does not significantly reduce the aircraft's weight before takeoff. To account for this, the MDTW is typically set slightly higher than the Maximum Design Takeoff Weight (MDTOW). For example, the Boeing 737 Max 8 has an MDTW of 182,700 lbs. and an MTOW of 182,200 lbs., a difference of 500 lbs. This small buffer ensures the aircraft remains within safe weight limits during taxiing while allowing for minor fuel burn adjustments to bring it under the MTOW before takeoff.

Adhering to the MDTW is essential for maintaining safety and operational flexibility. It ensures that the aircraft is properly prepared for takeoff under optimal conditions without exceeding its structural design limitations.

1.3.3 Maximum Design Takeoff Weight (MDTOW)

The **Maximum Design Takeoff Weight (MDTOW)**, also known as **Brake Release Gross Weight**, is the maximum weight at which an aircraft is designed and certified to take off safely. This weight includes the aircraft structure, passengers, cargo, crew, and fuel. Determined by the manufacturer and approved by aviation authorities such as the **FAA** (in the U.S.) and **EASA** (in Europe), MDTOW is a critical parameter influencing an aircraft's range, payload capacity, and operational flexibility.

Benefits and Challenges of Increased MDTOW

Increasing MDTOW offers airlines significant operational advantages, particularly in terms of range, payload, and versatility. These benefits allow airlines to optimize routes and meet market demands more effectively:

- **Extended Range:** A higher MDTOW allows the aircraft to carry additional fuel, enabling longer non-stop flights. This is essential for long-haul operations, facilitating direct routes over greater distances, reducing refueling stops, and improving per-trip fuel efficiency. These capabilities open new route opportunities and enhance operational efficiency.

- **Enhanced Payload Capacity:** Increased MDTOW supports additional cargo or passengers, offering flexibility to balance fuel load and payload based on flight requirements and market demand, thus improving operational versatility.
- **Broader Aircraft Utility:** Aircraft with higher MDTOW can serve a wider range of operations, from short-haul, high-density routes to long-haul flights, maximizing deployment options for airlines.

While the benefits of a higher MDTOW are substantial, they come with certain operational challenges. These challenges require careful consideration to ensure safety and efficiency:

- **Longer Takeoff Requirements:** Heavier aircraft need longer runways to reach safe takeoff speeds, potentially limiting operations at airports with shorter runway lengths.
- **Altered Climb Performance:** A higher takeoff weight can reduce climb performance, resulting in slower ascents to cruising altitude. This may increase fuel consumption during the climb phase and impact overall flight efficiency.

Industry Perspective 1-3. *Evolution of 777-200 MDTOW*

Figure 1-14 *illustrates how the MDTOW of the Boeing 777-200 evolved to meet growing operational demands. From its entry into service in 1995 to the introduction of the 777-200LR in 2006, the 777-200's MDTOW increased from 545,000 lbs. for the 777-200 A-market to 766,800 lbs. for the 777-200LR. This progression reflects Boeing's response to the increasing demand for greater payload and extended range capabilities.*

Figure 1-14. 777-200 MDTOW evolution

777-200 A-Market	777-200ER	777-200ER	777-200ER	777-200LR
1995 545,000-lb MDTOW Range: 5,120 nmi	1997 632,500-lb MDTOW Range: 6,940 nmi	1997 650,000-lb MDTOW Range: 7,370 nmi	1999 656,000-lb MDTOW Range: 7,510 nmi	2006 766,800-lb MDTOW Range: 9,290 nmi

Source: Author's analysis

To accommodate the increased MDTOW, Boeing implemented significant structural modifications, including:

- ***Reinforced wing structures***: *The wings were strengthened and redesigned to carry additional fuel and withstand higher loads.*
- ***Enhanced landing gear***: *The landing gear was upgraded to support the increased weight during takeoff and landing.*
- ***Larger fuel tanks***: *Expanded fuel storage capacity enabled the aircraft to achieve greater range capabilities.*

The evolution of the 777-200's MDTOW highlights how technological advancements and structural enhancements can expand an aircraft's operational capabilities. These upgrades allowed airlines to serve longer routes, showcasing the strategic importance of MDTOW in balancing operational efficiency, range, and market demand.

1.3.4 Maximum Design Landing Weight (MDLW)

The **Maximum Design Landing Weight (MDLW)** is the highest certified weight at which an aircraft can safely land, ensuring compliance with structural integrity requirements. This limit is determined based on the design strength of critical components such as the landing gear, wing structures, and fuselage, which endure significant stress during the landing phase. During landing, the aircraft experiences vertical deceleration and forward momentum, creating dynamic forces that must be absorbed without compromising structural integrity.

To certify aircraft for operations at MDLW, regulatory authorities such as the FAA have established stringent structural requirements to ensure safety during landings:

- **At MDLW:** The landing gear must withstand a touchdown sink rate of 10 feet per second without structural damage.
- **At Maximum Design Takeoff Weight (MDTOW):** The landing gear must tolerate a sink rate of 6 feet per second without structural damage.

In practice, typical touchdown sink rates range from 2 to 3 feet per second, even during hard landings, with sink rates exceeding 6 feet per second being rare. These conservative limits ensure a robust margin of safety under normal and extreme operational conditions.

By adhering to MDLW limits and accounting for regulated sink rates, manufacturers and operators ensure that the aircraft can safely endure the rigors of landing operations while maintaining structural integrity and airworthiness.

Benefits of Higher MDLW

Increasing MDLW provides significant operational advantages, enhancing an airline's flexibility and efficiency. Key benefits include:

1. **Carrying Additional Fuel for Long-Haul Flights**
   » A higher MDLW allows aircraft to land with more fuel onboard, providing flexibility for long-haul operations where substantial reserves may remain.
2. **Flexibility During Unplanned Diversions**
   » A higher MDLW enables safe landings at alternate airports during diversions, reducing or eliminating the need to jettison fuel, which enhances safety and adaptability.
3. **Strategic Fuel Management**
   » Airlines can carry additional fuel from departure airports where costs are lower, reducing operating expenses without compromising payload capacity.

Operational Impact of MDLW

In exceptional scenarios, such as in-flight turn-backs or emergency diversions, pilots may need to land at a weight exceeding the Maximum Design Landing Weight (MDLW)—a situation known as an **overweight landing**. Modern aircraft are engineered to handle such events without compromising structural integrity. However, overweight landings impose significant stress on critical components such as the landing gear, fuselage, and wing-root areas. Following an overweight landing, mandatory inspections are required to assess structural conditions and ensure airworthiness before returning the aircraft to service.

Maximum Design Landing Weight (MDLW) plays a critical role in balancing safety and operational flexibility during flight planning. It must exceed the combined weight of the Maximum Design Zero-Fuel Weight (MDZFW) and required fuel reserves to avoid constraints that could compromise payload capacity, fuel reserves, or safety margins. A low MDLW relative to MDZFW and fuel reserves can limit operational flexibility, potentially requiring payload reductions or reserve fuel adjustments that affect long-haul capability and safety margins.

Additionally, economic and safety considerations come into play, as constraints on MDLW can impact route profitability on high-demand routes and reduce safety margins during emergencies, such as diversions or holding patterns. Ensuring an optimal MDLW is essential for maintaining operational efficiency, safety, and profitability.

Scenario When MDLW < MDZFW + Fuel Reserve

When an aircraft's MDLW is less than the combined weight of its fully loaded payload (MDZFW) and required fuel reserves, it risks exceeding safe landing limits. This scenario arises because the aircraft's structural landing weight cannot accommodate both the desired payload and the necessary fuel reserves, forcing operators to make adjustments to ensure safe operations.

This creates several operational challenges, including:

- **Payload Reductions:** Limiting passengers or cargo to stay within MDLW directly impacts revenue and profitability on high-demand routes. Airlines must weigh the trade-off between maximizing payload and complying with landing weight constraints.

- **Reduced Fuel Reserves:** Operating with lower reserves to meet MDLW constraints reduces safety margins, limits diversion options, and may push fuel planning closer to regulatory minimums. This increases operational risk in unforeseen circumstances, such as weather disruptions or air traffic delays.

These operational challenges underline the importance of effective payload and fuel management to maintain safety, comply with MDLW, and optimize profitability.

EXAMPLE 1-9. The Interplay of MDLW, MDZFW, and Fuel Reserves
Case 1: MDLW Greater Than MDZFW + Fuel Reserve

- MDZFW: 200,000 lbs. (OEW + Payload)
- Fuel Reserve: 50,000 lbs.
- Ideal MDLW: Should be greater than 250,000 lbs. (200,000 lbs. + 50,000 lbs.)

This configuration allows the aircraft to land safely with a full payload and the required fuel reserve. It ensures operational flexibility and maintains safety margins without the need to adjust payload or fuel reserves.

Case 2: MDLW Less Than MDZFW + Fuel Reserve

- MDZFW: 200,000 lbs. (OEW + Payload)
- Fuel Reserve: 50,000 lbs.
- MDLW: 230,000 lbs.

In this scenario, the airline faces operational constraints and must choose between two options to ensure compliance with the Maximum Design Landing Weight (MDLW) of 230,000 lbs.: either reduce payload so that the combined Maximum Design Zero-Fuel Weight (MDZFW) and fuel reserve equals or stays below 230,000 lbs., or reduce fuel reserve to ensure the landing weight does not exceed 230,000 lbs. Maintaining an MDLW that exceeds the total of MDZFW and fuel reserves is essential for supporting operations without compromising payload capacity or safety margins, ensuring both operational efficiency and adherence to safety regulations.

1.3.5 Structural Design Weight and Regulatory Oversight

The Structural Design Weight of an aircraft refers to the maximum structural capacity it can safely support, which is a dynamic attribute influenced by factors such as the manufacturing timeline, technological advancements, and specific production line numbers. Older aircraft can also undergo modifications to increase structural capacities, but these changes require rigorous testing and certification to ensure safety. Understanding these variations is crucial for operators to manage payloads, plan operations, and strategize fleet modernization effectively.

Several factors influence an aircraft's Structural Design Weight, shaping its operational capabilities and long-term value. These include:

- **Manufacturing Timeline and Design**: Aircraft structural capacities evolve with advancements in engineering and materials science. Newer models often feature higher structural limit weights due to improved designs and the use of advanced materials, such as composites and lighter, stronger alloys. These innovations enhance strength and reduce weight, supporting increased payloads and improved fuel efficiency.
- **Line Numbers and Their Impact**: Structural capacities may vary even within the same aircraft model, depending on production sequence or "line numbers." As manufacturers refine processes and integrate new technologies, newer aircraft in a series may have enhanced structural limit weights, enabling greater payload capacities and extended range.
- **Upgrading Structural Capacities in Older Aircraft**: Upgrading older aircraft is possible but complex and costly. Techniques include reinforcing the frame, enhancing landing gear, and incorporating advanced materials. These modifications undergo extensive testing and certification to meet safety and regulatory standards, ensuring the aircraft maintains structural integrity.

Regulatory Oversight

The U.S. Federal Aviation Administration (FAA) and the European Union Aviation Safety Agency (EASA) play critical roles in setting and enforcing aircraft weight limits during the certification process. This process involves rigorous assessments of an aircraft's design and structural integrity to establish safe weight thresholds, ensuring operational safety under various conditions.

The FAA and EASA are tasked with responsibilities that ensure aircraft weight limits are met and maintained throughout an aircraft's lifecycle:

- **Certifying Weight Limits**: FAA and EASA evaluate and approve the aircraft's design to certify safe weight thresholds during initial production and post-modifications.
- **Ongoing Compliance**: Regular inspections and audits of airlines and aircraft ensure adherence to these weight limits.
- **Modification Approval**: Any upgrades or changes affecting weight limits require agency approval to confirm continued safety and compliance.

Through strict enforcement, the FAA and EASA uphold high safety and performance standards, ensuring safe and efficient aircraft operations globally. Together, advancements in aircraft design and rigorous regulatory oversight ensure the operational safety, efficiency, and reliability of modern aircraft fleets.

1.4 Certified Limit Weights

Certified Limit Weights refer to the maximum allowable operating weights for an aircraft, as selected by the operator and officially approved by aviation authorities, such as the FAA (Federal Aviation Administration) or EASA (European Union Aviation Safety Agency). These weights are specific to an individual aircraft or operator and are established based on operational requirements.

An operator determines these limits by considering factors like route planning, payload requirements, and efficiency considerations. Certified Limit Weights define the maximum allowable weight of the aircraft, excluding usable fuel, for normal operations. Importantly, these operational weights must always remain less than or equal to the maximum design structural weights set by the manufacturer.

Once approved, Certified Limit Weights become legally enforceable and are documented in the Aircraft Flight Manual (AFM) and the Certificate of Airworthiness (C of A). Operators retain the flexibility to adjust these limits through an AFM master change, enabling them to adapt to evolving operational needs while ensuring compliance with safety and regulatory standards.

Manufacturers like Airbus and Boeing offer multiple Certified Limit Weight options to accommodate diverse airline needs, enabling airlines to tailor aircraft configurations to meet specific operational goals.

Certified Limit Weights offer a range of advantages that enhance aircraft versatility, cost efficiency, and operational performance. These benefits include:

- **Aircraft Versatility**: Airlines operate across routes with varying distances, passenger loads, and cargo demands. By offering multiple Certified Limit Weight options, manufacturers enable airlines to adapt their aircraft to diverse operational scenarios, enhancing fleet utilization.
- **Cost Optimization**: Certified Limit Weights allow airlines to balance acquisition costs and operational benefits. Manufacturers often charge for incremental weight options above a baseline, making it critical for airlines to select a weight variant that aligns with anticipated usage. This minimizes unnecessary expenditures while maximizing aircraft utility.
- **Operational Savings**: Certified Limit Weights influence operating costs, particularly landing and navigation fees, which are often tied to Maximum Takeoff Weight (MTOW). Choosing a weight variant that meets operational needs without exceeding cost thresholds can generate significant savings.
- **Enhanced Performance Profiles**: Different weight variants provide distinct payload and range capabilities, enabling airlines to select configurations that meet performance requirements. Higher-weight variants are particularly suitable for long-haul routes or operations with high passenger and cargo demand, optimizing revenue and performance.

To illustrate the concept of Certified Limit Weights, consider how aircraft manufacturers provide Maximum Zero-Fuel Weight (MZFW) and Maximum Takeoff Weight (MTOW) options to align with the diverse operational needs of airlines. These options offer flexibility by enabling operators to configure their aircraft to prioritize either payload capacity or range, depending on specific mission requirements. Unlike operational weight limits set by airlines for particular routes, MZFW and MTOW are fixed structural constraints certified by manufacturers and regulatory authorities. Operators must select from the available MZFW and MTOW options, tailoring their choice to their unique operational strategies, but they cannot exceed the manufacturer-defined structural limits.

For instance, the Airbus A330-200F demonstrates this flexibility with its two distinct operational modes—Range Mode and Payload Mode—as outlined in **Table 1-2**. This adaptability allows airlines to optimize their operations for either maximum range or maximum payload, depending on the demands of the mission.

Table 1-2. A330-200F operational flexibility

	Range Mode	Payload Mode
Maximum Takeoff Weight	233 t	227 t
Maximum Landing Weight	182 t	187 t
Maximum Zero-Fuel Weight	173 t	178 t
Max Structural Payload	**65 t**	**70 t**
Range Capability	**4,000 nm**	**3,200 nm**

Source: Airbus "A330 Airplane Characteristics for Airport Planning" document, with modifications by the author [4]

In **Range Mode**, the aircraft operates with a lower MZFW, which allows it to carry more fuel, extending its range while reducing available payload capacity. This mode is ideal for long-haul operations, enabling airlines to perform non-stop flights over longer distances, minimizing refueling stops and optimizing overall efficiency.

Conversely, in **Payload Mode**, the aircraft operates with a higher MZFW, prioritizing maximum cargo or passenger capacity at the expense of range. This configuration is well-suited for short-haul or regional operations where high payload demand outweighs the need for extended range.

Manufacturers like Airbus enable this operational flexibility through a

weight variant system. This system specifies structural weight limits for key metrics, including MTOW, Maximum Landing Weight (MLW), and MZFW. By selecting the appropriate weight variant, operators can tailor their aircraft's configuration to match route demands, market conditions, and operational strategies.

Importantly, switching between weight variants does not require physical modifications to the aircraft. Operators leverage the aircraft's inherent capabilities, subject to regulatory approval, to adapt quickly to evolving market conditions. This strategic adaptability offers airlines a competitive advantage by allowing them to optimize payload and range for mission-specific operations while adhering to certified weight limits.

Certified Limit Weights: Manufacturer vs. Operator Certification

Certified Limit Weights define the maximum allowable operating weights of an aircraft, established by manufacturers and approved by aviation authorities to ensure safe operations within structural and performance limits. While these weights are primarily set by the manufacturer, they also accommodate operational flexibility, allowing airlines to tailor weight configurations to specific needs.

Aircraft weights can be categorized into two distinct groups: **manufacturer-certified weights** and **operator-certified weights**.

- **Manufacturer-Certified Weights:** These include Maximum Taxi Weight (MTW), Maximum Takeoff Weight (MTOW), Maximum Landing Weight (MLW), and Maximum Zero Fuel Weight (MZFW). These limits are determined during the aircraft design and certification process to comply with regulatory safety and structural integrity requirements. They are fixed values that cannot be altered without manufacturer approval, as they directly impact the aircraft's airworthiness and overall structural limits.
- **Operator-Certified Weights:** These include weights such as Operating Empty Weight (OEW) and Maximum Payload, which vary based on airline-specific configurations. OEW depends on how an airline equips the aircraft, including seating arrangements, galley installations, and optional onboard equipment. This information is documented in the **Aircraft Flight Manual (AFM)** and **Weight and**

Balance Manual (WBM). Similarly, Maximum Payload is defined by operators based on operational considerations, such as route structure, cargo capacity, and fuel requirements, ensuring compliance with Certified Limit Weights while optimizing efficiency.

Table 1-3 below provides a clear breakdown of these weights and their respective certification responsibilities.

By distinguishing between manufacturer-certified and operator-certified weights, Certified Limit Weights provide a structured framework that balances safety, structural limitations, and operational efficiency.

Table 1-3. Manufacturer-certified vs. operator-certified weights

Operational Weight	Manufacturer Certification	Operator Certification
Maximum Taxi Weight	Certified	Not Applicable
Maximum Takeoff Weight	Certified	Not Applicable
Maximum Landing Weight	Certified	Not Applicable
Maximum Zero Fuel Weight	Certified	Not Applicable
Operating Empty Weight	Operator-Specific	Certified (in AFM WBM)
Maximum Structural Payload	Not Defined	Certified (in AFM WBM)

Source: Author's analysis

Industry Perspective 1-4. *Certified Weight and Fleet Optimization*

In commercial aviation, Certified Limit Weights, such as Maximum Take-off Weight (MTOW), are critical for fleet planning and route optimization strategies. Aircraft offering multiple certified MTOW options allow airlines to tailor operations to specific mission profiles by balancing payload and range. This flexibility is especially valuable for airlines operating from weight-restricted airports or in regions with fluctuating demand.

*A practical example as illustrated in **Table 1-4** is the Boeing 787 family, which offers certified MTOW options for the 787-9 variant ranging from 545,000 lbs. to 571,500 lbs. This range enables airlines to select configurations that align with their network requirements:*

- ***Long-Haul Markets***: *Airlines serving extended routes might choose the higher MTOW variant to accommodate additional fuel for greater range.*
- ***Shorter, High-Density Markets***: *Carriers focusing on shorter routes with high passenger and cargo loads may opt for a lower MTOW to prioritize payload capacity and minimize landing fees.*

Table 1-4. 787-9 basic and maximum MTOWs

Basic **lb** (kg)	Maximum **lb** (kg)
545,000 (247,200)	**561,500** (255,372)

Source: Boeing "787 Airplane Characteristics for Airport Planning", document [2]

By leveraging the flexibility of multiple certified MTOW options, airlines can optimize fleet deployment, ensuring each aircraft is matched to routes that maximize revenue potential and operational efficiency. This adaptability underscores the strategic importance of certified limit weights in achieving a balance between operational effectiveness and economic performance.

EXAMPLE 1-10. Performance Benefits of Higher Certified Limit Weights

Figure 1-15 illustrates the performance benefits of selecting higher certified Maximum Takeoff Weights (MTOWs) for the A330-900. In its standard configuration, the A330-900 carries 278 passengers over a range of approximately 6,550 nautical miles (nm). At its maximum certified MTOW, the aircraft's capabilities expand—enabling either:

- An additional 650 nm of range, or
- An extra 4 tonnes (8,800 lbs.) of payload.

Figure 1-15. A330-900 certified MTOW tradeoffs

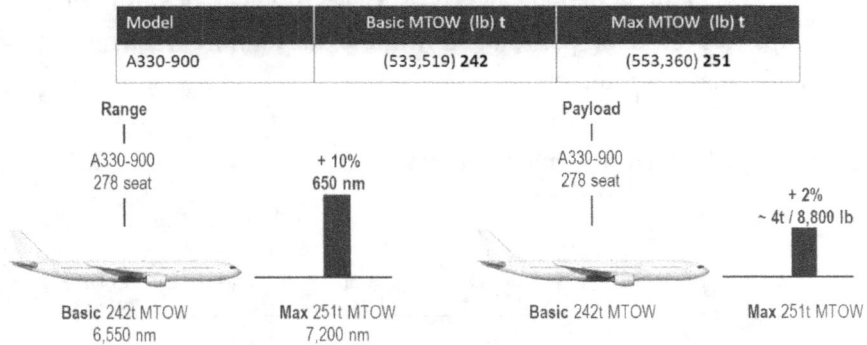

Model	Basic MTOW (lb) t	Max MTOW (lb) t
A330-900	(533,519) **242**	(553,360) **251**

Range

A330-900
278 seat
      + 10%
      650 nm

Basic 242t MTOW   **Max** 251t MTOW
6,550 nm   7,200 nm

Payload

A330-900
278 seat
      + 2%
      ~ 4t / 8,800 lb

Basic 242t MTOW   **Max** 251t MTOW

Source: Airbus "A330 Airplane Characteristics for Airport Planning", with analysis by the author [4]

This example demonstrates how higher certified weight limits provide airlines with greater operational flexibility, allowing optimization of payload capacity or extended routes based on market demand and mission requirements.

Operational and Economic Impact of MTOW

While increasing the Maximum Takeoff Weight (MTOW) enhances performance capabilities, it also introduces operational challenges and added costs. Airlines must carefully evaluate these trade-offs to strike the right balance between operational benefits and financial implications. Key considerations include:

- **Increased Purchase Price**: A higher MTOW typically raises the purchase price due to enhanced performance capabilities. Often achieved through a certification adjustment rather than physical modifications, this reflects added certification costs and operational flexibility.
- **Higher Operational Costs**: Landing fees and air navigation charges often scale with MTOW, increasing overall flight costs.

- **Increased Engine Direct Maintenance Costs**: Higher MTOW requires engines to produce more thrust, accelerating wear and increasing direct maintenance costs (DMC). This includes higher expenses for labor, parts, and downtime due to more frequent maintenance requirements.

Figure 1-16. MTOW economic tradeoffs

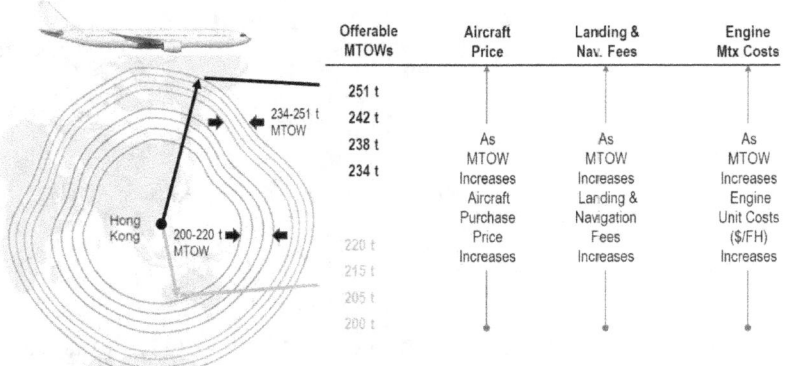

Source: Airbus, "The Leading Widebody Family," December 2019. [5]

***Industry Perspective 1-5.** MTOW Impact on Landing and Navigation Fees*

*The Maximum Takeoff Weight (MTOW) of an aircraft directly influences operational costs, particularly landing and navigation fees. Airports and **Air Navigation Service Providers (ANSPs)** calculate these fees based on the aircraft's certified MTOW, which determines its maximum authorized takeoff weight.*

*   *Figure 1-17* examines an Airbus A320 operating between Madrid and Amsterdam under two certified MTOW configurations:*

- *67 tonnes (t): Standard MTOW configuration.*
- *77 tonnes (t): Upgraded MTOW configuration.*

This example highlights how a higher MTOW increases operational fees:

- ***Landing Fees**: Increase by **15%** compared to the lower MTOW configuration.*

- **Navigation Fees**: *Rise by 8%, reflecting higher costs for air traffic control and en-route navigation services.*

Figure 1-17. A320 landing & navigation fees

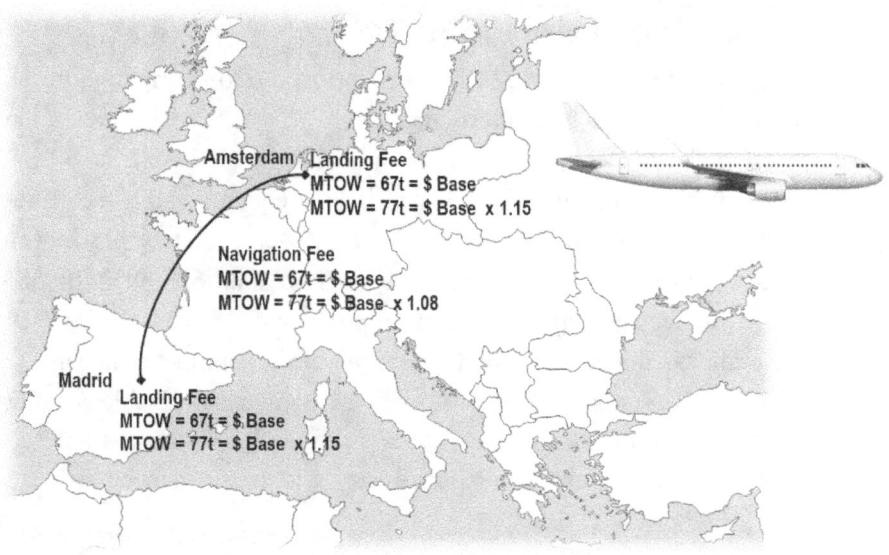

Source: Author's analysis

This industry practice demonstrates the cost implications for airlines operating heavier aircraft. While upgrading an aircraft's MTOW can increase payload capacity and revenue potential, airlines must carefully consider the associated rise in operational fees. Balancing these factors is essential for optimizing route economics.

Certified Weight Selection Process

Airlines operate across diverse routes, including short-haul (domestic), medium-haul (regional), and long-haul (international) flights. The selection of an aircraft's certified weights is largely influenced by the specific demands of these routes, ensuring operational efficiency and cost-effectiveness. Key considerations for route-specific weight requirements include:

- **Long-Haul Flights**: Higher Maximum Takeoff Weights (MTOWs) and Maximum Landing Weights (MLWs) are essential to accommodate the additional fuel and cargo required for extended distances. A lower Maximum Zero-Fuel Weight (MZFW) allows for greater fuel capacity, optimizing range without exceeding the MTOW limit.
- **Short-Haul Routes**: Lower MTOWs, MZFWs, and MLWs are often preferred, reducing fuel consumption and lowering landing fees, which enhances cost efficiency.

To meet specific operational needs, airlines frequently adjust certified weights across MTOW, MZFW, and MLW. However, selecting higher certified weights comes with operational and economic trade-offs, including increased acquisition costs, higher fuel consumption, and elevated landing fees, which are often calculated based on MTOW. Aircraft manufacturers, such as Airbus and Boeing, support this flexibility by offering customizable certified weight options, enabling airlines to tailor aircraft configurations to their specific operational requirements and balance costs with performance needs.

Airbus Weight Selection Approach

Airbus provides predefined Weight Variants (WVs), which combine options for MTOW, MLW, and MZFW, tailored for each aircraft model. This approach helps airlines optimize the balance between acquisition costs, operational expenses, and route-specific requirements, ensuring the best alignment with their fleet strategies.

EXAMPLE 1-11. A320 Weight Variants (WV) Tradeoffs
As illustrated in **Table 1-5**, weight variant selection for the Airbus A320 depends on an airline's operational requirements:

- **WV1**: Suitable for short-haul domestic flights, this variant features a lower Maximum Takeoff Weight (MTOW), offering cost savings in both acquisition and operational expenses.
- **WV3:** Designed for international long-haul routes, this variant includes a higher MTOW, enabling the aircraft to carry more fuel and support extended flight ranges.

Table 1-5. Airbus weight variants (WVs)

Weight Variant	MTOW (kg)	MZFW (kg)	Route Profile	Cost Considerations
WV002	70,000	60,500	Short-Haul	Lowest acquisition and operational costs
WV009	75,500	61,000	Medium-Haul	Moderate acquisition and operational costs
WV017	78,000	62,500	Long-Haul	Higher acquisition and operational costs

Source: Airbus "A320 Airplane Characteristics for Airport Planning" document, with analysis by the author [6]

Boeing Weight Selection Approach

Boeing offers greater customization flexibility than Airbus by providing a baseline of certified maximum operating weights for each aircraft model. Airlines can adjust these weights in precise increments—typically by 1,000 pounds—at a fixed cost per pound (e.g., $100/lb). This incremental approach enables airlines to fine-tune the Maximum Takeoff Weight (MTOW), Maximum Landing Weight (MLW), or Maximum Zero-Fuel Weight (MZFW) to align with their specific operational needs and strategic goals.

EXAMPLE 1-12: Customizing Certified Weights for Medium-Haul Flight Operations

An airline operating medium-haul routes may select certified weights that fall between the baseline and maximum limits, as shown in **Table 1-6**. This tailored approach strikes a balance between acquisition and operating costs while meeting the airline's payload and range requirements. It ensures cost efficiency and operational flexibility for routes with moderate fuel and payload demands.

Table 1-6. Boeing maximum weights

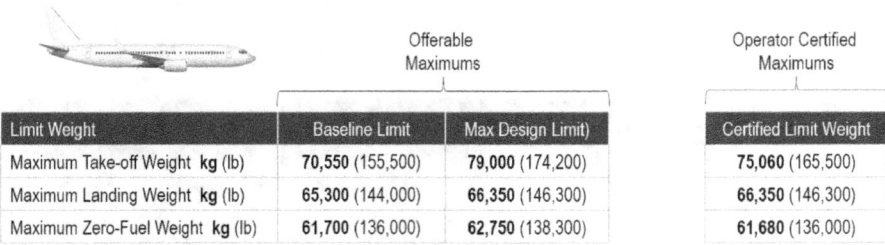

Limit Weight	Offerable Maximums		Operator Certified Maximums
	Baseline Limit	Max Design Limit)	Certified Limit Weight
Maximum Take-off Weight **kg** (lb)	**70,550** (155,500)	**79,000** (174,200)	**75,060** (165,500)
Maximum Landing Weight **kg** (lb)	**65,300** (144,000)	**66,350** (146,300)	**66,350** (146,300)
Maximum Zero-Fuel Weight **kg** (lb)	**61,700** (136,000)	**62,750** (138,300)	**61,680** (136,000)

Source: Boeing "737 Airplane Characteristics for Airport Planning" document, with analysis by the author [7]

***Industry Perspective 1-6.** Certified Weights and Appraised Value*

The selection of certified operating weights directly influences an aircraft's appraised value, with each weight variant adding performance capabilities that impact market valuation. For example, a higher Maximum Takeoff Weight (MTOW) typically increases an aircraft's appraisal due to enhanced operational flexibility and expanded route options.

*   **Table 1-7** illustrates this with a 2018 Boeing 737-800, where the market value reflects an $840,000 increase attributed to the higher MTOW certification. This demonstrates how certified weight options contribute to an aircraft's overall valuation.*

Table 1-7. MTOW market value adjustment example

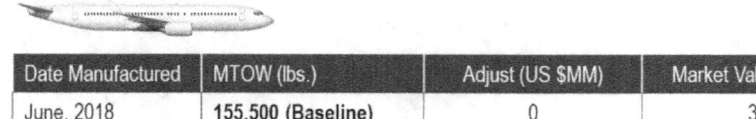

Date Manufactured	MTOW (lbs.)	Adjust (US $MM)	Market Value (US $MM)
June, 2018	**155,500 (Baseline)**	0	33.83
	174,200 (Maximum)	0.840	34.67

Source: AVITAS

In conclusion, certified operating weights are critical to an aircraft's market value, directly correlating with its appraised worth. Airlines must carefully evaluate these selections to optimize both the asset's current market value and its long-term economic potential.

1.5 Weight Efficiency

Weight efficiency in aircraft design involves balancing the aircraft's weight with material strength, durability, and production costs. The goal is to create an aircraft that is both lightweight and durable, improving fuel efficiency and performance while minimizing operational costs. Importantly, any weight reduction must uphold structural integrity and reliability to ensure safety.

While weight efficiency is a critical aspect of design, airlines typically prioritize payload-range performance and passenger capacity when selecting aircraft, as these factors have a more direct impact on revenue and route flexibility.

An aircraft's weight efficiency is assessed primarily through **structural efficiency** and **payload efficiency**. Evaluating these metrics offers valuable insights into how design and construction optimize the balance between weight, strength, and overall performance.

1.5.1 Structural Efficiency

Structural efficiency measures the relationship between an aircraft's structural weight and its capacity to carry fuel and payload. It is calculated as the ratio of the aircraft's Operating Empty Weight (OEW) to its Maximum Design Takeoff Weight (MDTOW):

$$\text{Structural Efficiency} = \text{OEW} / \text{MDTOW} \quad \text{(Eq. 1-11)}$$

A **lower ratio** indicates greater structural efficiency, enabling the aircraft to carry more payload or fuel relative to its own weight. Conversely, a **higher ratio** suggests a heavier structure, potentially limiting payload or range capabilities. Optimizing structural efficiency is critical for maximizing performance, fuel economy, and overall operational effectiveness.

EXAMPLE 1-13. Calculating the Structural Efficiency of the Boeing 787-8 Dreamliner

To analyze the structural efficiency of the Boeing 787-8 Dreamliner, consider the following specifications provided by Boeing:

- Operating Empty Weight (OEW): 229,501 lbs. (104,100 kg)
- Maximum Design Takeoff Weight (MDTOW): 502,500 lbs. (227,930 kg)

The structural efficiency can be calculated as:

$$\text{Structural Efficiency} = \text{MDTOW/OEW} = 502{,}500 \text{lbs.} \, / \, 229{,}501 \text{lbs.}$$
$$= 0.457 \text{or } 45.7\%$$

This result indicates that the 787-8's structure accounts for **45.7%** of its maximum takeoff weight, leaving the remaining capacity for fuel, payload (passengers and cargo), and other operational needs.

The **Boeing 787** and similar aircraft, such as the **Airbus A350**, achieve high structural efficiency by extensively using lightweight composite materials. These materials reduce structural weight while maintaining strength and durability, contributing to improved fuel efficiency and extended range capabilities.

1.5.2 Payload Efficiency

Payload efficiency measures an aircraft's ability to carry payload relative to its Maximum Takeoff Weight (MTOW). It is calculated by dividing the Maximum Structural Payload (MSP) by the Maximum Design Takeoff Weight (MDTOW):

$$\text{Payload efficiency} = \text{MSP} \, / \, \text{MDTOW} \quad \text{(Eq. 1-12)}$$

This metric evaluates how effectively an aircraft accommodates payload within its total weight limits. The following considerations highlight the implications of varying payload efficiency levels:

- **Higher** payload efficiency indicates greater payload capacity relative to structural weight, maximizing operational capacity.
- **Lower** payload efficiency suggests a heavier structure, which may restrict payload or range.

EXAMPLE 1-14. Calculating the Payload Efficiency of the Boeing 787-8 Dreamliner

Using the Boeing 787-8's specifications:

- Maximum Structural Payload (MSP): 129,499 lbs.
- Maximum Design Takeoff Weight (MDTOW): 502,500 lbs.

$$\text{Payload Efficiency} = \text{MSP} / \text{MDTOW} = 129{,}499 \text{ lbs.} / 502{,}500 \text{ lbs.}$$
$$= 0.25 \text{ or } 25\%$$

This result shows that approximately 25% of the 787-8's MTOW is allocated to payload, reflecting a high payload efficiency. This characteristic enhances the aircraft's ability to carry substantial payloads without compromising fuel efficiency.

Structural and Payload Efficiency Comparative Analysis

As illustrated in **Table 1-8**, comparing the Boeing 767-300ER, Airbus A330-200, and Boeing 787-8 reveals the 787-8's superior performance in both structural and payload efficiency. The following points highlight key advantages of the 787-8's design:

- A lower OEW to MDTOW ratio, attributed to its lightweight composite structure, enhancing structural efficiency and useful load capacity.
- Higher payload efficiency, allowing more payload relative to its MTOW, making it adaptable to diverse operational scenarios.

Table 1-8. Structural and payload efficiency of medium widebodies

Weight	767-300ER	A330-200	787-8
OEW	198,440	266,830	229,501
Payload	96,560	108,020	125,499
Fuel	117,000	138,915	147,500
MTOW	412,000	513,765	502,500
Structural Efficiency (OEW/MTOW)	48.2%	51.9%	45.7%
Payload Efficiency (Payload/MTOW)	23.4%	21.0%	25.0%

Source: Boeing, "767"; "787"; Airbus, "A330" Airplane Characteristics for Airport Planning" document, with analysis by the author [8]

This comparison underscores the advanced design and technology in modern aircraft like the 787-8. By optimizing structural and payload efficiencies, the 787-8 offers airlines greater operational flexibility, enhanced fuel efficiency, and the ability to maximize payload without sacrificing performance.

Industry Perspective 1-7. *Downsizing and Payload Efficiency*

When an aircraft is downsized, the fuselage length is typically reduced to accommodate fewer passengers, while essential components such as engines, landing gear, and wings are retained. This configuration often leads to decreased structural efficiency, as a larger proportion of the aircraft's total weight is allocated to these fixed structural assemblies, leaving less weight available for payload.

*For example, in the **737NG family**, as shown in **Table 1-9**, downsized models feature a shorter fuselage but retain the same engines and primary structural components—including wings, stabilizers, and landing gear—as their larger counterparts. This results in:*

- *Reduced payload capability relative to MTOW, as a higher fraction of the aircraft's weight supports its structure rather than carrying passengers or cargo.*
- *Lower structural efficiency, which limits the aircraft's operational flexibility and reduces its payload capacity.*

Downsizing highlights the trade-offs in structural and payload efficiency, emphasizing the importance of design optimization to maintain operational effectiveness in smaller aircraft models.

Table 1-9. Structural and payload efficiency of 737NG family

Weight	737-900ER	737-800	737-700	737-600
OEW	96,780	91,990	84,690	82,330
Payload	52,520	46,310	37,010	31,670
Fuel	38,400	35,900	32,800	31,500
MTOW	187,700	174,200	154,500	145,500
Structrual Efficiency (OEW/MTOW)	51.6%	52.8%	54.8%	56.6%
Payload Efficiency (Payload/MTOW)	28.0%	26.6%	24.0%	21.8%

Source: Boeing. "737 Airplane Characteristics for Airport Planning" document with analysis by the author [7]

Chapter 1. Key Takeaways

1. **Weight Groups**:
   - The chapter introduces key weight categories, including Operating Empty Weight (OEW), Zero-Fuel Weight (ZFW), Taxi Weight (TW), and Takeoff Weight (TOW).
   - These groups are critical for evaluating an aircraft's payload capacity, fuel requirements, and operational performance.
   - Understanding these categories enables operators to optimize flight planning, assess economic potential, and ensure operational flexibility.

2. **Gross Weights**:
   - Gross Weight represents the aircraft's total weight at any moment during operation, including passengers, cargo, and fuel.
   - Unlike ZFW, Gross Weight is dynamic and decreases as fuel is consumed.
   - Effective management of Gross Weight is vital for maintaining flight stability, optimizing fuel consumption, and ensuring safe and efficient operations across all flight phases.

3. **Structural Limit Weights**:
   - **Structural Limit Weights** include thresholds such as Maximum Design Takeoff Weight (MDTOW), Maximum Design Zero-Fuel Weight (MDZFW), and Maximum Design Landing Weight (MDLW).
   - These weights are set during the aircraft's design and certification processes to ensure safe operations by maintaining structural integrity across all flight phases.
   - They influence an aircraft's payload capacity, range, and safety margins.

4. **Certified Limit Weights**:
   - Certified Limit Weights are operational maximums approved by regulatory authorities and chosen by airlines. These include certified limits for MTOW, MLW, and MZFW.
   - Customizable options provided by manufacturers allow airlines to align weight configurations with specific route profiles, payload demands, and cost objectives, enhancing flexibility and controlling operating costs.

5. **Weight Efficiency**:
   - Weight efficiency evaluates how well an aircraft's structure supports its payload and fuel needs while maintaining durability, safety, and cost-effectiveness.
   - Metrics such as structural efficiency (OEW/MDTOW) and payload efficiency (MSP/MDTOW) provide insights into the aircraft's design optimization and performance.
   - High efficiency enhances operational capabilities by increasing useful load capacity and reducing fuel consumption.

6. **Impact of Design Choices on Weight Efficiency**:
   - Downsizing aircraft or selecting higher certified weights directly impacts structural and payload efficiency.
   - While downsizing can decrease structural efficiency by dedicating a larger proportion of weight to fixed assemblies, customizing certified weights influences acquisition and operational costs.

Case Study 1-1. Gross Weight Build-Up

Figure 1-18: 747-400 specification

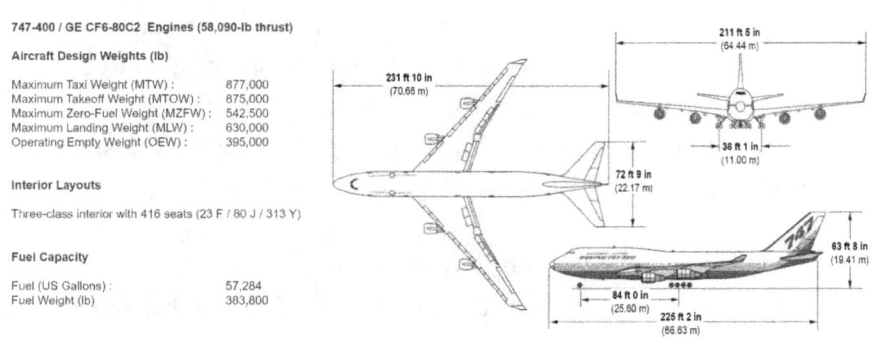

747-400 / GE CF6-80C2 Engines (58,090-lb thrust)

Aircraft Design Weights (lb)

Maximum Taxi Weight (MTW) :   877,000
Maximum Takeoff Weight (MTOW) :   875,000
Maximum Zero-Fuel Weight (MZFW) :   542,500
Maximum Landing Weight (MLW) :   630,000
Operating Empty Weight (OEW) :   395,000

Interior Layouts

Three-class interior with 416 seats (23 F / 80 J / 313 Y)

Fuel Capacity

Fuel (US Gallons) :   57,284
Fuel Weight (lb)   383,800

Source: Boeing. Startup Boeing [9]

Figure 1-19. 747-400 trip fuel LAX-SYD

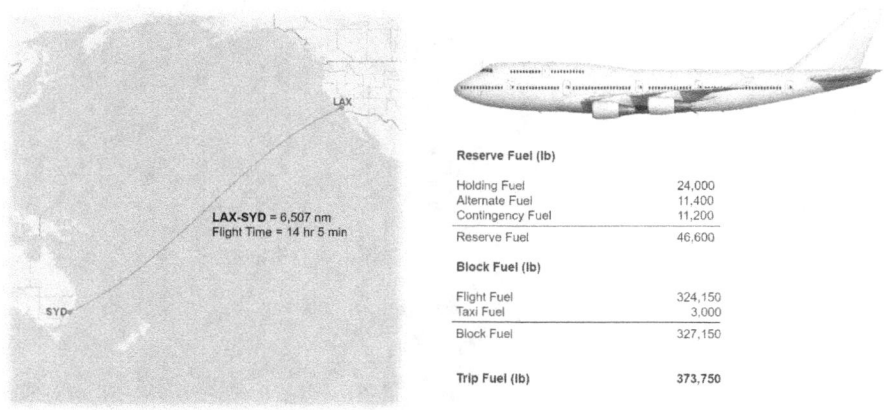

LAX-SYD = 6,507 nm
Flight Time = 14 hr 5 min

Reserve Fuel (lb)

Holding Fuel	24,000
Alternate Fuel	11,400
Contingency Fuel	11,200
Reserve Fuel	46,600

Block Fuel (lb)

Flight Fuel	324,150
Taxi Fuel	3,000
Block Fuel	327,150

Trip Fuel (lb)	**373,750**

Source: Great Circle Mapper [10]

Figure 1-20. 747-400 payload and fuel manifest

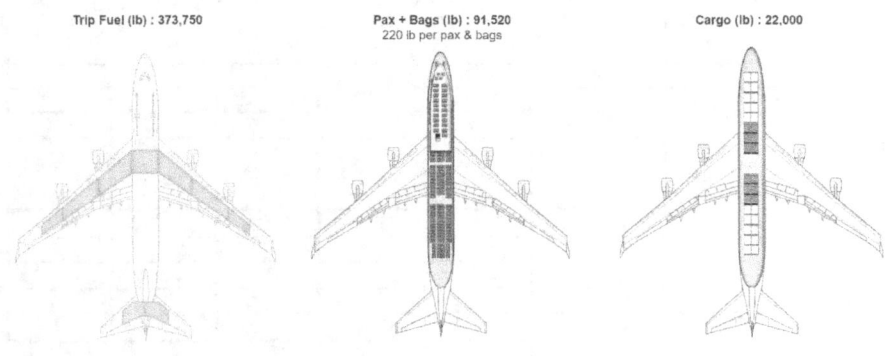

Trip Fuel (lb) : 373,750   Pax + Bags (lb) : 91,520   Cargo (lb) : 22,000
                             220 lb per pax & bags

Source: Images from, "AVIATION NOISE 101 Gregory Maxwell" [11]

Questions:

1. Analyze how the different weight components (Operating Empty Weight, Payload, and Fuel) contribute to the Total Takeoff Weight (TOW) for the Boeing 747-400 on the LAX-SYD route. Explain the significance of each component in determining the TOW.

2. Analyze the impact on the Total Takeoff Weight (TOW) and operational feasibility if the Operating Empty Weight (OEW) of the Boeing 747-400 is increased to 425,000 lbs. What adjustments might be necessary to comply with the Maximum Takeoff Weight (MTOW)?

3. Evaluate the implications of increasing the Maximum Zero-Fuel Weight (MZFW) of the Boeing 747-400 from 542,500 lbs. to 570,000 lbs. on its payload capacity and operational range. Consider the trade-offs and how these changes might affect an airline's operational strategy and revenue potential.

4. Evaluate the operational consequences of increasing the Maximum Takeoff Weight (MTOW) of the Boeing 747-400. How would such an increase influence decisions about fuel capacity and payload allocation?

Case Study 1-2. Weight Variant Analysis

Figure 1-21. A320-200 weight variants (WV010 – WV014)

Aircraft Characteristics		WV010	WV011	WV012	WV013	WV014
Maximum Ramp Weight (MRW)	Kilograms	77 400	75 900	77 400	71 900	73 900
Maximum Taxi Weight (MTW)	Pounds	170 638	167 331	170 638	158 512	162 922
Maximum Takeoff Weight (MTOW)	Kilograms	77 000	75 500	77 000	71 500	73 500
	Pounds	169 756	166 449	169 756	157 630	162 040
Maximum Landing Weight (MLW)	Kilograms	64 500	66 000	66 000	64 500	64 500
	Pounds	142 198	145 505	145 505	142 198	142 198
Maximum Zero Fuel Weight (MZFW)	Kilograms	61 000	62 500	62 500	61 000	61 500
	Pounds	134 482	137 789	137 789	134 482	135 584

Source: Airbus. "A320 Airplane Characteristics for Airport Planning" document [6]

Questions:

1. Compare the operational advantages and potential trade-offs between WV010 and WV013 for an airline operating high-density short-haul routes. Consider how differences in MTOW impact fuel capacity, payload capabilities, and range flexibility.

2. Considering that many airports calculate landing fees based on Maximum Takeoff Weight (MTOW), and the need to maximize payload on short-haul routes with limited fuel requirements, which weight variant (WV010 to WV014) offers the best balance between minimizing operating costs and maximizing payload capacity? Provide a recommendation, referencing MTOW, Maximum Zero Fuel Weight (MZFW), and overall cost efficiency.

3. How much more fuel can the A320 weight variant WV011 carry at MTOW compared to WV013?

4. Why would an airline operating the A320 weight variant WV012 potentially benefit from its higher Maximum Landing Weight (MLW) in terms of route planning flexibility?

References

[1] Supply Chain Management Blog, "The Global Partners of 787," Boeing 787 Dreamliner, Jan. 2013. [Online]. Available: https://cmuscm.blogspot.com/2013/01/is-boeing-787-really-dreamliner.html

[2] Boeing, "787 Airplane Characteristics for Airport Planning," Document D6-58333, Revision O, Feb. 2023. [Online]. Available: https://www.boeing.com/commercial/airports/plan-manuals

[3] Airbus, "Getting to Grips with Weight & Balance," p. 38. [Online]. Available: https://www.smartcockpit.com/docs/Getting_To_Grips_With_Weight_and_Balance.pdf

[4] Airbus, "A330 Aircraft Characteristics for Airport Planning," AC A330, Jul. 2023. [Online]. Available: https://aircraft.airbus.com/en/customer-care/fleet-wide-care/airport-operations-and-aircraft-characteristics/aircraft-characteristics

[5] Airbus, "The Leading Widebody Family," Presentation, Jul. 2019.

[6] Airbus, "A320 Aircraft Characteristics for Airport Planning," AC A320/A320neo, Jun. 2024. [Online]. Available: https://aircraft.airbus.com/en/customer-care/fleet-wide-care/airport-operations-and-aircraft-characteristics/aircraft-characteristics

[7] Boeing, "737 Airplane Characteristics for Airport Planning," Document D6-58325-7, Revision A, Mar. 2023. [Online]. Available: https://www.boeing.com/commercial/airports/plan-manuals

[8] Boeing, "767 Airplane Characteristics for Airport Planning," Document D6-58328, Revision J, Aug. 2023. [Online]. Available: https://www.boeing.com/commercial/airports/plan-manuals

[9] Boeing, "Startup Boeing." [Online]. Available: https://www.boeing.com/company/about-bca/startupboeing#selection

[10] Great Circle Mapper. [Online]. Available: http://www.gcmap.com/

[11] G. Maxwell, "Aviation Noise 101," Casper Airport Solutions, UC Davis Noise and Aviation Conference, [Online]. Available: https://aqrc.ucdavis.edu/sites/g/files/dgvnsk1671/files/inline-files/UC%20Davis%20Noise%20101_0.pdf

Chapter 2

Aircraft Capacities

This Chapter is About:

This chapter examines three essential aspects of aircraft capacity: **cabin capacity**, **fuel capacity**, and **cargo capacity**. These components are critical for understanding an aircraft's performance and economic efficiency, as they directly influence payload, range, and operational flexibility.

The following overview highlights how each capacity component impacts operational performance and economic outcomes:

- **Cabin Capacity:** Cabin configuration affects weight distribution, revenue potential, and overall performance. Optimizing the layout maximizes passenger capacity and space utilization, influencing weight and center of gravity (CG). High-density seating increases weight, potentially raising fuel burn and reducing range, while fewer seats may enhance fuel efficiency and extend range, though at a cost to maximum payload. Balancing passenger capacity, weight, and payload efficiency is vital for maintaining performance and maximizing revenue.

- **Fuel Capacity:** Fuel capacity defines an aircraft's range and route flexibility. Greater fuel storage supports longer non-stop flights, reducing stopovers and operational costs, enhancing route options, and boosting market competitiveness.
- **Cargo Capacity:** Cargo capacity is a key revenue factor, especially for freighters. Efficient cargo space management supports optimal payload. For e-commerce, low-density, high-volume goods demand ample cargo volume rather than weight, enabling efficient transport of lightweight, high-volume items. For passenger aircraft, balancing cargo and passenger space optimizes payload and increases revenue potential.

Optimizing cabin, fuel, and cargo capacities is essential to maximize payload, range, and economic efficiency, shaping an aircraft's overall competitiveness. The following sections explore each of these capacities in detail, assessing their individual and combined impacts on performance.

2.1 Cabin Capacity

Cabin capacity is a fundamental aspect of aircraft design, balancing performance, fuel efficiency, and payload capacity while shaping the passenger experience. Beyond seating arrangements, it encompasses features that drive operational efficiency and ensure passenger comfort and safety. Airlines must carefully consider these factors to achieve economic efficiency without compromising passenger satisfaction.

This section explores the core components of cabin capacity, highlighting the importance of optimizing layout, complying with safety standards, and meeting passenger needs. Key aspects include:

- **Seating Configuration:** This includes seat arrangement, rows per class (economy, business, first), seat pitch, and seats per row. Optimizing the layout is vital for maximizing passenger capacity while preserving comfort.
- **Cabin Optimization Features:** Airlines incorporate innovations like slim-line seats, which reduce space usage while maintaining comfort, allowing for increased seating capacity within the same area. Strategic rearrangement of lavatories and galleys further

expands space, particularly in the rear cabin, enabling additional rows without significant structural changes, thereby increasing passenger capacity and maintaining accessibility.

- **Cabin Exit Doors:** The configuration of exit doors directly influences maximum seating capacity. Manufacturers provide various door options, allowing airlines to match configurations to their operational needs. Larger or additional doors support higher passenger counts, provided safety regulations for emergency evacuations are met.

These elements illustrate how cabin layout affects an aircraft's performance, operational efficiency, and passenger satisfaction. The following sections delve into each component, revealing its role in optimizing cabin space and enhancing overall aircraft utility.

2.1.1 Seating Layouts

An aircraft's seating configuration is determined by key factors such as **seat pitch** (distance between rows), **seats abreast** (number of seats per row), and aisle configuration. These elements define cabin density, passenger comfort, and overall capacity, making them critical for both narrowbody and widebody aircraft.

Seating arrangement impacts not only passenger count but also weight distribution, center of gravity, and operational efficiency, influencing the aircraft's performance and economic potential.

Advances in cabin efficiency technologies provide airlines with flexibility to adjust seating layouts based on route profiles and passenger needs, optimizing both the passenger experience and economic outcomes. As a result, seating configuration plays a pivotal role in an airline's operational strategy and capacity management.

Seat Pitch

Seat pitch refers to the distance between a fixed point on one seat and the same point on the seat directly in front, typically measured in inches or centimeters. This measurement determines the amount of legroom available to passengers, significantly influencing comfort. The following highlights the implications of varying seat pitch configurations:

- A larger seat pitch offers more legroom, enhancing passenger experience.
- A smaller seat pitch allows for closer rows, increasing cabin density.

Figure 2-1 illustrates seat pitch variations across different airlines and aircraft configurations, highlighting the balance between passenger comfort and cabin capacity.

Figure 2-1. Seat pitch

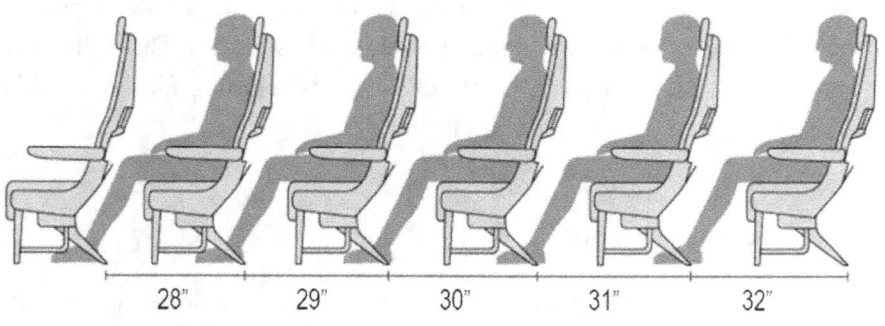

Source: Majekodunmi, Y. (2020). Review of Studies on Passenger Seat Size on Commercial Airplanes. [1]

EXAMPLE 2-1. 737-900ER Seat Pitch Configurations

The Boeing 737-900ER offers customizable seating layouts to align with operational requirements by varying seat pitch, as shown in **Figure 2-2**. The following seating configurations demonstrate how different layouts balance capacity, comfort, and operational priorities:

- **Two-Class Configuration:** Accommodates 185 seats, with 16 first-class seats at a 36-inch pitch and 166 economy seats at 31/32 inches. This configuration balances comfort with capacity, catering to both premium and economy travelers.
- **Single-Class Configuration:** A uniform 32-inch pitch allows seating for up to 199 passengers, maximizing capacity while maintaining a standard comfort level.

- **High-Density Layout:** For high-capacity routes, a 28/29-inch pitch fits up to 220 seats. This tighter configuration suits short-to-medium-haul flights where capacity optimization is prioritized over comfort.

Figure 2-2. 737-900ER seat pitch layouts

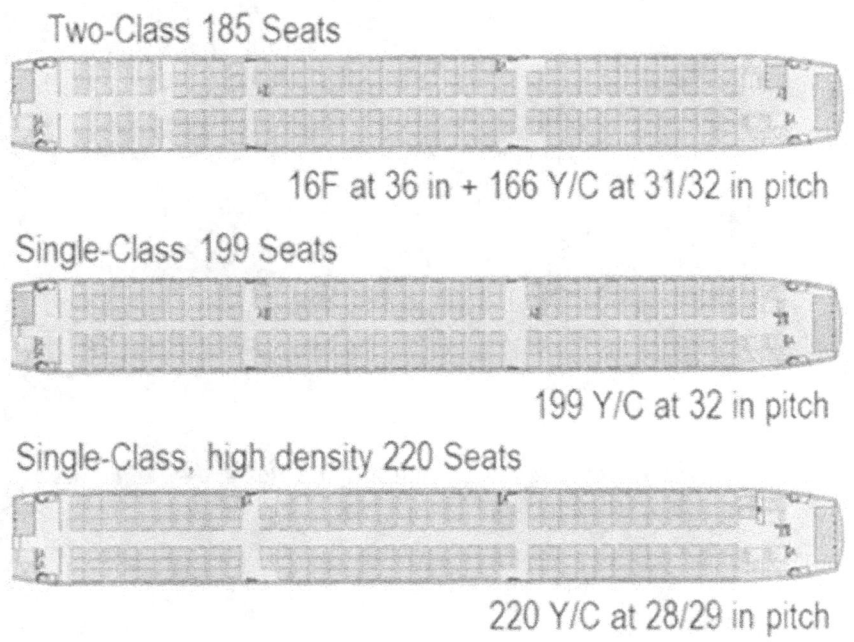

Two-Class 185 Seats

16F at 36 in + 166 Y/C at 31/32 in pitch

Single-Class 199 Seats

199 Y/C at 32 in pitch

Single-Class, high density 220 Seats

220 Y/C at 28/29 in pitch

Source: Boeing. Startup Boeing [2]

These configurations demonstrate how airlines can customize the 737-900ER's cabin layout to optimize capacity, comfort, and revenue potential based on route profiles and market demands.

Seat Pitch Trends

Industry trends indicate a shift toward denser seating layouts, as illustrated in **Figure 2-3**, which tracks changes in seat pitch within the A320 Family's single-class cabins from 2003 to 2020.

By 2020, the 28-inch pitch, once uncommon, had become the predominant configuration. This change reflects a strategic focus on maximizing seat numbers to increase revenue within the same cabin space. While this densification strategy boosts capacity, it often comes at the cost of passenger legroom, highlighting the industry's response to evolving market demands for high-capacity, cost-efficient operations.

Figure 2-3. A320 family seat pitch and capacity trends

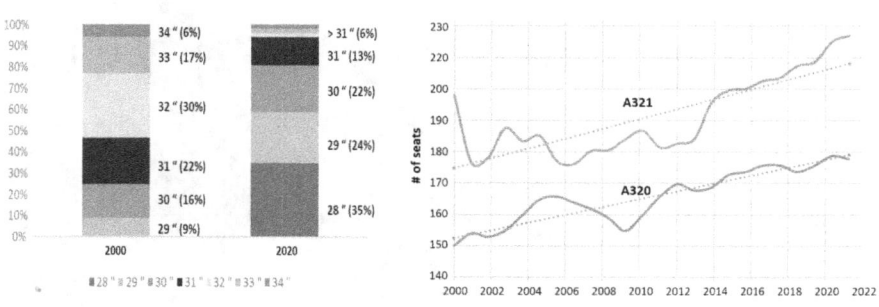

Source: Airbus. A320 Family production statistics for single-class cabins. [3], SMBC Aviation Capital. Fueling the future of flight, [4]

Seats Abreast

Adjusting the seats abreast (number of seats per row) is a strategic way to increase seating capacity without modifying cabin dimensions. For example, a typical widebody configuration with a **2-4-2** layout can be expanded to **3-4-3**, adding two additional seats per row. This adjustment significantly enhances passenger capacity while maintaining the same cabin width, making it an effective approach for airlines seeking to maximize revenue potential. **Figure 2-4** illustrates how seats abreast vary across different cabin classes and aircraft types, highlighting the balance between capacity and passenger comfort.

The following examples demonstrate how the number of seats abreast varies across cabin classes to meet specific passenger needs:

- **Standard Economy**: Typically features eight to ten seats abreast in widebody aircraft, maximizing capacity with higher density.

- **Premium Economy**: Offers six to seven seats abreast, prioritizing additional space and enhanced comfort.
- **First and Business Classes**: Designed for luxury and privacy, with three to four seats abreast, offering a superior passenger experience.

Figure 2-4. Widebody seating layouts

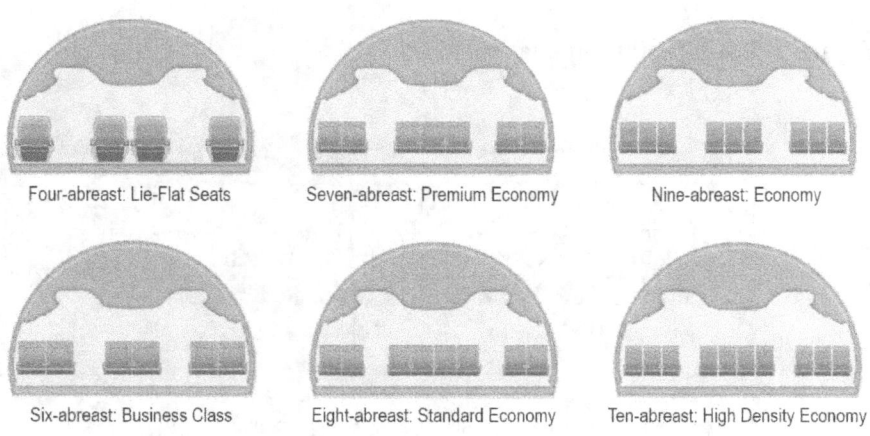

Credit: Boeing

These variations in seating layouts allow airlines to align cabin configurations with their operational goals, route profiles, and market demands, balancing passenger comfort and economic efficiency. This concept is further demonstrated in **Figure 2-5**, which illustrates two cabin configurations for the A330-300:

- The first layout, a dual-class configuration, accommodates 300 passengers, with 36 business class seats at a 60-inch pitch and 264 economy seats in an eight-abreast layout with a 32-inch pitch. This configuration suits long-haul flights, prioritizing comfort, and service differentiation.
- The second layout is high-density, single-class, seating up to 440 economy passengers. Ideal for short-to-medium-haul routes, this layout maximizes seat count, appealing to budget-conscious travelers.

Adjusting seats abreast and seat pitch gives airlines the flexibility to align cabin configurations with route profiles, demand, and revenue goals, while still considering passenger comfort. However, seating density directly impacts aircraft performance and operational costs. Denser layouts increase weight and fuel burn, potentially reducing range and efficiency, though they can lower per-seat costs, improving economic competitiveness. These trade-offs will be examined further in this section.

Figure 2-5. A330-300 cabin layouts

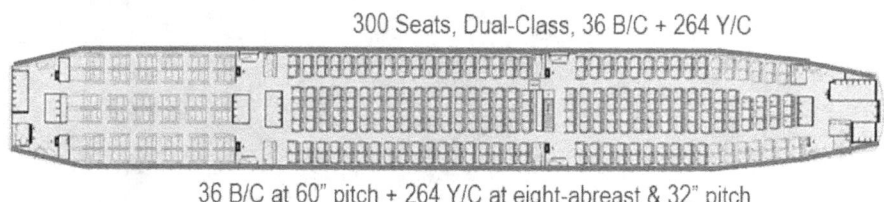

300 Seats, Dual-Class, 36 B/C + 264 Y/C

36 B/C at 60" pitch + 264 Y/C at eight-abreast & 32" pitch

Single-Class, High-density, 440 Y/C

440 Y/C at nine-abreast & 29/30" pitch *

* Requires Type A door aft of the wing

Source: Airbus, A330 Family Briefing [5]

Industry Perspective 2-1. *The LOPA Diagram*

The **Layout of Passenger Accommodations (LOPA)** *is a detailed diagram illustrating the placement of seats, galleys, lavatories, exits, and other key cabin elements within an aircraft. LOPA diagrams are critical for planning, designing, and certifying aircraft interiors, ensuring compliance with safety regulations, and optimizing operational efficiency.*

Beyond meeting regulatory requirements, the LOPA serves as a strategic tool for airlines, enabling them to optimize seating configurations and onboard services. By visually representing the cabin layout, the LOPA guides decisions that balance revenue potential, passenger comfort, and safety standards.

Figure 2-6 provides an example of a LOPA diagram, showcasing how cabin elements are arranged for a well-balanced configuration. This tool ensures:

- *Compliance with safety protocols, such as sufficient exit access for evacuations.*
- *Efficient placement of galleys and lavatories, ensuring accessibility without obstructing passenger flow.*
- *Identification of optimal seating configurations to enhance capacity and comfort while maintaining operational efficiency.*

Figure 2-6. Example LOPA diagram

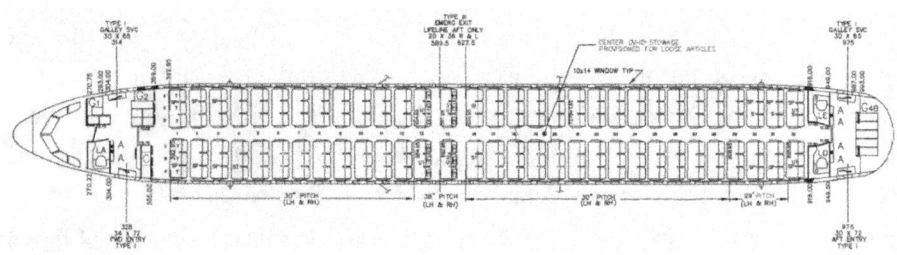

Credit: Boeing

2.1.2 Cabin Efficiency Enablers

In modern commercial aviation, airlines are continually optimizing aircraft interiors to enhance performance, passenger comfort, and economic efficiency. **Cabin Efficiency Enablers** play a pivotal role in achieving these goals.

One notable innovation is the **aft cabin redesign**, which reconfigures the rear galley and lavatories to create additional space for seating. This redesign, paired with **slim-line seats**—which reduce cabin weight while maintaining basic comfort—enables airlines to increase passenger capacity, lower unit costs, and improve economic efficiency within the same cabin footprint.

While these advancements boost revenue potential and operational efficiency, denser seating configurations may impact passenger comfort, as increased capacity often results in reduced personal space.

Aft Cabin Enhancements

Aft cabin innovations, such as the A320's **SpaceFlex** and the 737's **Pax-Plus** compact aft layout, improve space utilization and increase passenger capacity. These enhancements focus on reconfiguring the aircraft's rear section by redesigning the galley and relocating lavatories to more compact areas, achieving two primary objectives:

1. **Increased Passenger Capacity**: Frees up space to add more seats, thereby boosting total seating capacity.
2. **Enhanced Passenger Comfort**: Provides flexibility to increase seat spacing, offering additional legroom for passengers.

These innovations allow airlines to optimize cabin space, providing a cost-effective solution to increase capacity without investing in larger or more expensive aircraft. For example, the introduction of a new, more efficient rear galley and lavatory design means the A320 can be configured with up to an additional six seats. As shown in **Figure 2-7**, efficient space management enables airlines to tailor their strategy—accommodating more passengers for higher revenue or offering enhanced comfort to appeal to premium markets.

Figure 2-7. A320 Space Flex

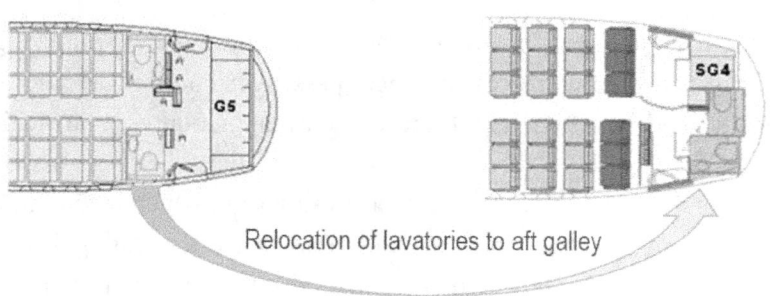

Relocation of lavatories to aft galley

Source: Airbus. Space-Flex: Innovative cabin option for A320 [6]

Slim-line Seats

Slim-line seats, as shown in **Figure 2-8**, represent a significant advancement in cabin interior optimization. These seats are lighter and more compact than traditional designs, typically reducing weight by **600–800 pounds** on narrowbody aircraft. This weight reduction contributes to lower fuel consumption and operational costs, improving overall efficiency. Additionally, their compact design allows for increased seating capacity within the same cabin footprint, enabling airlines to add more seats without modifying the aircraft's dimensions.

Figure 2-8. Slim-line seats

Credit: Recaro

Slim-line seating minimizes unit costs while maintaining acceptable comfort standards. The reduced weight decreases fuel use, directly impacting operating expenses, while the ability to accommodate additional seats enhances revenue potential. This approach is particularly beneficial for low-cost carriers and airlines operating on high-density routes, where maximizing seating capacity is critical for achieving cost efficiency.

2.1.3 Cabin Exit Doors

The **maximum seating capacity** of an aircraft is the highest number of passenger seats permitted by emergency evacuation standards established by regulatory bodies such as the **FAA** in the U.S. and the **EASA** in Europe. These regulations account for factors like aircraft design, the number and type of emergency exits, and evacuation procedures to ensure a safe and rapid evacuation for all passengers in emergencies. The maximum seating capacity, along with other specifications, is documented in the aircraft's **Type Certificate Data Sheet (TCDS)**, which defines the design, operational limits, and approved specifications of each model.

Exit Door Types and Classifications

Different exit types influence seating capacity limits based on their size, location, and evacuation capacity. Understanding these classifications is essential for assessing how aircraft configurations meet regulatory evacuation standards:

- **Type A/A+***, **Type B**, **Type C**, and **Type I**: Primary doors used for boarding, deplaning, and emergency exits.
- **Type II** and **Type III**: Overwing exits designed primarily for emergency evacuations. These are smaller than primary doors and commonly found on narrowbody aircraft.

* Type A+ Exits: Enhanced versions of Type A exits, designed to improve evacuation efficiency. For example, a pair of Type A exits can evacuate **110 passengers**, whereas Type A+ exits, with improvements like enhanced slide lighting and optimized procedures, increase capacity to **120 passengers** per pair.

For a comprehensive view of exit configurations and associated seating limits, refer to **Table 2-1**.

Table 2-1. Exit door limits

Configuration	Exit Limit	Configuration	Exit Limit
Type A / A+	110 seats / 120 seats	Type I	45 seats
Type B	75 seats	Type II	40 seats
Type C	55 seats	Type III	35 seats

Source: Author's analysis

EXAMPLE 2-2. Expanding Seating Capacity Through Exit Modifications

Aircraft manufacturers can increase seating capacity by modifying exit door configurations to meet regulatory safety standards. This process may involve adding new exit doors or adjusting existing ones to accommodate more passengers. For instance, the Boeing 737-900ER incorporates additional Type I exit doors, increasing its maximum seating capacity from 189 to 220 seats (see **Figure 2-9**). Additionally, a flat rear pressure bulkhead creates space for a new aft galley, optimizing cabin layout to support the increased seating capacity.

Figure 2-9. 737-900ER Type I exit doors

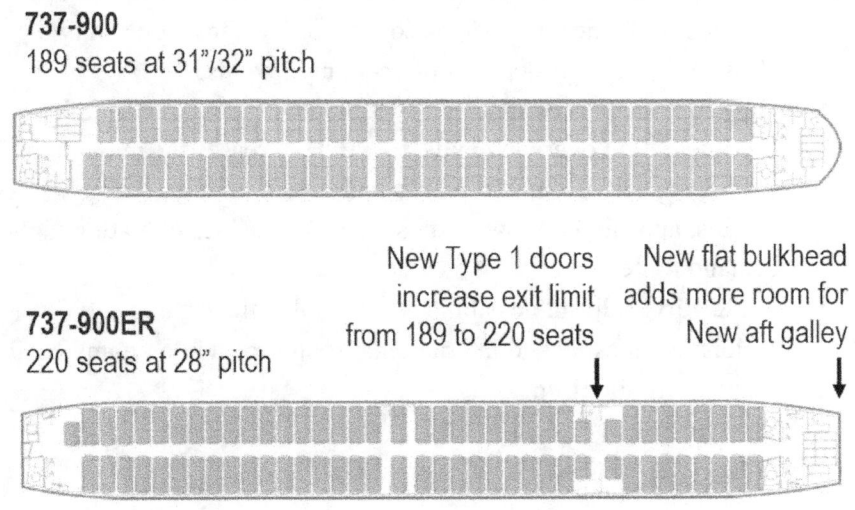

Source: Boeing. "737 Airplane Characteristics for Airport Planning" document [7]

By understanding regulatory requirements for emergency exits and strategically modifying door configurations, manufacturers like Boeing and Airbus can enhance passenger capacity while maintaining safety compliance. These design strategies maximize cabin utilization, enabling airlines to meet demand for increased seating capacity while balancing safety and operational efficiency.

EXAMPLE 2-3. The Airbus A321NEO ACF (Airbus Cabin Flex) Concept

The **Airbus A321NEO ACF (Airbus Cabin Flex)** introduces a versatile design, allowing operators to configure the aircraft to suit diverse operational and market demands. By modifying the fuselage structure, particularly the arrangement of exit doors and overwing exits, the ACF increases maximum seating capacity without changing the aircraft's dimensions. This innovation enhances cabin space utilization while adhering to evacuation safety standards.

The following highlights the key innovations that make the ACF a flexible and efficient solution for varying airline operations:

- **Flexible Exit Configurations**: The ACF supports multiple door activation setups to meet specific seating capacities and layouts. This flexibility accommodates configurations ranging from two-class cabins to high-density, all-economy layouts.
- **Higher Passenger Capacity**: By removing the second set of doors and integrating overwing exits, the ACF increases the maximum seating capacity from **220 to 240 passengers** in high-density layouts, appealing to low-cost carriers and airlines operating high-demand routes.
- **Versatility**: Adjustable cabin layouts enable the ACF to serve regional, domestic, and international routes, providing unmatched adaptability for airlines.

Figure 2-10. A321NEO ACF exit door configurations

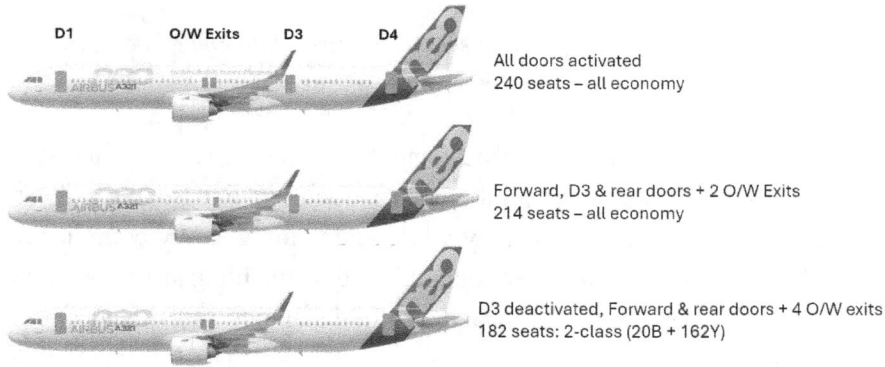

Source: Author's analysis

Figure 2-10 illustrates the flexibility of the A321NEO ACF through three distinct configurations, demonstrating its adaptability across various seating layouts:

- **240 Seats (High-Density Layout):** Activating all exit doors allows an all-economy configuration with 240 seats, ideal for low-cost carriers seeking maximum capacity.
- **214 Seats (Optimized Layout):** Utilizing forward, D3, rear doors, and two overwing exits, this configuration balances capacity and operational flexibility.
- **182 Seats (Two-Class Layout):** This configuration employs forward and rear doors with four overwing exits, prioritizing passenger comfort on mid-range routes.

The A321NEO ACF demonstrates how innovative design enhances operational flexibility, allowing airlines to optimize seating capacity while addressing varying market demands.

Industry Perspective 2-2. 737-10 MED Flexibility

*Aircraft manufacturers continually innovate to provide configuration flexibility, enabling operators to maximize capacity while meeting stringent safety regulations. Boeing's **mid-exit door design** for the 737-10, illustrated in **Figure 2-11**, demonstrates this adaptability by supporting multiple certification ratings—**Type III, Type I, and Type C**—without altering the door's physical dimensions.*

This flexibility is achieved through operational modifications around the exit door rather than changes to its size. Adjustments such as widening passageways, incorporating attendant assist spaces, or adding an attendant seat enable the same physical door to meet varying passenger evacuation capacities. These modifications comply with regulatory standards, ensuring safe emergency egress while allowing airlines to tailor the aircraft configuration to their operational needs.

Figure 2-11. 737-10 mid exit door

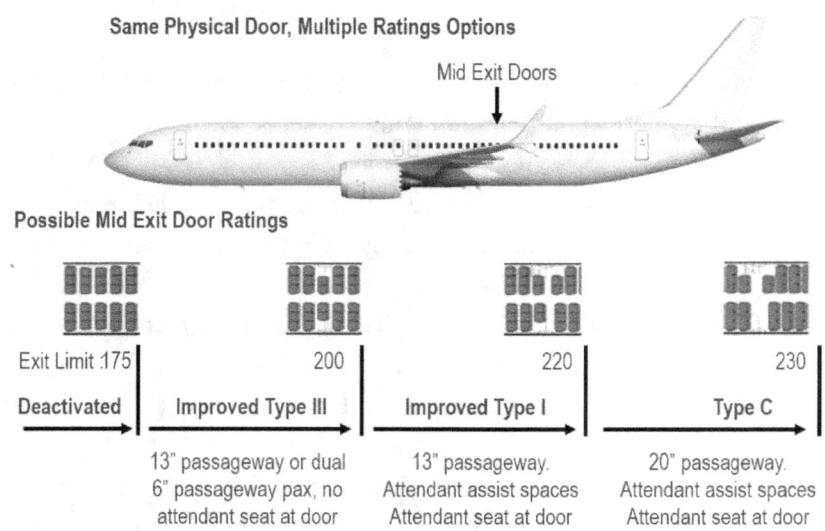

Source: Boeing, "737 Airplane Characteristics for Airport Planning" document along with modifications by the author [8]

From an operational perspective, this design offers significant benefits:

- *In **low-capacity layouts**, operators may deactivate the mid-exit door (certified as Type III) to reduce maintenance requirements or simplify cabin operations.*
- *In **high-density seating configurations**, the same door can be upgraded to a Type I or Type C rating by widening passageways and adding attendant support, allowing the aircraft to safely accommodate up to **230 passengers**.*

Widebody Modifications with Type A Doors

Strategic door configurations play a vital role in expanding the seating capacity of widebody aircraft. As illustrated in **Figure 2-12**, the addition of optional Type A doors allows aircraft like the Boeing 767-300ER and Airbus A330-300 to significantly increase their seating capacity, making them highly versatile for high-density routes.

The following examples demonstrate how Type A doors increase seating capacity in these aircraft:

- **Boeing 767-300ER**: Typically configured for 218 to 269 passengers, the addition of Type A doors increases its maximum seating capacity to 350 seats, enhancing its appeal for operations requiring higher passenger loads.
- **Airbus A330-300**: With a standard configuration seating 277 to 340 passengers, additional Type A doors enable a maximum capacity of 440 seats, making it suitable for high-demand routes.

Figure 2-12. Widebody Type A exit doors

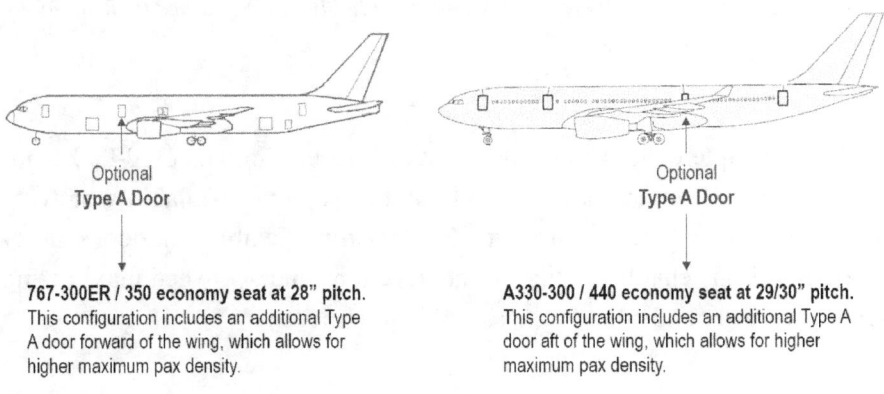

Optional
Type A Door

Optional
Type A Door

767-300ER / 350 economy seat at 28" pitch.
This configuration includes an additional Type A door forward of the wing, which allows for higher maximum pax density.

A330-300 / 440 economy seat at 29/30" pitch.
This configuration includes an additional Type A door aft of the wing, which allows for higher maximum pax density.

Source: Boeing & Airbus, "767 & A330 Airplane Characteristics for Airport Planning" document along with modifications by the author [9]

These modifications demonstrate how door configurations can optimize aircraft utility, balancing operational flexibility and passenger demand without altering the fuselage dimensions.

EXAMPLE 2-4. Passenger Emergency Exit Configurations for the A330-900
The Airbus A330-900 offers multiple emergency exit configurations, allowing airlines to adapt the aircraft to various operational needs while maintaining compliance with safety regulations. **Table 2-2** outlines these configurations, illustrating their impact on the maximum seating capacity based on the number and type of emergency exits.

Table 2-2. A330-900 layouts and maximum capacities

Configuration	Emergency Exits	Maximum Capacity
Basic	Three Pairs of Type A & One Type 1	375 Passengers
Option 1	4 Pairs of Type A	440 Passengers
Option 2	4 Pairs of Type A+	465 Passengers *

Source: Author's analysis
** Note: The A330-900's maximum seating capacity is limited to **465 passengers**, determined by the capacity of certified and installed life rafts, rather than solely by the number of emergency exits.*

This example demonstrates that seating capacity in the A330-900 is influenced by both emergency exit configurations and the availability of evacuation equipment, such as life rafts. By providing flexible exit door configurations, Airbus enables airlines to achieve a balance between maximizing seating capacity and adhering to safety requirements.

Aircraft Seating Impact on Aircraft Performance

An aircraft's seating configuration and density significantly impact its payload—the combined weight of passengers, baggage, and additional cargo. As illustrated in **Figure 2-13**, increasing seating density raises the weight attributed to passengers and baggage, which may reduce the available weight for cargo. This trade-off can limit cargo revenue on flights operating near their Maximum Takeoff Weight (MTOW).

Figure 2-13. Seating density and payload

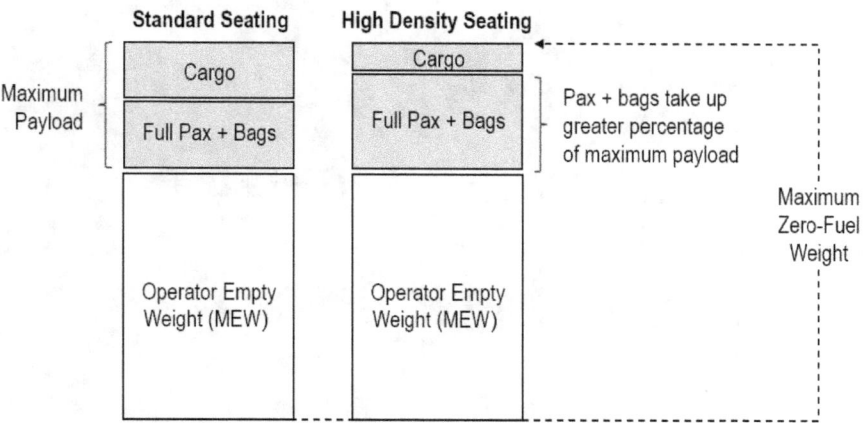

Source: Author's analysis

Seating configurations also influence overall aircraft performance. Adding more seats increases the payload, and under MTOW conditions, this may reduce fuel capacity. Each additional pound of passenger weight requires a corresponding reduction in fuel load, which can constrain the aircraft's range. Consequently, high-capacity seating configurations may limit the ability to operate longer routes efficiently, necessitating careful trade-offs between payload, fuel, and route distance.

EXAMPLE 2-5. Impact of Seating Density on Aircraft Range Performance

Figure 2-14 illustrates the impact of seating density on the maximum flight distances achievable with full passenger loads for the A330-300. Higher-density seating configurations typically reduce range, as the increased passenger and baggage weight requires a corresponding reduction in fuel to stay within the aircraft's Maximum Takeoff Weight (MTOW). This trade-off highlights the balance airlines must manage between seating capacity and range performance.

Figure 2-14. A330-300 seating density vs. range

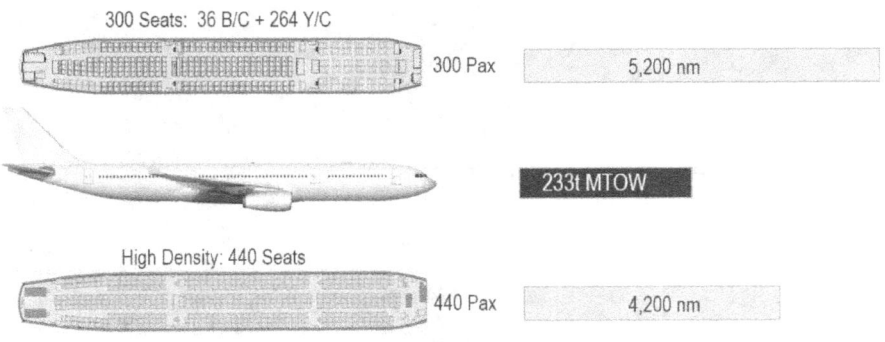

Source: Author's analysis

High-density seating configurations often align with the low-cost, long-haul (LCLH) model, which prioritizes maximizing seat numbers at the expense of range. This approach works well on shorter, more frequent routes where higher passenger volumes can be leveraged. It is particularly advantageous at airports with limited takeoff and landing slots, enabling airlines to maximize passengers per available slot.

For longer routes, lower-density layouts may be necessary to maintain sufficient fuel capacity and operational range. These configurations sacrifice some passenger capacity to ensure the aircraft can reach distant destinations without refueling, aligning better with long-haul operational demands.

Cabin configuration directly influences payload distribution and range performance. High-density seating increases passenger capacity but may limit range and cargo capacity, affecting revenue potential and route flexibility. By strategically managing seating density, airlines can optimize fleet utilization to align with their business models and market requirements.

Aircraft Seating Impact on Unit Costs

Benchmarking airliners using unit cost metrics is essential for comparing economic efficiency across different configurations. A key metric, **Available Seat-Miles (ASM)**, measures an airline's capacity by multiplying the number of available seats by miles flown over a specific period. For example, an aircraft with 180 seats on a daily 4,500-mile route generates 810,000 ASMs per day. ASM serves as a foundational measure for evaluating fleet utilization and capacity deployment across routes.

The following unit cost metrics provide airlines with insights into aircraft performance and operational efficiency:

- **Fuel Burn per ASM** and **Fuel Cost per ASM** measure fuel consumption and costs per seat-mile, respectively, highlighting the economic impact of fuel efficiency. Comparing the Fuel Burn per ASM of an Airbus A321NEO and a Boeing 737 MAX 9 on a 2,000-mile route, for example, reveals differences in fuel efficiency driven by seating configuration and weight.
- **Cash Operating Cost (COC) per ASM** includes direct costs like fuel, crew, and maintenance, while **Direct Operating Cost (DOC) per ASM** encompasses all operating expenses, offering a comprehensive view of financial efficiency.

EXAMPLE 2-6. Impact of Seat Density on Unit Cost Metrics

Increasing seat density is an effective strategy for reducing COC per ASM. For instance, adjusting a Boeing 777-300ER's cabin layout from a 2-4-2 to a 3-4-3 configuration increases seating capacity by two seats per row, distributing fixed costs over more seats and significantly lowering unit costs. Although tighter seating may reduce passenger comfort, the resulting decrease in COC per ASM is often substantial, benefiting low-cost carriers and operators prioritizing high-capacity short-haul routes.

Similarly, incorporating **slim-line seats** can yield similar efficiency gains. For example, replacing standard seats in an Airbus A321 with slim-line designs might increase capacity from 180 to 198 seats without requiring structural changes. This adjustment lowers COC per ASM by spreading fixed operating costs across more seats, increasing revenue potential per flight while maintaining operating expenses.

Understanding metrics such as Fuel Burn per ASM, Fuel Cost per ASM, COC per ASM, and DOC per ASM enables airlines to assess fleet efficiency and make informed decisions.

2.2 Fuel Capacity

Fuel capacity is a critical determinant of an aircraft's operational range and mission versatility. It refers to the total amount of fuel an aircraft can store, typically encompassing the primary tanks integrated into the wing structure and optional auxiliary tanks. Fuel capacity directly affects an aircraft's ability to operate on long-haul routes, meet reserve and contingency fuel requirements, and adapt to varying payload demands.

For commercial aircraft, balancing fuel capacity with payload and range requirements is essential. While greater fuel capacity enables extended-range missions, it also introduces trade-offs, such as increased weight, reduced cargo space, and higher fuel burn. Manufacturers and operators must carefully evaluate these factors to optimize performance and maintain economic efficiency.

This section examines the design and operational considerations related to fuel capacity, including auxiliary fuel tanks (ACTs), fuel volume limitations, and the trade-offs associated with expanded fuel storage. These insights highlight the critical role fuel capacity plays in shaping aircraft performance and route flexibility.

Auxiliary Fuel Tanks

Auxiliary Center Tanks (ACTs) are optional fuel tanks that provide additional fuel storage, enabling aircraft to extend their operational range and adapt to diverse route requirements. These tanks supplement the fuel stored in the primary wing tanks, offering greater flexibility for long-haul or specialized missions where standard fuel capacity may be insufficient. By integrating ACTs without requiring significant structural modifications, airlines can enhance an aircraft's performance versatility while maintaining operational efficiency.

The Airbus A321NEO highlights the benefits of **Additional Centre Tanks (ACTs)** in expanding operational range. With a Maximum Takeoff Weight (MTOW) of 89 tonnes and standard fuel capacity, the A321NEO achieves a range of 2,800 nautical miles (nm). However, the optional installation of up to three ACTs significantly increases its range, enabling transatlantic capabilities.

The following configurations illustrate how ACTs, combined with incremental MTOW increases, enhance the A321NEO's range potential:

- **One ACT at 93.5 tonnes MTOW:** Extends the range to 3,200 nm.
- **Three ACTs at 97 tonnes MTOW:** Reaches a range of 3,600 nm.

This increased range capability demonstrates the adaptability of the A321NEO to varying operational needs. For long-haul flights or specialized missions, airlines can install ACTs in the cargo hold to expand fuel capacity while maintaining safety and performance. Although ACTs may reduce cargo space, the added range flexibility enables airlines to explore new route opportunities, optimize aircraft utilization, and meet evolving market demands effectively.

Figure 2-15. A320NEO adaptive fuel capacity

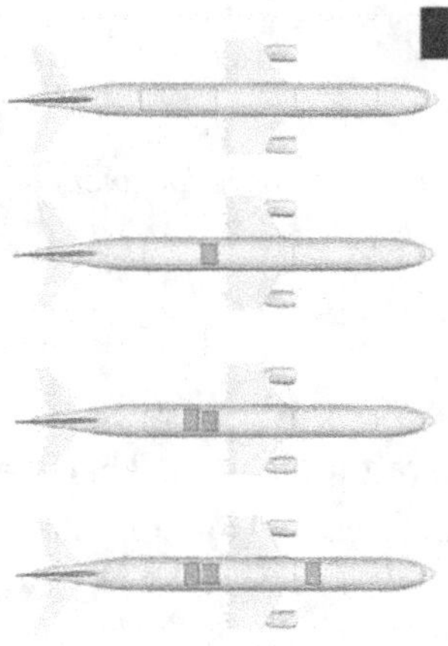

	ACTs	MTOW	Fuel, (gal) liters	Range (nm) *
	Basic (0)	89 t – 93.5 t	(6,229) 23,580	2,800
	1 ACT	89 t – 93.5 t	(7,053) 26,701	3,200
	2 ACT	89 t – 93.5 t	(7,877) 29,822	3,550
	3 ACT	89 t – 97 t	(8,701) 32,943	3,600

* 206 Pax + Bags

Source: Airbus, "A321 Airplane Characteristics for Airport Planning" document along with modifications by the author [10]

EXAMPLE 2-7. Range Enhancement through Optional Auxiliary Fuel Tanks in the 737-900ER

The Boeing 737-900ER can be equipped with up to two Auxiliary Center Tanks (ACTs), as illustrated in **Figure 2-16**. These optional tanks increase the aircraft's range by up to 715 nautical miles (nm) beyond its standard configuration. This enhancement allows operators to deploy the 737-900ER on longer routes, expanding its operational envelope and increasing route flexibility.

Figure 2-16. 737-900ER adaptive fuel capacity

Optional Tanks	Fuel, (gal) liters	OEW, lb (kg)	Range, (nm) km	Cargo Volume, ft³ (m³)
0	**(6,875)** 26,020	**96,780** (43,890)	**(2,845)** 5,265	**1,824** (51.7)
1	**(7,390)** 27,970 **(+515)** +1,950	**98,170** (44,520) **+1,390** (+630)	**(3,045)** 5,635 **(+200)** +370	**1,674** (47.4) **-150** (4.3)
2	**(7,837)** 29,660 **(+962)** +3,640	**98,510** (44,680) **+1,730** (+790)	**(3,200)** 5,980 **(+385)** +715	**1,585** (44.9) **-239** (6.8)

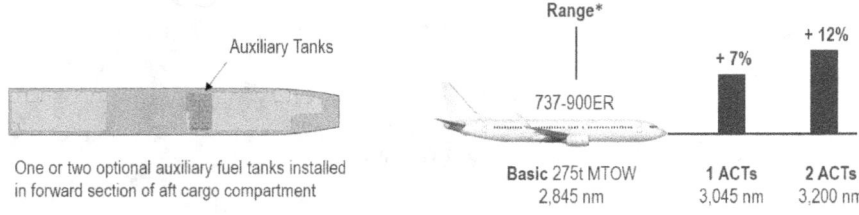

Auxiliary Tanks

One or two optional auxiliary fuel tanks installed
in forward section of aft cargo compartment

Range*

737-900ER

+ 7%   + 12%

Basic 275t MTOW   1 ACTs   2 ACTs
2,845 nm   3,045 nm   3,200 nm

* Pax = 180 lb (82 kg) / Bag = 40 lb (18 kg)

Source: Boeing. "737 Airplane Characteristics for Airport Planning" document along with modifications by the author [7]

By extending mission range and enhancing route flexibility, ACTs provide airlines with a versatile tool for optimizing aircraft utilization. This capability enables carriers to adapt to evolving market demands and explore new route opportunities effectively.

Trade-offs of Auxiliary Fuel Tanks (ACTs)

Installing Auxiliary Center Tanks (ACTs), whether detachable or fixed, involves modifications to the aircraft's fuel system, including specialized fuel lines, pumps, and hardware to manage fuel flow from the auxiliary tanks to the engines. ACTs significantly increase an aircraft's fuel capacity, enabling it to serve longer routes and enhancing route flexibility.

The following trade-offs illustrate the operational considerations airlines must evaluate when integrating ACTs:

- **Increased Operating Empty Weight (OEW):** The addition of tanks and associated hardware raises the aircraft's OEW, which can affect takeoff performance and fuel efficiency.

- **Reduced Cargo Space:** ACTs often occupy fuselage or cargo areas, limiting space available for freight and potentially reducing revenue on cargo-intensive routes.

By aligning ACT configurations with specific operational requirements, airlines can maximize aircraft utility for extended-range missions while maintaining flexibility for shorter, high-demand routes.

Fuel Volume Limitations

Fuel volume limitations occur when an aircraft's fuel tank capacity cannot store the amount of fuel required for a specific mission, despite the aircraft's Maximum Takeoff Weight (MTOW) allowing additional load. This constraint is driven by the physical volume available in the fuel tanks rather than weight limitations.

While Auxiliary Center Tanks (ACTs) can expand fuel capacity, some aircraft, such as the Boeing 777-200LR, may still face fuel volume limitations during extreme ultra-long-haul operations. For example, polar routes or missions with elevated reserve and contingency fuel requirements may exceed available tank volume.

Fuel volume limitations introduce several operational trade-offs:

- **Maximizing Range:** Optimized tank designs or auxiliary tanks can extend range, though this often reduces payload or cargo capacity.
- **Cargo and Payload Trade-offs:** Auxiliary tanks may occupy valuable cargo space, forcing airlines to balance revenue potential against operational requirements.
- **Efficiency and Economics:** Operating at or near maximum fuel capacity increases weight, leading to higher fuel burn and operating costs. Airlines must weigh the economic impacts of such configurations.

These constraints emphasize the need to balance fuel capacity, payload, and range for efficient mission performance. By addressing fuel volume limitations strategically, airlines can optimize fleet utilization for both operational flexibility and economic efficiency.

Industry Perspective 2-3. A350-900 ULR Fuel and Performance

The A350-900 benefits from a shared wingbox design with the larger A350-1000, enabling its fuel capacity to increase from 141,000 liters to 165,000 liters through internal fuel system modifications. These enhancements eliminate the need for auxiliary tanks while significantly extending the aircraft's range. This variant is designated as the A350-900 ULR (Ultra-Long-Range).

Figure 2-17 illustrates the improved performance of the ULR variant compared to the standard A350-900, emphasizing its extended range, and enhanced operational flexibility.

Figure 2-17. A350-900 adaptive fuel capacity

-900	Liters	US Gallons
Center	80,900	21,370
Wing (x2)	59,800	15,800
Total	**140,700**	**37,170**

-900 ULR	Liters	US Gallons
Center	105,200	27,790
Wing (x2)	59,800	15,800
Total	**165,000**	**43,590**

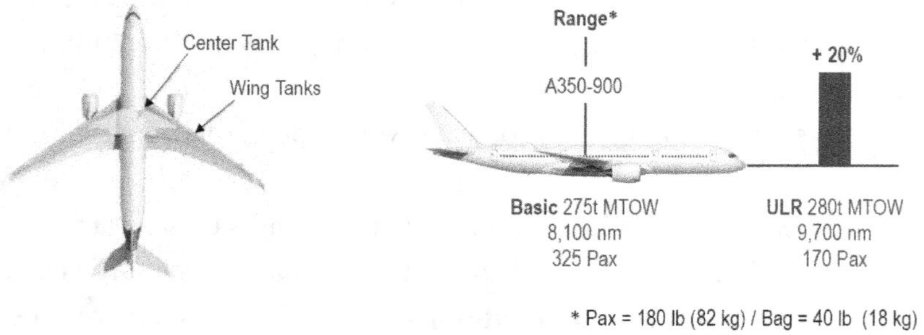

Source: Airbus. "A350 Airplane Characteristics for Airport Planning" document along with modifications by the author [11]

2.3 Cargo Volume Capacity

Cargo volume capacity refers to the maximum volume an aircraft can transport, constrained by its structural design and configuration. This capacity is typically measured in cubic feet or meters, reflecting the available space for cargo storage. While weight limits are also critical, the focus here is on the volumetric aspect of cargo, which varies significantly across aircraft models based on design trade-offs made during development.

Understanding cargo volume capacity is essential for evaluating an aircraft's freight potential. Airlines and logistics providers must consider not only the available space but also the accessibility and configuration of cargo compartments, as these factors significantly affect loading, unloading, and transport efficiency.

Cargo Volume Capacity in Widebody Passenger Aircraft

Widebody passenger aircraft provide **belly freight capacity**—cargo storage located beneath the main cabin. Although primarily designed for passenger transport, belly freight contributes significantly to operational profitability.

Key advantages of belly freight capacity include:

- **Lucrative Cargo Revenue**: On high-demand routes, increased cargo capacity can significantly boost revenue, particularly for time-sensitive or specialized freight commanding premium rates.
- **Operational Flexibility**: Spacious cargo holds allow airlines to adjust routes to align with cargo demand, ensuring a steady income even during passenger traffic fluctuations.
- **Revenue Diversification**: Substantial cargo capacity diversifies income streams, offering financial resilience during periods of reduced passenger demand, such as economic slowdowns.

EXAMPLE 2-8. Maximizing Cargo Capacity in the Boeing 787-9

The Boeing 787-9 conveys a balanced design that meets both passenger and cargo demands. As illustrated in **Figure 2-18**, the aircraft's lower hold accommodates up to 36 LD3 containers. Additionally, the forward hold can house six 96 x 125-inch pallets, while the aft hold provides space for four more pallets. This versatile configuration enables airlines to efficiently adjust to varying cargo demands, optimizing capacity and revenue potential.

Figure 2-18. 787-9 belly freight capacity

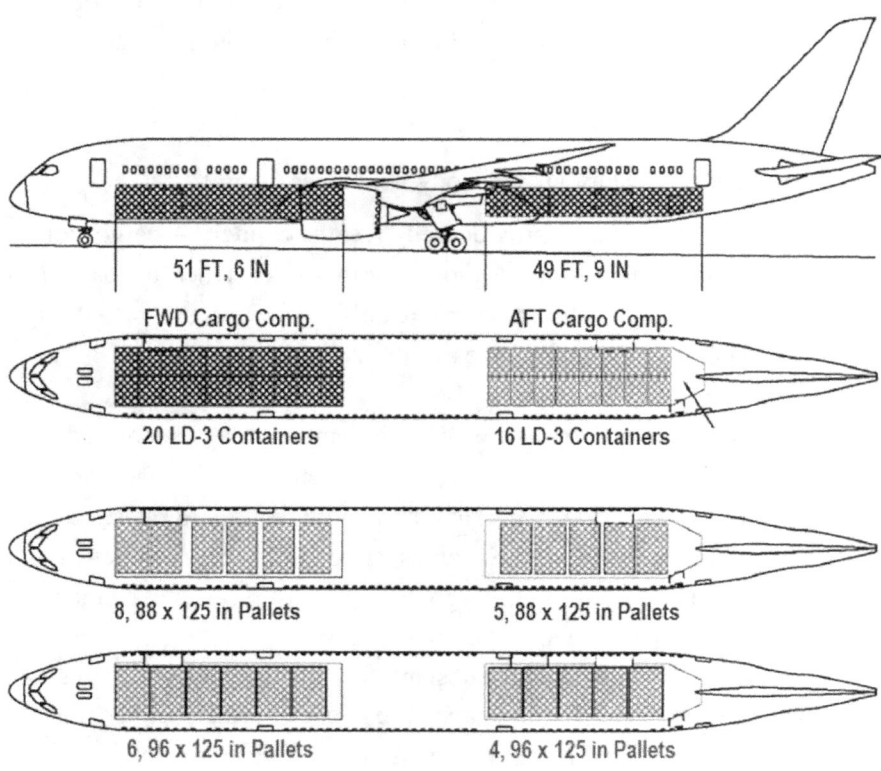

51 FT, 6 IN   49 FT, 9 IN

FWD Cargo Comp.   AFT Cargo Comp.

20 LD-3 Containers   16 LD-3 Containers

8, 88 x 125 in Pallets   5, 88 x 125 in Pallets

6, 96 x 125 in Pallets   4, 96 x 125 in Pallets

Source: Boeing. "787 Airplane Characteristics for Airport Planning" document [12]

Cargo Doors in Widebody Aircraft

Certain widebody aircraft, such as the **Boeing 767-300ER** and **777-300ER**, offer optional large cargo doors to enhance operational efficiency by accommodating oversized or non-standard cargo. These doors simplify loading and unloading processes, reducing turnaround times, and expanding the range of cargo the aircraft can carry.

While metrics like cargo volume and weight are paramount, practical design features—such as large cargo doors—are equally important in providing operational flexibility. This adaptability meets diverse logistical needs and offers airlines a competitive advantage. In a dynamic global market with shifting cargo demands, versatile aircraft capable of handling both standard and oversized cargo are vital for success.

The inclusion of large cargo doors broadens cargo operations beyond basic volume and weight limitations, allowing airlines to transport a wider range of freight. This versatility maximizes cargo capacity and strengthens an airline's position within the competitive air freight industry.

As depicted in **Figure 2-19**, the **777-300ER's optional large cargo door**, located on the left side of the fuselage, facilitates efficient handling of both standard pallets and uniquely shaped items, significantly enhancing cargo-handling capabilities and ensuring adaptability to diverse market requirements.

Figure 2-19. 777-300ER cargo door options

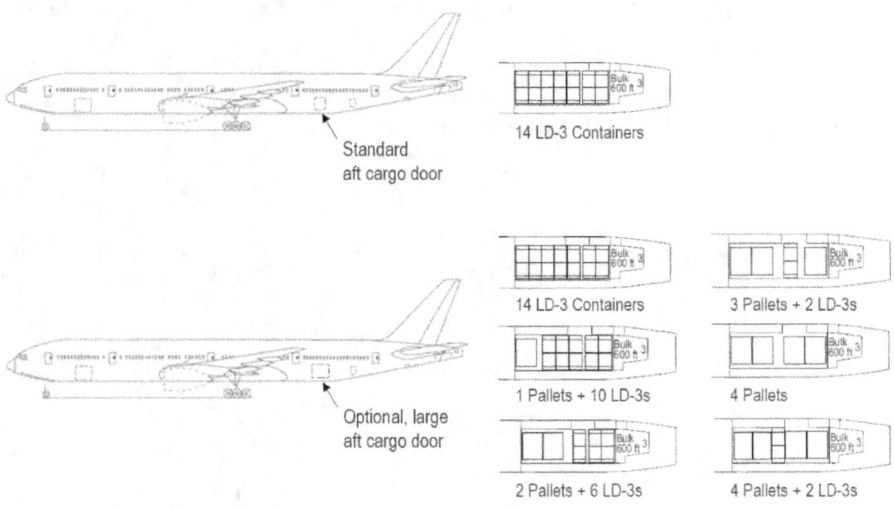

Source: "777 Airplane Characteristics for Airport Planning" document, along with modifications by the author [13]

2.3.1 Cargo Volume Capacity in Freighter Aircraft

The **cargo volume capacity** of freighter aircraft is a critical factor in aircraft selection, directly influencing the types of goods they can transport, operational efficiency, and revenue potential. This capacity encompasses the volumetric space available for cargo as well as the ability to accommodate high-density shipments, enabling operators to handle a wide spectrum of freight effectively.

Freighters like the Boeing 747-400BCF and 777 Freighter excel in versatility, making them indispensable for industries such as automotive, aerospace, and e-commerce. These aircraft are designed to transport both large volumes of low-density cargo and high-density items, such as machinery, electronics, and raw materials.

As illustrated in **Figure 2-20**, the Boeing 747-400BCF (Boeing Converted Freighter) leverages its main deck for palletized or containerized cargo using unit load devices (ULDs). The lower hold configuration varies by aircraft model, offering flexibility to accommodate a mix of containers, pallets, or bulk-loaded cargo. This adaptability ensures efficient handling of diverse freight types, from high-volume, low-density goods to dense, weight-intensive shipments.

Figure 2-20. 747-400BCF cargo layout

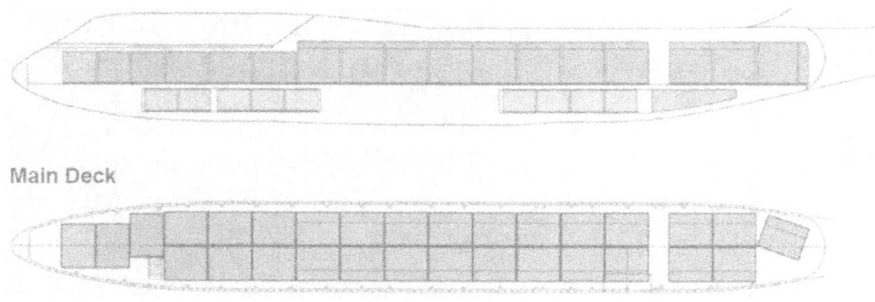

Main Deck

Source: Boeing. Startup Boeing [2]

Beyond its volumetric capacity, the Boeing 747-400BCF is optimized for high-density cargo, such as heavy machinery, industrial equipment, or other weight-intensive shipments. Its robust structural design and high revenue payload—the total weight of revenue-generating cargo—enables it to prioritize weight over volume when needed. This flexibility allows operators to maximize profitability by tailoring each flight to carry either high-density cargo or lower-density, high-volume shipments. This capability is particularly valuable for industries requiring dense material transport, enabling operators to balance high-volume and high-weight cargo based on mission requirements.

Aircraft with substantial volumetric capacity, such as the Boeing 747-400BCF, are especially advantageous for industries where cargo volume drives revenue. For instance, e-commerce and aerospace operations often require the transportation of bulky or irregularly shaped items that occupy significant space but may not be weight-intensive. Additionally, these freighters are optimized for carrying dense cargo, maximizing payload efficiency when freight costs are based on weight rather than volume.

Figure 2-21 highlights the total net available cargo volume of the Boeing 747-400BCF, a critical metric for logistics planning and load optimization. While the bulk area may not be explicitly itemized by pallet or container capacity, it significantly contributes to total cargo volume, ensuring the efficient use of every cubic foot for freight operations.

Figure 2-21. 747-400BCF available cargo volume

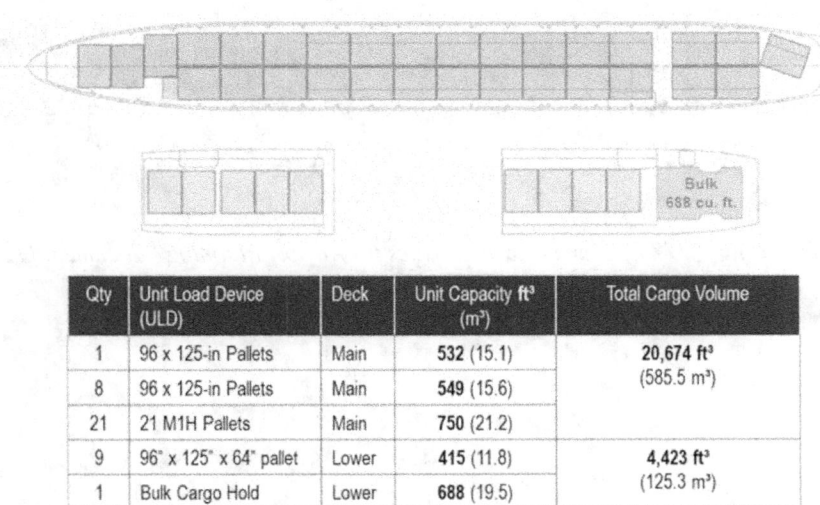

Qty	Unit Load Device (ULD)	Deck	Unit Capacity ft³ (m³)	Total Cargo Volume
1	96 x 125-in Pallets	Main	532 (15.1)	20,674 ft³ (585.5 m³)
8	96 x 125-in Pallets	Main	549 (15.6)	
21	21 M1H Pallets	Main	750 (21.2)	
9	96" x 125" x 64" pallet	Lower	415 (11.8)	4,423 ft³ (125.3 m³)
1	Bulk Cargo Hold	Lower	688 (19.5)	

Total = 25,097 ft³ (710.7 m³)

Source: Boeing. Startup Boeing [2]

Industry Perspective 2-4. *Main Deck Cargo Layout*

Figure *2-22 highlights the versatility of the **Boeing 777-200F** main deck cargo arrangement, showcasing its adaptability to a wide range of cargo types and volumes. This flexibility is a core feature of the aircraft's design, enabling operators to efficiently transport various freight, from standard containers to oversized cargo. The schematic demonstrates multiple configurations, incorporating different combinations of pallets and unit load devices (ULDs), emphasizing the aircraft's ability to optimize cargo hold layout for maximum space utilization and payload efficiency.*

This adaptability is particularly valuable for operators managing diverse cargo demands, including volumetric payloads, such as e-commerce shipments and lightweight goods, and high-density payloads, like heavy machinery and industrial equipment. By accommodating both types of freight efficiently, the 777-200F enhances operational flexibility and maximizes revenue potential for each flight.

Figure 2-22. 777-200F main deck cargo

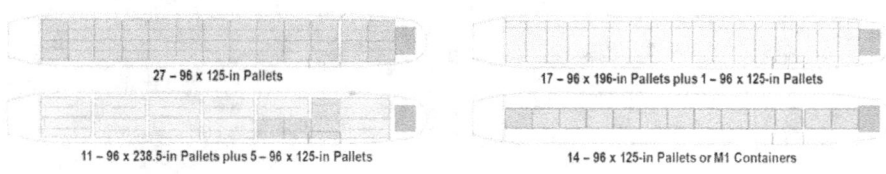

27 – 96 x 125-in Pallets

17 – 96 x 196-in Pallets plus 1 – 96 x 125-in Pallets

11 – 96 x 238.5-in Pallets plus 5 – 96 x 125-in Pallets

14 – 96 x 125-in Pallets or M1 Containers

Source: Boeing. "777 Airplane Characteristics for Airport Planning" document [13]

Chapter 2. Key Takeaways

1. **Cabin Layout**: Efficient cabin layouts, including seating configuration, space utilization, and innovations like aft cabin redesigns, balance passenger comfort and operational cost efficiency. By optimizing seat density and space usage, airlines can improve market competitiveness and enhance performance and economic positioning.

2. **Seating Layout**: Factors like seat pitch (distance between rows) and seats abreast (number of seats per row) significantly impact seating density, passenger comfort, and economic efficiency. High-density layouts maximize passenger capacity, making them ideal for high-demand routes, but may reduce range and cargo capacity, requiring careful planning to balance revenue and operational needs.

3. **Cabin Efficiency Enablers**: Innovations such as Space-Flex configurations, slim-line seats, and Smart-Lav designs increase passenger capacity, reduce cabin weight, and improve fuel efficiency. These enhancements optimize cabin space while maintaining or improving passenger comfort, directly contributing to economic efficiency and competitiveness.

4. **Cabin Exit Doors**: Exit door types and configurations determine maximum seating capacity by ensuring compliance with safety and evacuation standards. Strategic modifications, like adding additional exits or upgrading to larger door types (e.g., Type A), increase passenger capacity without compromising safety.

5. **Impact of Seating on Aircraft Performance**: Seating configurations affect payload distribution, range, and cargo capacity. High-density seating increases passenger numbers but may reduce available cargo space and limit range when operating at Maximum Takeoff Weight (MTOW). Airlines must carefully balance these trade-offs based on route profiles and revenue goals.

6. **Unit Cost Economics**: Metrics such as Available Seat-Miles (ASM), Fuel Burn per ASM, Fuel Cost per ASM, Cash Operating Cost (COC) per ASM, and Direct Operating Cost (DOC) per ASM are vital for

assessing fleet efficiency. These metrics inform decisions on seating configurations, fuel management, and operational cost optimization, ensuring economic viability and competitiveness.

7. **Fuel Capacity**: Fuel capacity determines range and route flexibility. Features like auxiliary center tanks (ACTs) and integrated fuel system modifications (e.g., in the A350-900 ULR) extend range capabilities, enabling airlines to serve longer routes and adapt to diverse operational needs without sacrificing performance.

8. **Fuel Volume Limitations**: Fuel volume limitations occur when tank capacity is insufficient to store the required fuel, even if the MTOW allows for additional load. This is common in ultra-long-haul operations and necessitates trade-offs such as reduced payload or cargo space. Understanding these constraints is vital for route planning and fleet utilization.

9. **Cargo Capacity**: Cargo capacity, particularly in widebody aircraft, drives significant revenue through belly freight. Effective management of volumetric payloads (low-density, high-volume goods) and high-density payloads (heavy goods) is essential for optimizing revenue and operational performance.

10. **Freighter Aircraft Cargo Capacity**: Freighter aircraft prioritize flexible volume and weight capabilities to manage diverse cargo types. Models like the Boeing 747-400BCF and 777 Freighter demonstrate versatility in addressing both volumetric and weight-intensive payload demands, serving industries like e-commerce and heavy manufacturing.

11. **Cargo Operations Versatility**: Features like large cargo doors and adaptable main deck configurations enhance the ability to transport oversized or non-standard items. This versatility strengthens an airline's position in the competitive air freight market by efficiently meeting diverse cargo needs.

Case Study 2-1. Exit Door Configurations

Figure 2-23. A321NEO ACF configurations

Feature	Standard A321NEO	A321NEO ACF
Maximum Seating Capacity	220 seats	240 seats
Exit Door Configuration	Door 1, Door 2, Door 3, Door 4	Door 1, Door 3 (relocated), Door 4, Two Overwing Exits
Max Takeoff Weight (MTOW)	93.5 tonnes (206.1 klb.)	97 tonnes (213.8 klb.)

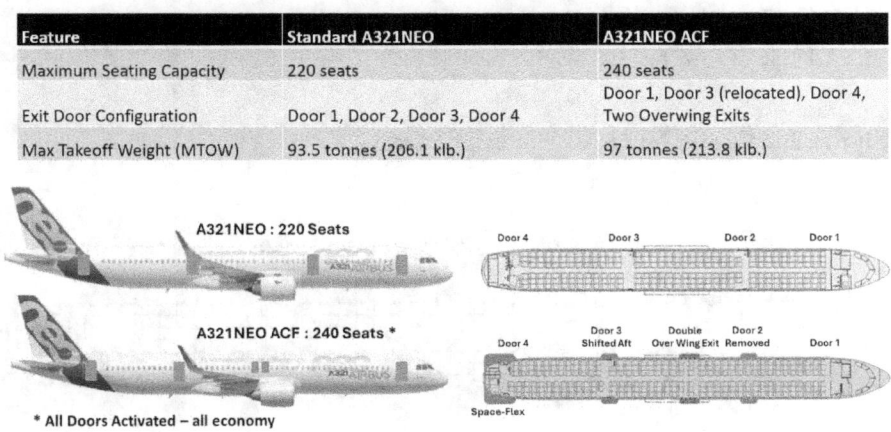

Source: Airbus and author's analysis

Questions:

1. Referring to the figure above, evaluate how the placement and modifications to cabin exit doors in the A321NEO ACF configuration influence the aircraft's maximum seating capacity and operational efficiency.

2. What are the potential performance tradeoffs airlines must consider with the increased seating capacity of the A321NEO ACF?

3. How does the space flex rear galley configuration contribute to the overall benefits of the Airbus A321NEO—ACF modification?

4. An airline is deciding between deploying the A321NEO (Standard) configuration or the A321NEO (ACF) configuration on a high-demand short-haul route with fluctuating seasonal passenger volumes. Evaluate the suitability of each configuration in terms of profitability, operational efficiency, long-term flexibility, and the implications of

landing and navigation fees. Provide a recommendation supported by your analysis.

5. Referring to the figure below, Analyze the impact of the removal of Door 2 on the cabin configuration and seating arrangement in the A321NEO ACF.

Figure 2-24. A321NEO ACF interior layout

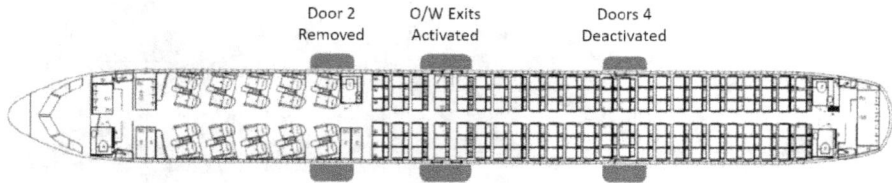

Credit: Airbus

Case Study 2-2. Fuel Capacity Evaluation

Figure 2-25. 777-200 family specifications

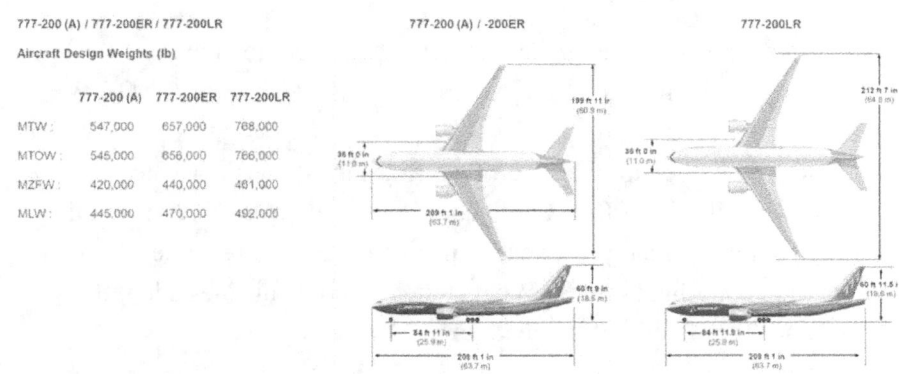

Source: Boeing. Startup Boeing [2]

Figure 2-26. 777-200 family fuel capacity

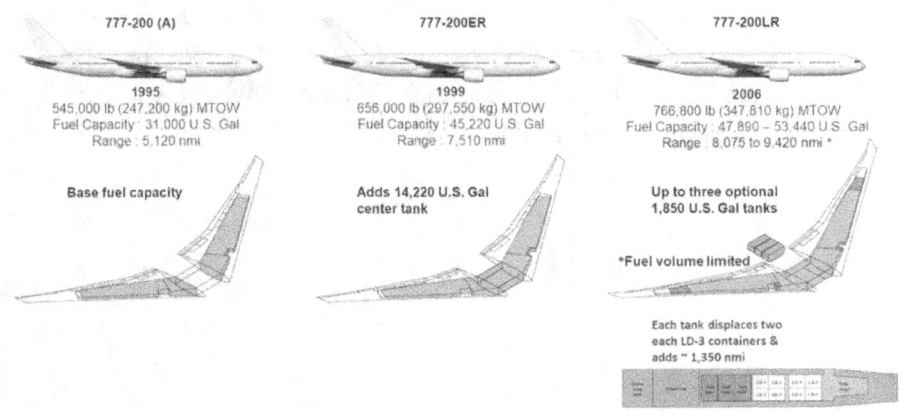

Credit: Boeing

Questions:

1. Why is a higher MTOW necessary for longer range flights, and how does it impact the range capabilities of the 777 variants?

2. What are some design and engineering considerations that manufacturers must consider when increasing an aircraft's MTOW?

3. Discuss the operational trade-offs airlines must consider when equipping the 777-200LR with additional fuel tanks. How does this decision impact cargo payload capacity, range, and revenue potential on ultra-long-haul routes? What strategies could airlines adopt to balance these trade-offs effectively?

4. An airline is evaluating whether to retain its fleet of 777-200 (A-Market) aircraft or upgrade to the 777-200ER to better serve medium- to long-haul routes. Evaluate the operational and financial trade-offs between these two variants, considering factors such as range, payload capacity, fuel efficiency, and market demand. Provide a recommendation supported by your analysis.

5. The 777-200LR has a stated design range of 9,420 nautical miles and is described as "fuel volume limited." What does this imply about the aircraft's design and operational capabilities?

References

[1] Y. Majekodunmi, "Review of Studies on Passenger Seat Size on Commercial Airplanes," Miami-Dade Auditor Library, Jan. 15, 2020. [Online]. Available: https://www.miamidade.gov/auditor/library/studies-on -passenger-seat-size-on-commercial-airplanes.pdf

[2] Boeing, "Startup Boeing." [Online]. Available: https://www.boeing. com/company/about-bca/startupboeing#selection

[3] Airbus, "A320 Family production statistics for single-class cabins," Airbus

[4] SMBC Aviation Capital, "Fueling the Aviation of Flight." [Online]. Available: https://www.smbc.aero/

[5] Airbus, "A330 Family Briefing," Reference CVM 310.0015 Issue 10, Sep. 2006.

[6] Airbus, "Space-Flex: Innovative cabin option for A320." [Online]. Available: https://www.noticiaslatamsales.com/noticias/april-2012 /space-flex-innovative-cabin-option-a320/

[7] Boeing, "737 Airplane Characteristics for Airport Planning," Document D6-58325-7, Revision A, Mar. 2023. [Online]. Available: https://www .boeing.com/commercial/airports/plan-manuals

[8] Boeing, "737 Airplane Characteristics for Airport Planning," Document D6-38A004, Revision J, Jan. 2024. [Online]. Available: https://www .boeing.com/commercial/airports/plan-manuals

[9] Boeing, "767 Airplane Characteristics for Airport Planning," Document D6-58328, Revision J, Aug. 2023. [Online]. Available: https://www.boeing .com/commercial/airports/plan-manuals

[10] Airbus, "A330 Aircraft Characteristics for Airport Planning," AC A330, Nov. 2024. [Online]. Available: https://www.airbus.com/aircraft /airport-operations/airport-planning-manuals

[11] Airbus, "A321 Aircraft Characteristics for Airport Planning," AC A321/A321neo, Jun. 2024. [Online]. Available: https://www.airbus.com /aircraft/airport-operations/airport-planning-manuals

[12] Airbus, "A350 Aircraft Characteristics for Airport Planning," AC A350-900/-1000/-1000F, May 2024. [Online]. Available: https://www .airbus.com/aircraft/airport-operations/airport-planning-manuals

[13] Boeing, "787 Airplane Characteristics for Airport Planning," Document D6-58333, Revision O, Feb. 2023. [Online]. Available: https://www.boeing.com/commercial/airports/plan-manuals

[14] Boeing, "777 Airplane Characteristics for Airport Planning," Document D6-58329-2, Revision F, Dec. 2022. [Online]. Available: https://www.boeing.com/commercial/airports/plan-manuals

Chapter 3

Aircraft Payloads

This Chapter is About:

This chapter delves into the critical role of payload in aircraft operations, expanding on concepts introduced earlier. Payload encompasses the combined weight of passengers, baggage, and cargo, and its capacity is determined by the structural design and spatial configuration of the aircraft. The fuselage's structural strength and internal dimensions dictate the maximum payload an aircraft can safely carry. Effective payload management requires balancing these factors to optimize operational performance.

The chapter is structured around three primary aspects of payload:

1. **Maximum Structural Payload (MSP):** The maximum weight the aircraft's structure can safely support while maintaining structural integrity under various loading conditions.
2. **Adaptive Payload:** The concept of adjusting the Maximum Zero Fuel Weight (MZFW) to accommodate flight length and fuel

requirements, often referred to as *dynamic payload management*, allows flexibility in optimizing payload capacity and efficiency.

3. **Volume-Limited Payload (VLP):** The constraints posed by the aircraft's internal dimensions, such as cabin layout and cargo hold size, which define the volume available for passengers, baggage, and cargo.

Special emphasis is placed on freighter aircraft, which prioritize maximizing cargo volume over passenger accommodations. Key considerations include:

- **MSP vs. VLP:** Balancing the aircraft's structural weight limits (MSP) with the spatial constraints of the cargo hold (VLP) is important for efficient cargo operations.
- **Revenue Payload:** Strategies for maximizing the weight of revenue-generating cargo within MSP and VLP limits to optimize profitability.
- **Packing Density:** A measure of how effectively cargo space is utilized, with high packing density directly impacting revenue and operational efficiency.
- **Running Load Limitations:** Managing cargo distribution to maintain the aircraft's center of gravity within safe limits, ensuring flight stability and performance.

By exploring these elements, the chapter highlights the important role of payload management in aviation, particularly for freighter operations. Readers will gain a comprehensive understanding of how payload dynamics influence aircraft performance, operational efficiency, and revenue generation in the aviation industry.

3.1 Maximum Structural Payload (MSP)

The **Maximum Structural Payload (MSP)** represents the highest payload weight—comprising passengers, baggage, and cargo—that an aircraft's structure can safely support, as certified by aviation authorities. It excludes fuel and ensures the aircraft operates within its structural design capacity, preserving integrity and preventing damage. MSP is documented in key resources like the **Aircraft Flight Manual (AFM)** and the **Weight & Balance Manual**.

The following considerations illustrate MSP's role in balancing payload, range, and regulatory compliance:

1. **Fuel and Range Trade-offs:**
   » The Maximum Structural Payload (MSP) is based on the aircraft's Maximum Zero-Fuel Weight (MZFW), which limits the maximum payload (passengers, baggage, and cargo) that can be carried, excluding fuel.
   » When operating near MSP (i.e., near the MZFW limit), the remaining allowable weight up to Maximum Takeoff Weight (MTOW) must be allocated to fuel. If the payload is heavy (approaching MSP), there may be insufficient margin to carry a full fuel load, which can limit range.
   » Conversely, when operating below MSP, additional weight capacity becomes available for fuel loading, allowing the aircraft to carry more fuel and extend its range.
2. **Structural and Stability Concerns:**
   » Exceeding MSP risks structural stress and potential damage.
   » Overloading can shift the aircraft's center of gravity (CG), compromising stability and control.
3. **Regulatory Compliance:**
   » Regulatory bodies like the FAA and EASA enforce adherence to MSP limits to ensure safety.
   » Violating MSP regulations can result in penalties, operational restrictions, or grounding of the aircraft.

MZFW Limitations

MSP is intrinsically linked to MZFW, which represents the maximum allowable weight of the aircraft excluding fuel. MSP cannot exceed the difference between MZFW and Operating Empty Weight (OEW), making MZFW a critical determinant of payload limits.

The formula for determining Maximum Structural Payload is:

$$MSP = MDZFW - OEW \quad \text{(Eq. 3-1)}$$

Where:

- MSP = Maximum Structural Payload
- MDZFW = Maximum Design Zero Fuel Weight
- OEW = Operating Empty Weight

While the MDZFW is fixed during the aircraft design and certification process, the OEW varies based on airline-specific customizations, such as cabin layouts, onboard equipment, and additional systems. These variations in OEW directly influence the Maximum Structural Payload (MSP), shaping payload capacity and operational efficiency.

The following examples illustrate how OEW impacts MSP:

- **Higher OEW:** Reduces MSP, limiting payload capacity and potentially impacting revenue potential on high-demand routes.
- **Lower OEW:** Increases MSP, allowing for additional passengers, cargo, or both without exceeding structural limits.

While MSP is capped by the aircraft's MDZFW, manufacturers can increase MSP through structural enhancements while maintaining integrity, which may involve:

- Using stronger, lightweight materials.
- Redesigning critical structural components.
- Adopting advanced manufacturing techniques to optimize strength and durability.

The Maximum Structural Payload (MSP) is not merely a weight limit but a key factor influencing aircraft performance, fuel capacity, and operational safety. Understanding and managing MSP ensures compliance with certification standards while optimizing operational efficiency and flexibility.

EXAMPLE 3-1. How Different Cabin Interiors Impact Maximum Structural Payloads

Consider two airlines operating the Boeing 777-300ER with distinct cabin configurations, as shown in **Figure 3-1**:

Figure 3-1. 777-300ER cabin configurations

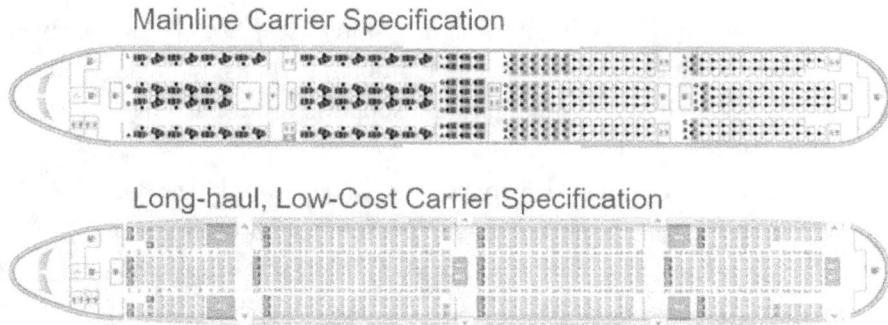

Mainline Carrier Specification

Long-haul, Low-Cost Carrier Specification

Source: https://www.seatguru.com/

- **Airline A:** A full-service mainline carrier with a premium cabin layout, including first, business, and premium economy classes.
- **Airline B:** A low-cost, long-haul (LCLH) carrier using an all-economy, high-density seating configuration.

The Boeing 777-300ER has a certified Maximum Design Zero Fuel Weight (MDZFW) of 524,000 lbs. **Table 3-1** compares how cabin layouts impact Operating Empty Weight (OEW) and Maximum Structural Payload (MSP):

Table 3-1. Cabin layout comparisons

Metric	Airline A (Premium Cabin)	Airline B (High-Density Economy)
MDZFW	524,000 lbs.	524,000 lbs.
OEW	~ 370,000 lbs.	~ 350,000 lbs.
MSP	154,000 lbs.	174,000 lbs.

Source: Author's analysis

The following insights demonstrate how cabin configurations influence OEW and MSP, shaping operational efficiency and market alignment:

- **Airline A:** The premium cabin layout increases OEW due to heavier seats, advanced amenities, and additional systems, reducing MSP to 154,000 lbs. This configuration supports fewer passengers but targets high-yield markets.
- **Airline B:** The high-density economy layout minimizes OEW, increasing MSP to 174,000 lbs. This setup supports a larger passenger load or more cargo, making it ideal for high-volume, cost-efficient operations.

This example highlights how cabin configurations influence payload capacity, showcasing the trade-offs airlines face in balancing operational efficiency, revenue potential, and market focus.

3.2 Adaptive Payload

Adaptive Payload refers to the operational strategy of tailoring an aircraft's payload, fuel distribution, and certified weight configurations to optimize performance for specific routes and market demands. This concept incorporates two key elements: **Dynamic Payload Management** and **Flexible Weight Variants (WV)**. Together, they enable airlines to enhance efficiency, minimize operating costs, and respond to seasonal or route-specific requirements—all while adhering to Maximum Takeoff Weight (MTOW) and payload limitations.

Dynamic Payload Management

Dynamic Payload Management involves adjusting the payload capacity—passengers, cargo, and baggage—within an aircraft's certified weight limits based on mission requirements.

For example:

- On shorter routes with reduced fuel needs, airlines can maximize payload by carrying additional passengers or cargo up to the Maximum Zero Fuel Weight (MZFW).

- On longer routes requiring greater fuel loads, payload must be reduced to stay within MTOW constraints, ensuring adequate fuel for range.

This dynamic adjustment helps airlines balance payload and fuel loads in real time, optimizing aircraft performance and revenue potential across diverse route networks.

EXAMPLE 3-2. A330-900 Dynamic Payload Capabilities

The A330-900 (A330NEO) illustrates dynamic payload management through its **Weight Variant (WV) 920**, which allows certified adjustments between WV921 and WV922 configurations, as shown in **Table 3-2**.

Table 3-2. A330-900 weight variants

Aircraft Characteristics	WV920 (e)	WV921	WV922
Maximum Taxi Weight (MTW)	251,900 kg (555,344 lb)	251,900 kg (555,344 lb)	247,900 kg (546,526 lb)
Maximum Take-Off Weight (MTOW)	251,000 kg (553,360 lb)	251,000 kg (553,360 lb)	247,000 kg (544,542 lb)
Maximum Landing Weight (MLW)	191,000 kg (421,083 lb)	191,000 kg (421,083 lb)	191,000 kg (421,083 lb)
Maximum Zero Fuel Weight (MZFW)	177,000 kg to 181,000 kg (390,218 lb to 399,037 lb)	177,000 kg (390,218 lb)	181,000 kg (399,037 lb)

Note: (e) Dynamic Payload between WV921 and WV922.

Source: "A330 Airplane Characteristics for Airport Planning" document [1]

The Weight Variant 920 offers significant operational adaptability through the following features:

- **Fixed MTOW:** The MTOW of 251,000 kg (553,360 lbs.) remains consistent, ensuring structural integrity and compliance during takeoff.
- **Adjustable MZFW:** The MZFW ranges from 177,000 kg to 181,000 kg, enabling tailored payload configurations:
- A **higher MZFW** allows for greater payload capacity on short-haul routes with lower fuel requirements.

- A **lower MZFW** optimizes the fuel-payload balance for long-haul missions, maximizing range within MTOW constraints.

This capability enables operators to align payload configurations with specific route demands, optimizing performance for high-demand, short-haul flights or long-haul missions requiring extended range. Transitioning between weight variants may require procedural adjustments and regulatory compliance, depending on the scope of the change.

Flexible Weight Variants (WV)

While Dynamic Payload Management focuses on adjusting payload within the aircraft's existing certified weight limits on a flight-by-flight basis, Flexible Weight Variants (WV) extend this flexibility by allowing airlines to modify the certified weight limits themselves to suit different operational requirements. Specifically, airlines can tailor an aircraft's Maximum Takeoff Weight (MTOW), Maximum Zero-Fuel Weight (MZFW), and Maximum Landing Weight (MLW) through certified weight variants. These variants enable operators to optimize aircraft performance for a range of missions—whether short-haul, high-frequency routes or ultra-long-haul flights—by selecting the most appropriate balance between payload capacity and fuel requirements.

By choosing the appropriate weight variant, airlines can optimize for different route lengths and payload demands while potentially lowering airport charges, navigation fees, and operating costs. Higher MTOW variants allow for increased fuel and payload capacity on long-haul and ultra-long-haul routes, while lower MTOW variants are optimized for shorter routes, reducing fuel burn and landing fees. Additionally, higher MZFW variants provide greater payload capacity—especially useful on high-density routes where fuel requirements are minimal—allowing airlines to maximize revenue potential while maintaining operational efficiency.

EXAMPLE 3-3. Airbus A350 Flexible Weight Variants
The Airbus A350 family exemplifies the use of Flexible Weight Variants, offering airlines the ability to adapt aircraft specifications to varying market needs and route structures.

A350-900 Variants:

- **Regional Variant:** Optimized for shorter-haul missions with lower MTOW, reducing operating costs.
- **Classic Variant:** Balanced range and payload capabilities for versatile medium- and long-haul operations.
- **Ultra Long Range (ULR) Variant:** Increased MTOW to carry more fuel for extended ranges (e.g., nonstop intercontinental flights).

A350-1000 Variants:

- Multiple weight variants are available, including the latest version featuring an increased MTOW, enabling extended range and higher payload capability.

Switching Between Variants:

Airlines may switch between weight variants (within certified limits) to match current route demands and load factors, enhancing operational flexibility and potentially reducing airport and navigation fees.

Key Advantages of Adaptive Payload

The integration of Dynamic Payload Management and Flexible Weight Variants offers operational and economic benefits:

- **Optimized Cost Efficiency:** Tailoring certified weight configurations and payload optimizes fuel consumption and reduces fees, lowering operating costs.
- **Maximized Revenue Potential:** Adjusting payload capacity to match demand increases revenue opportunities.
- **Enhanced Fleet Versatility:** Weight Variants offer operators flexibility to adapt aircraft performance without requiring additional fleet investments.
- **Improved Route Planning:** Airlines can fine-tune payload and range balance, enhancing network efficiency.

Adaptive Payload Limitations

Despite its advantages, Adaptive Payload strategies present limitations:
- Narrowbody aircraft generally offer fewer Weight Variant options due to standardized short-haul missions.
- Switching Weight Variants requires operational planning, including recalibration of payload limits, updates to performance data, and regulatory compliance.
- Adjustments must align with certifications from authorities like EASA and FAA, ensuring adherence to approved MTOW, MZFW, and MLW ranges.

3.3 Volume-Limited Payload (MSP)

Volume-Limited Payload (VLP) refers to the maximum payload an aircraft can accommodate, constrained by its internal space, including seating configurations, cargo hold volume, and baggage compartments. While VLP is primarily determined by an aircraft's dimensions and layout, payload weight must also remain within structural and certified limits, such as the Maximum Structural Payload (MSP) and Maximum Zero Fuel Weight (MZFW). Balancing volume and weight is critical for effective payload management and operational efficiency.

In passenger aircraft, VLP is typically less restrictive than in freighters, as cabin configurations and passenger luggage are optimized for efficient use of payload capacity. However, VLP becomes a constraint when carrying lightweight but bulky cargo, particularly alongside passenger luggage. This limitation is especially relevant on flights where cargo revenue is a significant factor.

For freighter aircraft, VLP is often the defining constraint. Bulky, low-density goods like textiles, electronics, or e-commerce packages can occupy the entire available cargo space before reaching MSP. In high-demand air cargo markets, managing the trade-off between volume and weight is vital to maximizing revenue potential.

Figure 3-2 compares MSP and VLP for a Boeing 737-800 configured with 178 seats. For operators, the more restrictive factor—whether MSP or VLP—ultimately determines the payload limit. Effective management of these constraints is essential to optimize operational efficiency and maximize payload capacity.

Figure 3-2. 737-800 MSP and VLP

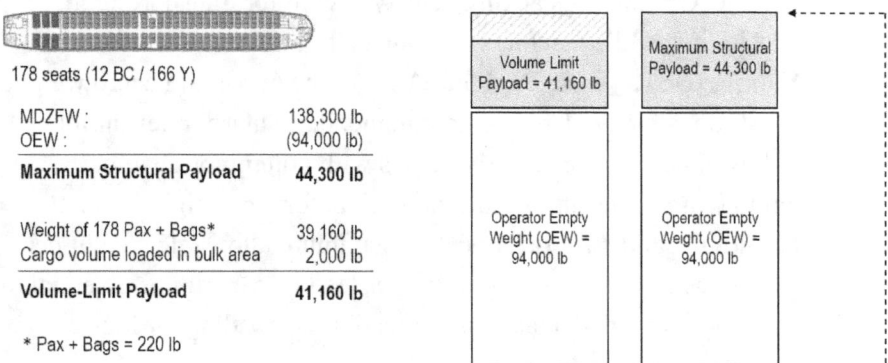

178 seats (12 BC / 166 Y)

MDZFW :	138,300 lb
OEW :	(94,000 lb)
Maximum Structural Payload	**44,300 lb**
Weight of 178 Pax + Bags*	39,160 lb
Cargo volume loaded in bulk area	2,000 lb
Volume-Limit Payload	**41,160 lb**

* Pax + Bags = 220 lb

Source: Author's analysis

3.4 Freighter Payload Metrics

Freighter aircraft are purpose-built for cargo transport, featuring large cargo doors, reinforced floors, powered loading systems, and efficient interior layouts. These design enhancements enable freighters to handle heavier, denser loads while optimizing available volume. Specialized loading systems streamline cargo operations, reducing turnaround times and improving overall efficiency.

While freighters share some payload characteristics with passenger aircraft, their focus on cargo transport necessitates unique performance metrics to evaluate operational efficiency and profitability.

The following metrics are critical for assessing the operational and revenue performance of freighter aircraft:

- **Maximum Structural Payload (MSP)**: The total weight the aircraft structure can safely support, including container and pallet tare weights. MSP ensures compliance with structural and airworthiness limits, crucial for managing overall weight capacity.
- **Maximum Revenue Payload:** The net weight of revenue-generating cargo, calculated by subtracting tare weights from MSP. This metric is central to evaluating an aircraft's revenue potential.

- **Maximum Packing Density:** The highest cargo density the aircraft can carry, calculated as payload weight divided by available cargo volume. Optimizing packing density is vital for transporting high-density items like machinery or raw materials.
- **Volumetric Revenue Payload (VLP):** The maximum cargo weight constrained by available cargo volume, particularly relevant for lightweight, bulky goods. On routes with voluminous cargo, the hold often reaches its volumetric limit before its weight limit.
- **Running Load Limitations:** The maximum allowable weight per square inch of the cargo floor. Proper load distribution is essential to prevent structural damage during loading, unloading, or flight.

Freighter aircraft must balance these metrics to optimize performance and revenue across varying cargo profiles:

- **Light, Bulky Cargo:** For goods like textiles or e-commerce packages, maximizing volumetric capacity while staying within structural limits is key.
- **Dense Cargo:** For weight-intensive items like industrial equipment, managing MSP and running load limitations is critical to maintaining safety and structural integrity.

By effectively applying these metrics, operators can optimize the utilization of freighter aircraft across diverse scenarios, ensuring efficient space and weight management while maximizing revenue potential.

3.4.1 Maximum Structural Payload

The **Maximum Structural Payload (MSP),** also referred to as **Gross Structural Payload**, is a key performance metric for freighter aircraft. MSP represents the maximum weight of cargo the aircraft's structure can safely carry, including the tare weight of containers and pallets. It is defined by the relationship between the aircraft's Maximum Zero Fuel Weight (MZFW) and Operating Empty Weight (OEW):

$$MSP = MZFW - OEW \quad \text{(Eq. 3-2)}$$

This metric is essential for freighter operations, as it sets the upper limit for cargo weight while ensuring structural integrity and operational safety.

The following features highlight MSP's critical role in freighter operations:

- **Structural Limitations:** MSP is constrained by MZFW, the highest allowable weight excluding fuel. Exceeding MSP or MZFW risks structural stress, particularly on critical components like the fuselage and wing-root areas, jeopardizing safety, and airworthiness.
- **Tare Weight Inclusion:** MSP accounts for the tare weight of loading equipment, such as containers and pallets. The remaining weight capacity, or **Maximum Revenue Payload**, excludes tare weight and represents the actual weight available for revenue-generating cargo.
- **Cargo Optimization:** Freighter aircraft prioritize MSP over passenger comfort, with specialized features such as reinforced floors, wide cargo doors, and powered loading systems. These enhancements maximize cargo efficiency and streamline operations.

Operating close to MSP maximizes revenue potential by fully utilizing the aircraft's cargo-carrying capacity:

- **Short-Haul, High-Density Routes:** Operators focus on maximizing MSP to accommodate dense cargo loads.
- **Long-Haul Operations:** MSP is balanced with fuel requirements to remain within the aircraft's Maximum Takeoff Weight (MTOW), ensuring optimal range and efficiency.

MSP Comparative Analysis

Table 3-3 highlights the structural payload capacities of Boeing 757 and 767 freighters, comparing production and converted models. This analysis emphasizes the trade-offs between payload capabilities and design specifications, demonstrating MSP's importance in operational planning and efficiency.

Table 3-3. Maximum structural payloads of 757 and 767 freighters

Aircraft	757-200PF *	757-200PCF **	767-300F *	767-300BCF **
MZFW (lbs)	200,000	200,000	309,800	309,000
OEW (lbs)	114,000	116,000	188,000	192,200
Maximum Structural Payload (lbs)	86,000	84,000	121,800	116,800

*Production Freighter / ** Converted Freighter*

Source: Author's analysis

Freighter aircraft are specifically designed to maximize MSP, prioritizing cargo transport over passenger amenities. Specialized features, including reinforced floors and efficient loading systems, enable freighters to handle dense and heavy loads effectively while complying with stringent safety standards.

By leveraging MSP, operators can optimize payload capacity and profitability. The balance between structural integrity and payload capacity ensures that freighters meet operational and economic goals, making MSP a cornerstone metric in evaluating freighter performance and revenue potential.

Maximizing Gross Structural Payloads in Freighter Aircraft

Increasing gross structural payloads in freighter aircraft is essential to meeting the demands of modern air cargo operations. This process involves optimizing the aircraft's weight and structural capabilities to handle higher payloads while maintaining compliance with design and regulatory limits. Two primary strategies are employed: **reducing Operating Empty Weight (OEW)** and **increasing Maximum Zero Fuel Weight (MZFW)**. By lowering OEW, passenger-related systems are removed, creating additional capacity for revenue-generating cargo. Increasing MZFW involves structural reinforcements to accommodate heavier loads safely. These approaches, often combined, exemplify how passenger-to-freighter (P2F) conversions and production freighters (PF) improve efficiency and payload performance. The following sections illustrate these strategies in action.

Category 1. Increasing Gross Structural Payloads by Reducing OEW

EXAMPLE 3-4. Precision A321 P2F Conversion

The Precision A321 P2F conversion showcases how OEW reductions enhance payload capacity. During the conversion, the Airbus A321CEO's standard OEW of **107,000 lbs.** is reduced to **98,105 lbs.**, as detailed in **Table 3-4**. This 8,895-pound reduction is achieved by removing passenger-specific systems such as seats, galleys, and lavatories, while optimizing the cargo compartment layout. The result is a **gross structural payload of over 59,000 lbs.**, making the A321-200PCF an attractive option for express and eCommerce markets. This weight optimization allows the freighter to meet or exceed performance targets without requiring additional certifications, offering operators enhanced operational flexibility and profitability.

Table 3-4. A321-200 to A321-200P2F conversion

	A321-200	A321-200 P2F
MTOW (lbs.)	196,210	196,210
MZFW (lbs.)	157,630	157,630
OEW (lbs.)	107,000	98,105
Gross Payload (lbs.)	50,630	59,525
Delta MSP (lbs.)		8,895

Source: Precision Aircraft Solutions [3]

EXAMPLE 3-5. A330-300 to A330-200 P2F Conversion

The A330-300 P2F conversion highlights a similar strategy for increasing payload through OEW reduction. The aircraft's original OEW of **277,560 lbs.** is reduced to **249,109 lbs.**, a significant weight savings of 28,451 pounds, as shown in **Table 3-5**. This transformation includes the removal of passenger-related systems such as seats, galleys, and overhead bins, replaced by reinforced cargo structures optimized for freighter operations. These changes increase the aircraft's maximum structural payload from **108,249 lbs.** to **136,700 lbs.**, an enhancement of over **28,000 lbs.** Remarkably, this payload improvement is achieved without altering the aircraft's MTOW or MZFW, emphasizing the efficiency of the P2F conversion process.

Table 3-5. A330-300 to A330-300P2F conversion

	A330-300	A330-300 P2F
MTOW (lbs.)	518,086	518,086
MZFW (lbs.)	385,809	385,809
OEW (lbs.)	277,560	249,109
Gross Payload (lbs.)	**108,249**	**136,700**
Delta MSP (lbs.)		*28,451*

Source: Airbus. "A330 Airplane Characteristics for Airport Planning" with analysis by the author [1]

Category 2. Increasing Gross Structural Payloads by Enhancing MZFW and Reducing OEW

EXAMPLE 3-6. 767-300ER to 767-300PF Conversion
The conversion of a 767-300ER passenger aircraft into a 767-300PF freighter demonstrates how a combination of increasing MZFW and reducing OEW enhances payload capacity. During the conversion, the aircraft's **MZFW increases from 295,000 lbs. to 309,000 lbs.**, while the OEW is reduced from **198,440 lbs. to 188,100 lbs.**, as presented in **Table 3-6**. These modifications result in a **24,340-lbs.** increase in gross structural payload capacity, rising from **96,560 lbs. to 120,900 lbs**. Structural reinforcements, particularly to the fuselage, wings, and floor beams, allow the freighter to handle these increased loads safely. This conversion highlights how targeted weight and structural optimizations can provide significant operational and economic advantages.

Table 3-6. 767-300ER to 767-300PF conversion

Limit Weight	767-300ER Passenger Variant lb (kg)	767-300PF Production Freighter lb (kg)	Delta
Max Takeoff Weight	412,000 (186,880)	412,000 (186,880)	
Max Zero-fuel Weight	295,000 (133,810)	309,000 (140,160)	+ 14,000 (6,350)
Operating Empty Weight	198,440 (90,011)	188,100 (85,321)	- 10,340 (4,690)
Max Payload	96,560 (43,799)	120,900 (54,839)	+ 24,340 (11,040)

Source: Boeing. "767 Airplane Characteristics for Airport Planning" with analysis by the author [4]

These examples illustrate the effectiveness of P2F conversions and production freighters in maximizing gross structural payloads. Whether achieved by reducing OEW, increasing MZFW, or employing both strategies, these enhancements transform passenger aircraft into high-performing freighters capable of meeting the growing demands of air cargo operations. By reallocating weight allowances and optimizing structural features, operators gain access to cost-effective and sustainable solutions for modern cargo transportation.

3.4.2 Maximum Revenue Payload

The **Maximum Revenue Payload**, also known as the **net structural payload**, is a key operational metric for freighter aircraft. It represents the actual weight of revenue-generating cargo after deducting the tare weight of containers, pallets, or Unit Load Devices (ULDs) from the Maximum Structural Payload (MSP). This metric directly reflects an aircraft's revenue potential.

The formula for determining Revenue Payload is:

$$\text{Maximum Revenue Payload} = \text{Maximum Structural Payload} - \text{Total Tare Weight} \quad \text{(Eq. 3-3)}$$

For a comparative analysis of the revenue payloads for Boeing 757/767 freighters, including tare weight considerations, see **Table 3-7**.

Table 3-7. Revenue payloads of 757 and 767 freighters

Aircraft	757-200PF *	757-200PCF **	767-300F *	767-300BCF **
MZFW (lbs)	200,000	200,000	309,800	309,000
OEW (lbs)	114,000	116,000	188,000	192,200
Maximum Structural Payload (lbs)	86,000	84,000	121,800	116,800
Total Tare Weight (lbs)	7,140	7,140	9,120	9,120
Maximum Reveune Payload (lbs)	78,860	76,860	112,680	107,680

*Production Freighter / ** Converted Freighter*

Source: Author's analysis

Key Differences Between MSP and Revenue Payload

- **Maximum Structural Payload (MSP):** Defines the total weight the aircraft can safely carry, including both cargo and tare weights.
- **Revenue Payload:** Refers to the net weight of revenue-generating cargo, excluding tare weight, making it the primary operational metric for profitability.

Freighter aircraft often operate near their MSP, a condition termed "**grossing out**," where the aircraft reaches its weight limit before exhausting available volume. This is typical for dense cargo types, such as machinery or raw materials, which fill the weight capacity before reaching the volumetric limit.

Maximizing Revenue Payload is significant for efficient freighter operations, ensuring optimal use of the aircraft's capacity for revenue generation. Additionally, high payload efficiency enhances fuel efficiency per ton-mile, critical for maintaining competitive costs in sectors like e-commerce and global trade.

Freighter operators employ several strategies to maximize revenue payload, focusing on reducing non-revenue weight and optimizing cargo configurations. The following approaches highlight key methods for enhancing payload efficiency:

- **Minimizing Tare Weight:** Employing lightweight containers and pallets reduces non-revenue weight, increasing available capacity for revenue-generating cargo.
- **Optimizing Packing Density:** Configuring cargo to balance weight and volume constraints effectively maximizes usable capacity.

These strategies not only improve revenue potential but also contribute to sustainable operations by reducing total weight and fuel consumption, aligning with industry goals for efficiency and environmental responsibility.

3.4.3 Maximum Packing Density

Maximum Packing Density represents the highest average density of revenue-generating payload that a freighter can accommodate within its containerized and palletized cargo volume, encompassing both the main deck and lower deck compartments. This metric is constrained by the aircraft's structural weight limits, including the Maximum Zero Fuel Weight (MZFW), floor load limits, and other operational parameters.

Typically, this calculation excludes bulk cargo volume, which is used for irregularly shaped items or smaller shipments that do not fit into standard **Unit Load Devices (ULDs)**. The certified cargo volume, defined in the aircraft's cargo specifications, is used for determining packing density.

The formula for determining Maximum Packing Density is:

$$\text{Maximum Packing Density} = \text{Maximum Revenue Payload} / \text{Total Containerized Cargo Volume} \quad \text{(Eq. 3-4)}$$

To compare Maximum Packing Density across different freighter models, including the Boeing 757/767 freighter family, both cargo volume and payload metrics are critical. Refer to **Table 3-8** for detailed comparisons.

Table 3-8. Maximum packing densities of 757 and 767 freighters

Aircraft	757-200PF *	757-200PCF **	767-300F *	767-300BCF **
MZFW (lbs)	200,000	200,000	309,800	309,000
OEW (lbs)	114,000	116,000	188,000	192,200
Maximum Structural Payload (lbs)	86,000	84,000	121,800	116,800
Total Tare Weight (lbs)	7,140	7,140	9,120	9,120
Maximum Reveune Payload (lbs)	78,860	76,860	112,680	107,680
Total Containerized Volume (cu ft)	8,390	8,390	15,469	15,469
Maximum Packing Density (lbs/cu ft)	9.40	9.16	7.28	6.96

*Production Freighter / ** Converted Freighter*

Source: Author's analysis

The following considerations demonstrate how maximum packing density influences freighter operations and efficiency:

- **Guidelines for Loading:** Maximum packing density provides a benchmark to ensure cargo operations stay within allowable weight and volume limits, avoiding underutilization of space (volume-limited scenarios) or exceeding weight constraints (weight-limited scenarios).
- **Efficiency Metrics:** Higher packing density indicates the freighter's capability to efficiently handle diverse cargo types—from low-density, bulky goods (e.g., e-commerce packages) to high-density shipments (e.g., machinery or raw materials).

In operational contexts, freighters encounter distinct constraints based on the nature of their cargo. When transporting high-density cargo, a freighter operating near its Maximum Revenue Payload typically "grosses out," reaching its weight limit before fully utilizing the available cargo volume. Conversely, with low-density cargo, characterized by lightweight, bulky goods, the freighter may "cube out" or "bulk out," reaching its volumetric limit before reaching its structural payload capacity. These scenarios underscore the importance of balancing payload weight and volume to optimize freighter performance and operational efficiency.

Industry Perspective 3-1. *The Role of Containerized Tare Weight and Volume in Packing Density Analysis*

*Understanding **Maximum Packing Density** is essential for optimizing freighter operations, as it ensures effective utilization of both structural and volumetric limits. Referencing **Table 3-9**, this example highlights the role of **containerized volume** and **tare weight** calculations in determining packing density and operational efficiency.*

Table 3-9. Containerized Volume, Tare Weight, and Maximum Packing Density for the 767-300ERSF

Aircraft	767-300ERSF
Gross structural payload-lbs	114,300
Type maindeck containers	88" X 125" X 96"/A2 ULD
Number maindeck containers	22/2
Unit volume maindeck containers-cu ft	502
Unit tare weight maindeck containers-lbs	240
Total volume maindeck containers-cu ft	11,884
Total tare weight maindeck containers-lbs	5,760
Type lowerdeck containers	LD-2
Number lowerdeck containers	30
Unit volume lowerdeck containers-cu ft	124
Unit tare weight lowerdeck containers-lbs	203
Total volume lowerdeck containers-cu ft	3,720
Total tare weight lowerdeck containers-lbs	6,090
Total volume all containers-cu ft	*15,604*
Total tare weight all containers-lbs	*11,850*
Net structural payload-lbs	102,450
Maximum packing density-lbs/cu ft	6.57

Source: Author's analysis

Step 1: Calculate Total Volume of All Containers

The total volume is the foundation for determining maximum packing density.

- *Main deck Volume: 22×502 = 11,884 cu ft.*
- *Lower Deck Volume: 30×124 = 3,720 cu ft.*
- ***Total Containerized Volume:** 11,884+3,720 = 15,604 cu ft.*

Step 2: Calculate Net Structural Payload

*The **Net Structural Payload** reflects the aircraft's payload capacity after deducting container tare weights:*

- **Total Tare Weight:** *5,760 lbs. (main deck) + 6,090 lbs. (lower deck) = 11,850 lbs.*
- **Net Structural Payload:** *114,300 lbs. (gross) − 11,850 lbs. (tare) = 102,450 lbs.*

Step 3: Calculate Maximum Packing Density

The **Maximum Packing Density** *is determined by dividing the* **Net Structural Payload** *by the* **Total Volume**:

$$Maximum\ Packing\ Density = Net\ Structural\ Payload$$
$$/ \ Total\ Containerized\ Volume$$

$$Maximum\ Packing\ Density = 102,450 \ / \ 15,604 \approx 6.57\ lbs./cu\ ft.$$

3.4.4 Volumetric Revenue Payload

Volumetric Revenue Payload (VLP), also known as "space-limited payload," measures the utilized cargo volume relative to the aircraft's total usable cargo space. Unlike weight-based constraints, VLP focuses on the physical dimensions of the cargo. When an aircraft "cubes out" or "bulks out," it means all available cargo space is filled before reaching the aircraft's weight capacity. This situation commonly occurs with low-density cargo, such as e-commerce shipments, where volume, rather than weight, becomes the limiting factor.

The formula for determining Volumetric Revenue Payload is:

$$Volumetric\ Payload = Total\ Containerized\ Volume$$
$$X\ Payload\ Packing\ Density \quad (Eq.\ 3\text{-}5)$$

Figure 3-3 illustrates how freighter aircraft often reach volumetric capacity before hitting maximum weight thresholds, particularly when transporting lighter, bulkier items. This emphasizes the importance of maximizing volumetric efficiency for goods that occupy significant space relative to their weight.

For example, freighters carrying e-commerce goods, such as electronics or apparel, may "cube out" before reaching their Maximum Structural

Payload (MSP), highlighting the operational need to balance cargo volume and weight for profitability.

Figure 3-3. Freighter volumetric capacity

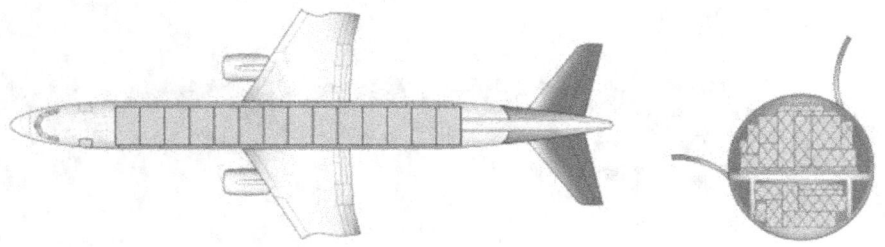

Credit: CargoJet

EXAMPLE 3-7. Calculating Volumetric Payload at 6.5 lb/ft³.
   Given:

   • Maximum Structural Payload: 100,000 lb
   • Total Containerized Cargo Volume: 15,000 ft³
   • Payload Packing Density: 6.5 lb/ft³

Calculation:

$$\text{Volumetric Payload} = \text{Total Containerized Volume} \times \text{Payload Packing Density}$$

   Volumetric Payload = 15,000 ft³ × 6.5 lb/ft³ = 97,500 lb

This result indicates the aircraft "**cubes out**" (fills its cargo space) before reaching its Maximum Structural Payload (MSP) of 100,000 lbs., illustrating the impact of low packing density on volumetric capacity.

   For a detailed comparison of Boeing 757/767 freighter family volumetric payloads at different packing densities (6.5, 7.0, and 7.5 lb/ft³), refer to **Table 3-10.**

Table 3-10. Volumetric payloads of 757 and 767 freighters

Aircraft	757-200PF *	757-200PCF **	767-300F *	767-300BCF **
MZFW (lbs)	200,000	200,000	309,800	309,000
OEW (lbs)	114,000	116,000	188,000	192,200
Maximum Structural Payload (lbs)	86,000	84,000	121,800	116,800
Total Tare Weight (lbs)	7,140	7,140	9,120	9,120
Maximum Reveune Payload (lbs)	78,860	76,860	112,680	107,680
Total Containerized Volume (cu ft)	8,390	8,390	15,469	15,469
Maximum Packing Density (lbs/cu ft)	9.40	9.16	7.28	6.96
Volumetric Revenue Payload @ 6.5lbs/cu ft	54,535	54,535	100,549	100,549
Volumetric Revenue Payload @ 7.0lbs/cu ft	58,730	58,730	108,283	107,680
Volumetric Revenue Payload @ 7.5lbs/cu ft	62,925	62,925	112,680	107,680

*Production Freighter / ** Converted Freighter*

Source: Author's analysis

At higher packing densities (e.g., 7.5 lb/ft^3), freighters like the Boeing 767-300F and 767-300BCF achieve volumetric payloads that align closely with their Maximum Revenue Payloads (net structural payloads). This packing density reflects a balance between weight and volume, fully utilizing the cargo hold without exceeding the aircraft's structural payload limits. For example:

- At 6.5 lb/ft^3, the aircraft is more likely to "cube out" due to the low packing density of the cargo.
- At 7.5 lb/ft^3, the aircraft achieves near-optimal utilization of both its volume and weight capacities.

Volumetric Revenue Payload (VLP) is a key factor in freighter operations, often becoming the primary limitation when transporting lightweight, bulky goods. Efficiently managing VLP is essential for optimizing profitability and operational efficiency, particularly on routes dominated by low-density cargo. For example, **e-commerce** shipments, such as packaged goods, apparel, and electronics, frequently result in "cubing out," where the cargo reaches the volumetric limit before weight constraints. Additionally, cargo distribution plays a key role, as efficient planning, and utilization of containerized or palletized cargo maximize available space while minimizing voids, ensuring effective use of the freighter's capacity. Managing VLP effectively is vital for sustaining operational success in low-density cargo markets.

Freighter Aircraft Categories

Freighter aircraft are specifically designed to accommodate various cargo profiles, balancing the trade-offs between volume and weight. **Figure 3-4** illustrates the distinct categories of freighter aircraft and their payload capabilities, highlighting how different designs cater to unique operational needs.

The following categories demonstrate how freighter types align with specific cargo requirements:

- **Express Cargo Freighters:** Cater to e-commerce, transporting parcels and lightweight goods with lower packing densities (~6.5 lb/ft^3). These aircraft prioritize volume over weight, often cubing out before grossing out.
- **General Cargo Freighters:** Handle dense cargo such as industrial equipment, prioritizing weight over volume with packing densities from 7.5 lb/ft^3 to 10 lb/ft^3.

Figure 3-4. Express vs. general freighters

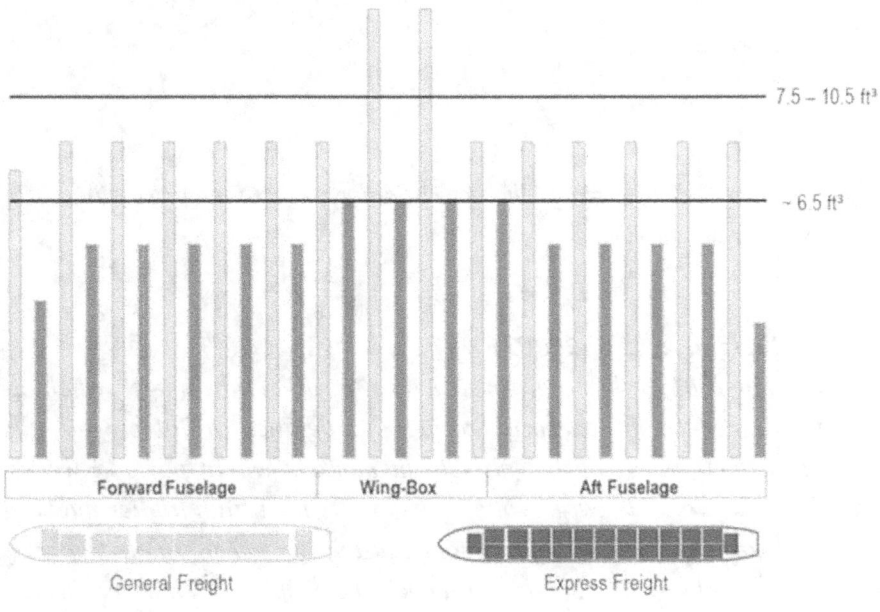

Source: Author's analysis

Industry Perspective 3-2. *A330P2F Payload Characteristics*

*When comparing the A330-200P2F and the A330-300P2F freighters, a clear divergence in their payload characteristics aligns with distinct operational use cases. As shown in **Table 3-11**, the A330-200P2F, with its higher maximum gross structural payload and robust packing density, is better suited for roles as a general-purpose freighter, excelling in transporting high-density cargo such as machinery, automotive parts, and industrial equipment. Conversely, the A330-300P2F, with its expanded volume capacity, proves to be an ideal platform for e-commerce operations, where cargo typically consists of lightweight, volumetric goods.*

Table 3-11. *A330-200P2F vs. A330-300P2F*

Aircraft	A330-200 P2F	A330-300 P2F
MTOW (lbs.)	518,086	518,086
MZFW (lbs.)	374,786	385,809
Gross Payload (lbs.)	132,300	136,700
Total Containerized Volume (cu ft)	**16,000**	**18,580**
Total Tare Weight (lbs.)	7,582	8,941
Net Structural Payload (lbs.)	**124,718**	**127,759**
Max Packing Density (lbs. / cu ft)	7.8	6.9
Volumetric Payload @ 6.0 lbs. / cu ft	*96,000*	*111,480*
Volumetric Payload @ 7.0 lbs. / cu ft	*112,000*	*127,759*
Volumetric Payload @ 8.0 lbs. / cu ft	*124,718*	*127,759*

Source: Airbus. "A330 Airplane Characteristics for Airport Planning" with analysis by the author [1]

General Freighter: A330-200P2F

*The **A330-200P2F** has a gross structural payload advantage, which allows for higher-density cargo operations. As detailed in **Table 3-10**, this characteristic is particularly valuable in markets where payload weight often exceeds available cargo volume. Its ability to sustain **higher packing densities** makes it the go-to option for industries requiring the transportation of dense, high-value goods. Moreover, the -200P2F's shorter fuselage reduces the available volume compared to the -300P2F, but its optimized payload-weight capabilities ensure its viability for missions emphasizing dense cargo loads.*

E-Commerce Freighter: A330-300P2F

*In contrast, the **A330-300P2F** leverages its extended fuselage to offer **increased cargo volume**, which is critical for e-commerce freight operations. The e-commerce sector thrives on transporting large volumes of lightweight goods, including parcels and consumer products. Despite its slightly lower packing density capability, the -300P2F compensates by accommodating **higher overall payload volume**, as illustrated in **Table 3-10**, allowing operators to maximize load factors on routes dominated by volumetric cargo.*

Production Freighters

Widebody freighters, such as the Boeing 777 Freighter (777F) and Airbus A350 Freighter (A350F), are engineered for versatility, combining the capabilities of both express and general cargo freighters. This flexibility enables a single aircraft type to handle diverse cargo missions, from transporting heavy machinery and industrial equipment to large volumes of consumer goods and medical supplies. The reliability and adaptability of these freighters improve operational efficiency, reduce costs, and minimize the need for a varied fleet, enhancing operational confidence for air cargo carriers.

EXAMPLE 3-8. Boeing 777F Payload Versatility

Figure 3-5 illustrates the Boeing 777F's performance, showcasing its ability to carry a maximum revenue payload over 4,970 nautical miles (9,200 kilometers). When transporting lighter, voluminous cargo at a packing density of 7 lb/ft^3, the 777F achieves ranges up to 7,000 nautical miles. This range versatility allows operators to plan effectively for different cargo types, from dense industrial equipment to lightweight e-commerce goods.

This adaptability is essential for cargo operators, enabling them to handle various cargo types without requiring specialized aircraft for each mission. The ability to efficiently transport both heavy and low-density goods enhances operational flexibility and revenue potential, providing a competitive advantage in today's fast-evolving air cargo market.

Figure 3-5. 777F payload versatility

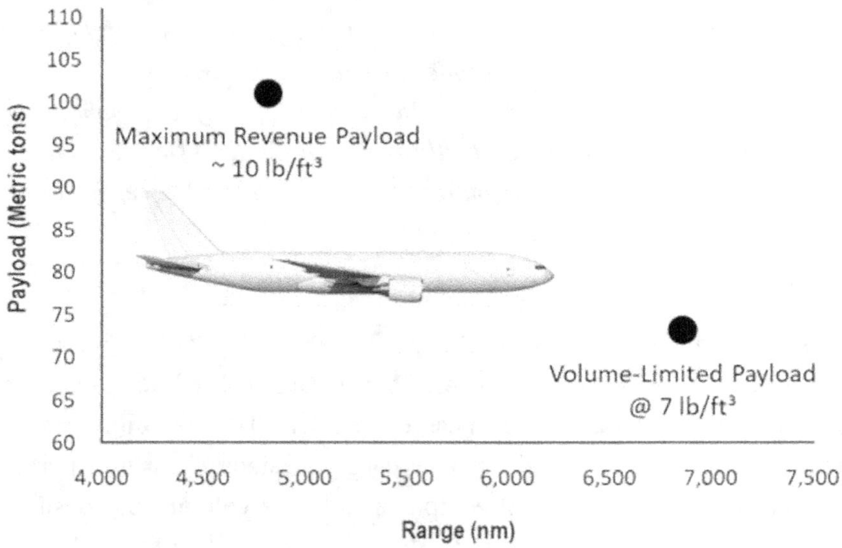

Source: Author's analysis

3.4.5 Running Load Limitations

Running load limitations define the permissible weight distribution along an aircraft's fuselage, specifying how much weight can safely be placed in each section of the cargo hold without exceeding structural limits. These loads are expressed in units such as pounds per inch (lb/in) or kilograms per centimeter (kg/cm) and vary across the aircraft, depending on its structural design and reinforcement.

In freighter aircraft like the 747-400F, as shown in **Figure 3-6**, running load limitations are essential for efficient cargo distribution and maintaining structural integrity. The fuselage is divided into zones, with each section having a specific load-bearing capacity dictated by its design. Adhering to these limits for both the main deck and lower cargo compartments is critical to ensuring safety and operational efficiency.

Freighter manufacturers provide detailed running load specifications in the **Weight & Balance Control and Loading Manual**, outlining allowable running loads for each fuselage section to guide proper cargo weight distribution.

Figure 3-6. 747-400F running load limitations

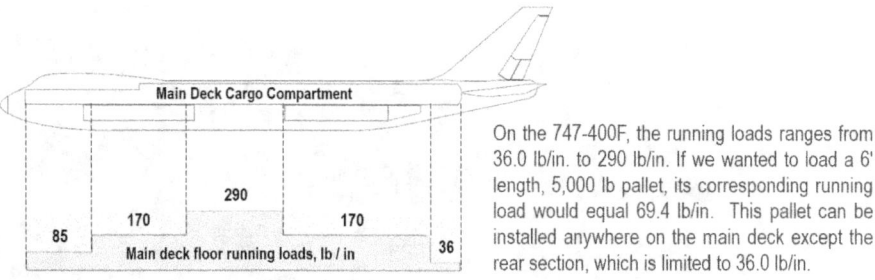

On the 747-400F, the running loads ranges from 36.0 lb/in. to 290 lb/in. If we wanted to load a 6' length, 5,000 lb pallet, its corresponding running load would equal 69.4 lb/in. This pallet can be installed anywhere on the main deck except the rear section, which is limited to 36.0 lb/in.

* The length to take into account is the length of the contact points on the floor.

Source: Boeing. Startup Boeing [2]

The following considerations illustrate the importance of adhering to running load limitations:

- **Cargo Distribution:** Proper alignment with running load specifications ensures that weight is distributed evenly to avoid overstressing specific fuselage sections.
- **Mixed Cargo Loads:** Balancing dense and lightweight cargo prevents imbalances that can lead to operational inefficiencies or safety concerns.
- **Structural Safety:** Adhering to running load guidelines maximizes the utilization of available space while maintaining the aircraft's structural integrity.

By complying with running load limitations, operators can enhance aircraft performance, maintain safety, and optimize cargo transport, even under complex loading conditions.

EXAMPLE 3-9. Optimizing Cargo Load for an A330-200F (**Figure 3-7**)
An operator needs to distribute three types of cargo—dense machinery, lightweight consumer goods, and bulk cargo—across an A330-200F, ensuring adherence to the aircraft's running load limits for optimal efficiency and structural safety.

Figure 3-7. A330-200F running load limitations

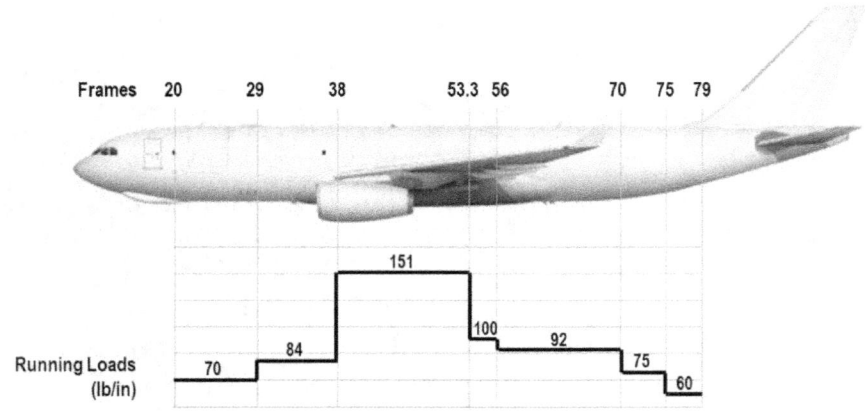

Source: Note. Airbus [5]

Cargo Details:

- **Machinery:** 10,000 lbs., length 30 ft (360 in)
- **Consumer Goods:** 15,000 lbs., length 40 ft (480 in)
- **Bulk Cargo:** 5,000 lbs., length 20 ft (240 in)

Cargo Distribution:

- **Machinery:** Placed in the aircraft's strongest section, between Frames 38–53.3, with a running load capacity of 151 lb/in. Given the 360 inches available, the maximum allowable load is:

    Max allowable load = 151lb/in × 360in = 54,360lbs.

This comfortably supports the 10,000 lbs. of machinery within the limit.

- **Consumer Goods:** These lighter but bulkier items are distributed between two forward sections. Part of the load is placed in Frames 29–38, with a running load capacity of 84 lb/in. For 240 inches of available space, the maximum load is:

$$\text{Max allowable load} = 84\text{lb/in} \times 240\text{in} = 20,160\text{lbs}$$

The remaining load is placed in Frames 20–29, which has a capacity of 70 lb/in. With an additional 240 inches, the maximum load here is:

$$\text{Max allowable load} = 70\text{lb/in} \times 240\text{in} = 16,800\text{lbs}$$

- **Bulk Cargo:** Positioned in the aft section between Frames 75–79, with a running load limit of 60 lb/in. For 240 inches, the maximum permissible load is:

$$\text{Max allowable load} = 60\text{lb/in} \times 240\text{in} = 14,400\text{lbs}$$

The 5,000 lbs. of bulk cargo is well within this limit.

Result: Cargo is distributed efficiently across the aircraft's hold per running load limits. The denser machinery is loaded in sections with the highest structural strength, while lighter cargo is placed in areas with lower capacities. This distribution maximizes structural capacity and maintains operational efficiency, ensuring both safety and optimal performance.

3.4.6 Payload-to-Fuel Ratio

The **payload-to-fuel ratio** is a metric in air cargo operations, representing the trade-off between cargo weight (payload) and the fuel weight required for a specific flight. Aircraft operate within a fixed Maximum Takeoff Weight (MTOW), which encompasses the empty weight, passengers, cargo, and fuel. Since MTOW is fixed, increasing fuel load for long-haul routes necessitates a reduction in payload. Conversely, shorter routes allow for reduced fuel loads, enabling aircraft to carry more cargo.

Optimizing this balance is essential for maximizing operational efficiency and profitability. The payload-to-fuel ratio directly impacts flight economics, requiring operators to determine the most effective way to allocate weight for cargo and fuel. For long-haul flights, cargo capacity may be reduced to ensure adequate fuel for the extended range. On shorter routes, the focus shifts to maximizing revenue-generating cargo by minimizing fuel weight.

EXAMPLE 3-10. Anchorage as a Strategic Fuel Stop

Anchorage International Airport (ANC) demonstrates a strategic approach to optimizing the payload-to-fuel ratio for trans-Pacific air cargo operations. Its geographical location and operational benefits make it a key refueling hub between North America and Asia.

The following advantages illustrate why Anchorage is a critical hub for maximizing the payload-to-fuel ratio:

- **Strategic Location:** Anchorage lies within a 10-hour flight to 90% of the industrialized world, providing access to major markets in Asia, Europe, and North America with minimal deviation from great-circle routes.
- **Payload Maximization:** Refueling at Anchorage enables operators to prioritize payload over fuel. Aircraft can load more cargo (up to their maximum structural payload) and only enough fuel for the segment to Anchorage. After refueling, the aircraft proceeds with a lighter fuel load to its final destination, such as Asia, maximizing cargo capacity on both legs of the trip.

Economic benefits of refueling strategies, such as those employed at Anchorage, are significant and enhance operational efficiency. By carrying less fuel, operators improve fuel efficiency, as a full fuel load for long-haul journeys increases weight and fuel consumption, while refueling mid-route can result in net fuel savings. Additionally, these strategies enable an increase in revenue by optimizing the payload-to-fuel ratio, allowing operators to transport additional revenue-generating cargo. For instance, a refueling stop may enable an aircraft to carry an extra 100,000 pounds of cargo, substantially boosting revenue potential. Moreover, the minimal time penalty of a 1-hour refueling stop is outweighed by the economic benefits, making this approach a practical solution for maximizing profitability.

Scenario: Chicago to Hong Kong with a Fuel Stop in Anchorage

Strategically managing routing and fuel stops can significantly enhance operational efficiency and revenue potential. The Chicago to Hong Kong route, with a fuel stop in Anchorage, demonstrates the benefits of dynamic payload and fuel management. **Figure 3-8** illustrates the great-circle route, highlighting Anchorage as a critical midpoint for optimizing performance.

Figure 3-8. GCD, Chicago – Anchorage – Hong Kong

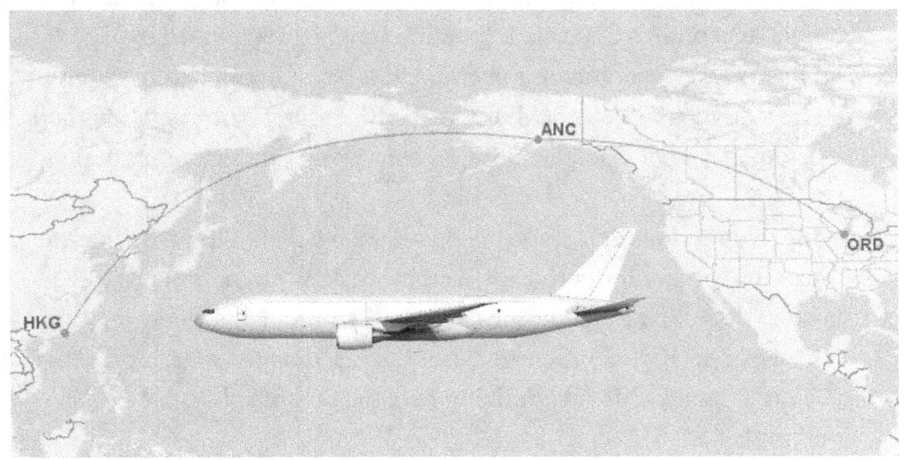

Source: Note. Great Circle Mapper [6]

The operational considerations for a direct flight versus a fuel stop in Anchorage include:

- **Direct Flight:** Flying directly from Chicago to Hong Kong requires carrying sufficient fuel for the entire journey, which may necessitate limiting payload to remain within MTOW, leaving potential revenue cargo behind.
- **Fuel Stop in Anchorage:** Stopping in Anchorage allows the aircraft to carry a larger payload for the first segment. After refueling, it continues to Hong Kong with an optimal balance of fuel and cargo, maximizing revenue potential across both legs.

Using Anchorage as a refueling stop illustrates how strategic route planning can optimize the payload-to-fuel ratio. By balancing cargo and fuel requirements through mid-route refueling, air cargo operators can maximize revenue-generating capacity while maintaining operational efficiency. This approach highlights the importance of payload-to-fuel optimization in achieving economic success for long-haul air cargo operations.

Chapter 3. Key Takeaways

1. **Maximum Structural Payload (MSP):** MSP is the maximum payload weight an aircraft's structure can safely support, determined by subtracting the Operating Empty Weight (OEW) from the Maximum Design Zero Fuel Weight (MDZFW). MSP ensures safe operations and is essential for payload planning and comparing different aircraft models.

2. **Adaptive Payload:** Adaptive payload management allows airlines to adjust the Maximum Zero Fuel Weight (MZFW) to optimize payload capacity based on route profiles and fuel requirements. This flexibility enhances operational efficiency, enabling carriers to balance passenger and cargo loads while maximizing revenue on both short- and long-haul routes.

3. **Volume-Limited Payload (VLP):** VLP refers to payload constrained by available cargo volume rather than weight. This is especially critical for freighters carrying low-density, high-volume goods, such as e-commerce shipments. Understanding the balance between structural payload capacity and cargo space ensures efficient operations and revenue optimization.

4. **Freighter Aircraft Payload Capabilities:** Freighters are purpose-built for cargo transport, featuring reinforced floors, large cargo doors, and optimized loading systems. Key metrics like MSP, Maximum Revenue Payload, and Maximum Packing Density are critical for evaluating and optimizing freighter performance, enhancing revenue generation and operational flexibility.

5. **Maximum Revenue Payload:** Also known as Net Structural Payload, this metric reflects the actual revenue-generating cargo weight, calculated by subtracting tare weight (e.g., containers and pallets) from MSP. It highlights an aircraft's economic efficiency and profitability potential across various freighter models.

6. **Maximum Packing Density:** Packing density measures the efficiency of space utilization within a freighter's cargo hold, expressed as weight per unit volume (e.g., lb/ft^3 or kg/m^3). Achieving high packing density

ensures optimal use of available space, whether transporting low-density goods or dense cargo, and is vital for maximizing revenue.

7. **Volumetric Revenue Payload (VLP):** VLP quantifies cargo volume utilization based on physical dimensions, focusing on situations where the aircraft "cubes out" (fills cargo space) before reaching weight limits. This metric is essential for freighters serving e-commerce markets, where lightweight, bulky goods dominate.

8. **Running Load Limitation:** Running load limitations govern the distribution of cargo weight along an aircraft's fuselage to ensure structural safety. Measured in pounds per inch (lb/in) or kilograms per centimeter (kg/cm), these limits vary by fuselage section and must be adhered to for safe and efficient cargo operations.

9. **Express vs. General Cargo Operators:** Express cargo operators prioritize volumetric payloads to accommodate lightweight, high-volume shipments typical of e-commerce. General cargo operators handle a broader range of cargo, focusing on maximizing structural payload for dense, heavy goods. Understanding these priorities is critical for selecting appropriate freighter types for specific market demands.

10. **Payload-to-Fuel Ratio:** This metric balances cargo weight and fuel load within the constraints of an aircraft's Maximum Takeoff Weight (MTOW). Optimizing the ratio maximizes revenue potential while ensuring safety and operational efficiency. Strategic refueling stops, such as in Anchorage, allow operators to enhance profitability on long-haul routes by maximizing payload on shorter flight segments.

11. **Versatility of Widebody Freighters:** Widebody freighters like the Boeing 777F and Airbus A350F combine the capabilities of express and general cargo operations, allowing them to efficiently transport both lightweight, high-volume goods and dense, heavy cargo. This versatility enhances operational flexibility, reduces fleet requirements, and ensures competitiveness in diverse cargo markets.

Case Study 3-1. Payload Capacity Assessment

Figure 3-9. A330-300 weight variants (WV080/WV081)

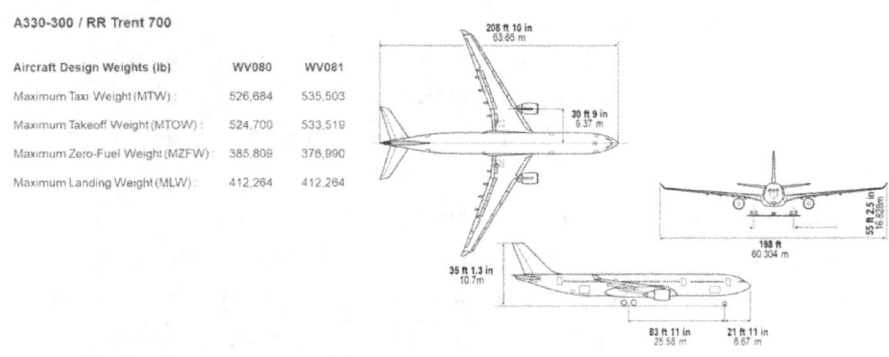

Source: "A330 Airplane Characteristics for Airport Planning," document [1]

Figure 3-10. A330-300 passenger and cargo manifest

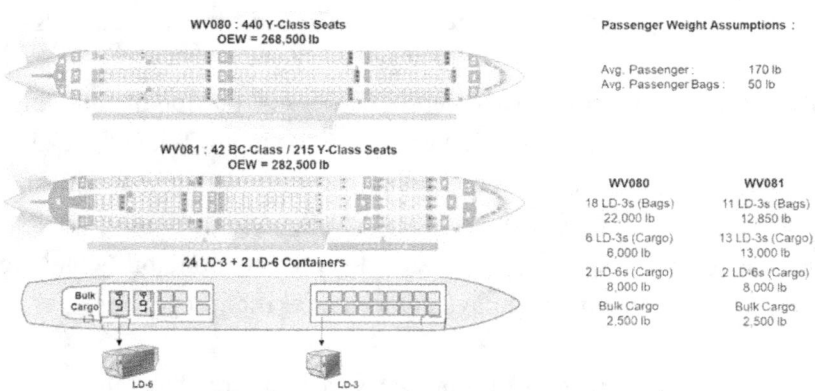

Source: https://www.seatguru.com & "A330 Airplane Characteristics for Airport Planning," [1]

Questions:

1. Given the differences in Maximum Zero-Fuel Weight (MZFW) and Maximum Takeoff Weight (MTOW) between the A330-300 WV080 and WV081 variants, evaluate which variant offers better operational flexibility and revenue potential for a carrier specializing in long-haul routes with significant cargo demand. Consider trade-offs related to payload capacity, fuel efficiency, and route flexibility.

2. Analyze how the MTOW differences between the two variants impact operational capabilities and cost structures for low-cost versus mainline carriers, considering factors such as route flexibility and operational efficiency.

3. Calculate the total passenger payload for both configurations and compare the results to determine the impact on overall payload capacity and operational efficiency.

4. Calculate the remaining cargo capacity for each variant when fully loaded with passengers and baggage, and evaluate how these differences reflect the aircraft's potential to generate additional revenue on cargo-intensive routes.

5. Compare the cargo hold configurations of both variants, determine which can accommodate more cargo, and analyze how these differences arise based on design weights and configurations.

6. Evaluate how the design weights of each variant align with the specific operational requirements of low-cost and mainline carriers, focusing on factors such as operational flexibility, cost efficiency, and route planning.

Case Study 3-2. Freighter Payload Metrics

Figure 3-11. 777-200F specification

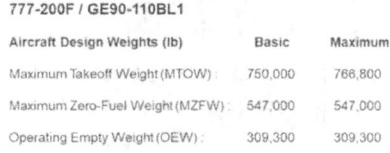

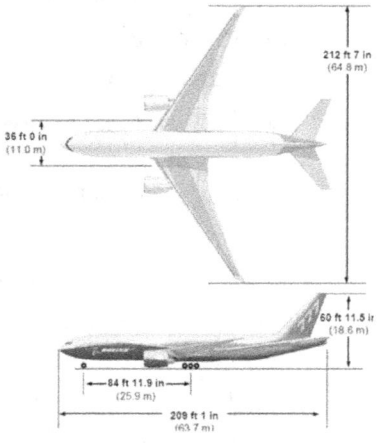

Source: Boeing. Startup Boeing [2]

Figure 3-12. 777-200F cargo manifest

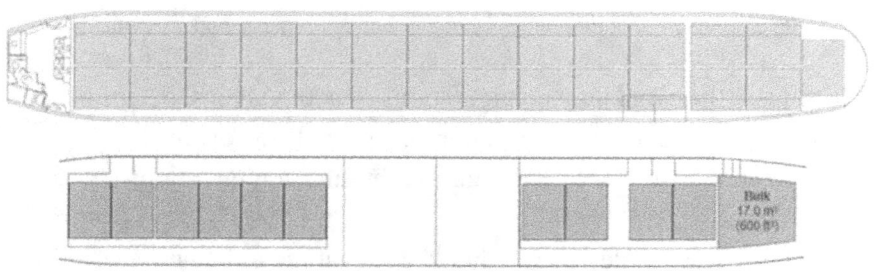

Qty	Container Types	Unit Tare Weight lb (kg)	Deck	Unit Capacity ft³ (m³)	Containerized Volume
22	96" x 125" x 118" pallet	300 (136.1)	Main	690 (19.5)	18,301 ft³ (518.2 m³)
4	96" x 125" x 116" pallet	300 (136.1)	Main	627 (17.8)	
1	96" x 125" x 8 ft pallet	300 (136.1)	Main	613 (17.4)	
10	96" x 125" x 64" pallet	290 (131.5)	Lower	407 (11.5)	4,070 ft³ (115.3 m³)

Total = 11,000 lb (4,999 kg)   Total = 22,371 ft³ (633.5 m³) *

* excludes bulk cargo

Source: Boeing. Startup Boeing [2]

Questions:

1. Calculate the following for the 777-200F:
   - Maximum Structural Payload
   - Maximum Revenue Payload
   - Maximum Packing Density
   - Volumetric Revenue Payload at 8.5 lb/ft^3

2. Evaluate how an airline operating the 777-200F should prioritize between maximizing structural payload and volumetric payload, considering different route types (short-haul vs. long-haul) and market demand for dense vs. lightweight cargo. Provide a recommendation supported by analysis.

3. How does the increase in MTOW for the Maximum specification impact the potential fuel load that can be carried, and how does this influence the aircraft's range?

4. How does cargo density influence the choice between maximizing volumetric payload and maximizing structural payload, especially when considering different types of freight (e.g., dense machinery vs. lightweight consumer goods)?

5. Assess the impact of the lower cargo holds configuration on the volume-limit payload capabilities of each variant. Which variant can accommodate more revenue cargo volume, and why?

References

[1] Airbus, "A330 Aircraft Characteristics for Airport Planning," AC A330, Jul. 2023. [Online]. Available: https://aircraft.airbus.com/en/customer -care/fleet-wide-care/airport-operations-and-aircraft-characteristics /aircraft-characteristics

[2] Boeing, "Startup Boeing." [Online]. Available: https://www.boeing .com/company/about-bca/startupboeing#selection

[3] Precision Aircraft Solutions, "Image of A321 Cargo Aircraft." [Online]. Available: https://www.precisionaircraft.com/a321-200pcf-freighter/, accessed Nov. 2024

[4] Boeing, "767 Airplane Characteristics for Airport Planning," Document D6-58328, Revision J, Aug. 2023. [Online]. Available: https://www.boeing .com/commercial/airports/plan-manuals

[5] Airbus, "Get a better return from your freighter: Introducing the A330-200F."

[6] Great Circle Mapper. [Online]. Available: http://www.gcmap.com/

Chapter 4

Engine Characteristics

This Chapter is About:

Engine Design Fundamentals explores the essential aspects of turbofan engine design, emphasizing their critical role in enhancing aircraft performance and fuel efficiency. Core parameters such as engine bypass ratio and pressure ratio are analyzed, as they are fundamental to optimizing fuel consumption and overall operational effectiveness. Additionally, various engine architectures, including twin-spool, tri-spool, and Geared Turbofan (GTF) designs, are examined to highlight their impact on engine efficiency and performance.

Engine thrust and power management focuses on strategies to align engine output with specific flight conditions. Features such as thrust bumps, which provide additional power during hot and high-altitude takeoffs, and thrust derates, which optimize fuel efficiency and extend engine life, demonstrate how operators balance performance with cost-effectiveness and engine longevity.

Engine Fuel Efficiency focuses on the metric of Thrust Specific Fuel Consumption (TSFC), which measures the fuel efficiency of an engine in producing thrust. TSFC is a key parameter in benchmarking engine performance, with a lower TSFC value indicating a more fuel-efficient design. By prioritizing improvements in TSFC, engine manufacturers aim to reduce fuel burn and emissions, ensuring engines are both economically and environmentally optimized for modern aviation demands.

Engine reliability and durability are equally critical in engine design, directly influencing operational safety, lifespan, and cost efficiency. High reliability minimizes unscheduled maintenance and downtime, while durable designs ensure consistent performance under frequent use, meeting stringent aviation safety and efficiency standards.

Engine noise and emissions have become a cornerstone of modern engine development. With growing regulatory emphasis on mitigating noise pollution and reducing harmful emissions, manufacturers are innovating to lower the environmental impact of engines, aligning with the industry's commitment to environmentally responsible aviation.

In summary, contemporary aircraft engines are defined by advancements in efficiency, reliability, durability, and sustainability. These factors collectively determine an engine's competitiveness and its contribution to the evolving demands of the aviation industry.

4.1 Engine Design Fundamentals

The design of turbofan engines plays a key role in determining aircraft performance and fuel efficiency. Two primary factors—**bypass ratio** and **overall pressure ratio**—are foundational to engine design. A higher bypass ratio improves fuel efficiency by increasing propulsion efficiency, enabling the engine to generate more thrust with less fuel. In contrast, the overall pressure ratio, which compares the compressor's discharge pressure to its inlet pressure, is vital for thermal efficiency. Higher pressure ratios allow the engine to extract more energy from the fuel, enhancing overall performance.

Another design consideration is the engine's **spool configuration**, which can be either twin-spool or tri-spool. This architectural choice affects how effectively the engine manages airflow and power generation, influencing both thrust and fuel economy.

The following sections delve into these factors, illustrating their contributions to engine efficiency and performance.

4.1.1 Bypass Ratio (BPR)

The **Bypass Ratio (BPR)**, illustrated in **Figure 4-1**, measures the ratio of air mass flow bypassing the engine core to the air mass flow passing through the core. In turbofan engines, the cooler bypassed air contributes significantly to fuel efficiency and noise reduction. While the engine core generates thrust and powers the fan, the bypassed air provides additional thrust, reducing specific fuel consumption (SFC) and enhancing overall engine performance.

Figure 4-1. Bypass ratio

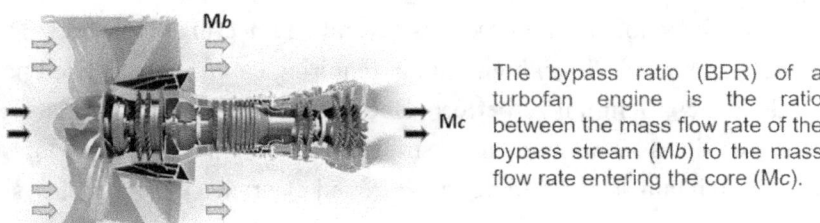

The bypass ratio (BPR) of a turbofan engine is the ratio between the mass flow rate of the bypass stream (Mb) to the mass flow rate entering the core (Mc).

Source: Author's analysis

The following considerations illustrate how the BPR impacts engine efficiency, operational benefits, and design trade-offs:

1. **Efficiency Gains from Higher Bypass Ratios**:
   » Higher BPRs improve fuel efficiency by reducing the reliance on the fuel-intensive engine core and increasing the contribution from bypassed air. This lowers SFC, particularly advantageous for long-haul operations.
   » The cooler bypass air also reduces noise emissions by buffering the high-speed jet exhaust from the core. This mitigates

noise pollution, aiding airport compliance and meeting environmental standards.

2. **Operational Benefits**:
   » High-bypass engines, such as the **GE90** (used on the 777) and the **LEAP** engine (found on the A320neo and 737 MAX), achieve remarkable efficiency gains. These engines deliver up to 15% better fuel economy than earlier generations, providing cost-effective solutions for airlines.

3. **Performance Trade-offs**:
   » While high BPR improves efficiency, it introduces challenges. Larger fan diameters increase drag and structural weight, necessitating advanced engineering solutions to ensure the efficiency gains outweigh these drawbacks.

Engineering Challenges

High-bypass engines necessitate larger fan diameters to increase bypass airflow, a design choice that introduces several engineering challenges. The increased fan size results in higher drag, requiring carefully optimized nacelle aerodynamics to minimize performance losses. Additionally, the larger and heavier engine assemblies demand stronger pylons and reinforced wing structures to maintain structural integrity. Ground clearance poses another significant challenge, especially for narrowbody aircraft. For example, the LEAP engines on the 737 MAX incorporate modified pylon designs to accommodate the larger fans while ensuring sufficient clearance from the ground.

The progression of **bypass ratios (BPR)** in turbofan engines underscores significant advancements in fuel efficiency and noise reduction. As illustrated in **Figure 4-4**, early turbofan engines featured bypass ratios near 1:1, where one pound of air bypassed the core for every pound that flowed through it. Modern engines, however, exceed bypass ratios of 10:1, with over ten pounds of air bypassing the core for every pound of core flow.

Historical Progression of Bypass Ratios

The evolution of bypass ratios reflects the ongoing technological advancements aimed at improving fuel efficiency, reducing noise, and adhering to environmental regulations. The following timeline highlights key milestones in BPR development:

- **Pratt & Whitney JT8D (1960s)**: With a bypass ratio just over 1:1, it powered aircraft like the Boeing 727 and 737-200, offering improvements over turbojets but with limited efficiency and higher noise levels.
- **CFM56 & PW4000 (1980s–1990s)**: Achieved bypass ratios of 5:1 to 6:1, powering popular aircraft like the Boeing 737 and Airbus A320.
- **Geared Turbofan (GTF)—PW1000G series & LEAP series (2010s–2020s)**: Engines like Pratt & Whitney's GTF (10:1–12:1) and the LEAP series reflect the trend toward higher BPRs, significantly improving fuel efficiency and noise reduction.

Figure 4-2. Bypass ratio trends

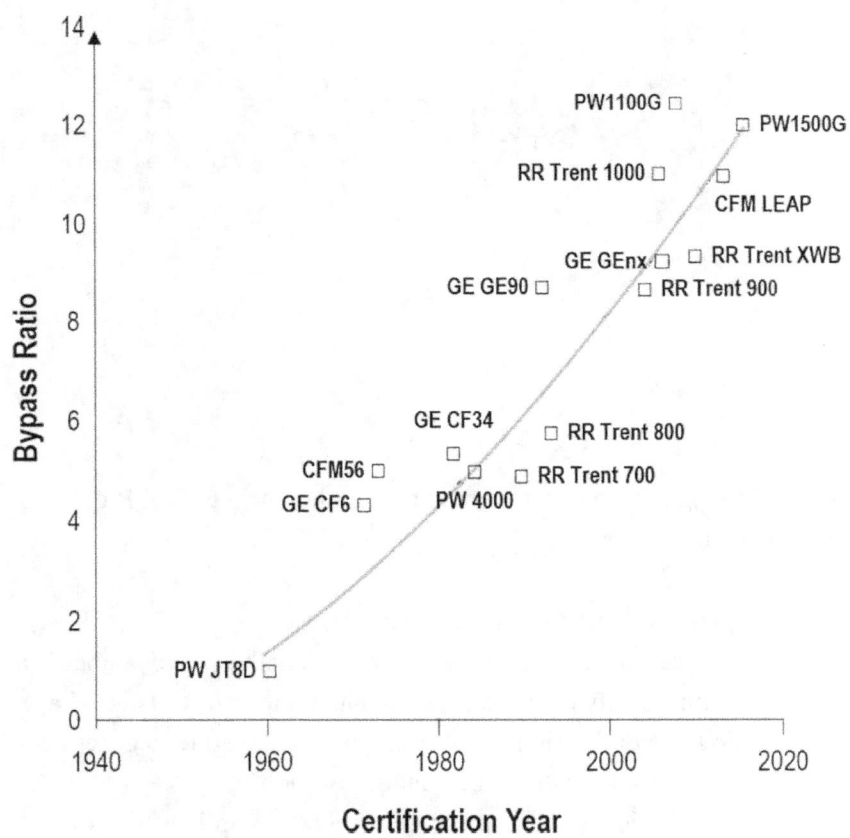

Source: Author's analysis

4.1.2 Overall Pressure Ratio (OPR)

The **Overall Pressure Ratio (OPR)** measures the engine's ability to compress incoming air as it passes through the fan and compressors before entering the combustion chamber. As shown in **Figure 4-3**, OPR is calculated as the ratio of the total air pressure at the exit of the high-pressure compressor (HPC) to the inlet air pressure at the engine's intake. This metric is fundamental to the thermodynamic efficiency of a turbofan engine, as it determines how effectively the engine converts fuel into thrust.

Figure 4-3. Overall pressure ratio

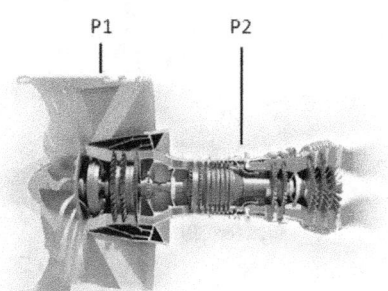

Overall (Compressor) Engine
Pressure Ratio = EPR = P2 / P1
Where P1 = air entering compressor,
and P2 = air exiting the compressor

Source: Author's analysis

The following key considerations illustrate the impact of OPR on engine performance and efficiency:

1. **Compression and Combustion Efficiency:**
   » A higher OPR means air entering the combustion chamber is at a significantly elevated pressure and temperature. This enhances the fuel combustion process, enabling the engine to generate more power for the same quantity of fuel.
   » This efficiency reduces specific fuel consumption (SFC), a critical factor for long-haul operations and economic performance.

2. **Modern Applications:**
   » Advanced turbofan engines, such as the GE9X (used on the Boeing 777X) and Pratt & Whitney's GTF series, leverage high OPR to deliver superior fuel efficiency. These engines achieve significant reductions in operating costs and environmental impact.

Engineering Challenges

High OPR engines face engineering challenges due to the elevated temperatures generated as air exits the high-pressure compressor, creating additional stress on downstream components like the combustion chamber and turbine. To address these demands, advanced materials such as single-crystal superalloys and ceramic matrix composites (CMCs) are employed for their ability to withstand extreme temperatures and pressures. Additionally, innovative cooling technologies, including air-cooled turbine blades and advanced thermal barriers, are essential to ensure component durability and maintain operational safety under high-stress conditions.

Fuel burn efficiency in a turbofan engine depends on effective air compression. Highly compressed air enhances the combustion process, allowing the engine to generate more power from the same fuel quantity. This makes the OPR a critical factor in engine performance.

The evolution of **Overall Pressure Ratios (OPR)** in turbofan engines highlights the significant strides made in jet engine technology over the decades. As shown in **Figure 4-4**, OPR has progressively increased, driving improvements in fuel efficiency, thrust, and environmental performance.

Historical Progression of Overall Pressure Ratios

The steady advancement of OPR reflects the industry's commitment to enhancing efficiency, meeting performance demands, and adhering to stricter environmental regulations. The following is a chronological overview of key milestones in OPR development:

- **Early Jet Engines (1960s):** The Pratt & Whitney JT8D, used on aircraft like the Boeing 727, had an OPR around 16:1, which was notable for its time.
- **High-Bypass Turbofans (1970s–1980s):** Engines like the CF6, powering widebody aircraft, achieved pressure ratios close to 20:1.

- **Advanced Turbofans (1990s–2000s):** Engines such as the CFM56 and PW4000 advanced to OPRs near 30:1, thanks to improvements in compressor design.
- **Latest Generation Turbofans (2010s–2020s):** Today's engines, such as the LEAP, Geared Turbofan (GTF), Trent XWB, and GE9X, operate at pressure ratios of 50:1 to 60:1, reflecting the industry's commitment to enhanced fuel efficiency and environmental performance.

Figure 4-4. Overall pressure ratio trends

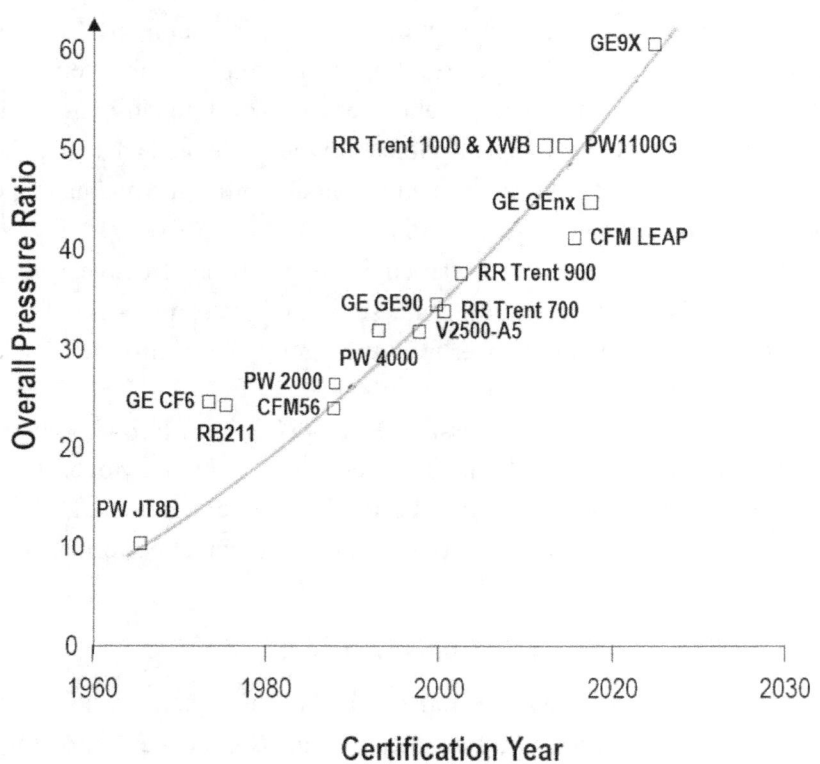

Source: Author's analysis

***Industry Perspective 4-1.** GTF and LEAP Efficiencies*

***Figure 4-5** illustrates the fuel efficiency advancements in **Pratt & Whitney's Geared Turbofan (GTF)** and **CFM International's LEAP** engines, both* *featuring high overall pressure ratios (OPRs) of 40:1 to 50:1. These high OPRs enable efficient air compression, generating greater thrust with lower fuel consumption.*

The GTF engine incorporates a unique gear system that allows the fan and core to operate at different speeds. This separation optimizes each component's performance, resulting in a higher bypass ratio and improved propulsive efficiency. By allowing a larger fan to rotate at slower speeds while the core operates faster, the GTF design boosts fuel efficiency and lowers noise emissions.

In contrast, the LEAP engine prioritizes thermodynamic efficiency through advanced core performance. It achieves this with materials like ceramic matrix composites that withstand higher temperatures, alongside optimized combustion processes for more effective fuel-to-energy conversion. While the GTF emphasizes aerodynamic efficiency through its geared mechanism, the LEAP's strength lies in maximizing fuel energy extraction via advanced core technologies.

Figure 4-5. *GTF and LEAP engines*

PW GTF: A design that enhances propulsive efficiency. Its gear system lets the fan turn more slowly than the low-pressure compressor and turbine, ensuring the fan works at peak efficiency.

CFM LEAP: A design focused on thermodynamic efficiency. Its high-efficiency compressor optimizes airflow and reduces energy losses. To withstand high pressures and temperatures, it incorporates advanced, lightweight, high-strength materials.

Source: CFMI and Pratt & Whitney

4.1.3 Engine Architecture

The architecture of turbofan engines significantly influences their performance, efficiency, and reliability. Three primary configurations—twin-spool, tri-spool, and geared turbofan (GTF)—each present unique advantages and engineering trade-offs. These designs focus on optimizing fuel consumption, thrust generation, and operational efficiency, reflecting key advancements in modern aviation technology.

- **Twin-Spool Engine Design:** A twin-spool engine comprises two rotor assemblies, each driven by a separate turbine (see **Figure 4-6**). The high-pressure turbine powers the high-pressure compressor, while the low-pressure turbine drives the low-pressure compressor. This arrangement allows each section to operate at optimal speeds, balancing efficiency, power output, and weight. Twin-spool engines are widely used for their simplicity, effectiveness, and versatility across various commercial applications. Notable examples include GE's CF6 and GE9X, Pratt & Whitney's PW4000, and CFM International's CFM56 and LEAP engines, powering aircraft from the Boeing 747 to the Airbus A320 family. While the design is straightforward and promotes ease of maintenance, it offers less optimization potential compared to more advanced architectures.

Figure 4-6. Twin-spool architecture

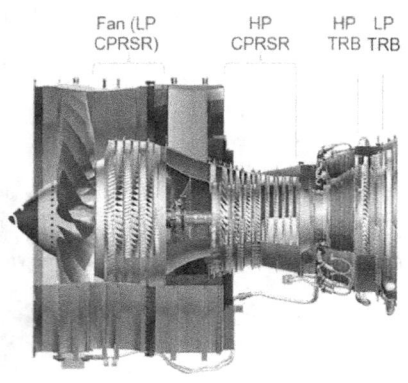

CFM CFM56-7B: This twin-shaft design features a Fan & Low-Pressure Compressor (LPC) powered by the Low-Pressure Turbine (LPT). Additionally, the High-Pressure Compressor (HPC) is driven by the High-Pressure Turbine (HPT).

Source: CFMI with modifications by the author

- **Tri-Spool Engine Design:** Tri-spool engines add a third, intermediate spool, with each spool independently driving its respective compressor stage (see **Figure 4-7**). This configuration allows for precise control over air compression, enhancing fuel efficiency and overall engine performance. The gradual, staged compression reduces thermal stress and extends engine life. Rolls-Royce pioneered this design, as exemplified by the RB211 and Trent engine series. The RB211, originally developed for the Lockheed L-1011 and later adopted by the Boeing 757 and 767, laid the groundwork for Rolls-Royce's tri-spool technology. The Trent series, powering the Boeing 787 and Airbus A350, further refined the architecture, achieving higher thrust and improved fuel efficiency. However, the added complexity and weight of the tri-spool design increase maintenance requirements.

Figure 4-7. Tri-spool architecture

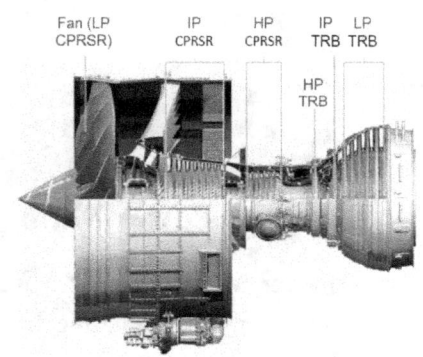

RR Trent 700: This three-shaft turbofan introduces an Intermediate Pressure Compressor (IPC) and Turbine (IPT) segment, nestled between the high-pressure compressor and turbine sections.

Source: Rolls-Royce with modifications by the author

- **Geared Turbofan (GTF) Engine by Pratt & Whitney:** Pratt & Whitney's Geared Turbofan (GTF) represents a transformative innovation in turbofan design. The GTF employs a reduction gearbox that allows the fan and low-pressure turbine to operate at independently optimized speeds, significantly enhancing propulsive efficiency. This setup enables a larger, slower fan to produce greater thrust, while the turbine runs at higher speeds to maximize energy extraction from exhaust gases (see **Figure 4-8**). The GTF achieves substantial improvements in fuel efficiency, noise reduction, and emissions performance, delivering up to 20% fuel savings compared to prior-generation engines. It powers aircraft such as the Airbus

A220 and A320neo, offering operators cost and environmental benefits.

Figure 4-8. GTF architecture

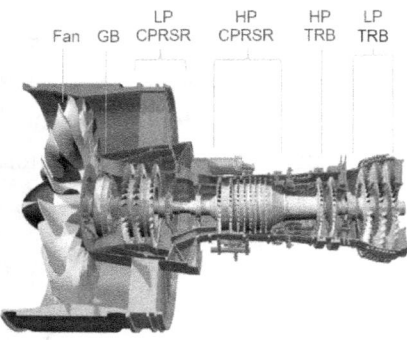

PW GTF: This design features a gear system allowing the fan to rotate independently of the low-pressure components. This enhances propulsive efficiency and leverages advanced aerodynamics and materials.

Source: Pratt & Whitney with modifications by the author

4.2 Thrust & Power Management

Thrust & Power Management focuses on ensuring optimal performance, efficiency, and safety by regulating an aircraft engine's power output across all flight phases. Key aspects of this process include thrust rating, thrust bump, and thrust derate, each designed to balance power requirements with efficiency and operational needs.

- **Thrust Rating**: Specifies the maximum certified power an engine can deliver. Calibrated to meet performance and safety standards, this rating ensures reliable operation under varying flight conditions.
- **Thrust Bump**: Temporarily allows the engine to exceed its certified thrust rating, providing additional power for takeoff in demanding conditions such as high-altitude airports or hot weather. This feature enhances safety and operational flexibility when extra thrust is required.
- **Thrust Derate**: Reduces engine power output during takeoff to save fuel, extend engine life, and adapt to specific operational scenarios, such as lighter payloads or shorter runways.

These strategies enable precise adjustment of engine power to match flight conditions, optimizing performance, fuel efficiency, and operational flexibility. Subsequent sections will explore each tool in greater detail.

4.2.1 Thrust Ratings

Thrust ratings are predefined engine power settings tailored to specific phases of flight, ensuring safe and efficient operation. These ratings are not the engine's absolute maximum output but calibrated configurations that meet operational demands without overstraining the engine. For example, the GEnx-1B76A engine, rated at 76,100 lbs. of thrust, refers to its **Maximum Takeoff Thrust (MTO)**—the peak thrust permitted during takeoff, which is sustainable only briefly to prevent excessive engine wear or overheating.

The following thrust ratings illustrate how engines adapt to different flight phases to optimize safety, performance, and efficiency:

- **Maximum Takeoff Thrust (MTO)**: Provides peak thrust during takeoff, essential for achieving required speed and climb gradients.
- **Maximum Climb Thrust (MCIT)**: Ensures efficient climb performance without overstressing the engine.
- **Maximum Cruise Thrust (MCrT)**: Balances performance and fuel efficiency for steady high-altitude cruising.
- **Maximum Continuous Thrust (MCT)**: Supports sustained high thrust for scenarios like engine-out operations or extended drift-downs without risking engine damage.
- **Go-around Thrust**: Delivers maximum power during low-speed maneuvers, such as missed approaches or go-arounds.

Selecting the appropriate thrust rating, particularly MTO, is essential for safe and efficient takeoff performance. Key factors include:

1. **Maximum Takeoff Weight (MTOW)**: Heavier aircraft near their MTOW require higher thrust ratings to achieve necessary takeoff power and climb gradients.
2. **Operating Environment**:
   - » **Altitude and Temperature**: High-altitude and hot conditions reduce air density (density altitude), diminishing engine output and necessitating higher thrust.

» **Runway Length**: Shorter runways demand higher thrust to reach takeoff speeds (V1 and Vr) within the available distance.
» **Fuel Efficiency**: Higher thrust settings increase fuel consumption. To optimize costs, operators may use derated or flex thrust operations under favorable conditions to save fuel and extend engine life.

Modern engines offer adjustable thrust options, allowing operators to match thrust settings to specific route profiles and environmental conditions. By balancing thrust requirements with MTOW, environmental factors, and runway constraints, operators can optimize performance, fuel costs, and operational efficiency across various scenarios.

EXAMPLE 4-1. Thrust Rating Options for the GEnx-1B Engine

Figure 4-9 illustrates the thrust rating options available for the GEnx-1B engine, which powers the Boeing 787-9 Dreamliner. This engine offers three Maximum Takeoff Thrust (MTO) ratings: 72,000, 74,000, and 76,000 lbs., allowing airlines to optimize engine performance based on specific operational requirements.

Selecting the appropriate thrust rating involves balancing operational demands with efficiency and cost considerations:

• **Fuel Efficiency:** Lower MTO ratings, such as 72,000 lbs., consume less fuel, making them ideal for routes where maximum takeoff power is unnecessary—such as those departing from airports with long runways or in cooler climates.
• **Performance in Challenging Environments:** Higher MTO ratings, such as 76,000 lbs., provide additional thrust for demanding conditions, including high-altitude airports or shorter runways. However, these settings may increase engine wear, potentially leading to higher maintenance costs over time.

The flexibility to select among multiple thrust ratings enables airlines to strategically balance fuel efficiency, engine wear, and performance, aligning engine output with route-specific and environmental demands. This adaptability ensures that the GEnx-1B remains a versatile and efficient powerplant for a wide range of operational scenarios.

Figure 4-9. GEnx-1B thrust ratings on 787-9

GEnx-1B

Engine Type	Takeoff Thrust (lbs.)
GEnx-1B70/75	70,200
GEnx-1B74/75	74,500
GEnx-1B76A	76,100

Source: GEnx-1B "Type Certificate Data Sheet (TCDS)", with analysis by the author [1]

4.2.1.1 Modifying Thrust Ratings

Adjusting a turbofan engine's thrust rating is a technical process that must adhere to strict regulatory and manufacturer standards to ensure safety and reliability. Modern engines utilize advanced electronic control systems to regulate performance, with thrust settings stored in a device known as the **rating plug.** Modifying thrust typically involves reprogramming or replacing this plug to adjust the engine's output.

In many cases, increasing an engine's thrust rating requires purchasing a new, pre-configured rating plug calibrated for the desired thrust level. Engine manufacturers often charge a premium for higher ratings, and upgrades may also necessitate software updates or, in some instances, physical modifications to support the increased thrust safely.

For engines with older analog control systems, the process is more complex. Physical alterations, such as replacing or adding components, may be required to manage higher power levels. These modifications demand careful execution to ensure the engine's long-term safety, performance, and reliability.

EXAMPLE 4-2. CFM56-7B engine's identification plug

The **CFM56-7B engine's identification plug** (see **Figure 4-10**) is a vital component of its **Electronic Engine Control (EEC)** system, providing essential data to ensure the engine operates with the correct thrust settings.

Figure 4-10. CFM56-7B rating plug

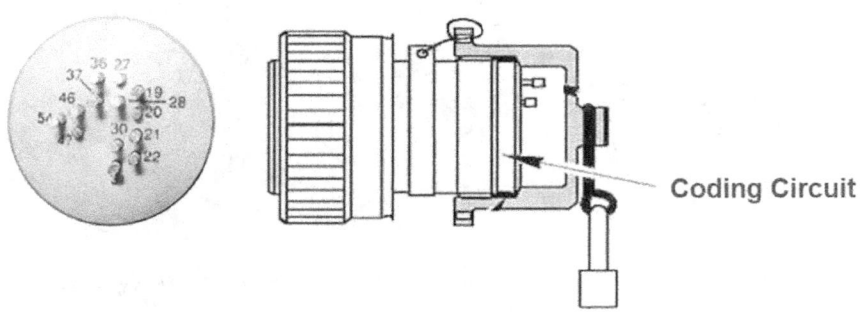

Source: CFMI with modifications by the author

The identification plug contains a circuit that facilitates signal flow throughout the engine. The **EEC** references this plug to determine the engine's configuration and optimize its performance. At startup, the EEC uses the identification plug to apply the correct settings, including:

- **Engine Family and Model**: Confirms the specific engine variant to ensure compatibility with performance adjustments.
- **Thrust Level**: Sets the engine's thrust capacity to its certified rating for safe and efficient operation.
- **Performance Optimization Adjustments**: Refines engine settings to enhance fuel efficiency and thrust output.
- **Optional Power Boosts (Thrust Bumps)**: Provides additional thrust capabilities for specific operational needs, such as high-altitude or short-runway scenarios.
- **Engine Monitoring Options**: Activates tracking and oversight features to maintain performance and reliability.

By supplying precise configuration data, the identification plug enables the **EEC** to manage thrust and performance settings accurately, ensuring the engine meets operational demands with safety and efficiency.

4.2.2 Thrust Derate

Thrust derate is a technique that intentionally reduces an engine's maximum thrust output during takeoff, as illustrated in **Figure 4-11**. This approach improves fuel efficiency, reduces mechanical stress on the engine, and extends its operational lifespan, leading to lower maintenance and operating costs for airlines.

Thrust derate is typically used in scenarios where full-rated thrust is unnecessary, such as:

- **Lighter payloads**: Reduced weight requires less power for takeoff.
- **Longer runways**: Additional distance allows for lower thrust during acceleration.
- **Favorable weather conditions**: Cooler temperatures and lower altitudes improve engine performance naturally.

Figure 4-11. Thrust derate

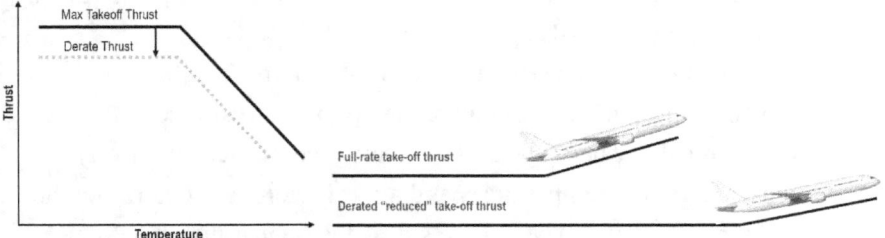

Source: Author's analysis

Conversely, full-rated thrust remains critical under more demanding conditions, including:

- **High-altitude airports**: Reduced air density limits engine performance, requiring maximum thrust.
- **Short runways**: Limited distance necessitates higher thrust for safe acceleration.
- **Maximum payload operations**: Heavier aircraft demand greater power to achieve required performance and safety margins.

Engines are designed to provide full thrust for peak performance scenarios. However, routine takeoff operations often do not require the full thrust capacity. By opting for derated thrust, pilots can reduce fuel consumption, minimize mechanical wear, and extend maintenance intervals without compromising safety.

Derate Implementation

Thrust derate can be implemented either manually by the flight crew or automatically through the aircraft's onboard systems, optimizing engine performance for specific takeoff conditions. The following methods illustrate how thrust derate can be applied to align engine performance with operational needs:

- **FLEX (Assumed Temperature) Derate Implementation**: The FLEX method reduces thrust by simulating a higher outside air temperature. Pilots input an assumed temperature into the flight management system, prompting the engine to adjust thrust as though operating in hotter conditions. This approach is ideal for scenarios where full power is unnecessary, such as on long runways or with light payloads.
- **Automatic Derate Implementation**: Modern aircraft with advanced systems can calculate the optimal thrust level automatically. These systems evaluate factors such as runway length, altitude, temperature, and aircraft weight to determine the appropriate derate. The engine's thrust is then adjusted without requiring manual intervention, ensuring a safe and efficient takeoff tailored to the operating environment.

FLEX derate remains a widely used technique in commercial aviation for its adaptability and efficiency. Meanwhile, the increasing adoption of automatic derate systems further enhances operational precision, reducing the need for manual adjustments while optimizing performance and cost-effectiveness.

4.2.3 Thrust Bumps

Thrust bumps provide a controlled, temporary increase in engine thrust, typically applied during takeoff to enhance performance under challenging conditions. This boost, often up to 10% or more above the engine's maximum rated thrust, is vital for ensuring safe and efficient operations in altitude-temperature ranges specific to the aircraft and engine type.

The thrust bump mechanism involves injecting additional fuel into the combustion chamber, raising the exhaust gases' temperature and pressure to produce extra thrust. Carefully regulated and applied only under defined operational limits, thrust bumps ensure engine integrity by minimizing mechanical stress. Procedures for thrust bump use are outlined in the Aircraft Flight Manual (AFM) to maintain safety and performance.

Thrust bumps are activated when specific environmental or operational conditions demand additional power. Once these conditions subside, the engine reverts to its standard thrust rating. Common scenarios include:

- **High-Altitude and Hot & High Conditions**: Reduced air density at high-altitude airports or in hot climates (high-density altitude) lowers engine performance and wing lift. Thrust bumps compensate by delivering the additional power needed for safe takeoff in these conditions.
- **Short Runways**: At airports with limited runway length, thrust bumps enable the aircraft to achieve required takeoff speeds within the available distance.
- **Obstacle Clearance**: Thrust bumps assist in quicker climb rates, ensuring the aircraft clears nearby obstacles safely during takeoff.
- **Payload Maximization**: When operating at maximum payload capacity, thrust bumps support higher takeoff weights, enhancing operational efficiency for cargo and passenger flights.

Thrust bumps can be tailored for specific needs. For example, the CFM56-7B engine offers optional thrust bump configurations, as shown in **Table 4-1**, detailing maximum thrust achievable based on hardware settings.

Table 4-1. CFM56-7B thrust bump options

Bump Suffix *	Bump Description	Aircraft Application
B1	Adds optimized thrust bump power management at takeoff	737-600,-700,-800,-900,-900ER
B1F	Adds optimized thrust bump power management at takeoff, and increased EGT limits	737-800,-900,-900ER
B2	Adds extended high altitude & temp rating above corner point takeoff	737-600,-700,-900ER
B2F	Adds extended high altitude and temp rating above corner point takeoff, and increased EGT limits	737-900ER
F	The Exhaust Gas Temperature (EGT) limitation is increased by 20°C.	737-700,-800,-900,-900ER

* Example: CFM56-7B26/3B1

Source: CFM56-7B "Type Certificate Data Sheet (TCDS)", with analysis by the author [2]

Figure 4-12 illustrates two types of thrust bumps, **Bump 1,** and **Bump 2,** highlighting variations in thrust and temperature enhancements. This visualization helps operators understand the specific capabilities provided under different bump configurations.

The following outlines the capabilities provided by each thrust bump configuration:

- **Bump 1:** Enhances thrust to increase engine temperature capabilities.
- **Bump 2:** Provides both temperature and thrust enhancements.

Figure 4-12. Thrust bumps

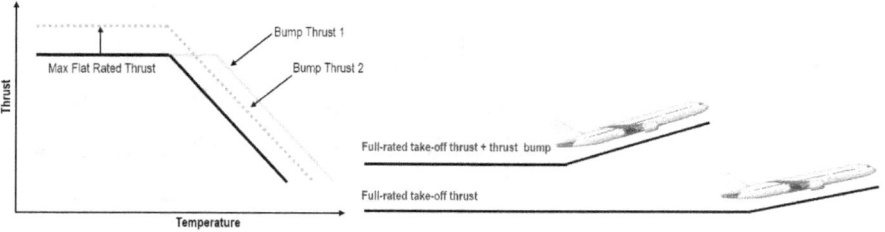

Source: Author's analysis

While thrust bumps offer critical performance benefits, they introduce operational trade-offs that require careful consideration. For instance, the additional thrust results in increased engine stress, accelerating engine wear, potentially shortening its operational lifespan, and raising maintenance frequency. Additionally, higher fuel consumption accompanies the elevated thrust, impacting operational costs and reducing fuel efficiency. Consequently, thrust bumps are typically employed only when essential, striking a balance between the need for additional power and the long-term considerations of cost and efficiency.

Thrust Bump Implementation

In modern turbofan engines equipped with electronic control systems, thrust bumps are implemented through adjustments to the engine's connector plug. This modification enables the Electronic Engine Control (EEC) to automatically fine-tune critical settings, such as fuel flow and turbine configurations, ensuring a safe increase in thrust within manufacturer-approved limits. The process is seamless, with the EEC autonomously managing the thrust boost, eliminating the need for direct input from the flight crew.

For older engines with analog control systems, thrust bumps must be manually engaged by the flight crew, following detailed procedures outlined in the Aircraft Flight Manual (AFM). This manual process requires pilots to closely monitor engine performance during activation to ensure the thrust bump operates within safe operational parameters.

4.3 Engine Fuel Efficiency

Engine fuel efficiency focuses on measuring how effectively aircraft engines convert fuel into useful work, primarily generating thrust to propel the aircraft. A key metric in assessing engine efficiency is **Thrust Specific Fuel Consumption (TSFC)**, which quantifies the amount of fuel required to produce a specific amount of thrust. A lower TSFC reflects higher efficiency, similar to a car achieving greater mileage per gallon of fuel. Engine manufacturers often emphasize cruise TSFC in performance specifications, as it serves as a critical benchmark for comparing fuel efficiency across different engine designs.

Thrust Specific Fuel Consumption (TSFC) is calculated as the ratio of the fuel flow rate to the thrust produced:

$$TSFC = \text{Fuel Flow Rate} / \text{Thrust} \quad \text{(Eq. 4-1)}$$

Where:

- **Fuel Flow Rate:** The rate at which fuel is consumed, typically measured in pounds per hour (lb/hr) or kilograms per hour (kg/hr).
- **Thrust:** The force generated by the engine, typically measured in pounds of thrust (for jet engines).

A lower TSFC reflects higher fuel efficiency, leading to reduced operating costs and environmental benefits, including lower fuel consumption and emissions. For example, an engine producing 25,000 lbs. of thrust with a fuel flow rate of 12,500 lbs./hr has the following TSFC:

$$TSFC = 12,500 \text{ lbs./hr} / 25,000 \text{ lbs.} = 0.5 \text{ lb/hr/lb}$$

This result indicates the engine consumes 0.5 pounds of fuel per hour for every pound of thrust produced.

Cruise TSFC

TSFC varies depending on flight conditions, but the cruise phase is particularly critical for fuel efficiency. Cruise represents the longest portion of most flights, requiring consistent thrust at steady speeds and altitudes. A lower cruise TSFC reflects an engine's ability to operate efficiently over extended distances, translating directly into fuel savings for airlines and reduced emissions.

EXAMPLE 4-3. Projected TSFC Improvements and Range Impacts

The Boeing 737-8 MAX, equipped with the LEAP-1B engine, is engineered to deliver a 15% improvement in Thrust Specific Fuel Consumption (TSFC) compared to its predecessor, the CFM56-7B26 used on the 737-800W. This improvement supports enhanced fuel efficiency and extended operational range. However, if the full improvement is not realized and a TSFC shortfall of 2.5% occurs, the aircraft's range decreases due to higher fuel consumption. Let us calculate the impact of this shortfall.

Step 1: Baseline TSFC and Range Assumptions

- Baseline TSFC (100% efficiency): 0.5 lb/hr/lb
- Projected improvement: 15%
- Resulting TSFC: $0.5 \times (1-0.15) = 0.425$ lb/hr/lb
- Range with projected TSFC improvement: 3,620 nm

Step 2: TSFC with a 2.5% Shortfall

- Actual TSFC (with shortfall): $0.425 \times (1+0.025) = 0.435$ lb/hr/lb

Step 3: Range Impact of Shortfall

Increased TSFC leads to higher fuel burn for the same mission profile. Using the **Breguet range equation**, a 2.5% higher TSFC reduces range by approximately 105 nm, resulting in a new maximum range of 3,515 nm.

This example illustrates the importance of achieving projected TSFC improvements. Even a small deviation, such as a 2.5% shortfall, can noticeably reduce the range capability, limiting operational flexibility and increasing fuel costs. Conversely, achieving, or exceeding TSFC targets ensures extended range, reduced fuel consumption, and lower emissions, aligning with the dual goals of economic and environmental sustainability.

Engine manufacturers continually optimize TSFC through advancements like higher bypass ratios, improved aerodynamics, and more efficient turbines. These innovations bolster fuel efficiency, providing airlines with operational advantages while supporting economic and environmental sustainability.

TSFC vs. Fuel Burn: Understanding the Differences

Thrust-Specific Fuel Consumption (TSFC) and fuel burn are both critical metrics for evaluating the efficiency of turbofan engines, but they serve distinct purposes:

- **TSFC:** A technical metric that measures an engine's efficiency in converting fuel into thrust. It allows direct comparisons between engines of different sizes or designs by normalizing fuel consumption to thrust. TSFC is particularly useful for assessing engine performance across various operating conditions, such as cruise, climb, and takeoff.

- **Fuel Burn:** Refers to the actual quantity of fuel consumed by an engine or an aircraft over a given period or distance. It reflects the combined effect of several factors, including the aircraft's weight, aerodynamics, mission profile, and engine efficiency.

For example, a high-efficiency engine with a low TSFC may still result in high fuel burn if the aircraft it powers is heavy or operates on long-haul routes.

In summary, TSFC is a technical measure of engine efficiency, while fuel burn is a practical measure of fuel usage during operations. Together, these metrics provide a comprehensive view of engine and aircraft performance.

Industry Perspective 4-2: *Lifecycle Compensation for Performance Shortfalls*

Engine manufacturers typically guarantee performance metrics, such as thrust-specific fuel consumption (TSFC), as a key indicator of engine efficiency. TSFC guarantees serve as a benchmark to ensure the engine meets the expected efficiency standards under specific conditions. However, any deviation from these guarantees can translate into higher fuel burn during operations, directly impacting airlines' operational costs and financial planning. To address such performance shortfalls, manufacturers often offer lifecycle compensation agreements to mitigate the economic impact on operators. These agreements may include:

- ***Financial Credits:*** *Direct compensation to offset increased operating costs.*
- ***Reduced Maintenance Costs:*** *Discounts or incentives during scheduled engine maintenance.*
- ***Performance Upgrades:*** *Enhancements integrated during overhauls to improve engine efficiency over time.*

By addressing performance shortfalls proactively, manufacturers ensure that the total cost of ownership remains consistent with initial expectations, supporting long-term partnerships with operators.

4.4 Engine Reliability & Durability

Aircraft engines are critical to aviation operations, where their **reliability** and **durability** are essential for ensuring safety, efficiency, and uninterrupted service. While interconnected, these terms address distinct aspects of engine performance that are pivotal for airlines and operators.

The following definitions highlight the unique yet complementary roles of reliability and durability in engine performance:

- **Reliability:** Measures an engine's ability to operate consistently without unexpected malfunctions or failures. A reliable engine delivers predictable performance across diverse operating conditions, minimizing disruptions caused by mechanical issues. High reliability reduces in-flight incidents, unscheduled maintenance, and delays, supporting operational stability and passenger satisfaction.
- **Durability:** Refers to an engine's capacity to withstand wear and tear over extended periods. A durable engine maintains performance over thousands of flight hours and cycles, requiring fewer major repairs. Durability is directly linked to long-term cost savings by reducing the frequency of overhauls and extending intervals between maintenance visits.

Together, reliability and durability underpin operational efficiency. Engines that perform consistently and resist degradation lower maintenance costs, enhance aircraft availability, and promote safety.

The following considerations highlight the primary drivers of engine reliability and durability:

1. **Engine Design**: The architecture, materials, and components of an engine significantly affect its reliability and longevity. Advanced materials, such as high-temperature alloys and composites, enable engines to endure the extreme stresses of high temperatures, pressures, and rotational speeds inherent to turbofan operation.
2. **Maintenance Practices**: Comprehensive maintenance programs aligned with manufacturers' specifications are vital. Airlines that prioritize consistent inspections and proactive maintenance can significantly extend engine lifespans and maintain reliability.

3. **Operating Conditions**: Environmental factors, including extreme temperatures, high altitudes, and operational demands, influence engine wear and tear.
    » **Hot and High Environments**: Engines face greater stress due to lower air density, affecting performance.
    » **Short-Haul Flights**: Frequent takeoff and landing cycles accelerate wear.

Reliability & Durability Metrics

Ensuring operational safety and efficiency requires rigorous monitoring of engine performance metrics by manufacturers, airlines, and regulatory authorities. These standardized metrics enable comparisons across engine types, identify areas for improvement, and establish critical benchmarks to support data-driven fleet management decisions. Two principal metrics used to assess reliability and durability are the **Shop Visit Rate (SVR)** and the **In-Flight Shutdown (IFSD) Rate**:

- **Shop Visit Rate (SVR)**: SVR measures the frequency of major overhauls or shop visits, typically expressed as the number of visits per 1,000 engine flight hours. A lower SVR indicates higher engine reliability and durability, reflecting fewer repair or overhaul requirements. This reduces maintenance costs and increases aircraft availability, enhancing fleet utilization and operational efficiency.
- **In-Flight Shutdown (IFSD) Rate**: The IFSD rate tracks unexpected engine shutdowns during flight, expressed per 1,000 engine flight hours. A low IFSD rate is a key indicator of engine reliability, signaling fewer unplanned shutdowns that could compromise flight safety. This metric is particularly vital for ETOPS-certified aircraft, as engine reliability determines the allowable operational range over remote areas or oceans. Low IFSD rates improve safety, operational dependability, and the ability to confidently operate extended routes without risking in-flight diversions or emergency landings.

Table 4-2 highlights benchmarks for these metrics, illustrating their role in assessing engine performance, reliability, and durability.

Table 4-2. Key engine reliability metrics

Reliability Metric	Description
Engine Shop Visit Rate (SVR) The SER & UER rate is expressed as the number of removals per 1,000 engine flight hours. (e.g., SER = .05 = 1 Scheduled Shop Visit per 20,000 EFH.	Engine SVR measures the frequency which an engine requires maintenance, repair, and overhaul/restoration services and is a important metric as it affects the overall cost of ownership and operation of an aircraft. An engine's Total SVR is composed of both scheduled and unscheduled engine removal rates (SER and UER). The SER measures how often a particular engine model is removed to address planned, or scheduled removals due to required maintenance actions. The UER measures how often an engine is removed for repair or refurbishment before the normal maintenance intervals are reached, or due to an unexpected engine anomaly preventing it from continued safe operation.
In-Flight Shutdown (IFSD) rate The IFSD rate is expressed as the number of incidents per 1,000 engine flight hours. (e.g., IFSD = .02 = 1 IFSD per 50,000 EFH)	IFSD rate is a measure of the number of times an aircraft's engine shuts down unexpectedly during a flight. The resulting rate provides a standardized measure for comparing engine reliability across different aircraft types or fleets.

Source: Author's analysis

These metrics provide airlines with critical tools for monitoring engine performance, identifying trends, and implementing strategies to ensure operational safety and efficiency. The following sections will explore these metrics in greater detail, offering insights into their application and significance in modern aviation.

4.4.1 Shop Visit Rate (SVR)

The **Shop Visit Rate (SVR)** is a key performance metric used to assess an engine's maintenance demands, durability, and operational reliability. It tracks the frequency of major maintenance events, such as overhauls and repairs, providing critical insights into both the planned and unplanned aspects of engine maintenance.

The SVR consists of two main components:

1. **Scheduled Engine Removal Rate (SER):** Measures the frequency of planned engine removals for maintenance, such as inspections or part replacements, based on predetermined service intervals. A **low SER** indicates strong adherence to expected durability standards,

allowing operators to efficiently schedule maintenance and avoid disruptions.

2. **Unscheduled Engine Removal Rate (UER):** Tracks the frequency of unexpected engine removals due to issues like malfunctions, failures, or performance concerns. A **high UER** signals potential reliability challenges, as it implies that the engine may not consistently perform between scheduled maintenance intervals.

The Shop Visit Rate (SVR) is calculated to provide insights into engine maintenance frequency and reliability. It is expressed as:

SVR = Number of Shop Visits / Total Engine Flight Hours (Eq. 4-2)

Where:

- Number of Shop Visits includes engine removals and major maintenance events.
- Total Engine Flight Hours represents the total operational usage over the period being analyzed.

This equation applies to Total SVR, Scheduled Engine Removal Rate (SER), and Unscheduled Engine Removal Rate (UER) by defining the Number of Shop Visits in the numerator:

EXAMPLE 4-4. Shop Visit Rate Calculation

Scenario: An airline operates a fleet of aircraft equipped with engines that collectively accumulate 50,000 Engine Flight Hours over a 12-month period. During this time:

- The engines undergo 8 Shop Visits, including both scheduled and unscheduled maintenance events.
- Out of the total shop visits, 6 are scheduled maintenance, and 2 are unscheduled maintenance events.

We will calculate the following:

1. Total Shop Visit Rate (SVR) = 8/50,000 = 0.00016 visits/hour or 1.6 visits per 10,000 hours.

2. Scheduled Engine Removal Rate (SER) = 6/50,000 = 0.00012 visits/hour or 1.2 visits per 10,000 hours.
3. Unscheduled Engine Removal Rate (UER) = 2/50,000 = 0.00004 visits/hour or 0.4 visits per 10,000 hours.

Figure 4-13 shows a 12-month rolling average of the Total Shop Visit Rate (SVR), Scheduled Engine Removal Rate (SER), and Unscheduled Engine Removal Rate (UER). The trends depicted in the figure provide insights into the maintenance dynamics of the fleet over time:

1. **Scheduled Engine Removal Rate (SER):** Represented by the middle line, the SER shows a gradual increase over time as engines approach their planned maintenance intervals. This reflects the predictable nature of scheduled maintenance, driven by operational usage and service life expectations.
2. **Unscheduled Engine Removal Rate (UER):** Represented by the lowest line, the UER exhibits a steady decline over time. This reduction highlights improvements in engine reliability, likely due to operational adjustments, better maintenance practices, or upgrades to engine components.
3. **Total Shop Visit Rate (SVR):** Represented by the top line, the Total SVR combines both scheduled and unscheduled events. Initially, the Total SVR increases due to the rising frequency of scheduled removals. Over time, as UER decreases and scheduled events stabilize, the Total SVR plateaus and eventually declines, reflecting an overall improvement in maintenance efficiency and engine reliability.

Figure 4-13. Engine shop visit rate (SVR)

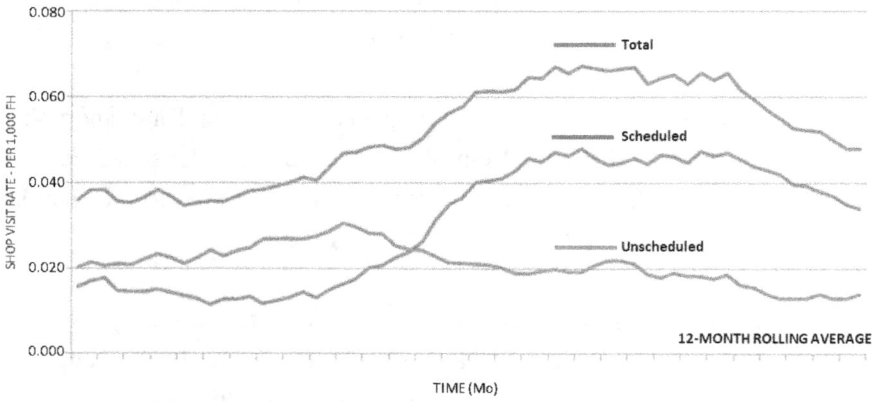

Source: Author's analysis

Implications of Elevated Engine Removal Rates

Elevated UER and SVR rates indicate disruptions in operational performance beyond planned maintenance schedules. This creates a cascade of challenges for airlines, including increased maintenance costs due to more frequent engine removals, potential operational downtime, and the added burden of sourcing replacement engines.

A high SVR—particularly when driven by frequent unscheduled removals—can significantly increase lifecycle maintenance costs, disrupt fleet operations, and reduce overall reliability. Conversely, a low SVR reflects robust engine durability and reliability, leading to lower maintenance expenses and improved operational efficiency. As shown in **Figure 4-14**, elevated removal rates have a direct impact on lifecycle maintenance costs, underscoring the importance of managing UER and SVR metrics for efficient fleet operations.

Figure 4-14. SVR impact on engine maintenance costs

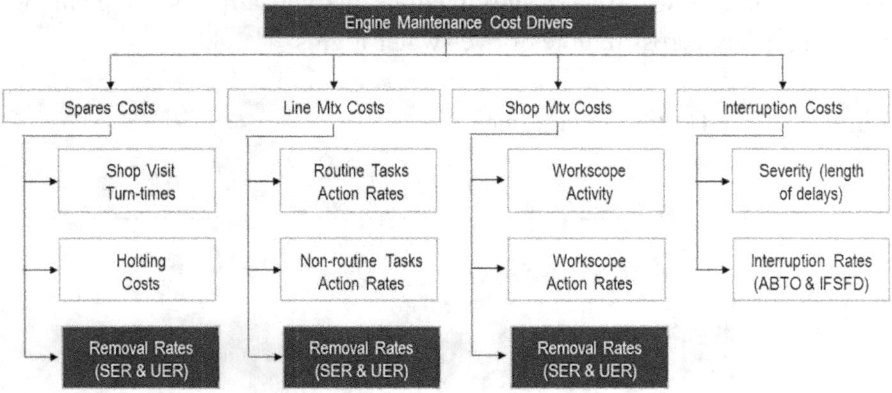

Source: Author's analysis

4.4.2 In-Flight Shutdown (IFSD) Rate

The **In-Flight Shutdown (IFSD) Rate** is a critical measure of engine reliability, tracking the frequency of unexpected engine shutdowns during flight. A low IFSD rate signifies high reliability, reducing safety risks, unscheduled diversions, and operational disruptions. For example, an IFSD rate of 0.02 corresponds to one shutdown per 50,000 flight hours, calculated as:

$$\text{IFSD Rate} = (1/0.02) \times 1000 = 50{,}000 \text{ flight hours per shutdown}$$

The IFSD rate is particularly significant for **Extended Twin-Engine Operations (ETOPS),** ensuring twin-engine aircraft can safely continue to an alternate airport after an engine failure. Regulatory standards include:

- **120-minute ETOPS:** IFSD rate better than 1 per 20,000 flight hours.
- **180-minute ETOPS:** IFSD rate better than 1 per 50,000 flight hours.
- **Beyond 180-minute ETOPS (e.g., 240 or 330 minutes):** IFSD rates approaching 1 per 100,000 flight hours, supported by rigorous operator assessments and route-specific certification.

Maintaining low IFSD rates preserves ETOPS certification, allowing airlines to operate extended routes confidently and cost-effectively. **Figure 4-15** highlights how ETOPS routes integrate alternate airports into planning, ensuring safety across remote or over-water flights.

Figure 4-15. ETOPS flight regime

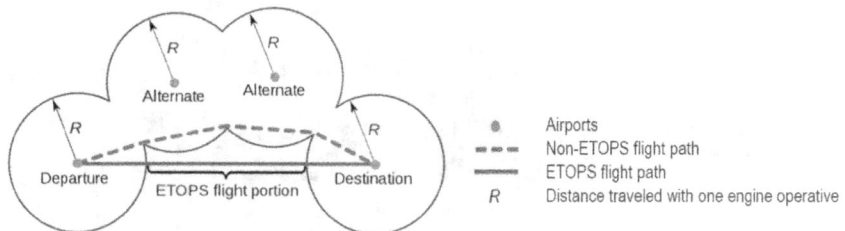

Source: Image from Wikipedia [3]

Operational Implications

Engines with low IFSD rates enhance operational flexibility and customer confidence, enabling airlines to plan extended-range flights with fewer restrictions. Conversely, elevated IFSD rates can result in ETOPS down-grades, limiting route options and increasing costs. By prioritizing engine reliability, airlines safeguard safety, operational efficiency, and long-term competitiveness.

Additionally, certification for routes exceeding 180 minutes is often granted on a city-pair basis, meaning the airline must demonstrate reliable ETOPS performance for specific route combinations. This ensures that both aircraft and operational practices meet the safety requirements for the unique challenges of each route.

Industry Perspective 4-3: Enhanced Reliability for 330-Minute ETOPS Certification

*As illustrated in **Figure 4-16**, achieving 330-minute ETOPS certification on the Boeing 787 demands exceptionally high reliability, especially within the propulsion system. ETOPS (Extended Twin-Engine Operations) regulations* *define the maximum duration twin-engine aircraft can operate safely on a single engine, primarily for routes far from suitable alternate airports.*

To qualify for the 330-minute ETOPS standard, the Boeing 787's propulsion system must demonstrate an In-Flight Shutdown (IFSD) rate of less than 0.01 per 1,000 engine flight hours. This rigorous threshold, translating to fewer than one engine shutdown per 100,000 flight hours, sets a high benchmark for engine reliability. Achieving this standard allows the aircraft to operate on extended, remote routes, such as transoceanic flights, with confidence that it can reach an alternate airport, if necessary, even from distant locations.

Figure 4-16. *787 IFSD rate for 330-minute ETOPS*

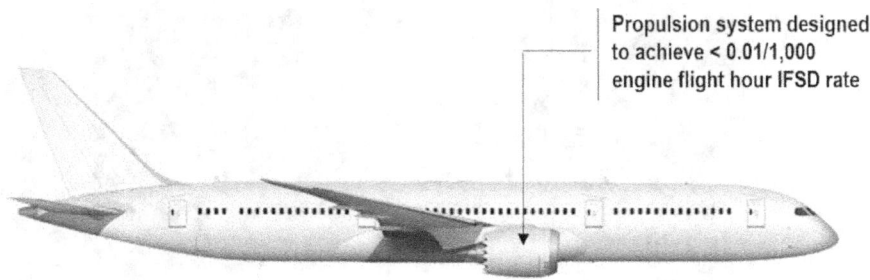

Propulsion system designed
to achieve < 0.01/1,000
engine flight hour IFSD rate

Source: Boeing with analysis by the author

4.5 Engine Noise & Emissions

The aviation industry faces increasing scrutiny over noise and emissions, particularly from pollutants like carbon dioxide (CO_2) and nitrogen oxides (NO_x). These issues have significant public health and environmental implications, prompting global regulatory bodies such as the International Civil Aviation Organization (ICAO), the Federal Aviation Administration (FAA), and the European Union Aviation Safety Agency (EASA) to enforce stricter environmental standards. Aircraft manufacturers and airlines are responding by driving innovation in engine technology, aiming to reduce emissions and noise levels while aligning with evolving sustainability goals.

4.5.1 Noise & Emissions-Based Charges

To address environmental challenges, many airports have introduced charges tied to noise and emissions levels. These charges are assessed based on pollution generated during landing, takeoff, and ground operations. As highlighted in **Figure 4-17**, the number of airports adopting such charges has significantly increased, reflecting the growing importance of engine technology in reducing aviation's environmental impact.

Figure 4-17. Airports levying noise and emission charges

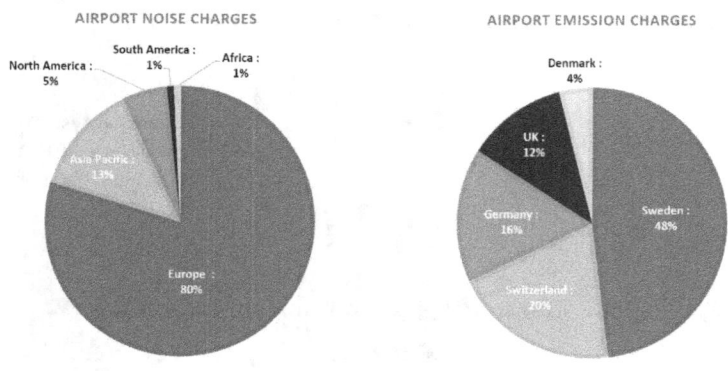

Source: Boeing "Airports with Noise and Emissions Restrictions," with analysis by the author [4]

European airports account for approximately 80% of global noise-based charges, demonstrating a strong commitment to mitigating noise pollution. Emissions-related charges are also concentrated in Europe, with Sweden leading at 48%, followed by Switzerland, Germany, and the UK at 20%, 16%, and 12%, respectively. These efforts underline Europe's leadership in fostering sustainable aviation practices.

The implementation of noise and emissions charges is driving advancements in quieter, more efficient aircraft, and engines. This shift reflects the industry's commitment to balancing operational efficiency with environmental responsibility.

Noise Assessment

Aircraft noise is assessed during certification to ensure compliance with regulatory standards. Most of the noise originates from engines, particularly during takeoff and climb. Key measurement points include:

- **Lateral (Sideline):** Positioned to the side of the aircraft's flight path during takeoff.
- **Flyover:** Directly below the aircraft as it ascends after takeoff.
- **Approach:** Positioned to capture noise during descent and landing.

These measurement locations, shown in **Figure 4-18**, provide a comprehensive noise profile across critical flight phases. Regulatory bodies evaluate these assessments to minimize disturbances to airport-adjacent communities and ensure environmentally responsible aviation practices.

Figure 4-18. Airport noise measurement locations

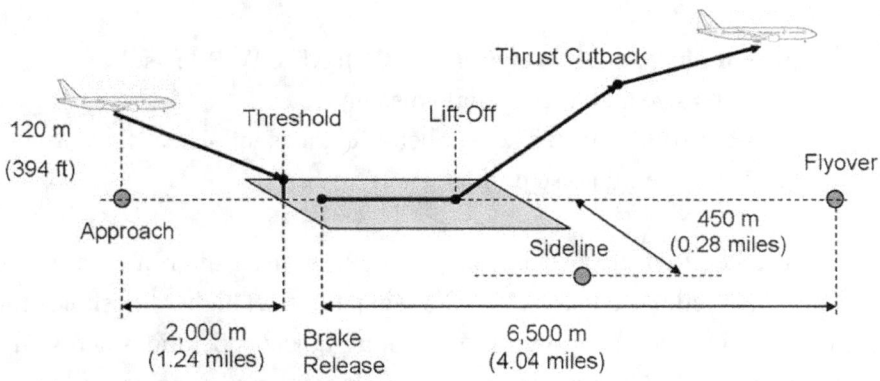

Source: Image from ResearchGate [5]

Noise data is detailed in Type Certificate Data Sheets (TCDS), published by authorities like EASA. These documents specify Effective Perceived Noise Levels (EPNLs) for lateral, approach, and flyover phases, ensuring compliance with regulatory limits. For example, the TCDS for the Airbus A320 series provides noise data essential for balancing operational efficiency with community impact (refer to **Table 4-3**).

Table 4-3. A320 noise limitations

EASA Record No.	Variant	Maximum Mass		Lateral EPNL		Flyover EPNL		Approach EPNL	
		Take-off[1] (kg)	Landing[1] (kg)	Level[1]	Limit	Level[1]	Limit	Level[1]	Limit
A12321	017	78,000	66,000	91.3	97.0	84.9	91.8	94.4	100.7
A619	015	78,000	64,500	91.3	97.0	84.9	91.8	94.3	100.7
A616	012	77,000	66,000	91.3	96.9	84.6	91.7	94.4	100.7
A611	007	77,000	64,500	91.3	96.9	84.6	91.7	94.3	100.7
A614	010	77,000	64,500	91.3	96.9	84.6	91.7	94.3	100.7
A615	011	75,500	66,000	91.4	96.9	83.9	91.6	94.4	100.6
A610	003	75,500	64,500	91.4	96.9	83.9	91.6	94.3	100.6
A613	009	75,500	64,500	91.4	96.9	83.9	91.6	94.3	100.6
A7544	016	73,500	66,000	91.4	96.8	83.1	91.5	94.4	100.5
A608	000	73,500	64,500	91.4	96.8	83.1	91.5	94.3	100.5

Source: A320 "Type Certificate Data Sheet (TCDS)" [6]

After assessing noise levels at designated certification locations, the International Civil Aviation Organization (ICAO) establishes noise standards for aircraft based on two main criteria:

1. **Maximum Takeoff Weight (MTOW):** MTOW reflects the aircraft's size and its potential noise impact.
2. **Number of Engines:** The number of engines influences the aircraft's overall noise profile.

These criteria ensure that larger, potentially noisier aircraft meet stringent noise reduction standards. ICAO's regulations set higher thresholds for noise mitigation on larger aircraft, promoting quieter operations across diverse categories and minimizing the environmental impact on communities near airports.

The **cumulative noise margin**, a key measure of compliance with ICAO standards, is calculated as:

$$\text{Cumulative Noise Margin} = (\text{Approach margin}) + (\text{Lateral margin}) + (\text{Takeoff margin})$$

$$\text{Cumulative Noise Margin} = (\text{LSNL}-\text{LCNL}) + (\text{ASNL}-\text{ACNL}) + (\text{TSNL}-\text{TCNL}) \quad \text{Eq (4-1)}$$

Where:

- LSNL is the Lateral Specified ICAO Noise Level
- LCNL is the Lateral Certificated Noise Level
- ASNL is the Approach Specified ICAO Noise Level
- ACNL is the Approach Certificated Noise Level
- TSNL is the Takeoff Specified ICAO Noise Level
- TCNL is the Takeoff Certificated Noise Level

Each term represents the difference between the specified and certificated noise levels at the corresponding measurement location. A **positive cumulative noise margin** indicates that the aircraft's noise emissions are below the specified limits, demonstrating compliance with ICAO's standards.

EXAMPLE 4-5. Calculate the cumulative margin for A320-200 Variant 007, MTOW = 77,000 kg

1. Certified Noise Levels (EPNLs): 91.3 Lateral (L), 84.6 Flyover (F), 94.3 Approach (A)
2. ICAO Specified Noise Levels (based on MTOW): 96.9 Lateral (L), 91.7 Flyover (T), 100.7 Approach (A)
3. Cumulative Noise Margin Calculation:

$$\text{Cumulative Noise Margin} = (96.9 - 91.3) + (100.7 - 94.3) + (91.7 - 84.6) = 19.1$$

The cumulative noise margin of **19.1 EPNdB (Effective Perceived Noise in Decibels)** confirms that the A320-200 Variant 007 complies with ICAO noise regulations for its MTOW category. Each positive margin ensures the aircraft's noise emissions are below allowable limits for lateral, approach, and takeoff measurements.

Noise Charging Model

The International Civil Aviation Organization (ICAO) establishes noise certification standards in *Annex 16*, which categorizes aircraft by noise compliance chapters: Chapter 2, Chapter 3, Chapter 4, and Chapter 14. Each successive chapter enforces stricter noise standards, ensuring that as technology advances, newer aircraft operate more quietly and with less environmental impact.

Noise certification levels are scaled to account for the aircraft's Maximum Takeoff Weight (MTOW) since larger, heavier aircraft generally produce more noise. This scaling ensures fair noise performance comparisons across different aircraft types, taking into consideration their size and weight. Noise certification involves measuring noise at three key locations:

1. **Approach** (during descent and landing)
2. **Lateral (Sideline)** (during takeoff)
3. **Takeoff** (as the aircraft ascends)

These measurements are then compared to ICAO's prescribed noise limits for the aircraft's specific weight category. The resulting **noise margin** is calculated by subtracting the measured noise levels from the ICAO limits. A larger noise margin reflects an aircraft's superior noise performance, as it operates below the maximum allowable noise levels.

Airports levy noise charges based on an aircraft's noise margin relative to its weight category, offering a standardized measure of noise performance. Aircraft that exceed noise standards by greater margins incur lower noise fees, encouraging quieter operations. For example, an aircraft certified under ICAO Chapter 4 with a substantial noise margin below Chapter 4 limits would typically face lower charges compared to an aircraft that only meets the baseline noise criteria.

By considering noise margins in fee structures, airports incentivize operators to use quieter aircraft and align with environmental goals, making informed decisions that balance operational demands with community impact.

EXAMPLE 4-6. Calculate the noise charge for an A320-200, Variant 007, with a Maximum Takeoff Weight (MTOW) of 77,000 kg. Details:

- Cumulative Noise Margin = 19.1, which qualifies as a Chapter 14 "High" classification.
- According to **Chapter 14 High** noise regulations (see **Table 4-4**), the applicable noise charge is $2,300.

Table 4-4. Example noise fees

Noise Chapter	Cumulative EPNdB	Noise Charge
Chapter 3	0 or more	$12,200
Chapter 4 high	10 or more	$5,300
Chapter 4 base	15 or more	$3,500
Chapter 14 high	17 or more	$2,300
Chapter 14 base	20 or more	$1,600
Chapter 14 low	23 or more	$980

Source: Author's analysis

This example demonstrates how noise charges are calculated by assessing an aircraft's noise performance relative to ICAO standards for its weight category. Airports may further adjust these charges by considering additional factors, such as the frequency of operations, time of day, and local environmental impacts.

By categorizing aircraft into distinct **noise performance tiers**, airports can implement a noise-related charging model that directly aligns charges with the degree to which an aircraft's noise performance exceeds the **ICAO Chapter 3** standard. For example, aircraft classified as **"Chapter 14 Low,"** which significantly surpass Chapter 3 requirements, incur the **lowest noise fees**. In contrast, aircraft that meet only the **Chapter 3** standards are subject to **higher charges** within their respective tier. This approach incentivizes operators to utilize quieter, more environmentally friendly aircraft while ensuring that charges reflect their relative noise impact.

This approach incentivizes quieter operations, allowing airports to align with environmental objectives by encouraging operators to prioritize aircraft with lower noise emissions.

Noise Reduction Efforts

Airports and aviation authorities are increasingly focused on mitigating aircraft noise pollution through stringent noise certification standards and promoting noise abatement procedures. Key initiatives emphasize advancements in engine technology, as engines are the principal source of aircraft noise. Modern engines are specifically engineered to be quieter, significantly reducing noise impacts on surrounding airport communities and the environment.

One prominent technological advancement is the high-bypass turbofan engine, which reduces noise emissions by channeling a larger volume of cooler air around the engine core. These engines not only assist airlines in meeting regulatory noise limits but also diminish noise exposure for communities near airports—especially important in urban areas with higher noise sensitivity and stricter operational restrictions.

For instance, as depicted in **Figure 4-19**, the Airbus A320NEO, featuring quieter and more fuel-efficient engines like the Pratt & Whitney Geared Turbofan (GTF) and the CFM International LEAP, achieves a noise footprint approximately 50% smaller than that of the older Airbus A320CEO. This noise reduction is most pronounced during takeoff and landing—the stages where aircraft noise typically peaks—reflecting the substantial benefits of modern engine technology in minimizing noise pollution.

Figure 4-19. A320NEO vs. A320CEO noise footprint

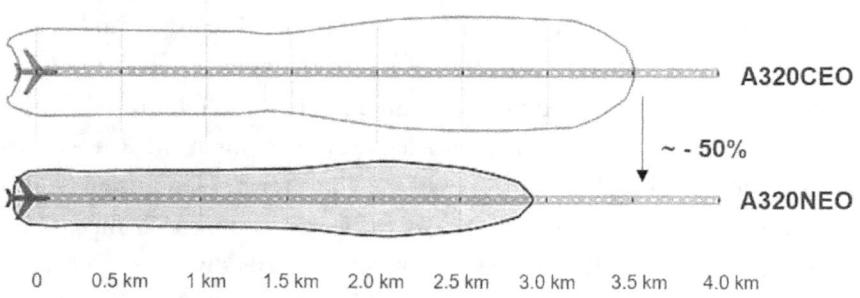

Source: Reduction of aircraft noise sources [7]

Reducing the noise footprint of modern aircraft brings both economic and environmental advantages. Airlines operating quieter models, such as the A320NEO, can achieve significant cost savings, especially at noise-sensitive airports like London Heathrow, where noise-related charges are calculated based on aircraft noise performance. By incurring lower noise charges, airlines can reduce operating costs while simultaneously adhering to stricter noise regulations.

Emissions Assessment

The commercial aviation industry is subject to stringent regulations aimed at reducing emissions, including the European Union's Emissions Trading System (EU ETS) and the International Civil Aviation Organization's (ICAO) Carbon Offsetting and Reduction Scheme for International Aviation (CORSIA). To comply with these initiatives, airlines and regulators rely on standardized estimation methods aligned with internationally recognized calculation standards.

Calculating CO_2 emissions is straightforward, as CO_2 production is directly proportional to fuel consumption. A widely accepted conversion factor in aviation is that burning 1 kilogram of jet fuel produces approximately 3.16 kilograms of CO_2. This allows airlines to estimate CO_2 emissions based on fuel burn data for each flight.

Formula for CO_2 Emissions:

$$CO_2 \text{ Emissions} = \text{Fuel Burned} \times CO_2 \text{ Emission Factor (Eq. 4-2)}$$

Example Calculation:

- Fuel burned during fight: 2,500 kg
- CO_2 Emission Factor: 3.16 kg of CO_2 per kg of fuel
- CO_2 Emissions = 2,500kg×3.16kg CO_2/kg fuel=7,900kg CO_2

Calculating nitrogen oxides (NO_x) emissions is more complex due to the non-linear relationship between fuel consumption and NO_x production. NO_x emissions depend heavily on engine type, operating conditions, and specific flight phases (e.g., takeoff, cruise, and landing). Standardized emission factors, predetermined based on engine performance data, simplify these calculations.

Formula for NO_x Emissions:

$$NO_x \text{ Emissions} = \text{Fuel Burned} \times NO_x \text{ Emission Factor (Eq. 4-3)}$$

Example Calculation:

- Fuel Burned: 2,500 kg
- NO_x Emission Factor: 0.040 kg of NO_x per kg of fuel
- NO_x Emissions=2,500 kg×0.040 kg NO_x/kg fuel = 100 kg Nox

Emissions Real-World Considerations

While these simplified calculations provide a foundational understanding, real-world emissions assessments require detailed inputs and models to account for variations in engine efficiency, flight phases, and operational conditions. Tools like the Aviation Environmental Design Tool (AEDT), developed by the U.S. Federal Aviation Administration (FAA), provide detailed modeling capabilities, enabling accurate emissions assessments that consider flight paths, fleet composition, and specific operational factors.

Emissions Charging Model

In support of environmental sustainability and reducing aviation's impact on climate change, many European airports have adopted emissions-charging models. These models incentivize airlines to minimize emissions of CO_2 and **NOx**, both significant contributors to aviation-related pollution. By levying fees based on emissions, airports encourage the adoption of fuel-efficient technologies and operational practices to reduce the industry's environmental footprint.

These models focus on two key emission types, each carrying distinct charges designed to address specific environmental concerns:

- **CO_2 Emissions:** Airports charge a fee for each kilogram of CO_2 emitted. These charges vary by airport, reflecting local environmental policies and regulations. This fee structure motivates airlines to improve fuel efficiency, optimize operations, and reduce their carbon footprint.
- **NOx Emissions:** NOx emissions, with their adverse effects on local air quality and role in ozone formation, incur separate charges. These fees are typically higher in regions with significant air quality challenges, driving investments in cleaner engine technologies and

operational methods, particularly during high-emission phases like takeoff and climb.

EXAMPLE 4-7. Calculate airport CO_2 and NOx emissions charges

This example demonstrates how emissions charges are calculated for a single flight based on fuel burned, emission factors, and airport-specific charge rates.

CO_2 Emissions Calculation

- CO_2 Emissions = 7,900 kg CO_2
- CO_2 Charge = CO_2 Emissions × Charge Rate = 7,900 kg CO_2 × \$0.05/kg CO_2 = \$395

NOx Emissions Calculation

- NOx Emissions = 100 kg NOx
- NOx Charge = NOx Emissions × Charge Rate = 100 kg NOx × \$0.15/kg NOx = \$15

Total Emissions Charges

- Total Fee = CO_2 Charge + NOx Charge = \$395 + \$15 = \$410

Chapter 4. Key Takeaways

1. **Bypass Ratio (BPR):** The BPR represents the ratio of air bypassing the engine core to the air passing through it. High-bypass engines improve fuel efficiency and reduce noise by channeling more airflow around the core. Modern engines achieve BPRs exceeding 10:1, reflecting significant advancements in propulsion efficiency and sustainability.

2. **Overall Pressure Ratio (OPR):** OPR measures the ratio of compressor discharge pressure to inlet pressure, enhancing thermal efficiency and power output. Higher OPRs improve fuel efficiency but require advanced materials, such as single-crystal superalloys and ceramic matrix composites, to withstand higher operating temperatures and stresses.

3. **Engine Architecture:**
   » **Twin-Spool Engines:** Feature two rotor assemblies, balancing efficiency, thrust, and fuel economy.
   » **Tri-Spool Engines:** Add an intermediate spool for enhanced compression control, improving performance and durability, though at the cost of added complexity and weight.
   » **Geared Turbofan (GTF):** Utilizes a reduction gearbox to optimize fan and turbine speeds independently, enabling greater fuel efficiency, noise reduction, and lower emissions.

4. **Thrust Ratings:** Predefined power settings tailored to specific flight phases. Examples include Maximum Takeoff Thrust (MTO) for takeoff and Maximum Cruise Thrust (MCrT) for efficient cruise operations, ensuring safe and effective engine performance across varying conditions.

5. **Thrust Derate:** A technique that reduces engine power output during takeoff to save fuel, reduce mechanical wear, and extend engine life. The FLEX derate method uses assumed temperature values to calculate thrust, optimizing efficiency under favorable conditions.

6. **Thrust Bumps:** Provide temporary thrust increases in challenging scenarios, such as high-altitude airports, hot-and-high environments, or short runways. Thrust bumps enhance takeoff performance while maintaining operational safety within manufacturer-approved limits.

7. **Thrust Specific Fuel Consumption (TSFC):** TSFC quantifies engine fuel efficiency, indicating fuel consumed per unit of thrust. Lower TSFC values reflect greater fuel economy, particularly critical during the **cruise phase**, which dominates fuel consumption in long-haul operations.

8. **Shop Visit Rate (SVR):** Tracks the frequency of major engine maintenance visits. A low SVR reflects high durability, reduced maintenance costs, and increased aircraft availability, contributing to better operational efficiency.

9. **In-Flight Shutdown (IFSD) Rate:** Measures unexpected engine shutdowns during flight. A low IFSD rate ensures safety and reliability, especially critical for ETOPS-certified aircraft, which operate extended routes far from alternate airports.

10. **ETOPS Certification:** Ensures twin-engine aircraft can safely operate extended routes. Specific IFSD rates are required, such as:
    » **120-minute ETOPS:** 1 shutdown per 20,000 flight hours.
    » **180-minute ETOPS:** 1 shutdown per 50,000 flight hours.
    » **Beyond 180-minute ETOPS:** Rigorous standards approaching 1 per 100,000 flight hours, supporting transoceanic operations.

11. **Noise Certification:** Aircraft noise is assessed at lateral, flyover, and approach locations. Modern high-bypass engines, like those on the Airbus A320NEO, significantly reduce noise emissions, helping operators comply with stricter standards and minimize community impacts.

12. **Emissions Metrics:**
    » **CO_2 Emissions:** Proportional to fuel consumption, with 1 kg of jet fuel producing approximately 3.16 kg of CO_2.
    » **NO_x Emissions:** Vary with engine type, operating conditions, and flight phase, requiring advanced modeling for precise assessments.

13. **Environmental Charges:** Airports levy fees based on CO_2 and NO_x emissions to encourage sustainable operations. Tiered fee systems incentivize reductions in emissions through advanced engine technologies, optimized operations, and cleaner practices.

14. **Noise Reduction Efforts:** Innovations like high-bypass turbofans reduce aircraft noise footprints by up to 50% compared to older models. Quieter aircraft, such as the Airbus A320NEO, benefit from lower noise-related charges and improved environmental compatibility.

15. **Emissions Compliance Programs:** Regulatory initiatives such as ICAO's CORSIA and the EU's ETS promote aviation sustainability by requiring airlines to measure, offset, and reduce carbon emissions. These programs drive innovation in engine technology and foster operational practices that align with global environmental goals.

Case Study 4-1. Thrust Bump Impact

Figure 4-20: V2527 thrust bumps

V2525E-A5 and V2527E-A5 Bump

The V2527E-A5 and the V2527E-A5 Bump are variants of engines designed for the A320 family, providing improved performance, especially for operations from high-altitude airports where thinner air can affect aircraft take-off performance.

V2527E-A5 Capabilities

- Thrust is increased for high altitude operations above the standard V2527 rating available on A320.
- The improvement increases from V2527 at sea level to match the V2530 (30,000 lb) rating used on A321 at 6,000 ft airport elevation.
- At 6000 ft airport, ISA+15°C, V2527E rating allows 7,700 lb. higher take-off weight; as payload, this is equivalent to 37 passengers.

V2527E-A5 Thrust Bump Capabilities

- V2527E Bump provides 33,000 lb engine thrust above 5,000 ft
- Increased thrust is targeted at operations from high and hot locations

Credit: IAE

Questions:

1. Evaluate the operational and economic impacts of adopting the V2527E-A5 versus the V2527E-A5 Bump engine for an airline with a mixed route network, including high-altitude but cooler airports like Quito (7,874 ft) and hot and high airports like Bogotá (8,360 ft and 15°C). Consider factors such as payload advantages, engine efficiency, maintenance requirements, and long-term route flexibility. Provide a recommendation for fleet integration based on your analysis.

2. What trade-offs do airlines face when selecting between the V2527E-A5 and the V2527E-A5 Bump engines, particularly when considering operational requirements at high-altitude airports versus hot and high conditions?

3. What operational limitations might arise from the V2527E-A5 Bump's increased thrust capability in hot and high conditions, and how do these compare to the benefits provided by the V2527E-A5 in high-altitude but cooler environments?

Case Study 4-2. Engine Shop Visit Rates

Figure 4-21. Total vs. UER shop visit rates

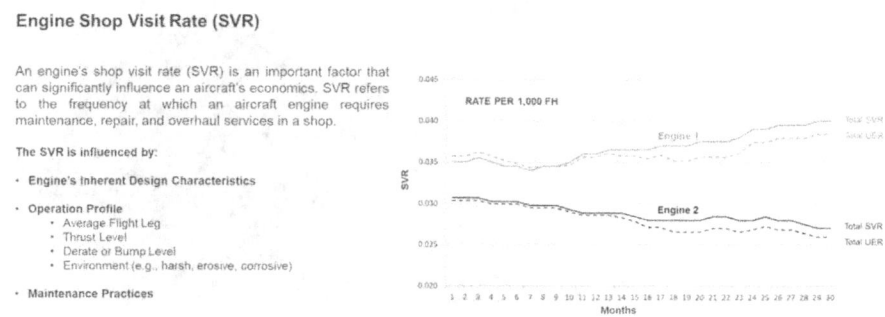

Source: Author's analysis

Questions:

1. How does an engine's shop visit rate (SVR) influence aircraft economics?

2. Evaluate how the observed differences in SVR and UER trends between Engine 1 and Engine 2 could influence an airline's long-term fleet planning and maintenance cost strategies. Consider factors such as engine reliability, maintenance intervals, and economic impacts. Provide a recommendation for engine selection based on your analysis.

3. How is an engine's reliability and durability impacted by its shop visit rate?

4. What does the disparity in the trend lines for Total SVR and Total UER between Engine 1 and Engine 2 suggest about their respective reliabilities?

5. How might the differences in SVR and UER between Engine 1 and Engine 2 affect an airline's operational and maintenance decisions?

References

[1] EASA, "GEnx-1B Type Certificate Data Sheet (TCDS)." [Online]. Available: https://www.easa.europa.eu/en/document-library

[2] EASA, "CFM56-7B Type Certificate Data Sheet (TCDS)." [Online]. Available: https://www.easa.europa.eu/en/document-library

[3] Wikipedia, "ETOPS." [Online]. Available: https://en.wikipedia.org /wiki/ETOPS

[4] Boeing, "Airports with Noise and Emissions Restrictions." [Online]. Available: https://www.boeing.com/commercial/noise

[5] ResearchGate, "CAO and FAR noise certification points." [Online]. Available: https://www.researchgate.net/figure/CAO-and-FAR-noise -certification-points_fig7_35440184

[6] EASA, "A320 Type Certificate Data Sheet (TCDS)." [Online]. Available: https://www.easa.europa.eu/en/document-library

[7] K. Haag, "Reduction of aircraft noise sources," Deutsche Lufthansa AG, 2016. [Online]. Available: https://www.umwelthaus.org/media/6 .icana2016_reduction_of_aircraft_noise_sources_dlh.pdf

Section 2

Aircraft Performance

Chapter 5

Study Flight Rules

This Chapter is About:

5.1 Mission Profile Rules
5.2 Cabin Configuration Rules

Analyzing aircraft performance requires standardized benchmarks to ensure accuracy, consistency, and fairness. **Study Flight Rules** provide the essential framework for comparing different aircraft types, offering structured guidelines to assess performance under uniform conditions. By adhering to these rules, the aviation industry can objectively evaluate aircraft across various models and configurations, enabling insightful and reliable comparisons.

The **Study Flight Rules framework** is divided into two primary categories:

1. **Mission Profile Rules**: These rules establish consistent parameters for evaluating aircraft performance across all phases of flight. They define critical metrics such as flight distance, speed, atmospheric conditions, and passenger and baggage weights. By applying these standardized conditions, Mission Profile Rules ensure fair comparisons of fuel efficiency, range, and payload capacity between aircraft.

2. **Cabin Configuration Rules**: These rules standardize interior layouts, including seat distribution, pitch, and width, enabling assessments of operational efficiency on a per-seat-mile basis. They also provide a basis for evaluating passenger comfort and operational performance across varying cabin configurations.

Together, these categories provide a comprehensive approach to aircraft performance analysis, addressing both technical and operational considerations. By adhering to **Study Flight Rules**, airlines, manufacturers, and operators can establish consistent benchmarks, ensuring fair and meaningful evaluations across the aviation industry.

5.1 Mission Profile Rules

Mission Profile Rules provide a standardized framework for evaluating and comparing aircraft performance across all phases of flight—taxi, takeoff, cruise, descent, and landing. By offering consistent benchmarks, these rules ensure fair and objective assessments of various aircraft types and models. Key areas addressed by Mission Profile Rules include route distances, cruise speeds, atmospheric conditions, fuel management, and passenger and baggage weights, alongside other critical considerations.

The following key areas highlight the comprehensive approach of Mission Profile Rules to aircraft performance evaluation:

*   **Route Distances**: Route distances are evaluated using metrics such as Great Circle Distance (GCD), Tracked Distance, and Equivalent Still Air Distance (ESAD). GCD represents the shortest theoretical route between two points, while Tracked Distance accounts for operational deviations from the theoretical path. ESAD provides a wind-neutral metric that reflects the impact of prevailing wind conditions on flight range. By combining these metrics, Mission Profile Rules enable accurate assessments of an aircraft's range capabilities, accommodating both ideal and real-world flight scenarios.
*   **Cruise Speeds**: Cruise speeds are another critical component of these rules, focusing on standardized speeds like Long-Range

Cruise (LRC) and Maximum-Range Cruise (MRC). LRC achieves a balance between speed and fuel efficiency, making it suitable for cost-effective operations, while MRC prioritizes maximum range at slightly reduced speeds. Evaluating aircraft performance at these speeds ensures consistent comparisons of fuel consumption and operational range.

- **Atmospheric Condition:** The International Standard Atmosphere (ISA) provides a uniform baseline for evaluating aircraft performance under consistent environmental conditions. Applying ISA standards ensures that comparisons between aircraft models are conducted under identical pressure, temperature, and air density settings, resulting in accurate assessments of operational capabilities.
- **Fuel Management and Reserve Contingencies**: Fuel management is integral to Mission Profile Rules, encompassing reserve contingencies for missed approaches, diversions, and holding patterns. Additional fuel requirements for approach and landing phases are also considered, ensuring a holistic view of an aircraft's operational efficiency. These standardized metrics support a thorough understanding of fuel consumption and long-term performance.
- **Passenger and Baggage Weights**: Passenger and baggage weight assumptions are similarly standardized to ensure consistency in fuel consumption and cost calculations. By applying average weight values across all assessments, Mission Profile Rules facilitate accurate model-to-model comparisons, enhancing the reliability of operational planning and aircraft selection processes.
- **Additional Considerations:** Beyond these core areas, the rules account for additional considerations such as engine aging and variations in fuel density, both of which can influence fuel consumption over time. By incorporating these real-world factors, Mission Profile Rules ensure that performance benchmarks remain relevant and comprehensive.

Together, Mission Profile Rules provide a structured and detailed approach to aircraft performance evaluation. By enabling consistent and accurate comparisons, they support informed decision-making in aircraft selection, operational planning, and route optimization.

5.1.1 Route Distances

Accurately assessing an aircraft's range is fundamental to understanding its performance and operational capabilities. Mission Profile Rules standardize this evaluation using three primary distance metrics:

1. **Great Circle Distance (GCD):** GCD represents the shortest theoretical path between two points on the Earth's surface, serving as a benchmark for the most efficient possible flight path. This metric establishes a baseline for evaluating the theoretical range capabilities of an aircraft.
2. **Tracked Distance:** Tracked Distance accounts for the actual flight path flown, which often deviates from the GCD due to factors such as Air Traffic Control (ATC) instructions, airway routings, and operational requirements (e.g., ETOPS for extended twin-engine operations). This metric reflects the real-world distance traveled, incorporating necessary adjustments for safety and operational efficiency.
3. **Equivalent Still Air Distance (ESAD):** ESAD calculates the effective distance an aircraft would travel in still air, neutralizing the effects of headwinds or tailwinds. As a wind-adjusted metric, ESAD provides a consistent basis for comparing aircraft range capabilities under standardized conditions.

By integrating these metrics, aviation professionals gain a comprehensive understanding of how operational factors—such as wind patterns and routing adjustments—affect range and fuel efficiency. These standardized measures ensure objective and reliable evaluations, forming a critical component of aircraft performance analysis.

Great Circle Distance (GCD)

The **Great Circle Distance (GCD)** represents the shortest path between two points on the Earth's surface, accounting for the planet's spherical shape. As the most direct route between two locations, GCD serves as a benchmark for evaluating an aircraft's theoretical range capabilities. Within the Mission Profile Rules, GCD provides a foundational metric for assessing an aircraft's ability to cover specific distances between airports or waypoints (see **Figure 5-1**).

Figure 5-1. GCD vs. tracked distance

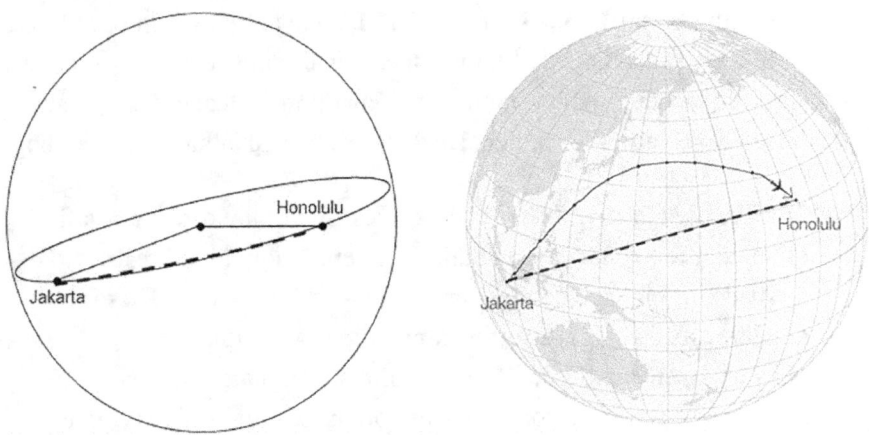

Source: Author's analysis

Standardizing GCD as a performance metric enables accurate and consistent comparisons across aircraft by focusing on their direct-flight range capabilities under ideal conditions.

The GCD is calculated using the geographical coordinates (latitude and longitude) of the origin and destination points and is typically expressed in nautical miles or kilometers. Tools such as the **Great Circle Mapper** (www.gcmap.com) simplify this process, offering quick and reliable estimates of GCD for various routes. By providing a uniform measurement, GCD supports fair and standardized evaluations of aircraft models based on their theoretical direct-flight range.

EXAMPLE 5.1. Calculating the Great Circle Distance between Jakarta and Honolulu

Using the **Great Circle Mapper** (www.gcmap.com), aviation professionals can calculate the GCD between **Jakarta (CGK)** and **Honolulu (HNL)** by entering the airport codes. The tool estimates the distance as approximately **5,844 nautical miles.**

This example demonstrates how accessible tools like the Great Circle Mapper assist in determining direct-flight distances, enabling precise and equitable comparisons of aircraft based on their theoretical range capabilities.

Tracked Distance

Tracked Distance represents the actual flight path taken by an aircraft, which often exceeds the **Great Circle Distance (GCD)** due to real-world operational factors. While GCD captures the shortest theoretical route between two points, tracked distance accounts for deviations that occur during actual flights. These deviations result from various operational and environmental influences, including:

- **Air Traffic Control (ATC) Directives:** ATC may direct aircraft to adjust their routes to maintain safe separation, avoid restricted airspace, or manage congestion in high-traffic regions. These adjustments can significantly extend the flight path.
- **Airway Routings:** Aircraft often follow designated airways or structured flight corridors to ensure organized and safe navigation. These routings may not align with the shortest path, leading to increased tracked distances.
- **ETOPS (Extended-range Twin-engine Operations):** Twin-engine aircraft operating over remote areas or oceans must comply with ETOPS requirements, which mandate staying within a specified distance of an alternate airport. These safety considerations can result in longer flight paths.
- **Environmental Factors:** Weather conditions such as storms, turbulence, or wind patterns may require deviations from the planned route. Headwinds and tailwinds also impact the actual distance flown, influencing flight efficiency.

Tracked Distance provides a realistic measure of an aircraft's operational performance by reflecting the complexities of real-world flight. This metric is particularly valuable for evaluating **fuel management** strategies, as it accounts for actual conditions rather than theoretical assumptions.

Unlike GCD, tracked distance captures the complexities of actual flight operations, making it essential for performance evaluations. **Figure 5-1** illustrates the relationship between Great Circle Distance and tracked distance, highlighting the potential for deviations from the shortest theoretical path.

Industry Perspective 5-1. *The North Atlantic Tracks*

*The **North Atlantic Tracks (NATs)** are structured high-altitude corridors that streamline transatlantic air traffic between Western Europe and North*

America's eastern coast. Managed by the **Shanwick Oceanic Centre** in Scotland and the **Gander Oceanic Centre** in Canada, NATs ensure safe and efficient transit across one of the world's busiest airspaces. The NAT system divides operations into distinct track structures, accommodating eastbound and westbound flights to maintain safety and efficiency:

- **Eastbound Tracks:** Allocated during designated hours for flights from North America to Europe, with systematic labeling for efficient management.
- **Westbound Tracks:** Similarly structured for flights from Europe to North America, supporting organized and safe operations.

The NAT system dynamically adapts to daily and seasonal variations in air traffic and atmospheric conditions, such as jet streams and wind patterns. This flexibility minimizes congestion, optimizes flight paths, and upholds strict safety standards, ensuring reliable and efficient transatlantic operations.

Figure 5-2. North Atlantic Tracks (NATs)

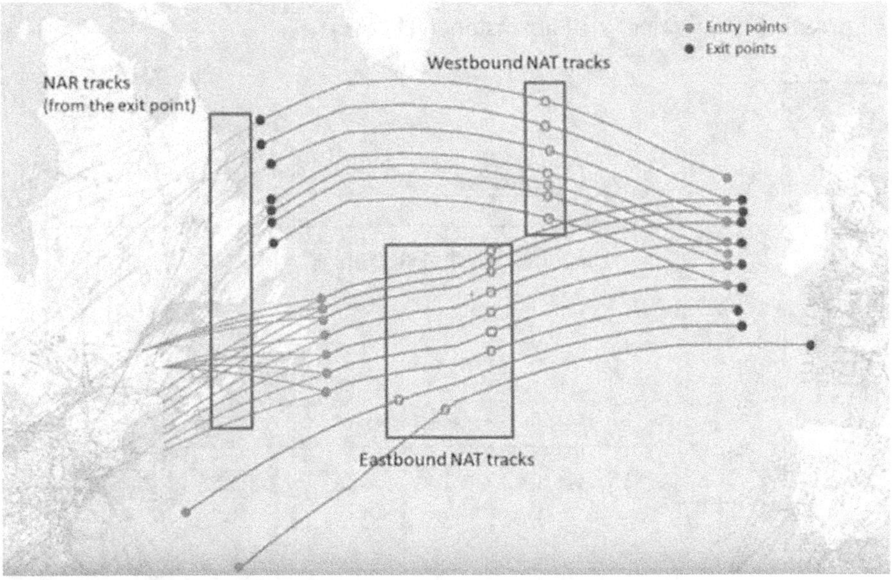

Source: Adapted from LinkedIn post [1]

Equivalent Still Air Distance (ESAD):

Equivalent Still Air Distance (ESAD) represents the theoretical distance an aircraft would cover in a wind-neutral environment, accounting for planned routes and fuel efficiency. Unlike Tracked Distance, which reflects actual flight paths influenced by operational and environmental factors, ESAD standardizes comparisons by neutralizing wind effects. This metric is essential for assessing range and fuel efficiency under consistent conditions, enabling fair performance evaluations across aircraft (see **Figure 5-3**).

As illustrated in **Figure 5-3**, **Equivalent Still Air Distance (ESAD)** provides a reliable basis for evaluating aircraft range capabilities by eliminating distortions caused by wind variability. By standardizing performance metrics, ESAD facilitates meaningful comparisons between aircraft models, offering valuable insights into operational efficiency and fuel requirements.

Wind conditions play a significant role in influencing ESAD: **headwinds** decrease ground speed, which increases ESAD, flight duration, and fuel consumption, whereas **tailwinds** increase ground speed, reducing ESAD and fuel requirements. This standardized approach ensures that performance evaluations remain consistent and unaffected by external environmental factors.

Figure 5-3. Equivalent still air distance (ESAD)

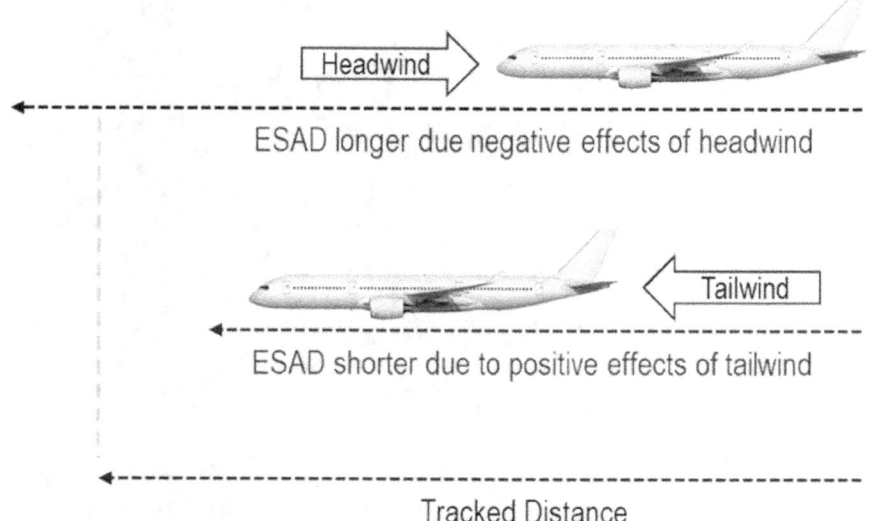

Source: Author's analysis

The calculation of ESAD is as follows:

$$ESAD (nm) = Ground\ Mileage \times (TAS / GS) \quad (Eq\ 5\text{-}1)$$

Where:

- TAS = True Airspeed (knots)
- GS = Ground Speed (knots) = (TAS + Wind Speed)

EXAMPLE 5-2. SEA—NRT (Seattle, Washington to Narita, Japan)

The wind conditions for the Seattle to Narita route in January are illustrated in **Table 5-1**, showing the standard deviations for typical wind conditions (i.e., Wind Velocity (WV) = Direct Winds)

Table 5-1: SEA to NRT flight profile

Origin	Dest.	GCD (nm)	Altitude	Air Speed	Month	Std. Dev	Rel	Direct Winds	ESAD (nm) Range	Return Winds	ESAD (nm) Range
SEA	NRT	4,133	33,000	463	Jan	17	85	-60	4,743	+18	3,980
							50	-42	4,540	+38	3,836

Source: Author's analysis

For Seattle to Narita:

- **Outbound:**
  TAS = 463 knots, WV = - 60 knots, Ground Mileage = 4,133 nm
  ESAD = 4,133 × [463 / (463 - 60)] = 4,748 nm
- **Return:**
  TAS = 463 knots, WV = +18 knots, Ground Mileage = 4,133 nm
  ESAD = 4,133 × [463 / (463+18)] = 3,978 nm

These results show ESAD variability of 770 nm due to wind conditions, highlighting the operational importance of adjusting fuel planning and flight strategies to account for wind effects.

ESAD plays a vital role in performance benchmarking, providing a wind-neutral basis for evaluating aircraft capabilities. By using ESAD, manufacturers deliver standardized performance data to airlines, facilitating fleet planning and route optimization. This metric ensures that long-term operational and investment decisions are based on consistent and comparable data.

Incorporating ESAD into Available Seat Mile (ASM) calculations improves the accuracy of capacity assessments. ASM, which reflects an airline's seating capacity by multiplying the number of seats by the distance flown, becomes more precise when ESAD is used to represent distance. This adjustment allows airlines to evaluate operational efficiency across aircraft types more effectively, ensuring balanced comparisons and informed decision-making.

EXAMPLE 5-3. Fuel Efficiency Benchmarking: Boeing 777-200ER vs. 777-300ER on the LHR-EZE Route

Table 5-2 compares the Boeing 777-200ER and 777-300ER on the London Heathrow (LHR) to Buenos Aires (EZE) route using ESAD and ASM calculations reveals differences in fuel efficiency:

- **Boeing 777-200ER:** Equipped with GE90-94B engines and 303 seats, it covers an ESAD of 6,564 nm, generating 1,995,456 ASMs while consuming 31,893 US gallons (USG) of fuel.
- **Boeing 777-300ER:** Equipped with GE90-115BL engines and 374 seats, it flies an ESAD of 6,531 nm, generating 2,494,842 ASMs and consuming 37,072 USG of fuel.

Table 5-2. ESAD and ASM fuel efficiency

City-Pair	Aircraft	Engine	Seats	ESAD-nm	ASM	Fuel-USG	Fuel/ASM
LHR-EZE	777-200ER	GE90-94B	304	6,564	1,995,456	31,893	0.0160
	777-300ER	GE90-115BL	382	6.531	2,494,842	37,072	0.0149

Source: Aircraft Commerce [2]

To calculate the unit cost of fuel per ASM:

- **777-200ER:** 31,893 USG ÷ 1,995,456 ASMs = 0.0160 USG per ASM
- **777-300ER:** 37,072 USG ÷ 2,494,842 ASMs = 0.0149 USG per ASM

Despite its larger capacity and higher overall fuel consumption, the 777-300ER demonstrates greater fuel efficiency per seat mile than the 777-200ER on this route, highlighting the benefits of using ESAD and ASM metrics for informed comparisons of fuel performance across aircraft models.

5.1.2 Cruise Speed

Cruise speed significantly impacts an aircraft's range and payload. Higher speeds increase fuel consumption, potentially reducing range and payload capacity, while lower speeds improve fuel efficiency but may affect economic viability. Efficient cruise speeds, such as Long-Range Cruise (LRC) and Maximum Range Cruise (MRC), balance fuel efficiency and flight duration, making them essential for optimizing long-haul operations.

Long Range Cruise (LRC) Speed

Long-Range Cruise (LRC) speed is the optimal cruise speed that balances fuel efficiency and practical flight times, making it ideal for long-haul operations. Slightly below an aircraft's maximum cruise speed, LRC maximizes range with a given fuel amount while conserving fuel without significantly increasing flight duration.

The goal of LRC is to achieve nearly minimal fuel consumption while maintaining practical flight times. Although LRC does not yield the absolute lowest fuel burn rate, it closely approaches it, offering a balanced trade-off between speed and fuel savings. The primary advantage of LRC is its fuel conservation, achieved without significantly increasing flight duration.

In practical terms, LRC aims to provide about 99% of the aircraft's maximum specific range. This balance involves a small reduction in range—typically around 1%—in exchange for a 2% to 4% increase in cruise speed. This trade-off is generally advantageous, as the slight increase in speed can offer operational benefits that often outweigh the minimal range reduction. **Figure 5-4** illustrates this concept, showing how LRC aligns speed, fuel efficiency, and range to optimize performance on long-haul flights.

Maximum-Range Cruise (MRC) Speed

Maximum-Range Cruise (MRC) speed is specifically designed to maximize an aircraft's fuel efficiency, allowing it to cover the greatest possible distance on a given amount of fuel. MRC typically involves flying at a lower speed than Long-Range Cruise (LRC), as it focuses exclusively on range rather than speed.

MRC is chosen when the primary goal is to optimize fuel use for the longest possible distance, accepting a slight reduction in speed compared to LRC. By prioritizing maximum fuel efficiency—measured as distance per unit of fuel—MRC helps extend range under fuel-conserving conditions. While LRC offers a balanced approach to fuel economy and flight time, MRC is solely dedicated to maximizing range. The selection between LRC and MRC depends on the specific operational needs of a flight, such as whether fuel conservation or time efficiency takes priority.

Figure 5-4. Long-range vs. max-range speed

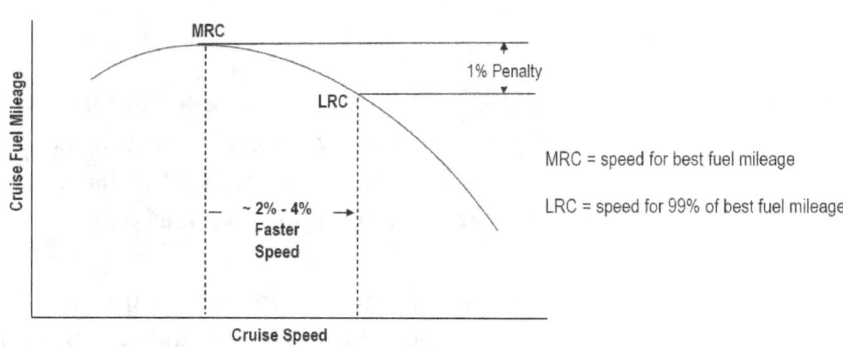

Source: Author's analysis

Standardized cruise speeds, such as Long-Range Cruise (LRC) and Maximum-Range Cruise (MRC), are essential benchmarks for evaluating aircraft performance across different models and manufacturers. These speeds provide consistent, objective reference points for analyzing capabilities under controlled conditions.

The following aspects highlight the importance of LRC and MRC in aircraft performance assessments:

- **Performance Metrics**: LRC and MRC establish standardized benchmarks for analyzing performance metrics, ensuring reliable comparisons across aircraft models.

- **Fuel Efficiency**: These speeds are vital for assessing fuel efficiency, helping identify models that offer operational cost savings.
- **Range Capability**: LRC and MRC benchmarks inform range assessments, providing critical data for route planning and operational flexibility.
- **Market Competitiveness**: Aircraft manufacturers leverage LRC and MRC to showcase performance advantages, such as superior fuel efficiency and range, aiding airlines in fleet selection decisions.

In summary, LRC and MRC speeds are foundational for evaluating fuel efficiency, range, operational planning, and competitive positioning, ensuring objective and standardized aircraft performance assessments.

Industry Perspective 5-2. ECON Speed and Cost Index

In commercial aviation, airlines optimize operational efficiency using ECON speed—a cruise speed derived from an airline's specific Cost Index (CI). While ECON speed is highly effective for operational optimization, it has limitations as a benchmark for comparing aircraft performance.

Cost Index (CI):
The Cost Index represents the balance between time-related costs (e.g., crew salaries, maintenance) and fuel costs, guiding the trade-off between speed and economy:

- *High CI: Prioritizes time savings, leading to faster ECON speeds and higher fuel consumption.*
- *Low CI: Focuses on fuel efficiency, resulting in slower ECON speeds and reduced fuel burn.*

ECON speed dynamically adjusts based on an airline's CI, optimizing flight operations by balancing economic factors like fuel prices and schedule requirements.

Limitations of ECON Speed:
Despite its operational value, ECON speed is unsuitable as a benchmarking metric due to:

- *Lack of Standardization:* Unlike LRC and MRC, ECON speed varies with each airline's CI, undermining consistency in comparisons.
- *Operational Specificity:* ECON speed reflects specific airline priorities and costs, limiting its relevance for industry-wide assessments.
- *Benchmarking Inconsistency:* Effective benchmarking requires uniform conditions, which ECON speed's variability across airlines does not provide.

5.1.3 Atmosphere Conditions

The **International Standard Atmosphere (ISA)** is an essential reference model in aviation that provides standardized atmospheric conditions for consistent aircraft performance evaluations. ISA establishes a baseline for temperature, pressure, and air density across various altitudes, creating a "universal standard" for assessing aircraft capabilities under uniform conditions. This model is essential because actual atmospheric conditions vary significantly with altitude, location, and weather, all which impact aircraft performance. By simulating a standardized environment, ISA enables fair comparisons between different aircraft models, ensuring evaluations are accurate and comparable across varying real-world conditions.

The following parameters form the foundation of the ISA model, enabling standardized assessments of aircraft capabilities:

- **Temperature:** At sea level, the ISA sets the standard temperature at 15°C (59°F). This temperature decreases at a standard lapse rate of approximately 1.98°C per 1,000 feet (or 6.5°C per kilometer) up to 11 kilometers (36,089 feet). Beyond this altitude in the tropopause the temperature stabilizes and remains constant at -56.5°C until 20 kilometers (65,617 feet).

  The ISA Temperature Lapse Rate Formula is:

  $$T = 15°C - (1.98°C \times \text{Altitude in 1,000 feet}) \text{ (Eq. 5-2)}$$

  This lapse rate is critical for evaluating aircraft performance, as temperature changes directly affect engine efficiency, fuel consumption, and aerodynamic lift. For example, deviations from this baseline, such as ISA+10°C, indicate that actual temperatures are 10°C higher than standard, requiring operational adjustments.

- **Pressure:** The ISA defines the standard atmospheric pressure at sea level as 1013.25 hPa (hectopascals or millibars). Pressure decreases with altitude, affecting both lift and engine thrust. Precise pressure measurements at various altitudes are essential to calculating true airspeed and assessing performance during all flight phases.
- **Density:** Air density at sea level is approximately 1.225 kg/m³. As altitude increases, air density declines, affecting the lift generated by the wings and the fuel needed for optimal engine performance. Lower air density at higher altitudes reduces engine thrust and lift, which may require longer takeoff rolls or specific flight configurations to maintain optimal performance.

Figure 5-5: ISA standard atmosphere

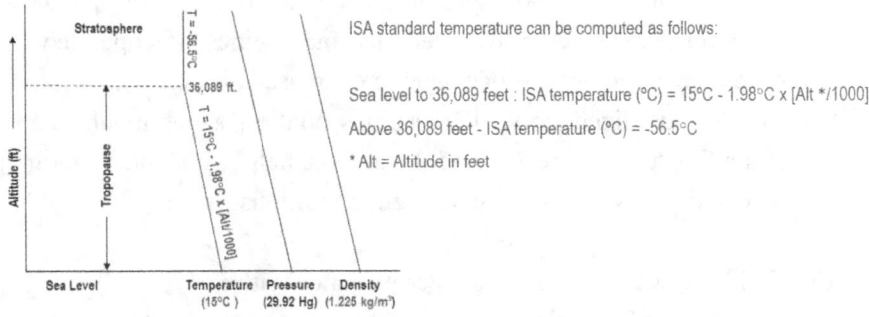

Source: Author's analysis

Figure 5-5 demonstrates how atmospheric conditions—temperature, pressure, and density—vary with altitude based on ISA standards, providing a consistent baseline for aircraft evaluations. This approach removes real-world fluctuations, allowing for fair comparisons of performance metrics like fuel efficiency, range, and engine performance under uniform conditions.

The following highlights why ISA is critical for consistent and reliable aircraft performance assessments:

- **Consistency:** ISA offers a uniform standard that engineers, manufacturers, and pilots use to assess aircraft under the same conditions. This consistency ensures that performance metrics such as speed, range, and fuel efficiency are accurately comparable across different aircraft types and models.
- **Predictability:** With ISA as a baseline, engineers can forecast how aircraft will perform in varied real-world conditions. Variations from ISA—such as on hotter or colder days—guide operational adjustments in engine power, fuel load, and runway requirements.
- **Role in Aircraft Design and Performance Evaluation:** Aircraft manufacturers rely on ISA conditions for defining performance metrics, ensuring unbiased comparisons between aircraft models. By filtering out environmental differences, ISA allows clear, direct evaluations of an aircraft's fuel efficiency, speed, and range.

While ISA provides a stable framework, actual conditions often deviate from these assumptions. Variations in temperature, pressure, and air density can meaningfully impact aircraft performance. For instance, on hot days, aircraft may require extended runway lengths, and engines may operate with reduced efficiency at higher altitudes due to decreased air density.

By using a standardized model, ISA enables aviation professionals to prepare for and adjust to these real-world deviations, helping maintain optimal performance and safety across diverse flight conditions.

EXAMPLE 5-4. Evaluating Aircraft Performance with ISA

Consider an aircraft cruising at 33,000 feet with an actual outside air temperature of -36°C. To evaluate performance under these conditions, we start by calculating the ISA standard temperature at this altitude:

$$\text{ISA Temperature} = 15°C - (\text{altitude in 1,000s of feet} \times 1.98°C)$$

$$\text{ISA Temperature} = 15°C - (33 \times 1.98°C) = 15°C - 65.34°C = -50.34°C$$
$$(\text{approximately } -50°C).$$

Comparing the actual temperature (-36°C) with the ISA standard (-50°C) reveals a deviation of +14°C, indicating that the aircraft is operating in ISA+14°C conditions. A warmer-than-ISA condition, such as ISA+14°C, means the air at 33,000 feet is less dense than predicted by the standard atmosphere model. This reduction in air density impacts several key performance areas:

- **Reduced Air Density:** Less dense air results in lower engine thrust and aerodynamic efficiency. Both engine performance and lift generation decrease, requiring more power to maintain altitude and speed.
- **Increased Fuel Consumption:** To offset the reduced efficiency, the aircraft must burn more fuel, directly affecting its operational range and fuel economy. Over extended distances, this can notably impact fuel efficiency and range.

In summary, real-world deviations from ISA (International Standard Atmosphere), such as ISA+15°C, highlight the significant impact of atmospheric conditions on aircraft performance. Variations in temperature, pressure, and air density influence engine thrust, fuel consumption, and climb efficiency, particularly on long-haul routes where these effects are magnified. A thorough understanding of these deviations is essential for accurate flight planning, allowing professionals to anticipate performance impacts, optimize fuel requirements, and ensure operational efficiency.

5.1.4 Fuel Management and Reserve Contingencies

A standardized flight profile framework, exemplified by the **Typical Mission Profile** in **Figure 5-6**, facilitates fair and consistent comparisons across aircraft models, with fuel management as a core component. Fuel management involves the precise calculation and planning of fuel requirements across all flight phases—taxi, takeoff, climb, cruise, descent, and landing—while incorporating reserve fuel contingencies. These reserves account for potential disruptions such as missed approaches, diversions, or holding patterns, ensuring safety and operational continuity under unforeseen circumstances.

Figure 5-6 provides a detailed visualization of the mission profile, illustrating the transition between the **Trip Profile** (planned operational fuel use) and the **Reserve Profile** (contingency planning). This framework highlights the critical role of reserve planning in achieving safe, efficient, and reliable operations.

Figure 5-6. Trip and reserve profile

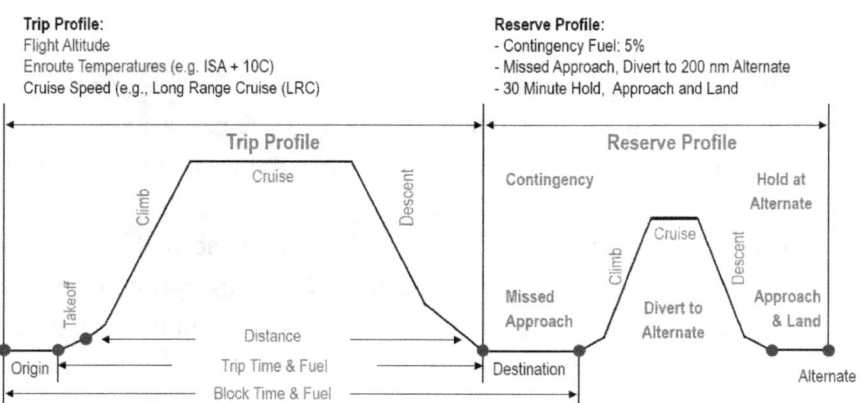

Source: Author's analysis

The following components highlight the structured approach to managing fuel for diverse flight scenarios:

- **Block Fuel:** Block fuel represents the total fuel loaded onto the aircraft before departure, covering all phases of the mission from departure to arrival. This includes fuel for taxiing, takeoff, climb, cruise, descent, and landing, along with allowances for contingency fuel and reserve fuel. Proper block fuel planning ensures operational needs are fully met, providing a comprehensive measure of the total fuel required for the flight.
- **Trip Fuel:** Trip fuel is the primary fuel needed to fly from departure to destination under standard conditions. It factors in variables like winds, weight, and cruise speed and includes all planned fuel for the en-route segment of the mission, excluding contingency and reserve fuel. Standardized Mission Profile Rules ensure consistent and unbiased assessments of trip fuel across different aircraft models.
- **Contingency Fuel:** Contingency fuel acts as a buffer for unforeseen en-route events, such as rerouting, unexpected weather changes, or Air Traffic Control (ATC) directives. It supports the safe completion of the flight when deviations from the planned route occur. Unlike reserve fuel, contingency fuel is planned for potential mid-flight

adjustments and is typically consumed before reserve fuel. Regulatory guidelines for contingency fuel vary based on operator practices and operational contexts.

- **Reserve Fuel:** Reserve fuel is a mandatory safety requirement to address unexpected contingencies at the destination or alternate airport. It is subdivided into three components:
  » **Missed Approach Fuel:** Allocated for additional landing attempts at the destination or for diversion to an alternate airport, ensuring the aircraft can manage failed approach scenarios safely.
  » **Alternate Fuel:** Required to divert to a pre-determined alternate airport in cases of adverse weather, runway unavailability, or other operational issues at the destination.
  » **Final Reserve Fuel:** A mandated minimum fuel amount sufficient for holding at 1,500 feet above the alternate airport (or the destination if no alternate is required) for at least 30 minutes. This safety buffer ensures the aircraft can handle emergencies effectively.

Reserve fuel is strictly reserved for emergencies and is not intended for routine consumption, as it is regulated by aviation authorities to maintain universal safety standards. Effective fuel planning incorporates fuel adjustment considerations, accounting for operational realities such as engine aging, which impacts fuel efficiency, and fuel density variations, which influence the actual weight of the fuel carried. These adjustments, aligned with Mission Profile Rules, reflect long-term performance trends, and support realistic assessments of aircraft capabilities. By adhering to these standards and considerations, reserve fuel ensures both safety and accurate operational planning.

Carrying reserve fuel, while critical for safety, directly impacts aircraft performance by increasing the overall weight of the aircraft. This added weight reduces fuel efficiency, requiring more fuel to sustain the same range, which in turn further compounds the weight penalty. Excessive reserve fuel beyond regulatory requirements amplifies this effect, leading to diminished climb rates, reduced cruise efficiency, and increased operational costs. Additionally, the higher weight affects payload capacity, potentially limiting revenue-generating opportunities, such as passenger or cargo load. Striking a balance between safety requirements and optimized fuel planning is essential to ensure reserve fuel is sufficient for emergencies without unnecessarily impairing aircraft performance and efficiency.

EXAMPLE 5-5. Reserve Fuel Penalties on an Ultra Long-Haul Flight (777-200LR)

Consider a Boeing 777-200LR operating an ultra-long-haul flight from Dubai (DXB) to Los Angeles (LAX), a route spanning approximately 7,300 nautical miles. The aircraft is loaded near its maximum takeoff weight (MTOW) of 766,000 pounds, with fuel accounting for nearly 50% of this weight. To meet regulatory requirements, the airline includes reserve fuel for contingencies, such as unplanned diversions or extended holding patterns at the destination.

For this mission, reserve fuel constitutes approximately 10% of the total fuel load, translating to an additional 15,000–20,000 pounds. This extra weight imposes a penalty on performance. The added reserve fuel increases the aircraft's induced drag (drag due to lift), requiring more thrust to maintain optimal cruising speed. Consequently, fuel consumption rises throughout the flight, reducing overall efficiency and cutting into the aircraft's operational range.

Moreover, the higher takeoff weight limits the payload capacity available for passengers and cargo. On this flight, the airline might need to restrict cargo loads or adjust passenger bookings to stay within MTOW limits, directly affecting revenue potential. Over a route of this length, these compounded penalties underscore the trade-offs involved in ultra long-haul operations.

Industry Perspective 5-3. Contingency vs. Reserve Fuel

In aviation fuel planning, distinguishing between Contingency Fuel and Reserve Fuel is essential for both operational efficiency and regulatory compliance. **Table 5-3** *outlines the key differences between these two categories:*

Table 5-3. *Differentiating contingency and reserve fuel*

Aspect	Contingency Fuel	Reserve Fuel
Purpose	Buffer for en-route uncertainties (e.g., headwinds, ATC)	Safety margin for destination and alternate scenarios
Regulatory Status	Often operator-defined; guidelines may vary	Mandated by aviation authorities
Scope	En-route deviations	Diversion and holding at alternate/destination
Consumption Priority	Used before reserve fuel	Reserved strictly for emergency scenarios

Source: Author's analysis

The integration of these fuel categories into the Typical Mission Profile, as shown in **Figure 5-7**, allows operators to optimize fuel planning while maintaining compliance and operational safety. For example, Boeing's Mission Profile Rules for the 737-500 include detailed contingency and reserve requirements, ensuring a consistent approach to fuel management.

Figure 5-7. Example typical mission profile rules

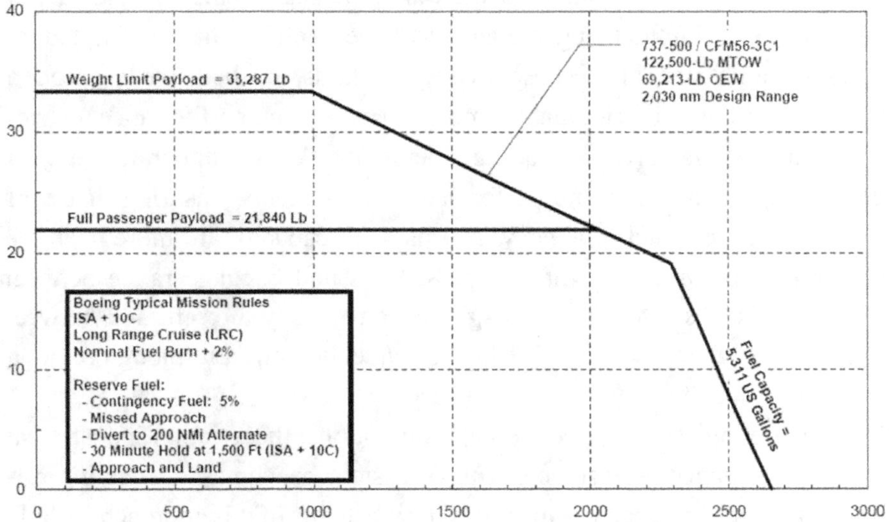

Source: Boeing Aircraft Trading Floor [3]

In conclusion, fuel management and reserve contingencies, as defined by Mission Profile Rules, provide a standardized framework for evaluating aircraft performance across models. By benchmarking fuel consumption and reserve requirements consistently, this framework enables objective, data-driven decisions in fleet planning and operational strategies.

5.1.5 Passenger & Baggage Weight

Accurate calculations of passenger and baggage weight are fundamental to airline operations, directly influencing seating capacity, payload limits, fuel requirements, and route planning. These calculations incorporate average passenger weights, including both checked and carry-on baggage, to ensure precise planning. Standardizing these estimates aligns operational processes with real-world travel patterns, enhancing both predictability and efficiency. Additionally, accurate weight data informs key aircraft performance metrics—such as takeoff parameters, cruising altitude, and fuel burn rates—essential for maintaining operational safety and cost-efficiency.

Historically, passenger weight estimates often excluded baggage, leading to discrepancies between projected and actual payloads. However, recent shifts in travel trends—such as increased baggage quantities and demographic changes influencing average passenger weight—have prompted updates to weight standards. These revised standards now better reflect modern travel conditions, contributing to improved safety and performance metrics.

Major manufacturers, including Boeing and Airbus, integrate these updated weight standards into performance assessments, ensuring that evaluations of range, fuel efficiency, and payload capacity are more accurate. Generally, combined weights for passengers and baggage range between **210 and 220 lbs. (90.7 to 99.7 kg)** for narrowbody aircraft, and between **220 and 250 lbs. (99.7 to 113.4 kg)** for widebody aircraft, though regional and airline-specific regulations may vary.

By adopting standardized weight assumptions, the aviation industry can align performance assessments with consistent benchmarks, enabling reliable evaluations and fair comparisons. Key benefits of this approach include:

- **Consistency in Performance Metrics:** Standardized weight calculations provide a reliable foundation for assessing aircraft models, ensuring that metrics like fuel efficiency, payload capacity, and operational range are evaluated using consistent data. Without standardization, comparisons could be skewed, especially when assessing aircraft for varying market needs.
- **Capacity and Range Evaluation**: Accurate weight estimates support precise seating configurations, payload limits, and range assessments. For long-haul flights, standardized weights help balance seating capacity with fuel requirements, avoiding issues such as fuel shortages from underestimating weight or inefficiencies caused by overestimations.
- **Fuel Consumption Analysis**: Passenger and baggage weight significantly impacts fuel consumption. Heavier loads increase drag and fuel demand, while lighter loads improve fuel economy.

Standardized weights allow airlines to calculate fuel needs more accurately, aiding in cost management and reducing environmental impacts. This data also supports adjustments during delays or weather-related deviations.

5.2 Cabin Configuration Rules

Cabin configuration rules are essential for accurately comparing aircraft models, as variations in cabin layout significantly impact operational metrics such as fuel burn per seat, passenger comfort, and Cost Per Available Seat Mile (CASM). These rules establish a standardized framework, ensuring fair and realistic comparisons that reflect typical airline operations.

By defining uniform assumptions about cabin characteristics—such as seat numbers, aisle widths, galley and lavatory space, crew rest areas, and fuel reserves—airlines can conduct consistent, 'apples-to-apples' assessments of aircraft performance. Standardized configurations enable meaningful evaluations of operational efficiency, fuel consumption, and cost-effectiveness, supporting strategic decision-making for fleet acquisitions and route planning.

By adopting standardized configurations, airlines can achieve consistent and objective assessments of critical operational metrics, enabling fair comparisons across aircraft models:

- **Consistency in Measurement**: Aircraft vary in seating density, service class offerings (e.g., economy, business, first class), and features like lie-flat seats or additional legroom. Standardizing these cabin elements eliminates discrepancies caused by layout differences, enabling fair comparisons of key metrics like fuel efficiency and CASM.
- **Industry Benchmarking**: Consistent cabin configurations enable industry benchmarking, allowing airlines to evaluate fleet performance relative to competitors. Metrics like CASM and fuel burn per seat, standardized across the industry, inform decisions about fleet modernization and route optimization.

Without a defined ruleset, comparisons risk being skewed by selective adjustments to cabin layouts, crew numbers, or fuel reserves. For instance, an aircraft configured with higher seat density or minimal fuel reserves may appear more efficient, but such setups often fail to represent real-world airline operations or passenger comfort.

Standardized cabin configurations ensure that evaluations are based on realistic and operationally viable setups, creating a level playing field for assessing the technical and economic performance of competing aircraft models.

5.2.1 Standardizing Cabin Configurations

A systematic approach to applying standardized cabin configurations ensures fair and accurate assessments of aircraft performance. This method removes variables that could lead to inconsistent results, focusing on each aircraft's inherent capabilities.

This structured methodology involves several key actions that promote reliable and consistent evaluations of performance metrics:

- **Maintaining Consistent Seat Ratios per Class**: Ensuring consistent ratios of seats among service classes (e.g., business, premium economy, and economy) across aircraft models is key for unbiased performance assessments. This method prevents discrepancies in cabin layout or class distribution from distorting metrics like fuel burn or Cost per Available Seat Mile (CASM), enabling comparisons to focus on the aircraft's design and efficiency.
- **Standardizing Seat Pitch and Seats Abreast**: Standardizing seat pitch (row spacing) and seats abreast (row width) is essential for fair comparisons. By aligning cabin density and comfort levels, analysts can objectively evaluate performance metrics such as fuel efficiency and passenger experience. This ensures that any observed variations are due to the aircraft's design rather than differences in cabin configuration.

EXAMPLE 5-6. Normalized Cabin Layout Comparison

Figure 5-8 illustrates a standardized dual-class cabin configuration applied to four different aircraft models: the 737-800, A320, 737-900ER, and A321. Each aircraft has consistent seating arrangements, with business class at a 36-inch pitch in a four-abreast layout and economy class at a 32-inch pitch in a six-abreast configuration. This normalization allows for direct, unbiased comparisons of performance metrics like fuel burn per seat and CASM, as all models are assessed under identical cabin conditions.

Figure 5-8. Standardized cabin layouts

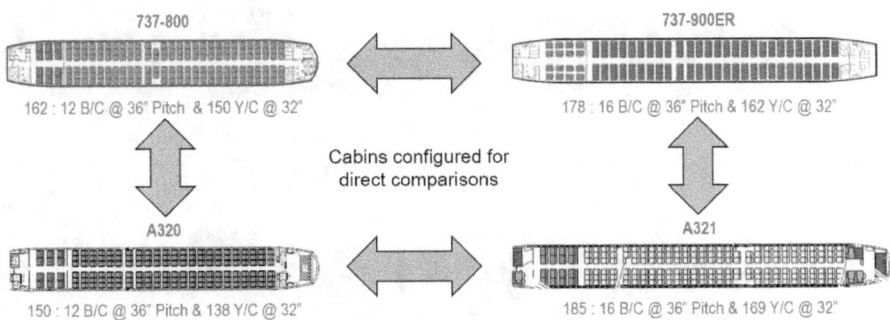

Source: Author's analysis

By ensuring uniform cabin parameters, this standardized approach reveals each aircraft's cost-effectiveness and fuel efficiency, supporting informed fleet and operational planning decisions.

EXAMPLE 5-7. Comparative Analysis of Cabin Configurations: A321NEO-LR (Long Range) vs. 757-200

When evaluating aircraft for specific missions, analyzing cabin configurations provides critical insights into operational capabilities, passenger comfort, and revenue potential. This example compares the A321NEO-LR with two configurations of the 757-200 (**Figure 5-9**) to determine the most suitable basis for comparison.

Figure 5-9: A321NEO-LR vs. 757-200 cabin configurations

AIRCRAFT	LIE-FLAT (60")	ECON-PLUS (37")	ECONOMY (31")	TOTAL
A321NEO-LR	16	48	98	162
757-200 _ Spec 1	16	52	108	176
757-200 _ Spec 2	16	48	108	172

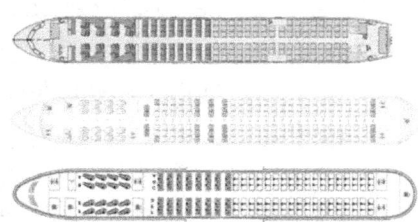

Source: Author's analysis

Cabin Layouts and Seat Counts

- **A321NEO-LR**: 162 seats (16 lie-flat Business Class seats + 48 Economy Plus seats + 98 Economy seats)
- **757-200 Configurations**:
  » **Spec 1**: 176 seats (16 Business Class seats + 52 Economy Plus seats + 108 Economy seats)
  » **Spec 2**: 172 seats (16 Business Class seats + 48 Economy Plus seats + 108 Economy seats)

Key Considerations for Comparison

1. **Business Class Alignment**: Both configurations of the 757-200 include 16 Business Class seats, matching the A321NEO-LR and ensuring parity in premium cabin capacity.
2. **Economy Plus Alignment**:
   » **Spec 2** aligns directly with the A321NEO-LR, offering 48 Economy Plus seats.
   » **Spec 1**, with 52 Economy Plus seats, introduces a higher count, potentially skewing comparisons of cost-per-seat metrics.
3. **Economy Seating**: Both 757-200 configurations provide 108 Economy seats, compared to the A321NEO-LR's 98 seats. While the increased capacity of the 757-200 may benefit high-density

routes, it also influences cost-per-seat and passenger comfort metrics, particularly on long-haul missions.

Conclusion: Among the two configurations, **757-200 Spec 2** is better aligned with the A321NEO-LR due to matching capacities in Business Class (16 seats) and Economy Plus (48 seats). This alignment facilitates a fair and consistent evaluation of operational efficiency, passenger experience, and cost-per-seat economics.

By using **Spec 2** for comparison, analysts can assess the A321NEO-LR's competitive positioning relative to the 757-200 under conditions that reflect market demands and operational strategies. This approach ensures reliable insights into the performance of both aircraft models.

Standardizing Cabin Configurations for Widebody Analysis

In widebody aircraft, standardizing cabin configurations becomes more intricate due to the varied needs of different flight profiles and premium seating requirements in classes such as First and Business. Ensuring consistency across high-density, medium-range, and long-range cabin setups is foundational for fair performance evaluations, as each configuration serves distinct operational goals and passenger expectations.

This approach involves categorizing and evaluating configurations based on their unique operational focus:

- **High-Density Operations:** Designed to maximize seat capacity, high-density configurations target revenue per flight by increasing the number of seats. This setup suits high-demand, shorter routes, or price-sensitive markets, where distributing operational costs over more seats lowers the cost per seat mile.
- **Medium-Range Operations**: Medium-range configurations aim for a balance between seating density and passenger comfort, especially in premium classes. These flights often require more amenities than short-haul operations but do not necessitate the ultra-dense layouts or extensive crew rest facilities of long-haul aircraft.
- **Long-Range Operations**: For long-haul flights, passenger comfort takes precedence due to extended flight durations. Premium seating configurations often include lie-flat seats, and dedicated crew rest areas are standard to meet regulatory requirements. In this setup, the

focus shifts toward balancing range, payload, and fuel efficiency—key factors that influence cost per seat mile over long distances.

Standardizing these configurations across various operational profiles allows for consistent performance evaluations. As illustrated in **Figure 5-10**, this approach helps airlines select the optimal aircraft based on route demands and mission-specific requirements, ensuring informed decisions that balance capacity, cost efficiency, and passenger experience across high-demand, medium, and long-haul routes.

Figure 5-10. 787-9 cabin layouts

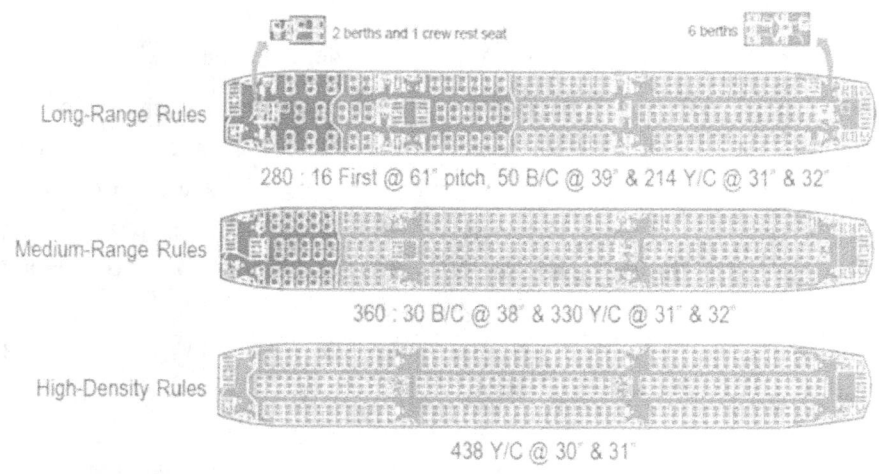

Credit: Boeing

Maintaining uniformity in seating distribution is essential for accurate comparisons of seating capacities and operational efficiency across different aircraft models. Premium seats, which occupy more space and yield higher revenue per seat compared to economy class, play a significant role in an aircraft's overall space utilization and cabin efficiency. Standardizing the ratio of premium to economy seating enables fair assessments of performance, especially when evaluating sections of the cabin that contribute most to revenue—an important factor for routes with high business travel demand.

The value of consistent seating configurations is further demonstrated in

Table 5-4, which normalizes seating layouts for aircraft models such as the 787-8/-9 and A330-800/-900. The table shows how a standardized approach to premium seating impacts total seat capacity, operational efficiency, and cost per seat mile, providing airlines with insights into each model's real-world performance.

Standardizing cabin layouts across different aircraft models enables airlines and manufacturers to make balanced evaluations, facilitating more informed decisions regarding aircraft acquisition, fleet optimization, and route planning.

Table 5-4. Standardized widebody layouts

Seating Capacity	787-8	A330-800	787-9	A330-900
Two-Class Configuration	243 32 B/C / 211 Y	248 32 B/C / 216 Y	292 40 B/C / 252 Y	294 40 B/C / 254 Y
Three-Class Configuration	222 28 B/C / 34 P/E 160Y	225 28 B/C / 34 P/E 163Y	260 32 B/C / 40 P/E 188Y	264 32 B/C / 40 P/E 192Y

P/E = Premium Economy

Source: Author's analysis

Industry Perspective 5-4. *From IAC to Standard Rules*

Boeing has updated its cabin configuration and performance standards, replacing the outdated Integrated Airplane Configuration (IAC) framework with the modernized "Boeing Standard Rules." These updates address evolving market trends, reflecting advancements in passenger preferences, payload requirements, and operational realities.

The IAC framework, established over 20 years ago, standardized parameters such as seat dimensions and passenger weights but failed to account for key industry shifts. Economy class densities increased, business class cabins grew more spacious, premium economy emerged, and first-class seating largely disappeared. Additionally, higher baggage and freight demands, driven by expanded belly-hold capacity, resulted in increased LD3 container weights. These outdated assumptions led airlines to configure aircraft with fewer seats than advertised, driving higher costs per available seat-mile (CASM) and reduced passenger comfort.

Under the Boeing Standard Rules, updated configurations feature increased seat pitch, fewer rows, optimized layouts for premium economy, and repositioned lavatories and galleys to maximize space efficiency. Revised payload assumptions now include higher LD3 container weights and expanded freight capabilities. These changes reflect a growing industry trend toward two-class configurations for long-range routes, with business, premium economy, and economy classes replacing first class to align with passenger and market demands.

Although Boeing's published performance metrics now show reduced ranges due to updated assumptions, actual aircraft performance remains unchanged. These adjustments provide more realistic and relevant data for comparing aircraft capabilities. **Table 5-5** highlights the specific changes introduced under the Boeing Standard Rules, offering a detailed comparison with the IAC framework.

For airlines, lessors, and operators, these updates emphasize the importance of evaluating aircraft based on tailored configurations that meet specific operational needs. Premium airlines often prioritize onboard features that increase empty weight, while low-cost carriers focus on simplicity and efficiency. The Boeing Standard Rules aim to support these decisions by offering accurate and industry-aligned performance metrics.

Table 5-5. Boeing seating rules before and after IAC rules

Aircraft	Seats Current 2-Class	Seats Current 3-Class	Seats Prior (IAC)	Range Current (nm)	Range Prior (nm)
737-700	126	N/A	126, 2 CL	3,010	3,445
737-800	162	N/A	162, 2 CL	2,935	3,085
737-900ER	178	N/A	180, 2 CL	2,950	3,050
737 Max 7	126	N/A	126, 2 CL	3,350	3,850
737 Max 8	162	N/A	162, 2 CL	3,515	3,660
737 Max 9	178	N/A	180, 2 CL	3,515	3,630
737 Max 200	200	N/A	200, 1 CL	2,700	3,345
787-8	242	N/A	242, 3 CL	7,355	7,850
787-9	290	N/A	280, 3 CL	7,635	8,300
787-10	330	N/A	323, 3 CL	6,430	7,000
777-8X	350-375	N/A	350, 3 CL	8,700	9,390
777-300ER	396	336	386, 3 CL	7,370	7,850
777-9X	400-425	N/A	400, 3 CL	7,600	8,200
747-8	N/A	410	467, 3 CL	7,730	7,790

Source: Leeham News & Analysis [4]

Standardizing Freighters

A systematic approach to standardizing cargo configurations ensures fair and accurate assessments of freighter aircraft performance. This method eliminates variables related to load and packing density, allowing evaluations to focus on the aircraft's inherent design and operational capabilities.

This structured methodology involves several key actions to promote reliable and consistent evaluations of performance metrics:

- **Maintaining Consistent Load Factors Across Payload Types**: Ensuring consistent ratios of volumetric, structural, and high-density payloads across aircraft models is critical for unbiased performance assessments. This approach prevents discrepancies in cargo type distribution from skewing metrics like fuel burn per ton-mile or operational cost efficiency, enabling comparisons to focus on aircraft performance.
- **Standardizing Cargo Packing Density and ULD Configurations**: Establishing consistent cargo packing densities and standardized unit load device (ULD) configurations ensures that differences in cargo storage methods do not distort performance metrics. By aligning load factors and packing efficiency, analysts can objectively evaluate metrics such as fuel efficiency and range, independent of variations in cargo handling practices.
- **Accounting for Tare Weight Consistently**: Normalizing tare weight (e.g., ULDs, pallets, and straps) across freighter models ensures that evaluations focus solely on the aircraft's operational efficiency and not on differences in handling equipment or packing methods.

By applying these standardization practices, performance analysis for freighter aircraft can achieve the same level of fairness and consistency as passenger aircraft assessments. This approach ensures that any observed variations in metrics like fuel burn, operational cost per ton-mile, or range reflect the aircraft's true design capabilities rather than differences in cargo configuration or handling practices.

Key Takeaways

1. **Mission Profile Rules**: Standardized guidelines for evaluating aircraft performance across all flight phases—taxi, takeoff, climb, cruise, descent, and landing. These rules ensure consistent and objective comparisons by accounting for factors such as route distances, cruise speeds, atmospheric conditions, fuel management, and passenger weights.

2. **Route Distances**:
   - **Great Circle Distance (GCD)**: The shortest theoretical route between two points, serving as a benchmark for evaluating range.
   - **Tracked Distance**: The actual flight path flown, accounting for deviations due to air traffic control directives, airway routings, or environmental factors.
   - **Equivalent Still Air Distance (ESAD)**: A wind-neutral measure for comparing range capabilities under standardized conditions, providing consistent performance assessments.

3. **Cruise Speeds**:
   - **Long-Range Cruise (LRC)**: Optimizes the balance between fuel efficiency and flight time, offering nearly maximum range with a small trade-off in fuel consumption.
   - **Maximum-Range Cruise (MRC)**: Focuses on achieving the maximum range by minimizing fuel consumption, ideal for fuel-conserving operations.

4. **Atmospheric Conditions**: The International Standard Atmosphere (ISA) serves as a baseline for evaluating aircraft performance under uniform conditions of pressure, temperature, and air density. This ensures fair comparisons between aircraft across various models and manufacturers.

5. **Fuel Management and Reserve Contingencies**: Comprehensive planning ensures all phases of flight, from taxi to landing, are accounted for, with reserves for contingencies such as missed approaches, diversions, or holding patterns. Key components include:
   - **Block Fuel**: Total fuel loaded before departure.
   - **Trip Fuel**: Fuel required for the planned en-route segment.

- **Alternate Fuel**: Fuel for diversion to an alternate airport.
- **Final Reserve Fuel**: Mandatory fuel for holding at a safe altitude for at least 30 minutes.

6. **Passenger and Baggage Weight**: Standardized weight assumptions for passengers and baggage provide consistency in evaluating aircraft performance. Recent updates to weight standards reflect modern travel patterns, improving safety, operational planning, and fuel calculations.

7. **Cabin Configuration Rules**: Standardized seat layouts, seat pitch, and class distribution enable fair comparisons of operational efficiency, fuel consumption, and cost per available seat mile (CASM). These rules ensure unbiased evaluations of aircraft performance across different configurations.

8. **Density Configurations**:
   - **High-Density Configurations**: Prioritize maximum seating capacity, typically used for short-haul operations.
   - **Medium-Density Configurations**: Balance seating capacity and passenger comfort for medium-range missions.
   - **Long-Density Configurations**: Optimize passenger comfort and payload for long-haul routes.

9. **Normalized Cabin Layouts**: Consistent cabin configurations, such as standardized ratios of business, premium economy, and economy seats, ensure unbiased evaluations of fuel efficiency, CASM, and operational capacity across aircraft models.

10. **Industry Evolution in Cabin Standards**: Updates in Boeing and Airbus configuration standards reflect advancements in aviation technology and shifting market demands. These changes ensure that modern performance metrics, such as range and fuel burn, accurately represent real-world operating conditions.

11. **Operational Impact of Configurations**: Cabin layouts directly influence payload limits, operational range, and CASM, highlighting the importance of aligning configurations with market needs and mission profiles.

12. **Role of Configuration in Benchmarking**: Standardized cabin configurations are essential for comparing aircraft performance objectively. They prevent discrepancies that arise from layout variations and ensure data-driven decision-making for fleet acquisitions and operational planning.

Case Study 5-1. Distance and Wind Effects

Table 5-6. Distance and wind values

ROUTE:	LHR - DEL	LHR - HKG	LHR - SIN
Great Circle Distance - nm	3,610	5,994	6,765
Tracked Distance - nm	3,738	5,572	6,034
Avg. Wind Component - kts	+28	+27	+16
ESAD - nm	3,526	5,263	5,832

Source: Author's analysis

Questions:

1. Analyze the discrepancies between the Great Circle Distance and Tracked Distance for each route. How do factors such as air traffic control, geographic constraints, and flight path optimization contribute to these variations?

2. Discuss how the Average Wind Component influences the ESAD compared to Tracked and Great Circle Distances. How do prevailing winds impact route planning and ESAD calculations?

3. Examine the role of the Average Wind Component in route optimization. If the wind profile shifted significantly (e.g., a +10 kt increase), how might this alter ESAD and subsequently the feasibility of the current flight plan?

4. Considering the variance in Average Wind Component across the three routes, what implications do headwind components have for fuel consumption and flight scheduling for airlines operating on these routes? How could this affect an airline's choice between different aircraft models?

Case Study 5-2. Standardized Layout Evaluation

You are tasked with evaluating the E195-E2 and A220-300 for potential fleet inclusion. To ensure an objective assessment, both aircraft have been standardized to a single-class Economy configuration with a 31-inch seat pitch. This eliminates variables like multi-class layouts or operator preferences. The E195-E2 accommodates 132 seats, while the A220-300 offers 145 seats, giving the A220-300 a 10% higher passenger capacity. See Figure 5-11 for a visual comparison of the cabin layouts.

Figure 5-11. E195-E2 and A220-300 cabin layouts

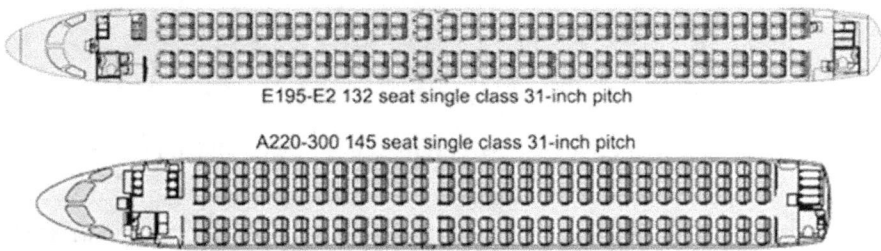

Credit: Embraer and Airbus

Questions:

1. Why is it critical to normalize cabin layouts for an apples-to-apples comparison when evaluating aircraft like the E195-E2 and A220-300? Identify potential biases normalization eliminates and explain how this enhances the objectivity of seat-mile cost comparisons.

2. How does standardizing seat pitch at 31 inches for the E195-E2 and A220-300 influence seat-mile cost evaluations? If an airline adjusts the seat pitch to 32 inches on one aircraft, how might this affect passenger yield, cabin utilization, and operational metrics? Discuss what changes would be necessary to maintain a fair comparison.

3. If the cabins were configured with a mix of Economy and Business classes, how might the seating capacity and layout comparison differ? Discuss how class transitions introduce biases and why a single-class configuration is more suitable for this analysis.

4. Given the normalized cabin configurations of the E195-E2 and A220-300 (single-class Economy, 31-inch pitch), propose a methodology for conducting a comparative analysis to evaluate aircraft suitability for short-haul operations, focusing on differences in Cash Operating Costs (COC).

References

[1] LinkedIn, "Image retrieved from Jainam Doshi: North Atlantic Tracks (NATS)." [Online]. Available: https://www.linkedin.com/posts/jainam -doshi-6288b01b4_north-atlantic-tracks-nats-are-daily-high-activity -7098988657268682752-0l3r/

[2] Aircraft Commerce Magazine, "A350-900/-1000 Fuel Burn & Operating Performance," Issue No. 121, Dec. 2018 / Jan. 2019. [Online]. Available: https://www.aircraft-commerce.com/

[3] Boeing, "737-500/CFM56-3C1 Aircraft Characteristics & Performance," Aircraft Trading Floor, Document D906Q3874, Oct. 2008.

[4] Leeham News & Analysis, "Boeing starts applying 'Standard Rules' to its and competitors' aircraft." [Online]. Available: https://leehamnews.com/

Chapter 6

Airport Characteristics

This Chapter is About:

6.1 Field Length
6.2 Field Environment
6.3 Performance Enhancements for Demanding Environments

Selecting the right aircraft for a route requires a thorough understanding of how airport characteristics influence performance. This chapter focuses on three primary elements: **Field Length**, **Environmental Factors** such as altitude, temperature, and humidity, and **Performance Features for Demanding Environments**, which include specialized aircraft modifications designed to enhance operational capabilities at challenging airports. These factors ensure that aircraft can take off and land efficiently and safely, even under less-than-ideal conditions.

- **Field Length:** Runway length is a vital determinant of an aircraft's takeoff and landing performance. At airports with shorter runways, aircraft may face restrictions on their maximum takeoff weight (MTOW), resulting in a **Regulated (or restricted) Takeoff Weight (RTOW)**. Understanding RTOW is essential for evaluating an aircraft's suitability for specific airport operations.

- **Field Environment:** The combination of **altitude**, **temperature**, and **humidity** at an airport defines its **density altitude**. Higher altitudes, warmer temperatures, and increased humidity reduce air density, negatively affecting engine performance and aerodynamic lift. These environmental conditions often necessitate RTOW adjustments to maintain safe operational margins.
- **Performance Enhancements for Demanding Environments:** Aircraft operating in challenging conditions, such as short runways or high-altitude airports, often require specialized design features. Examples include:
  » **Short-field performance packages** that improve takeoff and landing capabilities on limited runways.
  » **Thrust bumps**, providing additional engine power in high-altitude or hot conditions.
  » **Lower wing loading**, enabling more lift at lower speeds and enhancing operations in "hot and high" environments.

In the following sections, we will explore these factors in detail, examining how Field Length, Environmental Factors, and Performance Features shape aircraft performance. This discussion will address the operational challenges posed by varying airport environments and the adaptations necessary to achieve safe and efficient performance.

6.1 Field Length

Field length is an important factor in determining both the operational capabilities and economic efficiency of aircraft. It directly influences whether an aircraft can safely operate from a specific airport, shaping airline fleet decisions and route viability.

Longer runways offer operational advantages by allowing aircraft to accelerate more gradually, which often enables reduced engine power settings. This approach not only saves fuel but also minimizes engine wear, lowering maintenance costs over time. Additionally, longer runways facilitate a controlled deceleration during landing, reducing dependence on heavy braking or extensive reverse thrust and thereby extending the lifespan of brakes and engines.

Conversely, shorter runways impose operational limitations. Aircraft operating from shorter runways require higher power settings or steeper climb angles to achieve the necessary lift within the available space. These requirements increase fuel consumption and place additional strain on engines and brakes, resulting in more frequent maintenance and higher operating costs.

In addition, restricted runway length can limit an aircraft's maximum takeoff weight (MTOW), reducing fuel capacity and, subsequently, range. This limitation can have significant implications for route planning and network strategy. Aircraft that can maintain substantial fuel loads and extended range, even from shorter runways, provide airlines with enhanced operational flexibility and a competitive edge.

In summary, runway length is essential for ensuring safe and efficient aircraft operations, impacting decisions on allowable fuel load, payload capacity, and the selection of suitable aircraft for specific routes. Considering these factors allows airlines to balance operational requirements with economic outcomes effectively.

Practical Planning Tools

Aircraft performance planning relies heavily on tools that address runway length constraints. One key resource is the *Airplane Characteristics for Airport Planning* document, published by aircraft manufacturers. These documents provide detailed technical data for various aircraft models, including takeoff performance charts, such as those illustrated in **Figure 6-1**, which compare the performance of the Boeing 737-700W (winglet variant) and Airbus A330-300 under standard day conditions (15°C or 59°F). These tools enable informed decisions regarding runway utilization and aircraft selection.

Figure 6-1. 737-700 and A330-300 takeoff performance

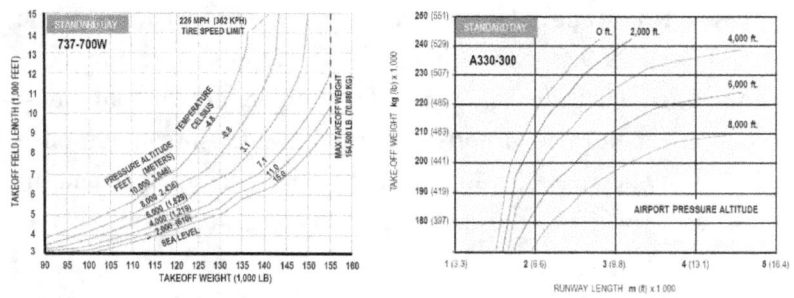

Source: Boeing 737 & Airbus A330 "Airplane Characteristics for Airport Planning" document, [1] [2]

Both Boeing and Airbus takeoff performance charts provide critical data for calculating maximum takeoff weight and runway requirements, though their designs differ:

- **Boeing Charts:** Organized with takeoff weight on the horizontal axis and takeoff field length on the vertical axis, these charts include curves for varying pressure altitudes. Additional data, such as temperature corrections and a tire speed limit line (indicating maximum tire speed during takeoff), are integrated into the main chart for ease of use.
- **Airbus Charts:** Displaying takeoff weight on the vertical axis and runway length on the horizontal axis, Airbus charts feature a grid layout that simplifies the visual relationship between weight and runway requirements. Supplementary details, like temperature adjustments and tire speed limits, are presented in separate tables or charts, resulting in a streamlined main chart.

While the layouts and presentation styles differ, both charts serve the essential function of determining maximum takeoff weight for specific runway length and airport pressure altitude combinations. These resources allow pilots and operators to account for variations in weight, altitude, and temperature, ensuring safe and efficient takeoffs.

Takeoff performance charts are vital for evaluating an aircraft's ability to safely operate under varying environmental and weight conditions. These charts provide essential metrics to determine whether an aircraft can achieve a safe takeoff based on runway length, atmospheric factors, and weight. Key components include:

- **Pressure Altitude:** Measured relative to a standard atmospheric pressure of 29.92 inches of mercury (in-Hg), pressure altitude impacts engine thrust and wing lift. At higher pressure altitudes—common at elevated airports or during low-pressure conditions—air density decreases, reducing both engine performance and lift. This directly affects the aircraft's ability to generate sufficient lift for takeoff.
- **Temperature:** Ambient temperature influences air density and, consequently, takeoff performance. Higher temperatures reduce air density, diminishing engine thrust and lift, and necessitate longer

runway lengths to achieve safe takeoff speeds. Performance charts account for temperature variations to ensure operational safety.

- **Takeoff Weight:** This is the total aircraft weight at takeoff, typically measured in thousands of pounds. Heavier aircraft require greater lift and, therefore, longer runway lengths to become airborne. Accurate weight calculations are essential for ensuring safe climb performance and efficient operations.
- **Required Runway Length:** This value represents the minimum runway length needed for a safe takeoff, given specific conditions of pressure altitude, temperature, and weight. As any of these factors increase, the required runway length rises accordingly. Ensuring the runway meets these requirements is essential for safe takeoff operations.

Takeoff performance charts also incorporate operational limits like the **tire speed limit**, which defines the maximum safe ground speed for the aircraft's tires during takeoff. High-density altitude conditions—common at elevated airports with reduced air density—can extend takeoff rolls and increase ground speeds, posing a risk of tire overheating or blowouts if this limit is exceeded.

EXAMPLE 6-1. Determining Takeoff Weight for a 737-700W at Chicago's Midway Airport

This example evaluates a Boeing 737-700W with a Maximum Design Takeoff Weight (MDTOW) of 154,500 pounds, preparing for departure from **Chicago Midway Airport**. The available runway length at Midway is 6,530 feet, imposing constraints on the allowable takeoff weight. Standard day conditions are assumed, with a pressure altitude matching Midway's elevation and an ambient temperature of 15°C (59°F).

To determine the maximum permissible takeoff weight, the aircraft's takeoff performance chart (**Figure 6-2**) is used. This chart illustrates the relationship between runway length, weight, and environmental conditions, ensuring safe and efficient takeoff operations.

Figure 6-2. 737-700 Midway Airport takeoff performance

Aircraft : 737-700W Engine : CFM56-7B22		MDTOW (lb) : 154,500				
Airport (Code)	Runway	Pressure Altitude (ft)	Field Length (ft)	Temperature (°C)	Takeoff Weight (lb)	Takeoff Limitation
Chicago (MDW)	31C	612	6,520	14.4	142,450	RTOW

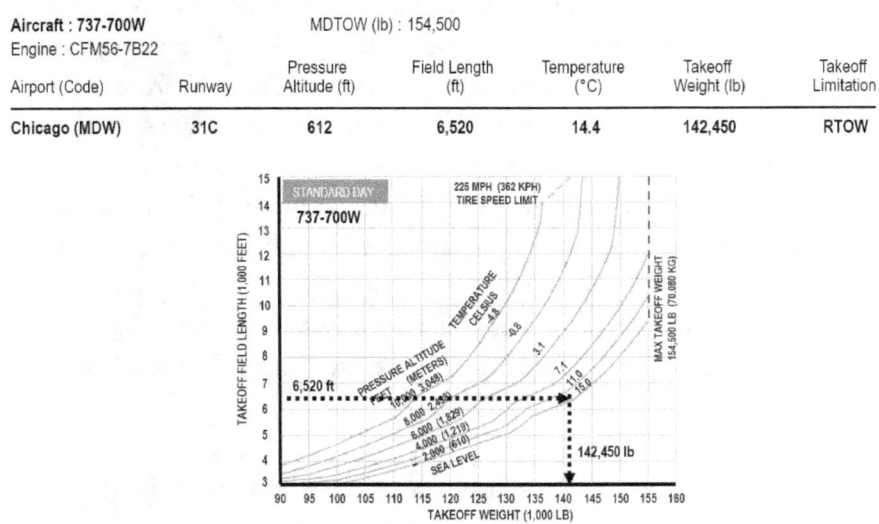

Source: "737 Airplane Characteristics for Airport Planning", document with modifications by the author [1]

Determining the Maximum Takeoff Weight:

1. **Identify the Sea-Level Line**: Locate the sea-level reference line on the chart, which establishes the baseline for pressure altitude under standard day conditions.
2. **Approximate Runway Length**: Match the 6,530-foot runway length to the closest value on the chart, typically 6,500 feet.
3. **Trace the Vertical Line**: Draw a vertical line upward from the 6,500-foot mark on the horizontal axis until it intersects the curve for standard day, sea-level conditions.

The intersection point indicates the **regulated takeoff weight (RTOW)**, approximately 142,450 pounds. This restricted weight ensures the aircraft can safely operate from Midway under the specified runway and environmental constraints.

Runway length significantly impacts an aircraft's operational range and flexibility. Shorter runways often limit the MTOW, as insufficient length may prevent the aircraft from achieving the required takeoff speed. Since fuel constitutes a significant portion of total weight, reduced takeoff weight frequently results in lower fuel loads, limiting the aircraft's range.

As shown in **Figure 6-3**, the Boeing 737-700W, at its **MDTOW** of 154,500 pounds, requires approximately **9,000 feet** of runway for takeoff on a standard sea-level day. At Midway, where the runway length is restricted to 6,530 feet, the takeoff weight must be reduced to **142,450 pounds**. This reduction directly impacts the aircraft's range capabilities.

Using the payload-range chart, the following implications are observed:

- **Full MDTOW**: The 737-700W achieves a range of 2,550 nautical miles.
- **RTOW at Midway**: Range decreases to approximately 1,500 nautical miles due to the shorter runway and reduced fuel load.

These constraints highlight the need for effective flight planning to balance runway limitations with operational requirements. Adjusting fuel loads to meet RTOW ensures safe takeoff while accounting for reduced range.

Figure 6-3. 737-700 takeoff performance and range

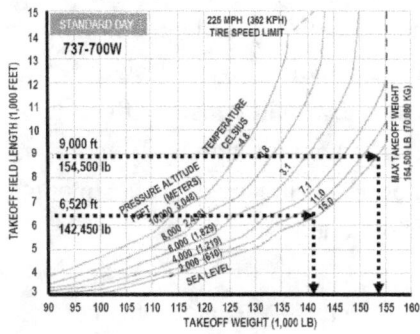 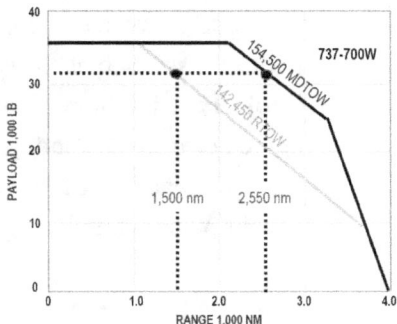

Source: "737 Airplane Characteristics for Airport Planning", document with modifications by the author [1]

6.2 Field Environment

Aircraft performance is highly sensitive to an airport's **field environment**, as atmospheric conditions directly impact critical factors like lift generation and engine efficiency during takeoff and landing. Variations in air density affect fuel consumption, payload capacity, and operational safety, making the airport's environmental characteristics an essential consideration.

The following environmental factors illustrate how atmospheric conditions impact aircraft performance:

- **Elevation:** Higher altitudes reduce air density, leading to diminished engine thrust and aerodynamic lift. This necessitates longer takeoff distances and higher takeoff speeds to achieve adequate lift, impacting climb performance and range capabilities.
- **Temperature:** Increased temperatures further lower air density, reducing engine output and lift capabilities. In hot conditions, aircraft require longer takeoff distances and consume more fuel, affecting operational efficiency and economic performance.
- **Hot & High Conditions:** Airports with both high altitude and high temperatures—referred to as "Hot & High" environments—present compounded challenges. The combination of reduced air density and increased takeoff requirements often necessitates specialized aircraft performance features to maintain safety and operational effectiveness, such as thrust bumps or modified wing designs.
- **Humidity:** High humidity levels also lower air density, affecting engine performance and lift. Aircraft operating in humid conditions may experience reduced climb rates, requiring careful adjustments in flight planning and weight distribution.

Understanding how these environmental factors—elevation, temperature, humidity, and their combined effects—affect aircraft performance is critical for evaluating an aircraft's technical and economic competitiveness. This knowledge supports informed decision-making in aircraft selection and operational planning, ensuring effective performance across diverse airport settings.

***Industry Perspective 6-1.** Density and Engine Performance*

*Air density, a critical factor for both engine performance and aerodynamic lift, decreases with rising temperatures. As illustrated in **Figure 6-4**, jet engines are designed to ingest a specific volume of air, but warmer air is less dense, containing fewer air molecules per unit volume. This reduction in air density lowers engine efficiency, resulting in decreased net thrust output as temperatures rise.*

The impact of high temperatures extends to aerodynamic performance. Reduced air density diminishes lift, requiring aircraft to achieve higher speeds to generate sufficient lift for takeoff. Consequently, longer runway distances are needed, and in some cases, operational adjustments—such as reduced climb rates or decreased payload—are necessary to ensure safe operations in high-temperature environments.

Figure 6-4. Air density and engine performance

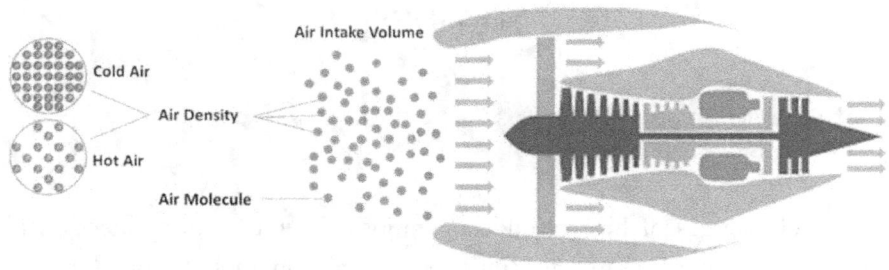

Source: Author's analysis

6.2.1 Elevation

At higher altitudes, where air pressure and density are lower, aircraft engines produce reduced thrust, and wings generate less lift. These conditions require longer takeoff distances to achieve the necessary speed for sufficient lift, resulting in extended takeoff rolls. As shown in **Figure 6-5**, takeoff field length increases with altitude, highlighting the additional runway distance required to compensate for reduced air density. Consequently, high-altitude airports often require longer runways to ensure safe and efficient operations.

Figure 6-5. Impact of altitude

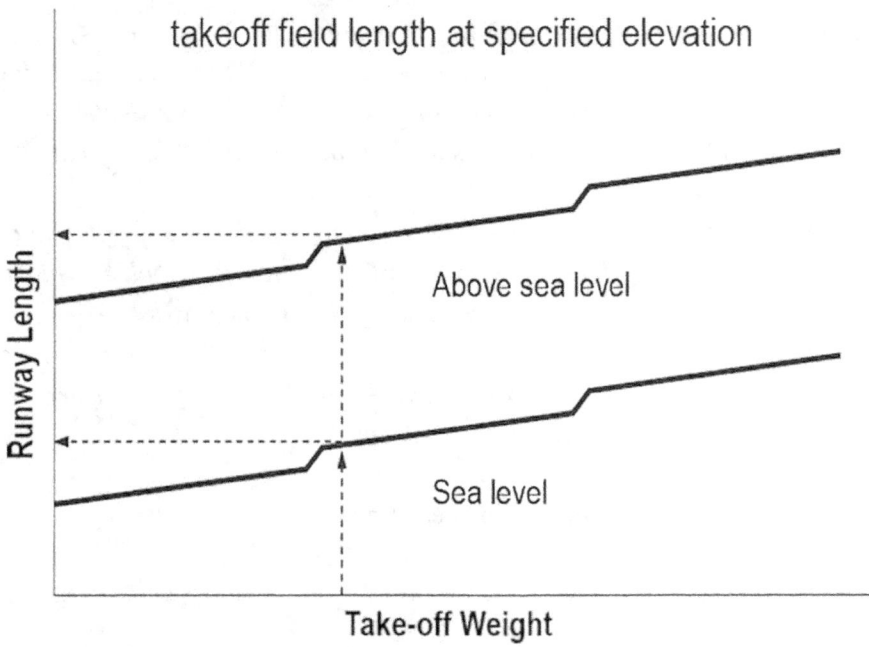

Credit: Boeing

The challenges of high-altitude operations extend beyond takeoff. Reduced air density also impacts climb performance, making it more demanding for aircraft to gain and maintain altitude. Similarly, during landing, diminished lift affects deceleration and descent rates, often necessitating longer runway distances to ensure safe landings. Operating in low-density environments requires careful planning of takeoff and landing procedures to mitigate these effects.

To illustrate, **Figure 6-6** compares two scenarios under standard day conditions: a Boeing 737-700W operating at sea level and at a pressure altitude of 8,000 feet, both with a temperature of +15°C and a takeoff weight of 130,000 pounds. At sea level, the aircraft requires a takeoff field length of 5,000 feet. However, at 8,000 feet, where air density is significantly lower, the same aircraft needs 8,000 feet of runway to achieve takeoff speed. This example underscores the operational challenges posed by higher altitudes, where thinner air reduces both engine performance and lift efficiency, necessitating longer takeoff distances.

Figure 6-6. 737-700 impact of elevation

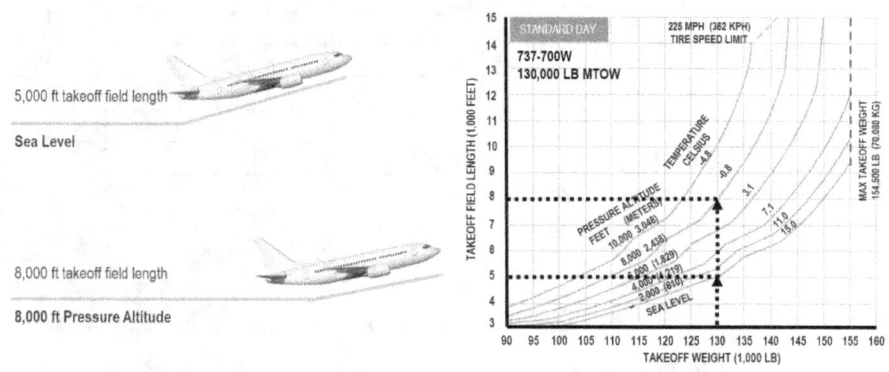

Source: "737 Airplane Characteristics for Airport Planning", document with modifications by the author [1]

To further illustrate the impact of elevation on aircraft performance, consider the takeoff capabilities of the Airbus A330-300 as shown in **Figure 6-7**. At sea level, the aircraft's certified MTOW is 242 tonnes, requiring a takeoff roll of approximately 8,800 feet. However, at a pressure altitude of 8,000 feet—where air density is significantly reduced—the aircraft's Regulated Takeoff Weight (RTOW) decreases to 210 tonnes, and the required takeoff roll extends to approximately 14,800 feet. This dramatic difference highlights how reduced air density at higher altitudes directly impacts takeoff performance, limiting both allowable weight and operational range.

Figure 6-7. A330-300 impact of elevation

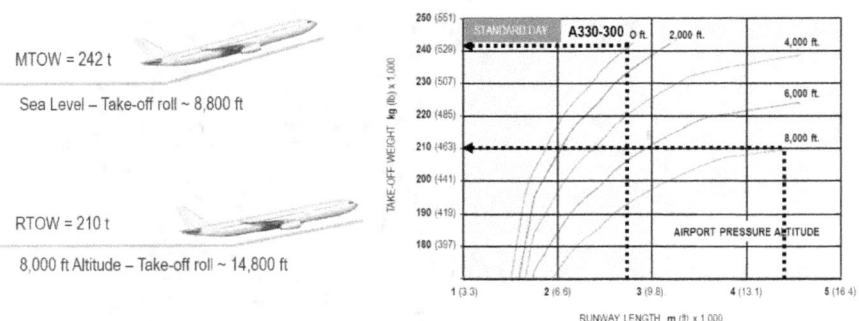

Source: "A330 Airplane Characteristics for Airport Planning", document with modifications by the author [2]

6.2.2 Temperature

Temperature significantly affects aircraft performance by reducing air density, effectively increasing the **density altitude**—the operational altitude adjusted for current air density rather than physical elevation. As shown in Figure **6-8**, higher temperatures above standard levels necessitate longer takeoff field lengths due to decreased engine thrust and aerodynamic lift.

Figure 6-8. Impact of temperature

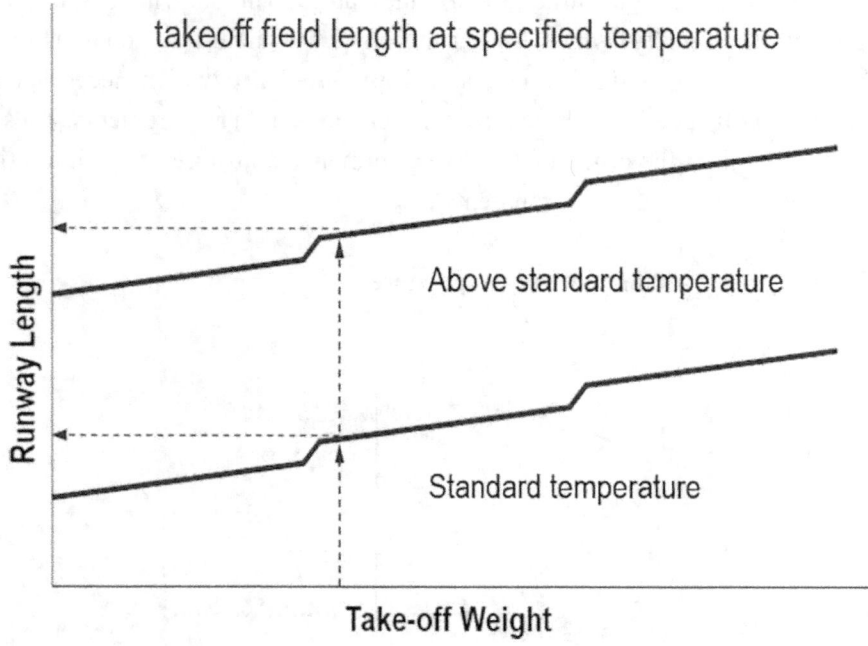

takeoff field length at specified temperature

Runway Length

Above standard temperature

Standard temperature

Take-off Weight

Credit: Boeing

Impact on Takeoff and Climb is significant in warmer conditions, where changes in performance necessitate careful planning. In such conditions, **engines produce less thrust**, resulting in reduced acceleration, while **wings generate less lift**, requiring higher takeoff speeds and longer runway distances. These factors underscore the importance of precise calculations for **takeoff distances** and **climb rates** to ensure safe and efficient operations under temperature-sensitive conditions.

Airlines often mitigate temperature effects by scheduling flights during cooler periods, such as early morning or late evening. Cooler conditions enhance engine thrust and lift, improving overall safety and performance, especially when operating near maximum performance limits.

Figure 6-9 demonstrates the impact of temperature on the takeoff performance of a **737-700W** under **STANDARD DAY + 40°F** conditions, representing a 22.2°C increase above the ISA baseline of 15°C at sea level. At sea level, the aircraft requires **6,200 feet of runway** for takeoff. However, at a **pressure altitude of 8,000 feet** with the same temperature, the required takeoff distance increases significantly to **10,000 feet**, underscoring the compounded effects of altitude and temperature. This is primarily due to **reduced air density**, which lowers the oxygen available for combustion, thereby reducing **engine thrust**, and **diminished lift**, which necessitates higher takeoff speeds, further increasing runway length requirements. These factors highlight the critical need for performance adjustments in high-altitude, high-temperature environments.

Figure 6-9. 737-700 impact of temperature

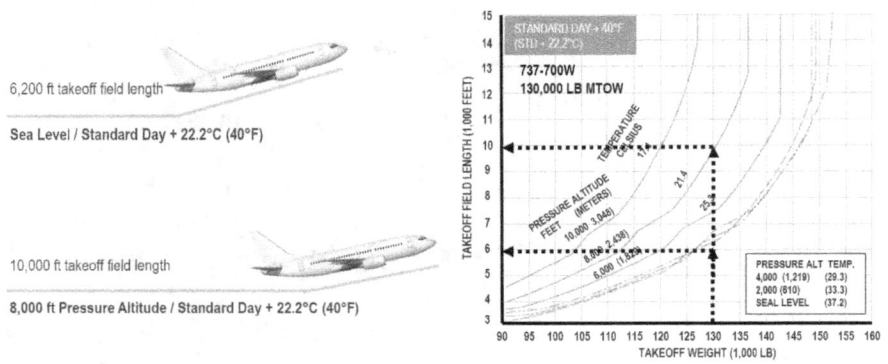

Source: "737 Airplane Characteristics for Airport Planning", document with modifications by the author [1]

6.2.3 Hot & High

"Hot and High" airports present significant operational challenges due to the combined effects of high altitude and elevated temperatures, which drastically reduce air density. Low air density impacts both engine thrust and aerodynamic lift, requiring longer takeoff distances and imposing stricter payload limitations.

Air density, a critical factor in aircraft performance, is commonly expressed as **sigma (σ)**—the ratio of air density at a given altitude and temperature to standard sea-level density. Sigma values near 1.0 indicate conditions similar to sea level, while lower sigma values, such as 0.60, reflect significantly reduced air density, which diminishes engine power and lift. For instance, at 80% of standard sea-level density, sigma equals 0.80, directly impacting takeoff weight, climb performance, and overall operational flexibility. Understanding and accounting for sigma values is essential for ensuring safe and efficient aircraft operations in varying environmental conditions.

Real-World Examples of "Hot and High" Airports:

Several well-known airports demonstrate the dual challenges of high altitude and elevated temperatures:

- **Benito Juárez International Airport, Mexico City** (7,349 feet, 27°C): Sigma = 0.7310 (73% of sea-level air density).
- **Albuquerque International Sunport, New Mexico** (5,312 feet, 33°C): Sigma = 0.7740 (77% of sea-level air density).
- **El Alto International Airport, La Paz** (11,942 feet, 20°C): Sigma = 0.6257 (63% of sea-level air density).
- **Sky Harbor Airport, Phoenix, Arizona** (1,117 feet, 45°C): Sigma = 0.8697 (87% of sea-level air density), showing the impact of extreme heat even at lower altitudes.

Performance Impact of Hot and High Conditions is driven by reduced air density, commonly referred to as low sigma, which significantly affects key operational factors. Takeoff distance increases as longer runway lengths are required to achieve the necessary takeoff speed due to diminished lift and thrust. Additionally, Regulated Takeoff Weight (RTOW) often necessitates reductions in payload and fuel capacity to remain within safe takeoff limits. Furthermore, climb performance is adversely impacted, as decreased air density limits climb rates, reducing safety margins. These factors highlight the operational challenges and critical adjustments required in hot and high environments.

Figure 6-10 compares the takeoff performance of a Boeing 737-700W under various conditions:

- **STANDARD DAY at sea level:** RTOW = 150,000 pounds.
- **22.2°C above baseline at sea level:** RTOW = 140,000 pounds, showing temperature's impact on performance.
- **8,000 feet at STANDARD DAY conditions:** RTOW = 125,000 pounds, demonstrating altitude's effect.

The combined challenges of high altitude and elevated temperatures can significantly restrict range and payload capacity. Effective flight planning must consider these factors, including adjustments to departure timing, payload, and fuel loads, to ensure safe and efficient operations.

Figure 6-10. 737-700 impact of elevation & temperature

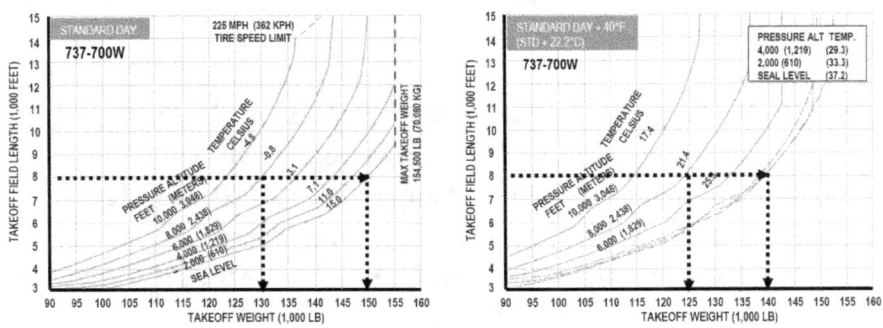

Source: "737 Airplane Characteristics for Airport Planning", document with modifications by the author [1]

At airfields with challenging conditions, aircraft often operate with a Regulated Takeoff Weight (RTOW) that is lower than their Maximum Takeoff Weight (MTOW). This limitation is particularly impactful for cargo aircraft, where maximizing payload is critical for operational efficiency. High-altitude airfields, characterized by thinner air, elevated temperatures, and shorter runways, frequently necessitate a lower RTOW. This reduction directly limits payload, especially on long-haul routes requiring the aircraft's full range.

Cargo aircraft performance under hot and high airfield conditions is a critical measure of their operational capability. These environments present some of the most demanding challenges, where altitude, elevated temperatures, and limited runway lengths combine to significantly reduce air density. This reduction impacts takeoff performance, limiting maximum takeoff weight (MTOW) and, consequently, both payload and range. While all aircraft experience restrictions in regulated takeoff weight (RTOW) and payload under such conditions, the degree of performance degradation varies by model. Selecting the right aircraft for operations involving hot and high airfields is essential to ensuring operational efficiency, safety, and profitability.

For example, as shown in **Figure 6-11**, the **MD-11F** can carry a full payload of 198,300 pounds over a range of 4,000 nautical miles under sea level and International Standard Atmosphere (ISA) conditions. However, on shorter flights from high-altitude airports like Bogotá or Quito to Miami, its payload capacity becomes restricted due to the effects of high-density altitude and limited runway length. These constraints significantly affect operational range and, consequently, the airline's economic performance.

Figure 6-11. MD-11F impact of elevation & temperature

Aircraft Type	MD-11F
Engine type	CF6-80C2
MTOW (lb)	630,500
MLW (lb)	491,500
MZFW (lb)	461,300
OEW+Tare Weight (lb)	263,000
Net Available Payload	**198,300**

Airport	Elevation (ft)	Runway Length (ft)	Ambient Temperature	MIA Route (nm)	Payload (lb)
Mexico City, Mexico	7,316	12,960	30°C / 86°F	1,108	198,300
Quito, Ecuador	7,874	13,451	26°C / 79°F	1,553	128,087
Bogota, Colombia	8,355	12,467	28°C / 84°F	1,309	184,640

Source: Aircraft Commerce Magazine [3]

Industry Perspective 6-2. *High Altitude Airports and Tire Speed*

Operating aircraft from hot and high airports introduces unique challenges, particularly concerning tire speed limits. At these airports, where high-density altitude results from reduced air density due to altitude and temperature, aircraft must achieve higher ground speeds during takeoff to generate sufficient lift. This increased ground speed can approach the tires' maximum rated limits, raising safety concerns.

For example, at **Mexico City International Airport** *(7,349 feet elevation, 27°C), the elevated density altitude significantly increases the required takeoff speed, bringing ground speed closer to the tire limit. To mitigate this, airlines often reduce takeoff weight by adjusting passenger, cargo, or fuel loads, which impacts payload capacity and operational efficiency.*

Aircraft operating in such environments may become **tire-speed-limited***,* *necessitating careful weight management to prevent exceeding safe tire speeds. Airlines address these constraints through strategies such as reducing takeoff weight, scheduling flights during cooler periods, or equipping aircraft with tires rated for higher speeds.*

Effectively managing tire speed limits is essential for ensuring safe and efficient operations. By optimizing weight, timing, and tire specifications, airlines balance the trade-offs between payload capacity and operational efficiency in challenging hot and high conditions.

6.2.4 Humidity

In addition to elevation and temperature, **humidity** plays a role in aircraft performance, particularly by influencing engine efficiency and takeoff performance. While its impact on aerodynamics is less direct than altitude or temperature, humidity affects engine power output by altering the air's composition.

Humidity refers to the amount of water vapor in the air. As humidity increases, a greater portion of the air consists of water vapor, which does not support combustion. This reduces the oxygen available for combustion, leading to decreased engine efficiency. The effect is most noticeable in hot conditions, where the air holds significantly more water vapor. For example, at 96°F (35.5°C), the water vapor content can be up to eight times greater than at 42°F (5.5°C). This amplifies the loss of engine power and performance on particularly humid, hot days.

While high humidity and high-density altitude do not always coincide, their combined effects can significantly impact performance. A general rule of thumb is to add 10% to the computed takeoff distance in humid conditions and anticipate a reduced climb rate. These adjustments compensate for the loss of engine power, ensuring adequate safety margins during takeoff and the initial climb.

Considering humidity alongside elevation and temperature allows flight planners and pilots to make more accurate performance calculations. This comprehensive approach ensures that all relevant environmental factors are addressed, supporting optimal safety and operational reliability across a wide range of conditions.

6.3 Performance Enhancements for Demanding Environments

Operating in challenging environments—such as those with short runways, high altitudes, or high temperatures—requires specific aircraft performance attributes to ensure efficiency and safety. To address these demands, many aircraft incorporate specialized features and modifications that enhance operational capability under such conditions. Three key attributes play an essential role in supporting performance in these environments:

1. **Short-Field Performance Packages**: These integrated or optional features enable safe takeoffs and landings on shorter runways, which are often found at remote or space-constrained airfields. Enhanced braking systems, optimized flap settings, and improved takeoff performance are common elements of these packages.
2. **Thrust Bumps**: Thrust bumps provide additional engine power to compensate for reduced air density at high-altitude or hot airports. This ensures sufficient thrust during takeoff, enabling safe operations even in environments where engines perform less efficiently.
3. **Low Wing Loading Aircraft**: Aircraft with lower wing loading—defined as the ratio of an aircraft's weight to its wing area—are better suited for hot and high-altitude conditions. Lower wing loading enhances lift generation at lower speeds, reducing the runway length required for takeoff and landing. Examples include minor family variants like the Airbus A319CEO/NEO, A330-200, Boeing 737-700/MAX7, and 787-8, which are specifically designed to perform effectively in such demanding environments.

The following sections explore each of these performance-enhancing features in detail, illustrating their impact on operational adaptability and efficiency across diverse airport environments.

Short-field Performance Packages

Short-field performance packages, available as optional enhancements for aircraft like the Boeing 737-800 (see **Figure 6-12**), are designed to optimize takeoff and landing capabilities on shorter runways. These packages incorporate key modifications that enhance safety and operational flexibility in environments with limited runway length. The following key features demonstrate the value of short-field performance packages:

- **Increased High-Lift Device Extension**: Extended deployment of high-lift devices, such as flaps and slats, enables the aircraft to generate additional lift at lower speeds. This feature is critical for safe takeoffs and landings on short runways, as lower speeds improve safety margins.
- **Enhanced Spoiler Deflection on Ground**: Improved spoiler deflection increases braking efficiency by enhancing deceleration after landing. This reduces the required stopping distance, a significant advantage for operations from short runways.
- **Extended Tail Skid**: A longer tail skid provides protection against tail strikes during landing, allowing for steeper descent profiles and higher angles of attack. This modification reduces the runway length required for safe landings.

These enhancements collectively improve aircraft performance in short-field settings, enabling safe and efficient operations from airfields with runway constraints. By incorporating these features, airlines gain greater operational versatility and reliability, supporting a wider range of route and airport options.

Figure 6-12. 737-800 short-field performance package

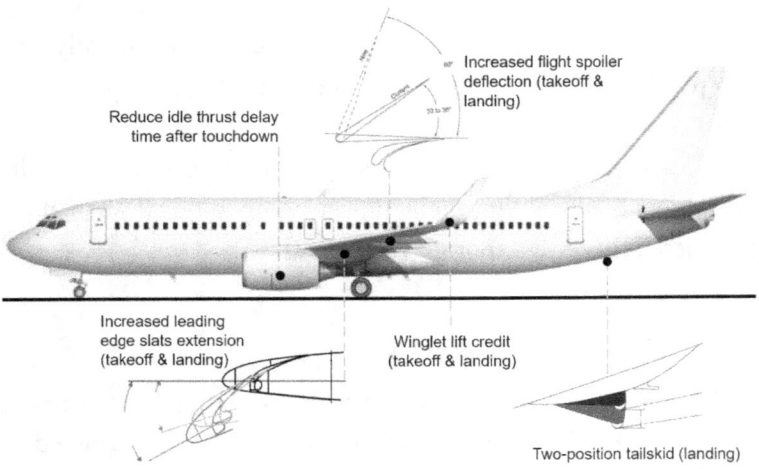

Source: Flight Global with modifications by the author [4]

Engine Thrust Bumps

Thrust bumps are optional engine enhancements that increase maximum thrust output, enabling aircraft to maintain optimal performance in environments with reduced air density, such as hot or high-altitude conditions. As shown in **Table 6-1**, thrust bumps are applied selectively within the altitude-temperature envelope to provide additional power where it is most needed.

Table 6-1. GE90 thrust bumps

Engine Model	Thrust (lb)	Description
GE90-110B1L	110,100	Baseline model
GE90-110B1L1	110,100	Thrust-bump providing additional thrust at selected low-altitude & hot-day conditions
GE90-110B1L2	110,100	Thrust-bump providing additional thrust at selected high-altitude & hot-day conditions
GE90-115B1L	115,300	Baseline model
GE90-115B1L1	115,300	Thrust-bump providing additional thrust at selected low-altitude & hot-day conditions
GE90-115B1L2	115,300	Thrust-bump providing additional thrust at selected high-altitude & hot-day conditions

Source: GE90 "Type Certificate Data Sheet (TCDS)" [5]

For example, GE90 engines used on Boeing 777-300ER and 777-200LR models feature thrust bump options tailored to specific environmental challenges. The GE90-110B1L1 variant is designed for low-altitude, high-temperature operations, while the GE90-110B1L2 variant delivers additional thrust for high-altitude, hot-day environments. These enhancements ensure the aircraft can achieve necessary thrust during takeoff and climb, even under conditions where reduced air density compromises engine performance. The benefits of these thrust bumps include:

- **Enhanced Operational Versatility**: Thrust bumps enable aircraft to carry greater payloads and maintain safety margins during critical flight phases.
- **Adaptability in Extreme Conditions**: Airlines operating in regions with challenging environmental conditions benefit from added flexibility to meet diverse operational demands.

Thrust bumps are not universally applicable and require careful evaluation of operational factors such as runway length, weather conditions, and aircraft weight. A comprehensive assessment is essential to ensure thrust bump usage meets specific performance requirements while maintaining safety and efficiency.

By augmenting engine thrust in demanding environments, thrust bumps provide a valuable tool for enhancing aircraft performance and expanding operational capabilities.

EXAMPLE 6-2. GE90-110B1 Engine Model Selection for 777 Freighter Operators in Dubai, UAE and Addis Ababa, Ethiopia

Two airlines operating Boeing 777 Freighters illustrate the importance of selecting the appropriate GE90 engine variant to address specific environmental conditions:

Dubai-Based Operator: Operating from Dubai International Airport (DXB), located at a low altitude (62 feet/19 meters) but characterized by extreme summer temperatures averaging 41°C (106°F) and often exceeding 45°C (113°F).

- **Recommended Engine Model: GE90-110B1L1**: This variant is optimized for low-altitude, high-temperature environments. It provides the additional thrust required to counteract reduced air density caused by extreme heat, ensuring safe and efficient takeoff performance during peak summer conditions.

Addis Ababa-Based Operator: Operating from Addis Ababa Bole International Airport (ADD), situated at a high altitude of 7,657 feet (2,334 meters) and subject to both moderately hot temperatures (summer averages 23°C/73°F) and high-altitude conditions. The combination of reduced air density due to elevation and moderately high temperatures compounds the challenges to engine thrust and lift.

- **Recommended Engine Model: GE90-110B1L2:** Designed for high-altitude operations, this variant delivers increased thrust to overcome the reduced air density typical of elevated airports. Its capability to perform reliably under the dual conditions of moderate heat and high altitude ensures the aircraft achieves necessary takeoff power safely and effectively.

Summary

Selecting the appropriate engine variant is critical for optimizing aircraft performance in diverse environmental conditions. For low-altitude, high-temperature operations in Dubai, the **GE90-110B1L1** provides the necessary thrust, while for high-altitude and moderately hot conditions in Addis Ababa, the **GE90-110B1L2** ensures safe and reliable performance.

Low Wing Loading Aircraft

Minor family variants, such as the Airbus A319CEO/NEO, A330-200, Boeing 737-700/MAX7, and 787-8, are characterized by having lower wing loading, a key advantage in demanding environments such as hot and high airports. Wing loading, a key performance measure, influences an aircraft's takeoff, climb, and landing capabilities under challenging conditions. It is calculated as the ratio of an aircraft's weight to its wing area and is expressed in pounds per square foot:

$$\text{Wing Loading} = \text{Aircraft Weight} / \text{Wing Area} \quad (\text{Eq. 6-1})$$

Where:

- **Aircraft Weight:** Typically represented by the maximum takeoff weight (MTOW) for performance evaluations.
- **Wing Area**: The total surface area of the aircraft's wings.

For instance, the Airbus A319CEO, with an MTOW of 166,500 lbs. and a wing area of 1,330 ft^2, has a wing loading of:

$$\text{Wing Loading} = 166{,}500 \text{ lbs.} / 1{,}330 \text{ ft}^2 \approx 125.2 \text{ lbs./ft}^2$$

This lower wing loading enables the A319CEO to achieve lift at lower speeds, making it well-suited for high-altitude airports such as Bogotá (El Dorado, 8,360 ft) or La Paz (El Alto, 13,325 ft), where thin air requires higher takeoff speeds and longer runways.

In comparison, the Airbus A320CEO, with an MTOW of 172,000 lbs. and the same wing area, has a wing loading of:

$$\text{Wing Loading} = 172{,}000 \text{ lbs.} / 1{,}330 \text{ ft}^2 \approx 129.3 \text{ lbs./ft}^2$$

The higher wing loading of the A320CEO necessitates longer takeoff rolls and higher speeds to achieve sufficient lift, making the A319CEO, with its lower wing loading, better suited for operations in hot and high conditions.

Aircraft like the A319CEO, 737-700, and 787-8 leverage their lower wing loading and larger wing area to generate lift more efficiently, particularly in high-density altitude scenarios where reduced air density increases takeoff speeds and runway requirements. This design advantage enables reliable performance, including takeoff, climb, and landing, even in the most challenging airport environments.

EXAMPLE 6-3. Evaluating the Boeing 787 Family for Hot & High Operations

The Boeing 787 family consists of three variants—the 787-8, 787-9, and 787-10—that share the same wing design and area but differ in Maximum Takeoff Weights (MTOWs), impacting their suitability for challenging environments. In hot and high operations, where reduced air density demands greater lift and engine thrust during takeoff, the 787-8 stands out due to its lower wing loading.

As shown in **Table 6-2**, the wing loading for each variant is as follows:

- **787-8**: 143.50 lbs./ft²
- **787-9**: 163.20 lbs./ft²
- **787-10**: 164.00 lbs./ft²

This lower wing loading enables the 787-8 to generate more lift at lower speeds, resulting in shorter takeoff distances and improved climb performance. These attributes are particularly valuable for operations from high-altitude airports like **Bogotá (El Dorado, 8,360 ft)** and **Addis Ababa (Bole, 7,657 ft)**, where thin air requires aircraft to achieve higher speeds for takeoff.

The 787-8's ability to perform efficiently under low-density air conditions provides a clear operational advantage over its higher-weight siblings. Its shorter takeoff rolls and better climb performance make it well-suited for challenging environments, reducing the need for payload limitations or extended runway lengths. This capability enhances both operational flexibility and cost efficiency for routes originating from hot and high airports.

Table 6-2. 787 family wing loading comparison

Model	Wing Area (ft²)	MTOW (lbs.)	Wing Loading (lbs. / ft²)	Suitability
787-8	3,501	502,500	143.50	Market Opener, Thin Routes, Hot & High Operations
787-9	3,501	571,500	163.20	Network Growth & Expansion, More Seats & Cargo, More Range
787-10	3,501	574,000	164.00	Larger Demand Markets, Higher Profitability

Source: "787 Airplane Characteristics for Airport Planning", document with modifications by the author [6]

Industry Perspective 6-3. *737-700 Takeoff Enhancements*

*Operating in challenging environments requires strategic adaptations to optimize aircraft performance. The Boeing 737-700, a smaller variant within the 737NG family, is particularly well-suited for such conditions due to its lower wing loading and the option to employ engine thrust bumps. These features enable operators to increase the Takeoff Gross Weight (TOGW), making the 737-700 an effective choice for high-altitude airports like **Paro International Airport** in Bhutan.*

Situated at 7,300 feet elevation and surrounded by peaks reaching 18,000 feet, Paro International presents unique operational challenges. In February 2003, Boeing conducted flight demonstrations to evaluate how engine thrust bumps could enhance the 737-700's performance, specifically using the CFM56-7B26 engine.

Initially, the 737-700 was tested at the highest thrust rating certified for the model. The engine was then enhanced with the CFM56-7B26/B2 thrust bump, which increased thrust output by at least 2% over the standard rating. This additional thrust provided approximately 2,100 pounds (953 kg) of extra takeoff weight capacity—a critical improvement for operations at high-altitude airports, where runway length and surrounding terrain impose strict limits.

By leveraging the 737-700's the added thrust capability of the CFM56-7B26/B2 engine, operators can achieve greater takeoff weights, enhancing payload capacity and route flexibility in high-altitude environments.

Key Takeaways

1. **Field Length**: Runway length critically affects aircraft takeoff and landing performance. Shorter runways often necessitate Restricted Takeoff Weight (RTOW), limiting fuel capacity, payload, and range. Understanding these constraints is vital for operational planning and assessing aircraft suitability.

2. **Field Environment**: **Density altitude**, influenced by altitude, temperature, and humidity, directly impacts lift, engine performance, and required takeoff distance. Higher altitudes and warmer temperatures reduce air density, requiring adjustments to payload and fuel loads to ensure safe operations.

3. **Hot & High Airports**: Airports with both high altitudes and elevated temperatures, such as Mexico City and La Paz, pose operational challenges due to reduced air density. These conditions necessitate careful payload management, increased takeoff distances, and specialized performance adaptations.

4. **Short-Field Performance Packages**: These enhancements improve operations on short runways through features such as increased high-lift device deployment, enhanced spoiler deflection, and extended tail skids, enabling safer and more flexible operations.

5. **Thrust Bumps**: Engine thrust bumps boost maximum thrust output, compensating for reduced air density in hot and high environments. This allows aircraft to carry higher payloads and ensures reliable takeoff and climb performance.

6. **Wing Loading**: Aircraft with lower wing loading, such as the Boeing 737-700 and Airbus A319, generate lift more efficiently at lower speeds, reducing takeoff distances and improving performance in high-altitude or short-runway conditions.

7. **Humidity Effects**: High humidity decreases air density by reducing oxygen available for combustion, affecting engine performance. This

may necessitate longer takeoff distances and reduced payloads to maintain operational safety.

8. **Takeoff Performance Charts**: These charts provide critical metrics for determining runway length requirements based on aircraft weight, altitude, temperature, and humidity. They are essential tools for flight planning and ensuring operational safety.

9. **Impact of Elevation**: High-altitude airports require longer takeoff rolls and reduced takeoff weights due to lower air density, which affects both payload and range. Effective planning is essential to mitigate these challenges.

10. **Tire Speed Limits**: In hot and high environments, reduced air density results in higher ground speeds during takeoff, which can push tires to their performance limits. Managing tire speed constraints is essential for safe operations.

Case Study 6-1. Hot-and-High Operations

Airport Details:

- **Altitude:** Bogotá El Dorado International Airport (IATA: BOG, ICAO: SKBO) is situated at an elevation of approximately 2,548 meters (8,360 feet) above sea level.
- **Average Hot Day Temperatures:** The average high temperature in Bogotá typically ranges between 18°C to 20°C (64°F to 68°F), with occasional peaks up to 21°C to 22°C (70°F to 72°F) during the warmest months.
- **Runway Length:** The airport has two runways, each 3,800 meters (12,467 feet) long, which are designed to accommodate large aircraft under challenging "hot and high" conditions.

Bogotá El Dorado International Airport, located in Colombia, is a key hub for both passenger and cargo operations in South America. However, operating at high-altitude airports like Bogotá presents unique challenges for airlines, particularly regarding aircraft performance during takeoff. The reduced air density at higher altitudes affects engine performance, requiring higher thrust levels to achieve the necessary lift. This can lead to compromises in payload and range, impacting the overall operational efficiency of flights departing from Bogotá.

Questions:

1. How does the high altitude of Bogotá El Dorado International Airport impact air density, engine thrust, and lift, and how do the runway length and elevation interact to influence aircraft takeoff performance?

2. How does operating out of Bogotá's high altitude affect an aircraft's payload and range, particularly for long-haul routes?

3. What operational strategies could an airline employ to mitigate the challenges of operating from a high-altitude airport like Bogotá?

4. How might the combination of high altitude and high temperature at Bogotá affect the wear and tear on aircraft engines?

Case Study 6-2. Takeoff Performance Metrics

Figure 6-13. 787-8 takeoff charts

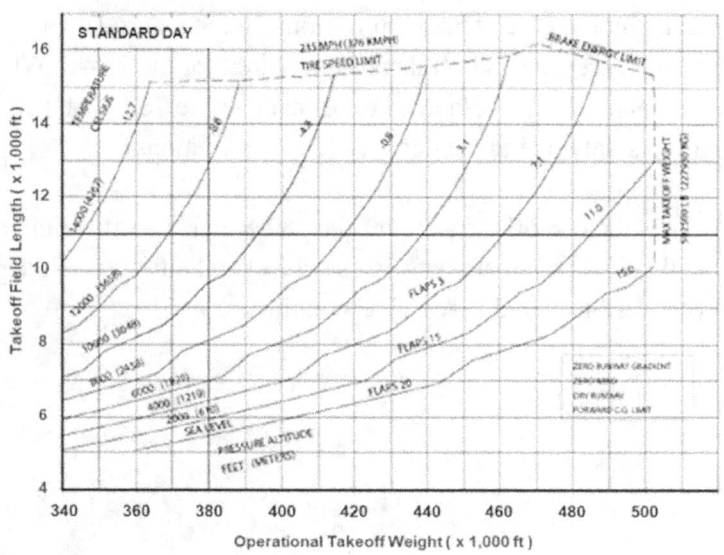

FAA/EASA Takeoff Runway Length Requirements - Standard Day, Dry Runway: Model 787-8 (Typical Engines)

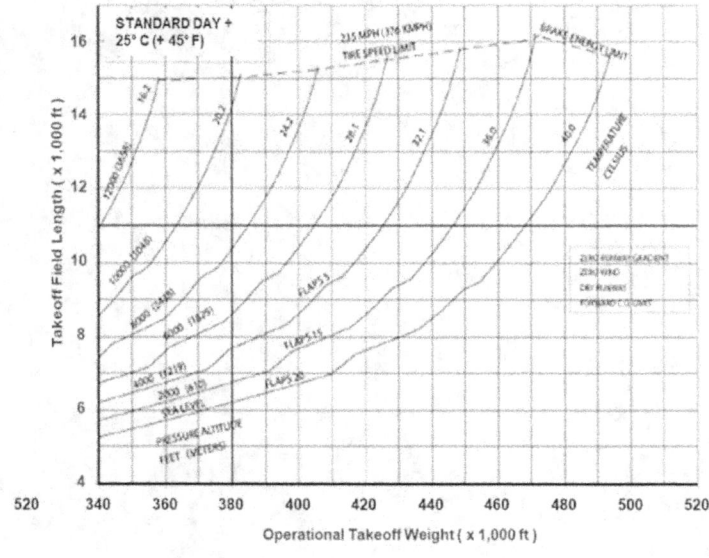

FAA/EASA Takeoff Runway Length Requirements - Standard Day + 45°F (STD + 25°C), Dry Runway: Model 787-8 (Typical Engines)

Source: "787 Airplane Characteristics for Airport Planning", document [6]

Questions:

Referring to the charts at sea level conditions, compute the takeoff runway length at ISA Standard Day conditions and ISA +25°C for a 460,000-pound Takeoff Weight (TOW).

1. Explain why increased temperature from ISA Standard Day to ISA +25°C increases the takeoff distance required for the 787-8. What adjustments, if any, would need to be made to the 787-8's takeoff weight to safely operate under ISA +25°C conditions?

2. How does the takeoff distance for the 787-8 at a takeoff weight of 420,000 pounds compare between sea level and 4,000 feet under both ISA Standard Day and ISA +25°C conditions?

References

[1] Boeing, "737 Airplane Characteristics for Airport Planning," Document D6-58325-7, Revision A, Mar. 2023. [Online]. Available: https://www .boeing.com/commercial/airports/plan-manuals

[2] Boeing, "777 Airplane Characteristics for Airport Planning," Document D6-58329-2, Revision F, Dec. 2022. [Online]. Available: https://www .boeing.com/commercial/airports/plan-manuals

[3] Airbus, "A330 Airplane Characteristics for Airport Planning," AC A330, Jul. 2023. [Online]. Available: https://aircraft.airbus.com/en /customer-care/fleet-wide-care/airport-operations-and-aircraft -characteristics/aircraft-characteristics

[4] Aircraft Commerce Magazine, "Hot & High Performance of Freighters," Issue 3, Jan./Feb. 1999. [Online]. Available: https://www .aircraft-commerce.com/

[5] Flight Global, "Short-field 737 Goes into Flight Test," Jan. 2006. [Online]. Available: https://www.flightglobal.com/short-field-737-goes -into-flight-test/64695.article

[6] EASA, "GE90 Type Certificate Data Sheet (TCDS)." [Online]. Available: https://www.easa.europa.eu/en/document-library

[7] Boeing, "787 Airplane Characteristics for Airport Planning," Document D6-58333, Revision O, Feb. 2023. [Online]. Available: https://www .boeing.com/commercial/airports/plan-manuals

Chapter 7

Performance Analysis

This Chapter is About:

7.1 Payload Range Diagrams

7.2 Expanded Payload Range Diagrams

7.3 Advanced Payload Range Considerations

7.4 Factors Influencing Payload Range Performance

7.5 Circle Charts

7.6 Seat-Range Diagrams

Having established a solid foundation in study flight rules—including operational guidelines, aircraft performance regulations, and airport-specific considerations such as runway length, altitude, and environmental factors—we now turn to a detailed exploration of key aircraft performance characteristics.

This chapter focuses on three essential analytical tools: Payload Range Charts, Circle Charts, and Seat-Range Diagrams. Each provides a structured, data-driven approach to evaluating and comparing aircraft performance across critical parameters, enabling precise and objective assessments.

1. **Payload Range Charts**: These charts depict the relationship between an aircraft's payload capacity and its achievable range under no-wind conditions. They are essential for understanding

how different aircraft balance payload and range, offering valuable insights into performance under various operational constraints.

2. **Circle Charts**: Incorporating average monthly cruise wind speeds, Circle Charts provide a nuanced view of how wind conditions impact an aircraft's range and fuel efficiency. By factoring in wind effects, these charts allow a more realistic comparison of aircraft performance under real-world flight conditions.

3. **Seat-Range Diagrams**: These diagrams compare seating capacity with range capabilities, typically based on a standard seating configuration. While they offer a high-level perspective on how seating arrangements influence range, it is important to consider airline-specific customizations, such as unique seating layouts or added amenities, which can affect range and should be included in comparative analyses.

With accompanying visual diagrams, this chapter provides a comprehensive framework for analyzing and comparing aircraft performance across a variety of conditions. By mastering these tools, you will gain critical insights into the comparative dynamics of aircraft performance—an essential component of effective aircraft benchmarking.

7.1 Payload Range Diagram

The Payload Range Diagram is a core tool for evaluating and comparing aircraft performance. It graphically represents the relationship between an aircraft's payload capacity—comprising passengers, baggage, and cargo—and its range, defined as the maximum distance the aircraft can travel. By visualizing this relationship, the diagram highlights an aircraft's operational limits, enabling clear comparisons of how different models balance payload and range under varying conditions.

These diagrams are indispensable for understanding performance trade-offs. They reveal how design features, fuel efficiency, and weight constraints influence an aircraft's ability to carry payload over specific distances. Advanced Payload Range Diagrams extend this analysis by incorporating factors like fuel consumption and aerodynamic efficiency, offering deeper insights often used in educational and research contexts.

Practical applications include determining the maximum payload an aircraft can carry over a specific route or identifying the farthest range achievable with a given payload. These scenarios help in comparing aircraft models objectively, showcasing their strengths and limitations in similar operational settings.

By mastering the use of Payload Range Diagrams, you will acquire a foundational skill for aircraft performance analysis. This tool is essential for evaluating operational capabilities, optimizing route planning, and conducting meaningful comparisons across different aircraft models.

Factors Influencing the Payload Range

The Payload Range Diagram is a fundamental tool for understanding the relationship between an aircraft's payload capacity and its range. Frequently included in aircraft performance documentation, this diagram highlights key factors that influence operational limits, including:

- **Aerodynamic Design:** Features like optimized wing shapes, fuselage contouring, and high-lift devices (e.g., winglets, slats) improve efficiency by reducing drag. These enhancements enable longer flights on the same fuel load or allow increased payload for a given range—critical for long-haul operations.
- **Structural Limitations:** Weight constraints such as Maximum Takeoff Weight (MTOW), Maximum Zero Fuel Weight (MZFW), and Maximum Landing Weight (MLW) define the diagram's boundaries. For instance:
  » MZFW indicates the maximum payload without fuel.
  » MTOW defines the maximum allowable weight for takeoff, determining the balance of payload and fuel.
- **Engine Technology:** Engine efficiency and thrust capacity play a vital role. Advances like high bypass ratios, geared turbofans, and improved thermal efficiency enable increased range and payload flexibility while reducing fuel consumption.
- **Payload and Fuel Trade-offs:** The diagram visually depicts the trade-off between payload and fuel. For longer missions, more fuel reduces payload, while shorter missions allow maximum payload with reduced fuel loads. This balance is central to optimizing performance for specific routes.

Elements of the Payload Range Diagram

Figure 7-1 illustrates a conventional payload range diagram. The outer boundary of the diagram is shaped by **structural limits**, defining the maximum payload at various ranges and the inherent trade-offs between payload and fuel. The interior of the diagram reflects the aircraft's performance capabilities as influenced by aerodynamic design, engine efficiency, and mission-specific requirements.

Figure 7-1. Payload range diagram

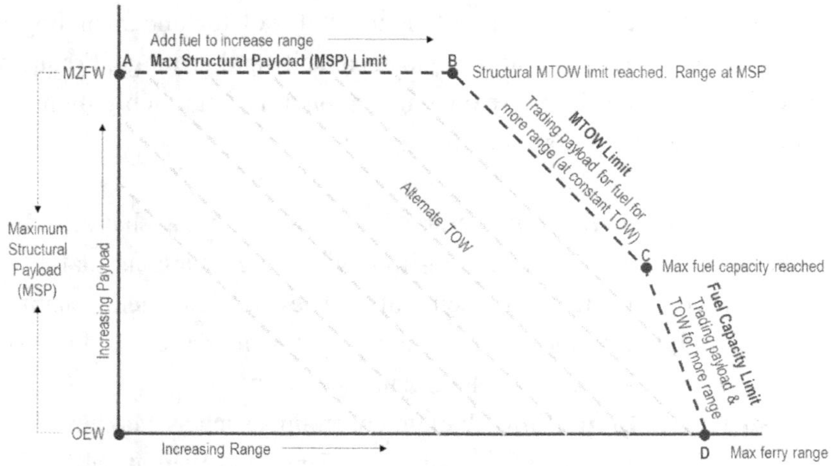

Source: Author's analysis

The diagram highlights the operational trade-offs and boundaries defined by payload and range. The key elements include:

- **Point A:** The aircraft's Maximum Zero Fuel Weight (MZFW)—the maximum payload weight excluding fuel. For passenger aircraft, this includes passengers and baggage; for freighters, it represents cargo.
- **Segment A to B:** Shows the addition of fuel while carrying maximum payload, constrained by MZFW. This represents the range achievable with full payload.

- **Point B**: At MTOW, the aircraft achieves maximum range with full payload. Further range extension requires reducing payload to accommodate additional fuel.
- **Segment B to C**: Illustrates the trade-off as payload decreases, enabling increased fuel and extended range.
- **Point C:** At full fuel capacity, the aircraft carries the maximum fuel load allowable while retaining a substantial payload. This configuration is structurally optimized but may limit economic efficiency due to payload restrictions.
- **Segment C to D**: Represents further range extension achievable only by significantly lowering payload, a scenario typically applied to missions requiring maximum range without substantial payload. The aircraft is constrained by Maximum Fuel Capacity (MFC) in this phase.
- **Point D:** Indicates maximum ferry range with no payload, where the aircraft operates at Operator's Empty Weight (OEW).

Inside the Diagram Boundary: The area within the diagram represents feasible Payload-Range combinations. Contour lines parallel to the MTOW boundary indicate alternative authorized MTOWs. Selecting a lower MTOW affects both payload and range and can be tailored for specific operational needs or restrictions.

Based on data from the Boeing 787-9 *Airplane Characteristics for Airport Planning (ACAP)* document, **Figure 7-2** illustrates the aircraft's Payload Range capabilities. This diagram is instrumental for analyzing key weight metrics at Points A, B, C, and D, providing a detailed understanding of payload capacity and range under various operational scenarios.

Figure 7-2. 787-9 payload range diagram

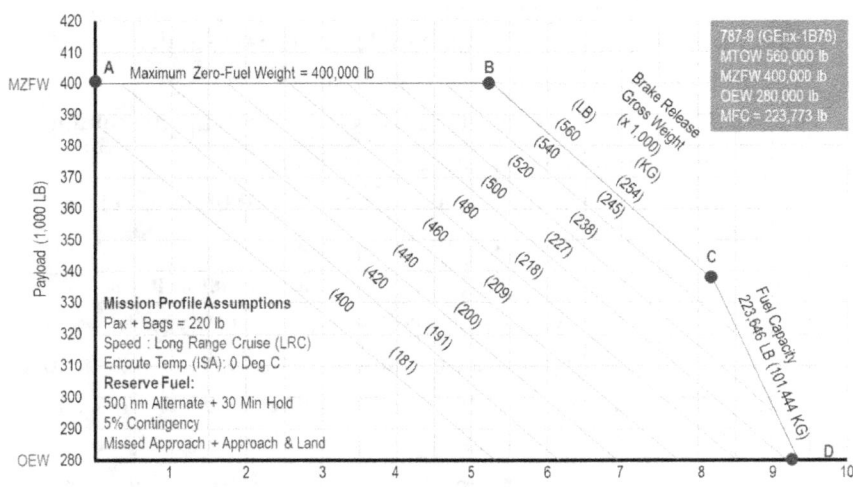

Source:"787 Airplane Characteristics for Airport Planning" document, with
modifications by the author [1]

Points on the Payload Range Diagram:

- **Point A (Maximum Zero Fuel Weight – MZFW):** At the Maximum
  Zero Fuel Weight (MZFW) of 400,000 lbs., the Boeing 787-9
  achieves its Maximum Structural Payload (MSP), calculated as:

$$MSP = MZFW - OEW = 400,000 \text{ lbs.} - 280,000 \text{ lbs.} = 120,000 \text{ lbs.}$$

  This represents the maximum payload the aircraft can carry
  without fuel. Point A provides a baseline for evaluating payload
  capacity in zero-fuel conditions, emphasizing the aircraft's
  operational flexibility for shorter missions or cargo-heavy routes.

- **Point B (Maximum Takeoff Weight):** At this point, the aircraft
  operates at its Maximum Takeoff Weight (MTOW) of 560,000 lbs.,
  carrying the same payload as at Point A (120,000 lbs.) but with
  additional fuel to reach MTOW. The fuel load is:

$$\text{Fuel Load} = MTOW - MZFW = 560,000 \text{ lbs.} - 400,000 \text{ lbs.} = 160,000 \text{ lbs.}$$

This point represents the maximum range achievable with a full payload, under MTOW limitations, without requiring a reduction in payload. It illustrates the aircraft's capability to carry maximum payload and the largest possible fuel load, highlighting its performance at full capacity.

- **Point C (Maximum Fuel Capacity):** At Point C, the aircraft carries its Maximum Fuel Capacity (MFC) of 223,646 lbs., with a reduced payload to stay within MTOW. The remaining payload is:

Remaining Payload = MTOW – OEW – MFC = 560,000 lbs.
         – 280,000 lbs. – 223,646 lbs. = 56,354 lbs.

This point illustrates the trade-off between payload and fuel in payload-range performance. It demonstrates the aircraft's ability to operate long-haul routes with maximum fuel while accepting a reduced payload to stay within structural weight limits.

- **Point D (Operating Empty Weight):** At this point, the aircraft operates at its **Operating Empty Weight (OEW)** of 280,000 lbs., carrying only fuel and no payload. The total weight is:

Total Weight = OEW + MFC = 280,000 lbs. + 223,646 lbs. = 503,646 lbs.

This configuration achieves the maximum ferry range, suitable for delivery flights or repositioning operations where payload is unnecessary.

The diagram illustrates key considerations for balancing payload, fuel capacity, and range, highlighting trade-offs, operational flexibility, and cost efficiency to support optimized decision-making for various mission profiles.

- **Trade-Off Analysis**: Points B and C highlight the trade-offs between maximizing payload (for shorter routes) and prioritizing fuel capacity (for extended-range missions).
- **Operational Flexibility**: Understanding these points allows airlines to optimize the aircraft for specific mission profiles, balancing fuel, payload, and range to meet route demands efficiently.
- **Fuel Efficiency and Costs**: The interplay of payload and fuel at different points directly affects fuel consumption and operational costs, guiding informed decision-making for fleet optimization.

By leveraging these insights, operators can assess the 787-9's suitability for specific routes, ensuring efficient and effective performance across diverse operational conditions.

Mission Profile Assumptions

When aircraft manufacturers present performance data, they embed **Mission Profile Assumptions** into Payload Range diagrams to standardize the analysis of aircraft capabilities under typical operating conditions. These assumptions create a consistent framework, allowing for meaningful comparisons across aircraft models by normalizing performance-influencing factors. Key assumptions include:

- **Temperature Assumptions**: Manufacturers commonly use the **International Standard Atmosphere (ISA)** as the baseline, which defines standard temperature, pressure, and air density at various altitudes. Adjustments, such as **ISA + 10°C**, simulate operations in warmer climates or more challenging conditions, impacting engine performance and fuel consumption. These adjustments provide a realistic depiction of aircraft range and payload capabilities under diverse thermal conditions.
- **Cruise Speed**: The **Long-Range Cruise (LRC)** speed is typically assumed for most Payload Range calculations. LRC represents the optimal balance between fuel efficiency and travel time, ensuring the diagrams realistically portray performance over long-haul flights while accounting for operational efficiency.
- **Reserve Fuel Policies**: To align with regulatory safety standards, Payload Range diagrams incorporate reserve fuel requirements, which typically include:
  - » **Contingency Fuel**: Set at 5% of trip fuel to cover unforeseen delays or deviations.
  - » **Alternate/Diversion Fuel**: Ensures the aircraft can divert safely to an alternate airport if necessary.
  - » **Missed Approach Fuel**: Accounts for fuel needed during a go-around in case of a missed approach.
  - » **Approach and Landing Fuel**: Covers fuel for descent, approach, and landing phases.

Standardizing these assumptions removes variability from environmental or operational factors, ensuring that Payload Range diagrams accurately represent an aircraft's performance and allow for fair comparisons between models.

Understanding the role of these Mission Profile Assumptions is important for accurately interpreting Payload Range diagrams. For a deeper dive into these principles, refer to **Chapter 5: Study Flight Rules**, which explores their implications for operational planning and fuel management.

Deconstructing the Payload Range Diagram

Figure 7-3 presents the Boeing 787-9's Payload Range diagram, which illustrates the balance between payload and range. The Y-axis represents the Zero Fuel Weight (ZFW) — the combined weight of the Operating Empty Weight (OEW) and payload —while the X-axis represents the achievable range at varying payload levels.

Let us walk through two cases to interpret this diagram effectively:

Figure 7-3. Deconstructing the payload range diagram

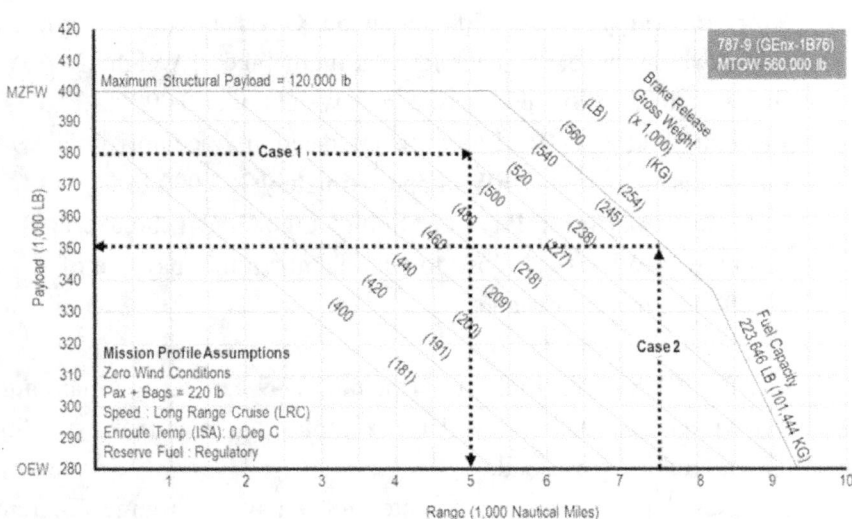

Source: "787 Airplane Characteristics for Airport Planning" document, with modifications by the author [1]

Case 1: Determining Maximum Range with 100,000 lbs. Payload at 520,000 lbs. TOW

1. **Calculate ZFW:** Add the payload (100,000 lbs.) to the OEW (280,000 lbs.) to get a ZFW of 380,000 lbs.
2. **Locate ZFW on Y-axis:** Find 380,000 lbs. on the Y-axis and draw a horizontal line until it meets the diagonal Brake Release Gross Weight line, corresponding to a TOW of approximately 520,000 lbs.
3. **Trace to X-axis for Range:** From this intersection, draw a vertical line down to the X-axis, which intersects at 5,000 nautical miles (nm), indicating the maximum range for this payload and TOW.

Result: The Boeing 787-9 can achieve a range of up to 5,000 nm with a payload of 100,000 lbs. at a TOW of 520,000 lbs. This case demonstrates the trade-off: increasing payload reduces the aircraft's maximum range.

Case 2: Determining Maximum Payload for a 7,500 nm Flight

1. **Start at Range:** Locate 7,500 nm on the X-axis and draw a vertical line upward to meet the diagonal Maximum Takeoff Weight (MTOW) line, which has a Brake Release Gross Weight of 560,000 lbs.
2. **Find ZFW at MTOW:** From this intersection, trace horizontally to the Y-axis, showing a ZFW of approximately 350,000 lbs.
3. **Calculate Maximum Payload:** Subtract the OEW (280,000 lbs.) from the ZFW (350,000 lbs.) to obtain a maximum payload of 70,000 lbs. for this distance.

Result: For a 7,500 nm flight, the Boeing 787-9 can carry a maximum payload of 70,000 lbs. at MTOW. This example illustrates that extending range requires reducing payload.

These cases demonstrate how to interpret a Payload Range diagram, showcasing the interplay between Zero Fuel Weight (ZFW), Operating Empty Weight (OEW), and payload. Key operational boundaries—including Maximum Takeoff Weight (MTOW) and Maximum Zero Fuel Weight (MZFW)—are visualized within the diagram, providing clear guidelines for balancing payload and range while ensuring structural integrity and compliance with safety limits.

Payload Range Diagram Limitations

The Payload Range diagram effectively illustrates the relationship between an aircraft's fuel load, payload, and range, providing a clear framework for comparing models. By visualizing the trade-offs between payload capacity and distance, it supports mission-specific evaluations and helps optimize aircraft performance. However, this tool has several limitations:

- **Omission of Key Operational Factors**: The diagram does not account for takeoff and landing performance, climb rates, or variations in fuel efficiency during different flight phases (e.g., takeoff, cruise, and descent). These factors, along with operational constraints such as runway length requirements and airport elevation, significantly influence an aircraft's real-world performance.
- **Exclusion of Wind Effects**: Payload Range diagrams assume zero-wind conditions, which simplifies comparisons but does not reflect real-world flight scenarios. Wind adjustments, such as the impact of headwinds or tailwinds, are better visualized through **Circle Charts**, which incorporate average monthly wind conditions for a more nuanced evaluation.
- **Potential Bias in Data Representation**: Manufacturers may highlight an aircraft's strengths by emphasizing idealized conditions. Comparisons based solely on Payload Range diagrams might not reflect a model's full operational capabilities or limitations.
- **Narrow Focus**: The diagram represents only one aspect of aircraft performance. Critical elements, such as runway requirements, climb gradients, and airport-specific constraints, require supplementary analysis for a comprehensive assessment.

To address these constraints, decision-makers should complement Payload Range diagrams with additional performance tools, including Circle Charts (for wind effects), takeoff performance charts (for runway requirements), and data on operational characteristics such as runway lengths, climb gradients, and airport-specific constraints. This comprehensive approach ensures a well-rounded evaluation, enabling better-informed aircraft selection tailored to specific operational demands.

Industry Perspective 7-1. *Underutilization of Maximum Performance Capabilities*

*Aircraft are designed with inherent flexibility to accommodate a wide range of missions, enabling airlines to operate efficiently under varying payload and range conditions. However, as illustrated in the graphs (**Figure 7-4**), real-world flight operations for the A320 and 737-800 reveal that no flights utilize the aircraft's full payload and range capabilities simultaneously.*

Figure 7-4. *Real-world operations vs. maximum performance limits*

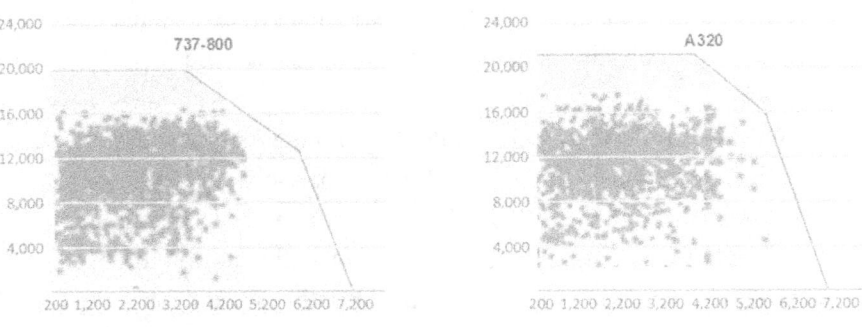

Source: Trends in Aircraft Efficiency and Design Parameters [2]

The observed "void region" in the graphs underscores a notable gap between an aircraft's theoretical performance envelope and how it is actually utilized in service. This discrepancy highlights the practical reality that airlines rarely operate near these extreme limits due to a combination of operational, economic, and logistical factors. Instead, aircraft are typically deployed within an optimal performance range that aligns with the specific needs of a given route or mission.

This underutilization emphasizes the importance of designing aircraft with the versatility to handle diverse operational scenarios while meeting airlines' economic and efficiency goals. Furthermore, it suggests that future advancements in aircraft technology—such as improved fuel efficiency, lighter materials, and refined aerodynamics—might prioritize optimizing performance for "typical mission profiles" rather than pushing the boundaries of maximum payload or range capabilities.

Critical Range Metrics

Payload Range charts are indispensable for evaluating an aircraft's operational capabilities, highlighting key performance boundaries that reflect its design strengths and limitations. These charts focus on three primary range scenarios: **Design Range** for passenger aircraft and **Maximum Payload Range** and **Volume-Limited Range** for freighter operations. Each scenario underscores the trade-offs between payload and range under specific operating conditions.

- **Design Range (Passenger Aircraft):** The Design Range represents the nominal maximum distance a passenger aircraft can achieve under standard conditions while carrying its nominal passenger load and baggage. Constrained by either Maximum Takeoff Weight (MTOW) or Maximum Fuel Capacity (MFC), this range reflects optimal fuel efficiency and serves as a benchmark for long-haul performance.
- **Maximum Payload Range (Freighter Aircraft):** This range indicates the farthest distance a freighter can operate while carrying its Maximum Structural Payload (MSP), constrained by Maximum Zero Fuel Weight (MZFW) and MTOW. It is critical for assessing revenue-generating potential on payload-intensive missions.
- **Volume-Limited Range (Freighter Aircraft):** This scenario applies when a freighter's cargo hold is fully occupied by low-density cargo (e.g., textiles, electronics) before reaching weight limits. The aircraft operates at a reduced weight, enabling an extended range relative to full-weight operations while maximizing cargo volume efficiency.

By analyzing these scenarios, Payload Range charts provide valuable insights into operational trade-offs between payload, fuel capacity, and range, assisting in evaluating an aircraft's suitability for specific routes and mission profiles.

EXAMPLE 7-1. Applying the Concepts of Design Range for the 787-9

Figure 7-5 illustrates how varying payload configurations impact the Boeing 787-9's range, showcasing trade-offs between passenger capacity and fuel load under MTOW limits. Two configurations are compared:

- **Mainline Operation Configuration:** In this standard setup, the 787-9 carries 290 passengers and achieves an operational range of approximately 7,900 nautical miles. The lighter payload allows for greater fuel capacity, optimizing the aircraft for long-haul routes where range is critical. This configuration balances fuel load and passenger payload, supporting efficient intercontinental operations.
- **High-Density Configuration:** With 438 passengers, the aircraft's range is reduced to approximately 6,000 nautical miles. The increased payload, including additional baggage and provisions, limits available fuel load under MTOW constraints. This configuration prioritizes passenger volume over range, making it suitable for high-density, shorter long-haul segments where maximizing seat capacity is more critical than extending range.

This comparison highlights how payload variations impact the 787-9's range and operational efficiency. Long-range configurations focus on balancing payload and fuel load, prioritizing extended operational distances, making them ideal for mainline carriers with long-haul routes. In contrast, high-density configurations maximize revenue potential by increasing seat count, though this setup reduces range and may compromise fuel efficiency and passenger comfort. These trade-offs illustrate the importance of tailoring aircraft configurations to align with specific route and market demands.

In summary, operators must carefully balance range, payload, and passenger experience. While higher capacity increases revenue potential, it also limits fuel load and range. A clear understanding of these dynamics is essential to align aircraft capabilities with mission-specific requirements.

Figure 7-5. Example design ranges

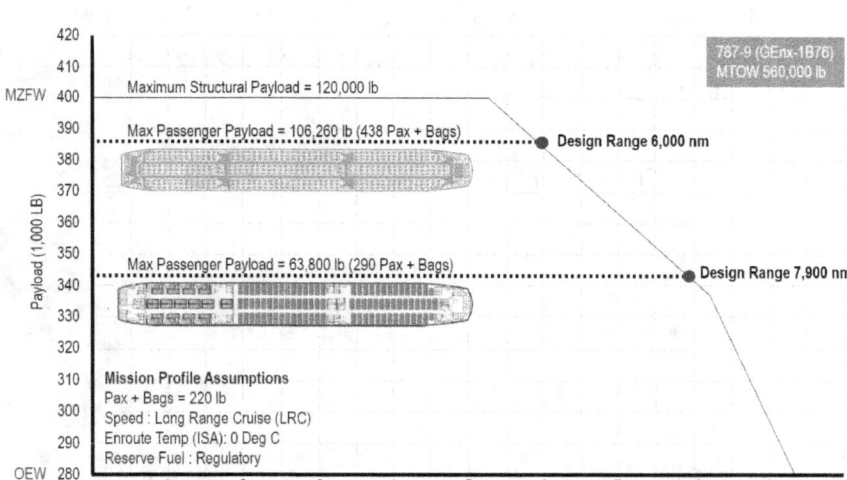

Source: Boeing. "787 Airplane Characteristics for Airport Planning" document, with modifications by the author [1]

EXAMPLE 7-2. Applying the Concepts of Maximum Payload Range and Volume-Limit Range for the 777-200F

Figure 7-6 illustrates the 777-200F's performance across various cargo densities and payload configurations, highlighting the relationship between payload density and operational range.

- **Low-Density E-Commerce Configuration:** At a cargo density of 6.5 lb/ft³, the 777F achieves a volume-limited range of 7,500 nautical miles, carrying a payload of 149,311 lbs. This configuration is ideal for lightweight, bulky items, such as e-commerce goods, where volume limits payload before weight. It maximizes range while accommodating low-density cargo efficiently.
- **General Freight Configuration:** With a cargo density of 8.5 lb/ft³, the 777F supports a payload of 195,253 lbs., reducing its range to 6,000 nautical miles. This setup balances payload capacity and range, making it suitable for denser cargo that requires moderate flight distances.

- **Maximum Structural Payload:** At its Maximum Structural Payload of 226,700 lbs., the 777F achieves a range of 4,880 nautical miles. This configuration prioritizes payload capacity over range, making it ideal for shorter routes where maximizing cargo weight is critical.

Figure 7-6. 777-200F maximum payload and volume-limit range

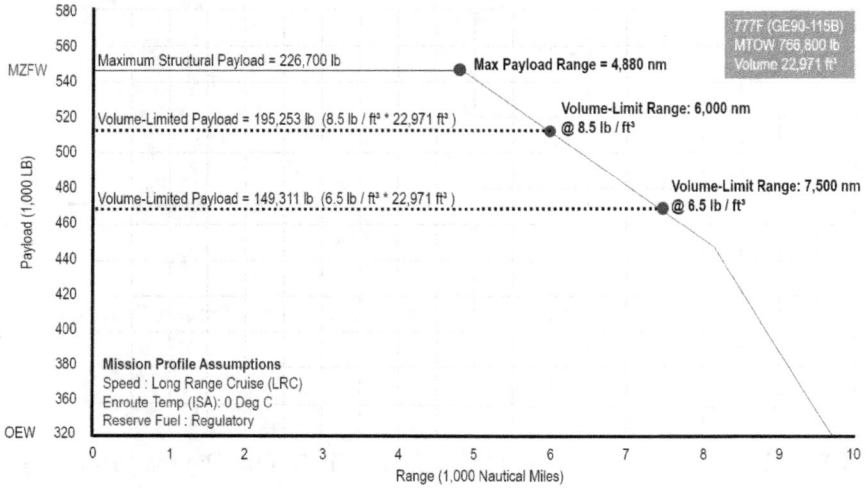

Source: Boeing. "777 Airplane Characteristics for Airport Planning" document, with modifications by the author [3]

Key insights reveal the operational trade-offs between payload and range, driven by cargo characteristics and aircraft limitations. In volume-limited operations, lightweight, low-density cargo enables extended ranges, as the aircraft reaches its volumetric capacity before weight limits are exceeded. Conversely, weight-limited operations involve high-density cargo that maximizes payload weight but reduces range due to Maximum Takeoff Weight (MTOW) constraints. Operating at maximum structural payload further shortens range, making it suitable for missions prioritizing weight over distance. These dynamics highlight the need to tailor operations to cargo type and mission requirements to optimize performance and efficiency.

For the 777-200F, understanding these trade-offs is essential to optimizing deployment across varied mission profiles. On long-haul routes, volume-limited operations are ideal for lightweight, high-volume goods like e-commerce shipments, maximizing range without exceeding structural limits. For shorter routes, weight-limited configurations allow the freighter to carry its full structural payload, prioritizing payload weight for higher revenue potential. Packing density also plays a vital role in fuel efficiency; higher cargo densities increase fuel burn, affecting operating costs. Balancing these factors is essential for cost-effective fleet utilization and aligning operations with logistical objectives.

The 777-200F's design is optimized for cargo transport, contrasting with the passenger-centric efficiency of the 787-9. While the 787-9 excels in maximizing passenger efficiency over long distances, the 777-200F adapts its payload capabilities to diverse mission profiles through flexibility in packing density and range.

By leveraging these trade-offs, operators can refine route planning and cargo-loading strategies to ensure the 777-200F achieves both operational and financial efficiency under varying conditions.

Payload Range Diagram and Comparative Analysis

The Payload Range Diagram is a powerful tool for comparing aircraft revenue-generating potential and operational flexibility, which are critical considerations in commercial aviation.

Using **payload** on the vertical axis instead of **Maximum Zero Fuel Weight (MZFW)** enhances comparative analysis by emphasizing the usable weight available for passengers, baggage, and cargo after accounting for fuel weight. While MZFW defines structural limits, focusing on payload provides a direct measure of revenue-generating capacity, particularly for long-haul operations where fuel load significantly affects available payload. The following summarizes the advantages of adopting a payload-centric approach for aircraft analysis:

- **Route Optimization:** For long-haul routes, where fuel efficiency and payload capacity must be balanced, comparing payload capacities helps identify the most profitable aircraft for high-revenue routes.

- **Fleet Management:** Payload-focused comparisons assist airlines in evaluating fleet models, identifying aircraft that maximize payload and revenue potential on specific routes.
- **Competitive Analysis:** Comparing payload-centered diagrams across manufacturers highlights designs that offer greater revenue capacity over similar ranges, aiding in selecting models aligned with revenue goals and operational needs.

EXAMPLE 7-3. Analysis for Payload & Range Efficiency
Figure 7-7 compares the payload and range capabilities of Aircraft A and Aircraft B, revealing critical differences in efficiency and flexibility:

- **Payload Efficiency at Design Range:** At the design range (~7,000 nm), Aircraft B carries an additional 10,000 kg (22,000 lbs.) of payload compared to Aircraft A. This makes Aircraft B more suited for cargo-heavy or high-demand passenger routes where payload capacity drives profitability.
- **Extended Operational Reach:** Beyond Aircraft A's design range, Aircraft B offers an additional 1,000 nautical miles of operational range while maintaining comparable payload capacity. This extends its versatility on long-haul routes requiring both extended range and competitive payload.

This comparison underscores how Aircraft B's higher payload efficiency and extended range provide greater operational flexibility. These attributes are particularly valuable for airlines seeking to optimize fleet performance across a mix of high-capacity and long-haul routes, enabling Aircraft B to address a broader range of mission profiles effectively.

Figure 7-7. Payload-range comparative analysis 1

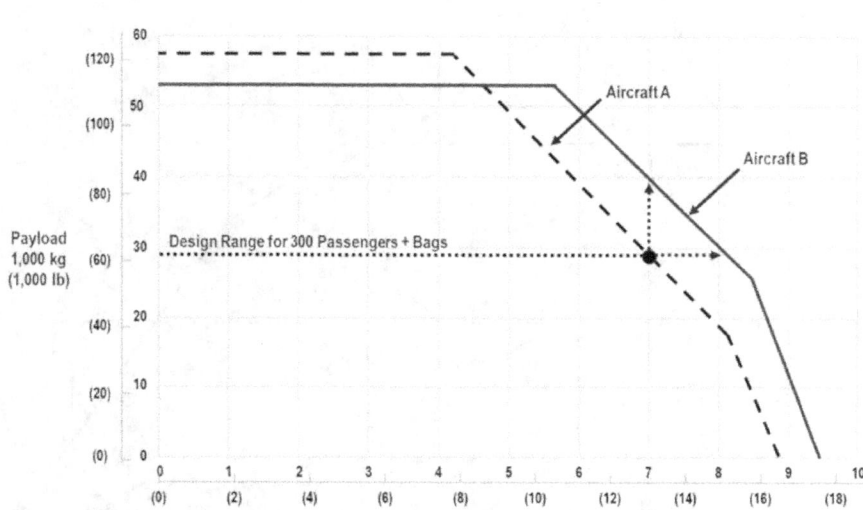

Source: *Author's analysis*

EXAMPLE 7-4. Analysis of Long-Range and Ultra Long-Range Aircraft

Figure 7-8 compares the operational profiles of Aircraft A and Aircraft B, emphasizing their suitability for different market demands based on payload and range.

- **Leisure Operations:** Aircraft B, configured for 400 passengers and a payload capacity of 40 metric tons over a range of 5,000 nautical miles, is optimized for high-density, long-range leisure routes. This setup suits markets prioritizing passenger volume, such as holiday destinations or charter operations, where range requirements are moderate compared to capacity demands.
- **Mainline Operations:** Aircraft A is tailored for ultra-long-range missions, carrying 20 metric tons of payload (~200 passengers and baggage) over 9,000 nautical miles. This configuration is ideal for premium, low-density routes requiring extended reach, such as intercontinental or business-focused travel, where range takes precedence over payload capacity.

Figure 7-8. Payload-range comparative analysis 2

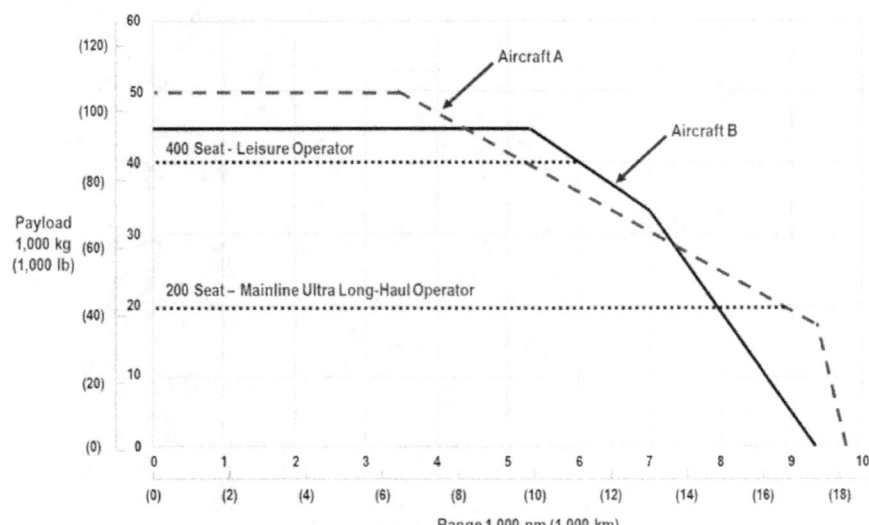

Source: Author's analysis

This analysis highlights the operational trade-offs between payload and range. Aircraft A's ultra-long-range capabilities serve premium mainline routes requiring maximum reach, while Aircraft B's high-capacity design supports leisure operations that prioritize passenger volume. Understanding these distinctions allows operators to align fleet strategies with specific market demands, optimizing route planning and operational efficiency.

EXAMPLE 7-5. Analysis for Cargo Operations

Figure 7-9 compares two freighters with a similar volume capacity of **16,000 cubic feet**, highlighting their specialization in different cargo types and operational needs.

Freighter A Performance Characteristics:

• **Payload Density:** Optimized for high-density cargo, capable of supporting densities exceeding 9 pounds per cubic foot.

- **Payload Capacity:** Higher maximum structural payload of approximately 70,000 kg (154,000 lbs.), making it ideal for industries requiring the transport of dense, compact goods (e.g., automotive parts, machinery).
- **Range:** Operates efficiently on short-to-medium haul routes up to 3,200 nautical miles, where payload capacity is prioritized over range.

Freighter B Performance Characteristics:

- **Payload Density:** Suited for lower-density cargo, accommodating densities between 6.5 and 7.5 pounds per cubic foot.
- **Payload Capacity:** Slightly lower maximum structural payload of around 65,000 kg (143,000 lbs.), offset by its extended range capabilities.
- **Range:** Achieves up to 4,750 nautical miles with cargo at 7.5 pounds per cubic foot and up to 5,500 nautical miles at 6.5 pounds per cubic foot, making it ideal for long-haul and global logistics, particularly for volume-intensive loads like e-commerce shipments or textiles.

Figure 7-9. Payload-range comparative analysis 3

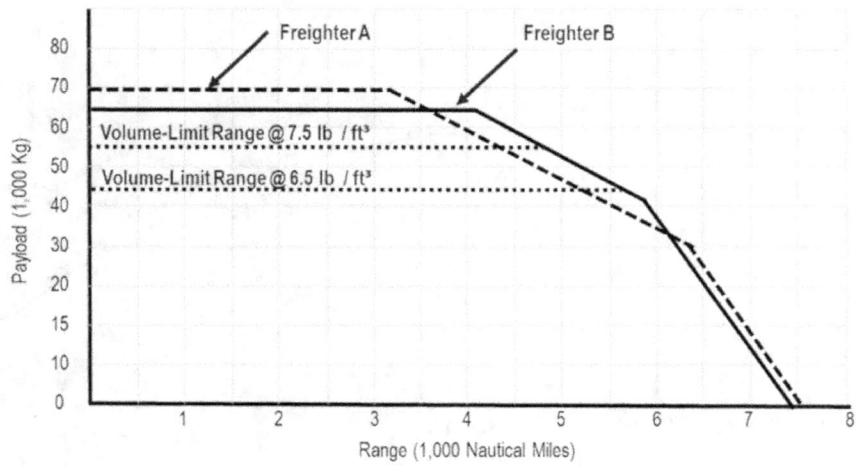

Source: Author's analysis

This comparison demonstrates Freighter A's suitability for high-density, shorter-range operations, while Freighter B excels in long-haul operations with lighter cargo at densities of 6.5 to 7.5 pounds per cubic foot. Freighter B's extended range at these densities highlights its operational efficiency for global routes, enabling operators to align fleet strategies with specific market demands.

7.2 Expanded Payload Range Diagram

An **Expanded Payload Range Diagram**, shown in **Figure 7-10**, provides a deeper understanding of how weight limitations influence an aircraft's range and efficiency. This diagram builds upon the basic Payload Range Diagram by detailing the interactions among payload, fuel, and range, offering a more comprehensive view of an aircraft's capabilities. Expanded diagrams are particularly valuable in engineering, research, and education for explaining the variables that shape performance.

Figure 7-10. Expanded payload range diagram

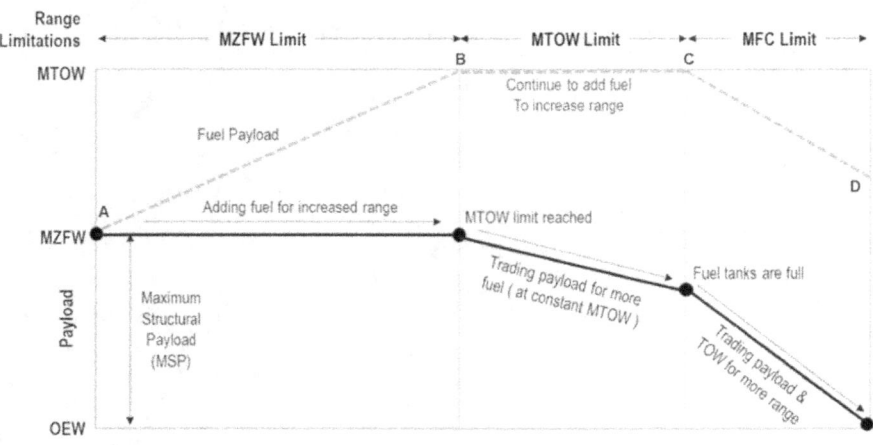

Source: Author's analysis

The expanded diagram incorporates key elements that illustrate the interplay between payload, fuel, and operational range, providing a clear framework for understanding aircraft performance. Key components include:

- **Weight Limitations:** Critical weight thresholds such as Maximum Takeoff Weight (MTOW), Maximum Zero Fuel Weight (MZFW), and Maximum Fuel Capacity (MFC) establish operational boundaries. These weights clarify how payload and fuel interact to define range limits. **Table 7-1** summarizes these key points and their associated weights.

Table 7-1: Key points & their associated weights

Point	Payload	Takeoff Weight	Fuel Weight
A	MSP (MZFW - OEW)	MZFW	Zero
B	MSP (MZFW - OEW)	MTOW	MTOW - MZFW
C	MTOW – OEW - MFC	MTOW	MFC
D	Zero	OEW + MFC	MFC

Source: Author's analysis

- **Fuel Representation:** Varying slopes on the diagram illustrate fuel loads at different stages. The vertical line from the Operating Empty Weight (OEW) to Point A represents the Maximum Structural Payload (MSP) at MZFW. Between Points A and B, the slope reflects additional fuel load extending range within MTOW constraints. The MFC limit identifies the farthest achievable range with full fuel capacity, albeit at the expense of payload to remain within MTOW.
- **Range Limitations:** The MTOW line indicates the maximum range achievable with full fuel and payload. The MFC limit marks the range with maximum fuel but reduced payload. Together, these lines reveal the relationship between range and payload under operational constraints.
- **Operational Envelope:** The diagram's operational envelope defines the performance boundaries between MZFW and MTOW. It indicates the maximum payload achievable at MZFW and the corresponding fuel load required to reach the maximum range at MFC.
- **Trade-offs:** The expanded diagram clearly highlights the trade-offs between payload and fuel. Between Points B and C, extending range

requires trading off payload for fuel while maintaining MTOW. The steeper slope from Point C to Point D reflects the condition where the aircraft carries full fuel capacity but no payload, representing the maximum range at MFC.

The expanded Payload Range Diagram primarily serves as an **academic tool**, offering a detailed framework for understanding the intricate trade-offs between payload, fuel, and range. By highlighting key performance boundaries, such as Maximum Zero Fuel Weight (MZFW), Maximum Takeoff Weight (MTOW), and Maximum Fuel Capacity (MFC), the diagram provides valuable insights into the theoretical limitations and capabilities of an aircraft. This visualization aids in educating engineers, researchers, and aviation professionals, enabling a deeper understanding of how operational constraints influence performance metrics.

EXAMPLE 7-6. Payload-Range Analysis of the Boeing 737-700W

Building upon the theoretical framework and the expanded Payload Range Diagram introduced earlier, the performance data and payload-range diagram of the Boeing 737-700W, shown in **Figure 7-11**, offer a practical illustration of how operational limitations such as Maximum Zero-Fuel Weight (MZFW), Maximum Takeoff Weight (MTOW), and Maximum Fuel Capacity (MFC) interact to shape an aircraft's payload and range capabilities.

Figure 7-11. Payload-Range Analysis of the Boeing 737-700W

Aircraft:	737-700W	Max TO Weight:	154,500 lbs.		Max Structural Payload:	36,610	lbs.
Interior:	126	Max Zero-Fuel Weight	154,500 lbs.		Pax + Bag Payload:	26,460	@ 210 lbs. each
Fuel Capacity (USG):	6,875	Op Empty Weight	85,090 lbs.		Revenue Cargo:	10,150	lbs.

Route	ESAD Range (nm)	Block Hours (hrs)	Total Fuel (lbs.)	Pax	Pax Payload (lbs.)	Cargo Payload (lbs.)	Total Payload (lbs.)	Zero-Fuel Weight (lbs)	Take-off Weight (lbs.)		Range Limit (nm)
1	200	0.928	9,825	126	26,460	10,150	36,610	121,700	131,295	▲	MZFW
2	857	2.375	17,102	126	26,460	10,150	36,610	121,700	138,571	MZFW Limit	MZFW
3	1,514	3.839	24,861	126	26,460	10,150	36,610	121,700	146,329	▼	MZFW
4	2,171	5.310	33,030	126	26,460	10,150	36,610	121,700	154,500	▲	MTOW
5	2,496	6.026	36,428	126	26,460	6,752	33,212	118,302	154,500	MTOW Limit	MTOW
6	2,820	6.747	39,668	126	26,460	3,512	29,972	115,062	154,500		MTOW
7	3,150	7.520	43,223	126	26,640	0	26,640	111,730	154,500	▼	MTOW
8	3,419	8.198	46,063	112	23,520	0	23,520	108,610	154,500	▲	MFC
9	3,582	8.577	46,063	82	17,220	0	17,220	102,310	148,263		MFC
10	3,745	8.975	46,063	54	11,340	0	11,340	96,430	142,455	MFC Limit	MFC
11	3,908	9.389	46,063	26	5,460	0	5,460	90,550	136,555		MFC
12	4,050	9.828	46,063	0	0	0	0	85,090	130,923	▼	MFC

Source. Author's analysis

Key Elements of the 737-700W Payload-Range Analysis

1. Weight Limitations and Range Implications

   The table and payload-range diagram in **Figure 7-11** highlight critical operational boundaries. For the 737-700W, the following weight limits dictate its performance:

   » **MZFW**: The maximum structural payload is capped at 36,610 lbs. For shorter routes, this limit governs performance, as the aircraft is capable of carrying its full payload without requiring significant fuel.

   » **MTOW**: At greater ranges, the payload must be reduced to accommodate additional fuel within the MTOW of 154,500 lbs. This balance reflects the trade-offs between payload and fuel weight for medium- to long-haul missions.

» **MFC**: For maximum range scenarios, the aircraft carries full fuel (46,063 lbs.) but sacrifices payload to stay within weight limits. At the design range of 3,150 nautical miles, the payload is reduced to 26,640 lbs.

2. Payload-Range Trade-offs

The payload-range diagram in **Figure 7-11** visually represents the interplay between payload and range.

» From 0 to approximately 2,171 nm, the payload remains constant at 36,610 lbs., as the MZFW limits take precedence.

» Beyond 2,171 nm, payload reductions become necessary to load additional fuel. This is evident in the slope of the line as the range increases between Points 4 and 7.

» At the design range of 3,150 nm, the payload reduces to 26,640 lbs., balancing the MTOW with fuel requirements.

» Beyond the design range, payload continues to decline as the aircraft approaches its maximum range (approximately 4,050 nm) with full fuel and no payload, demonstrating the limits of its operational envelope.

This example illustrates the nuanced trade-offs that airlines must navigate when planning operations. By analyzing weight limitations, fuel capacity, and payload configurations, operators can tailor the aircraft to maximize revenue and efficiency within its operational constraints. The payload-range diagram in **Figure 7-11** serves as a valuable tool for visualizing these interactions, offering a clear framework for understanding how weight and fuel impact range and performance.

Illustrating the Effects of Higher MTOW

The expanded Payload-Range Diagram in **Figure 7-12** illustrates how changes in Maximum Design Takeoff Weight (MTOW) influence an aircraft's performance. By increasing the MTOW (as shown by MTOW 2), the aircraft gains greater operational flexibility, allowing it to carry additional payload or extend its range.

Figure 7-12. Visualizing the effects of higher MTOW

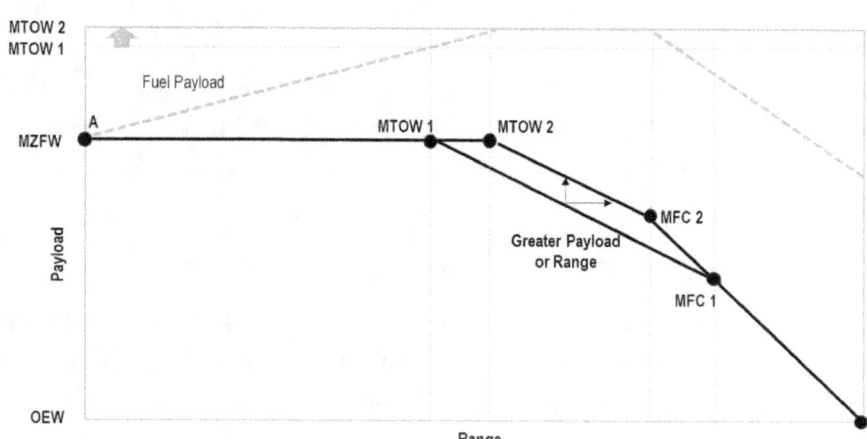

Source: Author's analysis

Higher Maximum Takeoff Weight (MTOW) introduces several performance enhancements, allowing aircraft to meet diverse operational requirements with increased flexibility. Key Features of Higher MTOW include:

- **Fuel and Range Considerations:** At MTOW 2, the aircraft can accommodate additional fuel within the new structural limits. However, extended range depends on whether the fuel tanks can store the extra fuel. Increasing MTOW without corresponding fuel tank capacity improvements does not inherently add range. If extra capacity exists, the additional MTOW allows airlines to trade payload for fuel, enhancing range on long-haul missions.
- **Payload Optimization:** Higher MTOW can be utilized to prioritize payload for shorter, high-demand routes, offering flexibility to match operational needs across varying flight lengths.

This enhanced flexibility broadens the aircraft's performance envelope, making it adaptable for diverse mission requirements. For example, airlines can optimize configurations for payload-heavy regional routes or fuel-intensive long-haul flights.

Trade-offs of Higher Maximum Takeoff Weight (MTOW) involve balancing operational advantages with associated costs. While an increased MTOW allows for greater payload and extended range, it also results in higher fuel consumption and greater structural stress, leading to elevated maintenance costs over time. Operators must carefully evaluate these trade-offs to optimize aircraft utilization, ensuring that the benefits of increased payload and range outweigh the additional operational expenses.

Illustrating the Effects of Maximum Fuel Capacity (MFC)

Figure 7-13 in the expanded Payload Range Diagram illustrates how changes in Maximum Fuel Capacity (MFC), often achieved by adding auxiliary fuel tanks, influence the trade-offs between payload and range. Increasing MFC enables the aircraft to carry more fuel, extending its range capabilities. However, this enhancement comes with notable trade-offs related to Operational Empty Weight (OEW) and payload capacity. The following are key insights from this diagram:

- **Impact on OEW and Payload:** Adding auxiliary fuel tanks increases OEW due to the structural weight of the tanks and associated systems. Since Maximum Zero Fuel Weight (MZFW) remains constant, any rise in OEW reduces the available Maximum Structural Payload (MSP). As depicted in **Figure 7-13**, OEW 2 reflects the inclusion of auxiliary tanks, resulting in a reduced payload at MZFW.
- **Extended Range with Trade-offs:** The increased MFC allows the aircraft to achieve extended range limits, as seen in the progression from Points C1 to C2 and D1 to D2. However, achieving this extended range requires a lighter payload to stay within operational weight limits.

Figure 7-13. Visualizing the effects of higher MFC

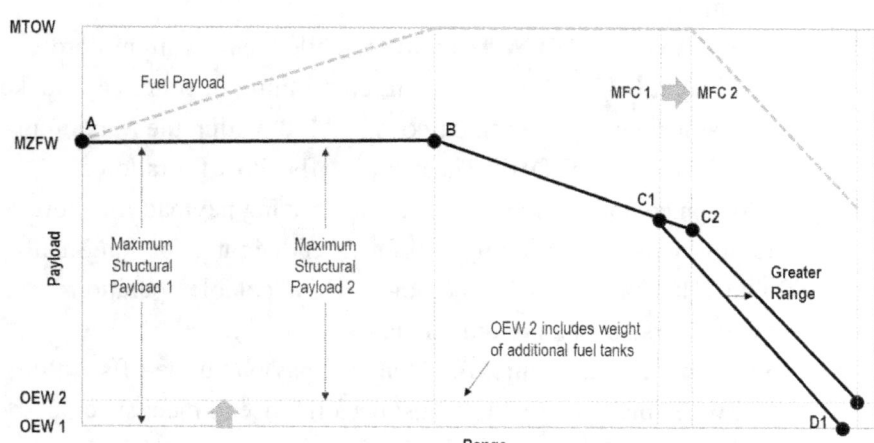

Source: Author's analysis

While additional fuel capacity enhances range for long-haul missions, it comes at the cost of reduced payload flexibility. This trade-off requires careful planning to align with mission profiles, balancing range requirements with payload limitations. The expanded Payload Range Diagram provides valuable insights into the interplay between fuel capacity and payload. While increased MFC allows for extended range, it also imposes constraints on payload, making it essential to understand these dynamics for optimizing aircraft performance across diverse operational scenarios.

7.3 Advanced Payload Range Considerations

This section explores advanced concepts that illuminate the complexities of payload-range dynamics, essential for optimizing and fully understanding aircraft performance. The following highlights key considerations:

- **Maximum Landing Weight (MLW) Limitations:** MLW restricts the aircraft's weight at the point of landing. For routes with high payload demands or potential diversions, exceeding MLW may necessitate payload reductions or, in rare cases, fuel jettisoning.

Understanding MLW constraints is critical for maintaining safety and efficiency, especially on missions with significant fuel burn en route.

- **Linear MTOW/MZFW Tradeoffs:** While the Maximum Zero Fuel Weight (MZFW) is a fixed structural limit, operators can make linear adjustments between payload and fuel within the Maximum Takeoff Weight (MTOW). These trade-offs allow for tailored performance optimization, such as maximizing payload for short-haul missions or prioritizing fuel for extended range on long-haul flights. This balance ensures efficient and adaptable operations across diverse mission requirements.

- **Dynamic Payload Tradeoffs:** Dynamic payload trade-offs within MTOW enable operators to adjust performance to meet specific mission needs. For instance, payload can be maximized for short-haul flights by reducing fuel loads, while range can be extended for long-haul missions by prioritizing fuel capacity over payload. This adaptability enhances operational flexibility across varied route profiles.

- **Fuel Volume-Limited Range:** In some scenarios, an aircraft's fuel tanks reach their maximum physical capacity before MTOW is achieved. This limitation prevents further range extension despite the structure's ability to carry additional weight. Fuel volume-limited range is particularly relevant for long-haul operations, where balancing fuel load and payload is vital for achieving mission-specific performance.

These advanced considerations offer valuable insights into how various factors and trade-offs shape an aircraft's payload-range capabilities. This deeper understanding supports precise aircraft benchmarking and optimization, enabling decision-makers to select aircraft that best meet specific operational requirements.

Maximum Landing Weight (MLW) Limitation

The **Maximum Landing Weight (MLW)** is a critical parameter in operational planning, defining the maximum certified weight at which an aircraft can land safely without compromising structural integrity. For freighters like the 747-400ERF, operational flexibility often hinges on managing trade-offs between payload, fuel capacity, and range. These constraints are shaped by two interrelated factors: linear MZFW/MTOW trade-offs and the payload break, a point where the MLW becomes the governing limitation.

The **payload break** occurs when the aircraft's payload capacity is limited by MLW rather than Maximum Takeoff Weight (MTOW). This concept is vital in scenarios where the aircraft operates at or near its Maximum Structural Payload (MSP), particularly on short-to-medium haul routes. As fuel burn during flight decreases the aircraft's weight, planning must ensure the aircraft's landing weight complies with MLW limits. Failure to account for this balance can lead to payload restrictions or inefficient fuel use, impacting operational and economic performance.

Both the MZFW/MTOW trade-off and the MLW constraint play essential roles in shaping an aircraft's payload-range performance, particularly for freighters operating at maximum payload. Understanding these interdependencies helps operators optimize route planning, payload distribution, and overall efficiency.

EXAMPLE 7-7. Maximum Landing Weight (MLW) Limitation Using the 747-400ERF

The payload-range diagram in **Figure 7-14** highlights the impact of MLW constraints for the **Basic** and **Optional** configurations of the 747-400ERF (Extended Range Freighter).

Figure 7-14. 747-400ERF MLW limitations

Weight Category	Basic	Option
Max Takeoff Weight (MTOW)	**412,770 kg** (910,000 lb)	**367,860 kg** (811,000 lb)
Max Zero-Fuel Weight (MZFW)	**277,140 kg** (611,000 lb)	**283,030 kg** (635,000 lb)
Max Landing Weight (MZFW)	**296,200 kg** (653,000 lb)	**302,090 kg** (666,000 lb)

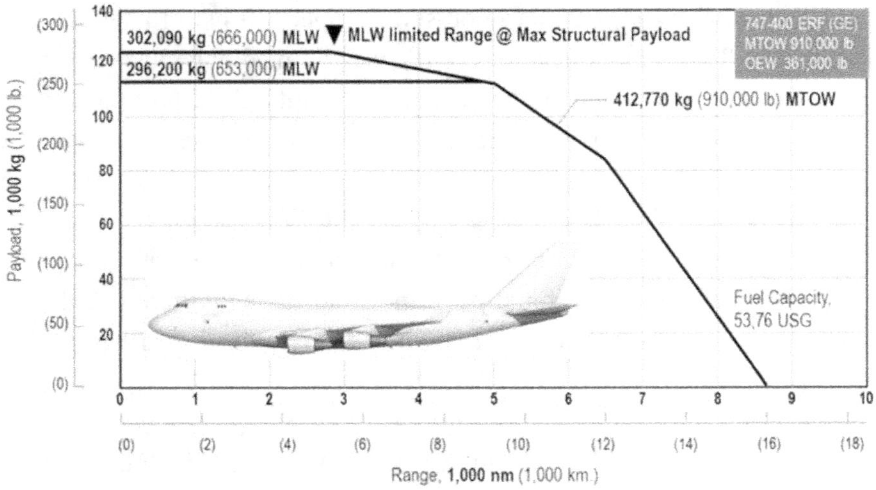

Source: Boeing. "747 Airplane Characteristics for Airport Planning" document, with modifications by the author [4]

1. **Basic MLW 296,200 kg (653,000 lb):** This configuration's lower MLW supports operations at maximum structural payload (MSP) up to the MTOW, particularly on medium-haul routes. It allows the aircraft to utilize its full structural payload capacity without encountering MLW constraints during landing, as sufficient fuel burn occurs during flight to ensure compliance with landing weight limits. At shorter ranges, this ensures that payload capacity can be maximized without compromising operational flexibility.
2. **Optional MLW 302,090 kg (666,000 lb):** This configuration's higher MLW caps the range at maximum structural payload (MSP) to approximately 2,825 nm. This is because adequate fuel must be burned during the flight to reduce the aircraft's landing weight below the MLW upon arrival. Beyond this range, operators must reduce payload to accommodate additional fuel required for longer

missions, as the increased MLW offers less flexibility for extended fuel loads at full payload capacity.

Key findings underscore the essential role of MLW in route and payload planning, particularly for freighters like the 747-400ERF operating at or near full payload. Effective fuel burn management is essential to ensure compliance with MLW, especially on routes where payload and range constraints intersect, safeguarding structural integrity while maintaining operational efficiency. Higher MLW options enhance operational flexibility, enabling freighters to support a broader range of route profiles and maximize payload capacity on shorter missions. These considerations are critical for optimizing freighter performance and efficiency.

Freighters are particularly susceptible to Main Landing Gear (MLG) limitations due to their frequent operation at Maximum Structural Payload (MSP) to maximize cargo revenue. Unlike passenger aircraft, where payload can vary based on passenger loads and cabin configurations, freighters typically aim to utilize their full structural payload capacity, especially on short-to-medium-haul routes.

Operating at MSP increases the likelihood of approaching or exceeding MLG load-bearing limits, particularly during taxiing, takeoff, and landing. This operational constraint often necessitates adjustments to payload or fuel distribution to ensure compliance with MLG limits while maintaining operational safety and efficiency.

Understanding the interaction between payload, MLW, and MLG limitations is critical for freighter operators. Exceeding MLG load limits not only risks structural damage but also compromises safety and efficiency. As a result, managing MLG constraints is a significant factor in freighter route planning and payload optimization.

Linear MTOW/MZFW Tradeoffs

The relationship between Maximum Takeoff Weight (MTOW) and Maximum Zero Fuel Weight (MZFW) is fundamental to balancing payload and fuel capacity within structural limits. The following outlines key definitions and considerations for understanding this trade-off:

- **MTOW:** The maximum certified weight an aircraft can carry during takeoff, including fuel, passengers, cargo, and other loads.

- **MZFW:** The maximum structural weight excluding usable fuel. This includes the aircraft's empty weight and payload (passengers and cargo).

Understanding the MTOW/MZFW trade-off enables operators to optimize payload and fuel capacity, particularly in freighter operations where route-specific adjustments are critical. This balance between payload and fuel load is key to maintaining operational flexibility across varying route profiles.

Higher MTOW enables increased fuel loads for extended range, while some designs reduce MZFW proportionally to stay within structural limits. Shorter routes prioritize payload by maximizing MZFW, whereas longer routes require payload reductions to accommodate additional fuel and achieve greater range within MTOW constraints.

The trade-off is illustrated by how payload increases at lower MTOW due to reduced fuel requirements, while higher MTOW enables more fuel but reduces payload capacity to remain within certified weight limits. Mastering this balance is essential for aligning aircraft performance with mission-specific requirements, ensuring efficiency across varying payload and range scenarios.

EXAMPLE 7-8: Linear MTOW/MZFW Trade-off Relationship Using the 747-400ERF

The payload-range diagram for the 747-400ERF, with an MTOW of 910,000 pounds, illustrates how payload and fuel load are balanced as range increases (see **Figure 7-15**).

Figure 7-15. 747-400ERF linear MTOW-MZFW tradeoff

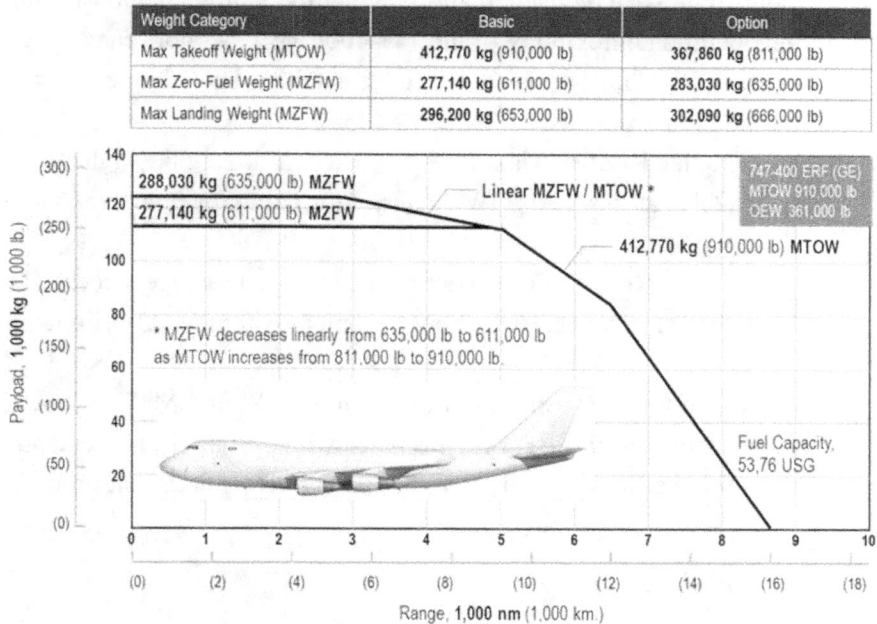

Weight Category	Basic	Option
Max Takeoff Weight (MTOW)	412,770 kg (910,000 lb)	367,860 kg (811,000 lb)
Max Zero-Fuel Weight (MZFW)	277,140 kg (611,000 lb)	283,030 kg (635,000 lb)
Max Landing Weight (MZFW)	296,200 kg (653,000 lb)	302,090 kg (666,000 lb)

Source: Boeing. "747 Airplane Characteristics for Airport Planning" document, with modifications by the author [4]

1. **At Maximum MZFW (635,000 pounds):** The aircraft achieves a range of approximately 2,825 nautical miles while carrying its full structural payload. This represents the upper limit of payload capacity without exceeding MZFW, as the fuel load required for this range is within MTOW limits. No further reduction in payload is necessary to meet this range.

2. **Beyond This Range:** To extend the aircraft's range beyond 2,825 nautical miles, additional fuel must be loaded. However, since the MTOW cannot be exceeded, the MZFW is reduced linearly as the MTOW increases from 811,000 pounds to 910,000 pounds. This reduction accommodates the added fuel while maintaining compliance with structural weight limits. For example, at the maximum MTOW of 910,000 pounds, the MZFW decreases to 611,000 pounds, enabling extended range but requiring a proportional reduction in payload.

3. **Dynamic Trade-Off:** This trade-off creates the linear descending trend observed in the payload-range diagram. As range increases, payload must be reduced to allow for additional fuel, demonstrating the operational flexibility of the 747-400ERF. Operators can strategically adjust payload and fuel capacities depending on mission requirements:

   » **Shorter Routes:** Maximize payload by utilizing the higher MZFW at lower MTOW values, prioritizing revenue-generating cargo.

   » **Longer Routes:** Prioritize fuel load to extend range, accepting necessary payload reductions to remain within MTOW limits.

By leveraging this linear trade-off between MZFW and MTOW, operators can align the 747-400ERF's performance with specific route demands, achieving optimal efficiency and flexibility across diverse mission profiles.

Dynamic Payload Tradeoffs

The **dynamic payload** system offers a flexible approach to managing payload and fuel capacity, surpassing the fixed ratios of the linear Maximum Takeoff Weight (MTOW) and Maximum Zero Fuel Weight (MZFW) trade-off.

In a **linear trade-off**, any increase in fuel load at MTOW requires a corresponding one-to-one decrease in payload, as determined by MZFW. While straightforward, this approach imposes rigid limits, potentially constraining operational adaptability in diverse scenarios.

The dynamic payload system, however, introduces greater flexibility by allowing variations in MZFW within a predefined range, all while maintaining MTOW constant. This adaptability enables operators to fine-tune the balance between payload and fuel based on specific mission needs, optimizing performance under a variety of conditions.

Such a system proves particularly advantageous for operations requiring variable configurations, such as adjusting for shorter flights with heavier payloads or extending range for long-haul missions. By offering refined control over payload and fuel distribution, adaptive payload trade-offs enhance operational efficiency and mission-specific performance.

EXAMPLE 7-9. Dynamic Payload Trade-off Relationship Using the A330-200F (Production Freighter)

The A330-200F freighter is derived from the A330-200 passenger variant and benefits from the **higher design weights** of the A330-300, providing enhanced payload and range capabilities. Specifically, the Maximum Zero-Fuel Weight (MZFW) was improved to increase payload capacity. The freighter can carry **up to 70 tonnes of payload over 3,200 nm**, meeting the requirements of the general cargo market. This combination of design enhancements and flexibility makes the A330-200F a versatile option for a wide range of operational needs.

The A330-200F illustrates the concept of adaptive payload through **three Weight Variants (WV)**, each tailored for specific missions (see **Figure 7-16**):

Figure 7-16. A330-200F dynamic payload tradeoff

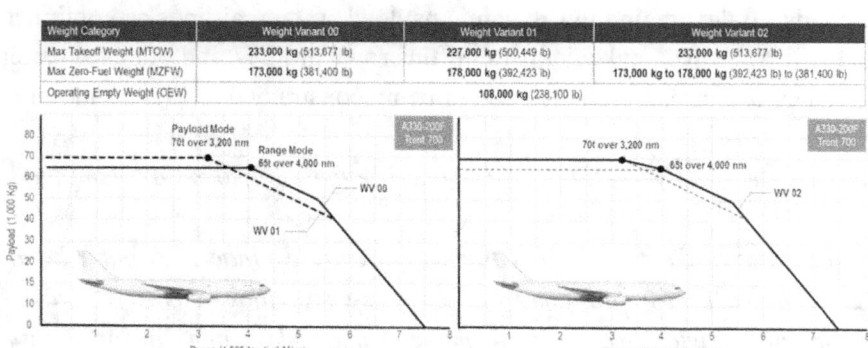

Source: Airbus. "A330 Airplane Characteristics for Airport Planning" document, with modifications by the author [5]

1. **WV00 – Range-Optimized Variant: MTOW:** 233,000 kg (513,677 lb), **MZFW:** 173,000 kg (381,400 lb)
   Purpose: Designed for long-range operations, this variant prioritizes maximizing fuel capacity to extend range while carrying a moderate payload.
2. **WV01 – Payload-Optimized Variant: MTOW:** 227,000 kg (500,449 lb), **MZFW:** 178,000 kg (392,423 lb)

Purpose: Ideal for short to medium-haul operations, this variant maximizes payload capacity at the expense of reduced fuel capacity and range.

3. **WV02 – Dynamic Payload Variant: MTOW:** 233,000 kg (513,677 lb), **MZFW:** Variable between 173,000 kg (381,400 lb) and 178,000 kg (392,423 lb)

   Purpose: Offers a **linear trade-off** between MZFW and MTOW, translating into a **variable structural payload** ranging from 65 to 70 tonnes. This mode enhances operational flexibility, allowing operators to adjust payload and range based on specific mission requirements. For example, payload capability increases by up to **2.5 tonnes** on routes between 3,200 and 4,000 nm.

With **Dynamic Mode (WV02)**, the A330-200F provides unmatched versatility, enabling operators to adapt payload and range to meet diverse market demands. By leveraging this dynamic payload system, airlines can optimize fleet utilization, respond quickly to shifting route profiles, and achieve greater efficiency in cargo operations without being constrained by rigid trade-offs.

Industry Perspective 7-2. Why MLW and Dynamic Payloads Are Omitted

Manufacturers like Boeing and Airbus typically exclude Maximum Landing Weight (MLW) limitations from payload-range diagrams to emphasize an aircraft's payload-range performance under Maximum Takeoff Weight (MTOW) and Maximum Zero Fuel Weight (MZFW) conditions. MLW constraints, tied to landing performance, depend on variables like fuel burn, route length, and environmental conditions, making them more suitable for operational planning than high-level comparisons.

Similarly, dynamic payload trade-offs, which allow operators to adjust payload and fuel within MTOW constraints, are rarely depicted. These trade-offs vary by mission, such as prioritizing fuel for long-haul routes or maximizing payload on shorter ones, adding complexity that could obscure the diagrams' focus on baseline capabilities.

Including MLW or adaptive trade-offs would shift the diagrams' purpose from marketing potential to highlighting operational constraints. By simplifying the visualization, manufacturers ensure these tools remain intuitive and effective for comparative analysis, while operational considerations like landing weight compliance and payload adjustments are handled through flight planning resources and manuals.

7.3.1 Fuel-Volume Limited

Fuel-volume limitation occurs when an aircraft's range is constrained by the physical capacity of its fuel tanks rather than its Maximum Takeoff Weight (MTOW). This limitation is particularly significant for long-haul operations, where the tanks are filled to capacity, preventing additional fuel from being carried to extend range, even if the aircraft remains below MTOW.

To address fuel-volume limitations on long-haul routes, manufacturers provide solutions like **Auxiliary Center Tanks (ACTs)**, which increase the aircraft's fuel capacity by utilizing available cargo space. By sacrificing some payload volume, ACTs enable extended range without exceeding the aircraft's structural weight limits. This trade-off highlights the critical need to balance payload and fuel to meet mission-specific requirements. Understanding when to prioritize fuel capacity over cargo volume ensures that operations remain both efficient and adaptable across various route profiles.

EXAMPLE 7-10. Fuel Volume Limitation Using the 757-200

The payload-range diagram for the 757-200, shown in **Figure 7-17**, illustrates how fuel-volume limitation impacts range when operating with a full passenger load of 200 passengers. Two configurations are compared:

Figure 7-17. 757-200 fuel volume limitation

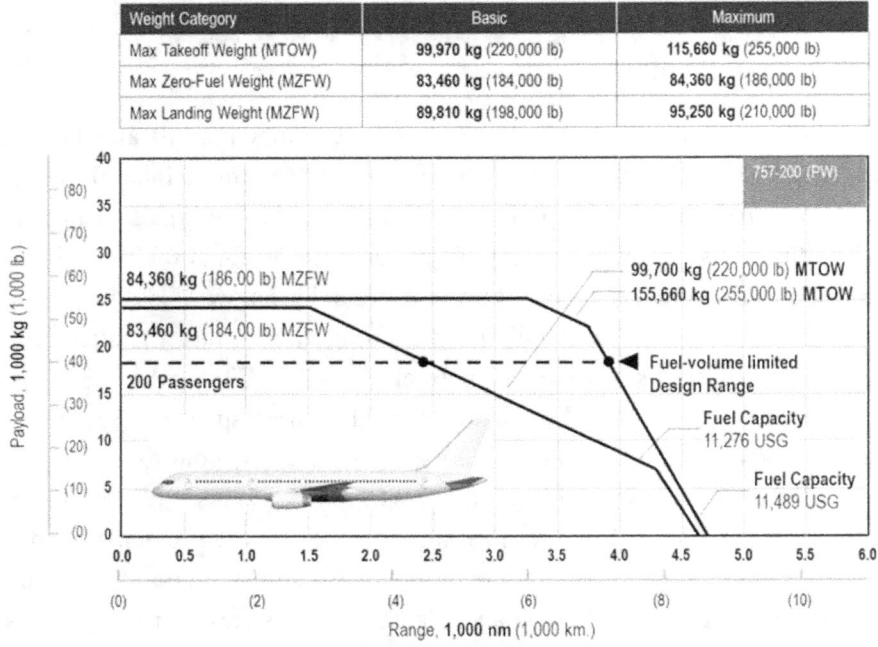

Weight Category	Basic	Maximum
Max Takeoff Weight (MTOW)	99,970 kg (220,000 lb)	115,660 kg (255,000 lb)
Max Zero-Fuel Weight (MZFW)	83,460 kg (184,000 lb)	84,360 kg (186,000 lb)
Max Landing Weight (MZFW)	89,810 kg (198,000 lb)	95,250 kg (210,000 lb)

Source: Boeing. "757 Airplane Characteristics for Airport Planning" document, with modifications by the author [6]

1. **Basic Configuration:** In the **Basic Configuration**, the aircraft's design range is constrained by the **MTOW** (99,970 kg / 220,000 lb), not by fuel volume. At this lower MTOW, the aircraft's range is limited by the balance between payload, fuel, and structural constraints, as the MTOW does not allow full utilization of both payload and fuel capacity simultaneously. The range is determined by how much fuel the aircraft can carry while staying within its MTOW.

2. **Maximum Configuration:** In the **Maximum Configuration**, the design range of **3,915 nautical miles** is constrained by the **Maximum Fuel Capacity (MFC)**. This range represents the farthest distance achievable with full fuel tanks and a full passenger load. Beyond this range, the aircraft is **fuel-volume limited**, as it cannot carry additional fuel to extend range due to tank capacity

limitations, even though the aircraft remains below its MTOW of **115,660 kg (255,000 lb).** Adjustments such as reducing passenger numbers or payload can improve range slightly by lowering fuel burn. However, the maximum achievable range is ultimately capped by the physical capacity of the fuel tanks.

By understanding fuel-volume limitations, operators can optimize payload and fuel distribution to balance efficiency and mission requirements. This knowledge is critical for managing long-haul operations effectively while adhering to the aircraft's design constraints.

7.4 Factors Influencing Payload-Range Performance

This section explores the primary factors influencing an aircraft's payload-range performance, categorized into three areas: **Aircraft Specifications**, **Aircraft Operations**, and **Environmental Conditions**. Understanding these factors is essential for effective benchmarking, as they directly affect operational efficiency and economic performance.

The following outlines key aspects of **Aircraft Specifications** that shape payload-range dynamics:

- **MTOW and MZFW Adjustments:** Changes to MTOW and MZFW affect payload capacity and range, determining how much cargo or how many passengers can be transported over specific distances.
- **OEW and Cabin Density:** Increases in OEW reduce payload capacity, while denser cabin layouts can compromise passenger comfort and affect range, especially in high-density configurations.
- **Aerodynamic Enhancements:** Features such as low-drag winglets improve range and fuel efficiency by reducing drag during flight. These enhancements enhance aerodynamic performance without directly affecting payload capacity.
- **Fuel Capacity Extensions:** Solutions like Auxiliary Center Tanks (ACTs) increase an aircraft's fuel capacity, enabling extended range for long-haul operations. However, ACTs trade cargo or payload volume for additional fuel storage, potentially impacting payload flexibility.

The following outlines key aspects of **Aircraft Operations** that shape payload-range dynamics:

- **Cruise Speed Adjustments**: Optimizing cruise speed balances fuel efficiency and travel time, but higher speeds increase fuel burn, reducing range.
- **Altitude Considerations**: Flying at optimum altitudes enhances efficiency, while constant-altitude operations, often due to air traffic control, increase fuel consumption.
- **Regulated Takeoff Weight (RTOW) Restrictions**: Short runways, high temperatures, or other constraints limit takeoff weight, affecting both range and payload capacity.
- **Contingency Fuel and Alternate Distance Adjustments**: Reducing fuel reserves or modifying alternate route distances increases payload flexibility but may lower safety margins.
- **Aging Effects**: Over time, increased drag and fuel burn due to structural wear or modifications reduce range and efficiency.

The following outlines the key **environment condition** that shapes payload-range dynamics:

- **High Temperatures**: Elevated enroute or airport temperatures reduce air density, adversely impacting engine performance, lift, payload, and range, especially at hot-and-high airports.

By considering these factors, airlines can better compare aircraft models, assessing their efficiency, cost-effectiveness, and adaptability for specific missions. This holistic understanding ensures that decisions align with both operational needs and economic goals.

7.4.1 Aircraft Specification Features

This section explores key specification features that influence an aircraft's payload-range performance, helping operators align aircraft capabilities with operational requirements.

Effect of Operating at Higher Certified MTOW

Operating at a higher Maximum Takeoff Weight (MTOW) allows an aircraft to carry additional payload or fuel, extending its range and enhancing flexibility for long-haul missions, as illustrated in **Figure 7-18**. A higher MTOW provides versatility to support varied operational needs, from increased cargo loads to longer routes.

However, the benefits of a higher MTOW come with added costs. In regions like Europe, navigation and landing fees are calculated based on MTOW, reflecting the greater strain heavier aircraft place on airport infrastructure such as runways and taxiways. These fees can significantly impact operational budgets. To optimize costs, operators may opt to certify aircraft at a lower MTOW, balancing the operational advantages of increased capability against the financial implications.

Figure 7-18. Effect of operating at higher certified MTOW

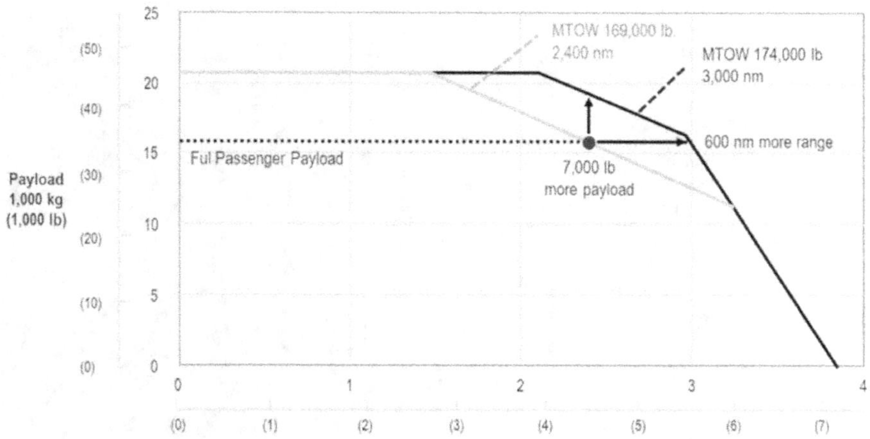

Source: Boeing. "737NG Airplane Characteristics for Airport Planning" document, with modifications by the author [7]

Effect of Lower Certified Maximum Zero-Fuel Weight (MZFW)

As shown in **Figure 7-19**, the Maximum Zero-Fuel Weight (MZFW) represents the maximum allowable payload (passengers, cargo, and baggage) an aircraft can carry, excluding fuel. When the MZFW is reduced, the payload must also decrease to ensure the total weight, once fuel is added, stays within the Maximum Takeoff Weight (MTOW)—the safe limit for takeoff, including payload, fuel, and the aircraft's Operating Empty Weight (OEW).

A higher MZFW, on the other hand, increases payload capacity but reduces the allowable fuel load due to the fixed MTOW. This trade-off limits range as the combined payload and fuel weight cannot exceed MTOW. By prioritizing payload through a higher MZFW, operators may face range constraints, particularly on long-haul routes requiring substantial fuel reserves.

To enhance flexibility, manufacturers often offer optional MZFW configurations, allowing operators to tailor the balance between payload and fuel based on mission requirements. For short- and medium-haul routes, a higher MZFW supports greater payload, maximizing revenue potential. For long-haul operations, a lower MZFW increases fuel capacity, extending range. These configurable options enable airlines to optimize aircraft performance for diverse operational needs, achieving both economic and operational efficiency.

Figure 7-19. Effect of lower certified MZFW

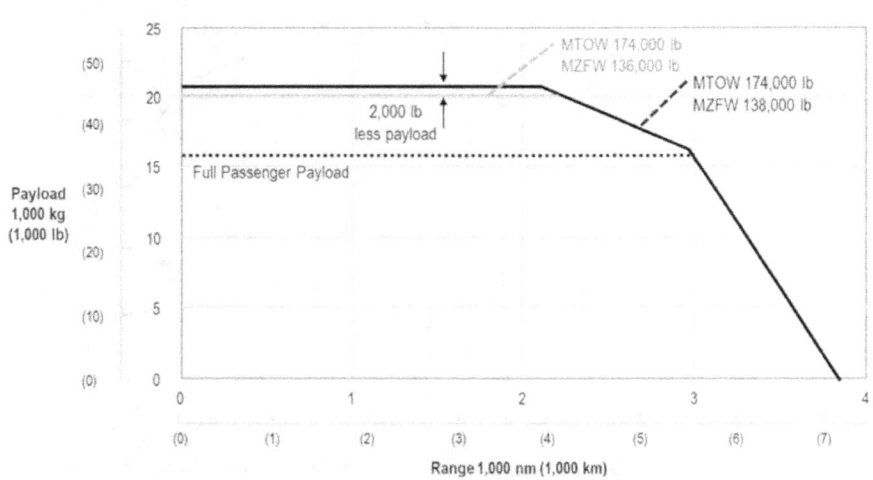

Source: Boeing. "737NG Airplane Characteristics for Airport Planning" document, with modifications by the author [7]

Effect of Higher Operating Empty Weight (OEW)

As shown in **Figure 7-20**, an increase in an aircraft's Operating Empty Weight (OEW) reduces both its maximum payload capacity and range. A higher OEW limits the payload the aircraft can carry and increases fuel burn to sustain the additional weight, further constraining range. Consequently, aircraft with elevated OEW have diminished payload and range capabilities compared to lighter counterparts, assuming all other factors remain constant.

OEW is influenced by the design choices and configurations airlines select when procuring an aircraft. Airlines customize their fleet based on brand identity, customer experience goals, and operational priorities, balancing additional amenities and features with the impact on weight. Customizations like premium seating, in-flight entertainment systems, galley and lavatory setups, and material choices for cabin interiors contribute to the OEW. While these features enhance passenger comfort and service quality, they also increase the aircraft's weight, directly affecting fuel efficiency, operating costs, and route viability.

This balance between OEW and service levels allows airlines to optimize aircraft configuration for specific missions, tailoring weight management to achieve both operational and economic efficiency.

Figure 7-20. Effect of higher OEW

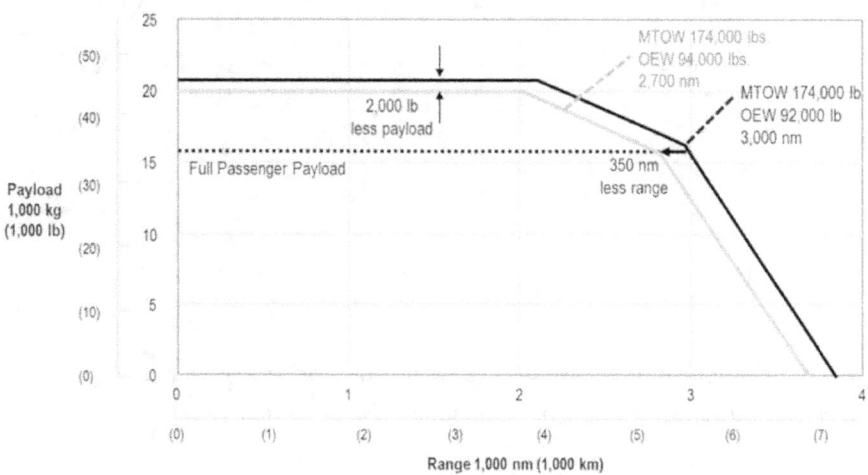

Source: Boeing. "737NG Airplane Characteristics for Airport Planning" document, with modifications by the author [7]

Effect of Higher Cabin Density

As shown in **Figure 7-21**, increasing cabin density—by adding seats or re-configuring the layout to accommodate more passengers—can enhance revenue potential but introduces significant trade-offs. Higher passenger capacity increases the aircraft's total weight, leading to greater fuel consumption as engines must work harder to sustain flight, particularly on longer routes.

This increased fuel burn directly impacts the aircraft's range. Additional fuel may be required to support the extra weight, reducing the fuel available for extended routes. In some cases, airlines may need to limit payload or adjust flight plans to stay within operational and safety constraints.

Airlines must carefully weigh the revenue benefits of higher cabin density against the implications for range and fuel efficiency. Striking this balance is essential for maintaining profitability while ensuring operational performance aligns with route and mission requirements.

Figure 7-21. Effect of higher cabin density

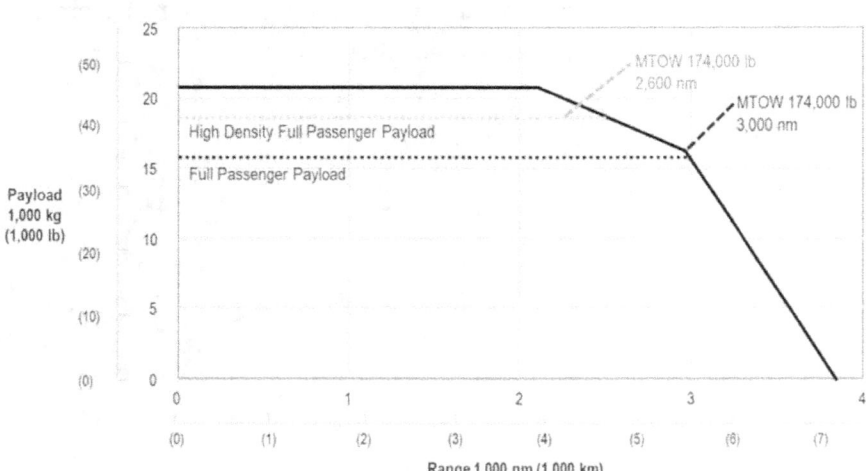

Source: Boeing. "737NG Airplane Characteristics for Airport Planning" document, with modifications by the author [7]

Effect of Winglets

As shown in **Figure 7-22**, winglets reduce aerodynamic drag by minimizing wingtip vortices—circular airflows formed at the wingtips during flight that increase drag and fuel consumption. By reducing this drag, winglets enhance the aircraft's fuel efficiency, allowing it to maintain speed with less energy.

Lower fuel consumption from winglets directly impacts range and payload capacity. With reduced fuel burn, the aircraft can carry additional payload or extend its range without exceeding weight or fuel limitations. This improvement is particularly beneficial for long-haul operations, where enhanced efficiency supports profitability and operational flexibility.

Figure 7-22. Effect of winglets

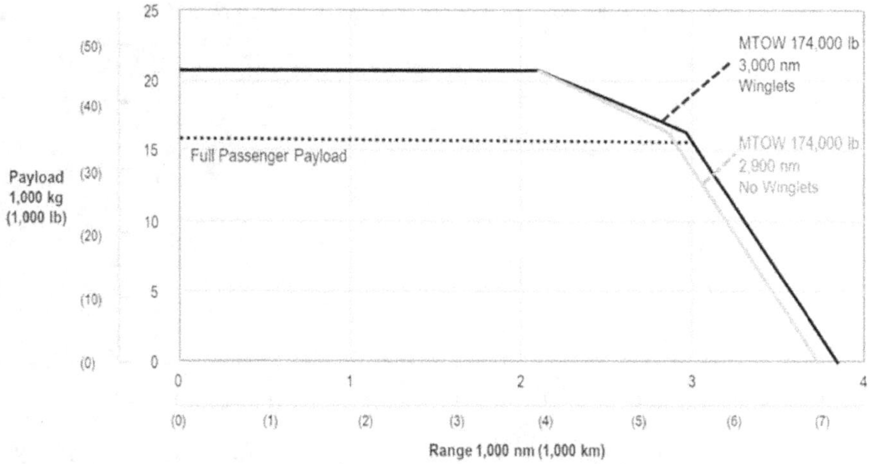

Source: Boeing. "737NG Airplane Characteristics for Airport Planning" document, with modifications by the author [7]

Effect of Adding Auxiliary Fuel Tanks

As illustrated in **Figure 7-23**, auxiliary fuel tanks increase an aircraft's fuel capacity, extending its range and making them particularly valuable for long-haul routes or operations in regions with limited refueling infrastructure. By enabling longer flights, these tanks enhance operational flexibility and route planning for carriers.

However, adding auxiliary fuel tanks comes with trade-offs. The additional tanks increase the aircraft's Operating Empty Weight (OEW), reducing the available payload capacity for passengers, cargo, or other revenue-generating items. This increased weight allocation to fuel storage can limit the aircraft's operational efficiency on routes where payload is a priority.

Operators must carefully evaluate whether the extended range provided by auxiliary fuel tanks justifies the reduction in payload capacity, ensuring that configurations align with both route demands and overall profitability.

Figure 7-23. Effect of adding auxiliary fuel tanks

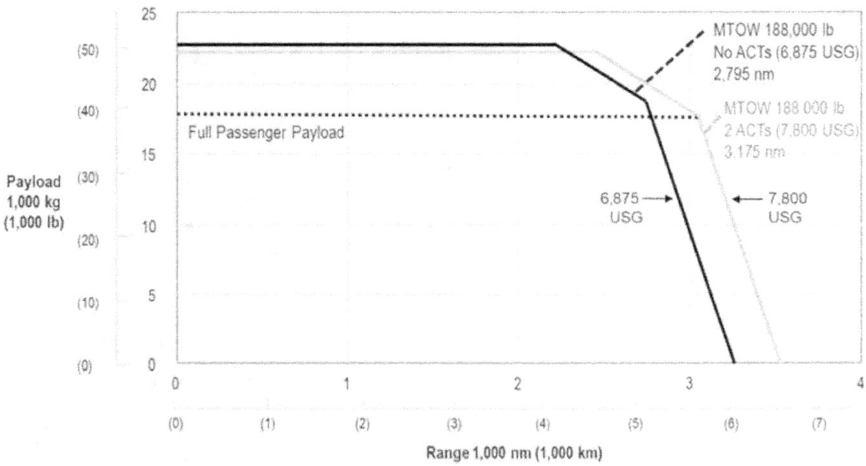

Source: Boeing. "737NG Airplane Characteristics for Airport Planning" document, with modifications by the author [7]

7.4.2 Aircraft Operation

This section examines operational strategies that affect an aircraft's payload-range performance. Decisions such as cruise speed, altitude selection, and fuel management play a significant role in optimizing flight efficiency and range. These choices directly impact fuel consumption, route planning, and operational flexibility, ultimately influencing how well an aircraft meets its performance goals.

Effect of Altering Cruise Speed

As illustrated in **Figure 7-24**, an aircraft's cruise speed has a significant impact on fuel efficiency and range. The Maximum Range Cruise (MRC) speed maximizes fuel efficiency, allowing the aircraft to cover the greatest distance possible with a given fuel load. MRC is ideal for long-haul operations where extending range is a priority. However, it results in longer flight durations, which may not align with routes that prioritize minimizing travel time.

The Long-Range Cruise (LRC) speed strikes a balance between fuel efficiency and reduced flight time. While slightly less efficient than MRC, LRC enables the aircraft to fly faster, shortening travel time. This comes at the cost of reduced range, as the increased fuel consumption per mile decreases the total distance the aircraft can travel on a single tank.

Selecting between MRC and LRC involves weighing the trade-off between fuel efficiency and travel time. This decision allows airlines to tailor operational strategies to specific route requirements, optimizing performance to align with passenger expectations and cost considerations.

Figure 7-24. Effect of speed schedule

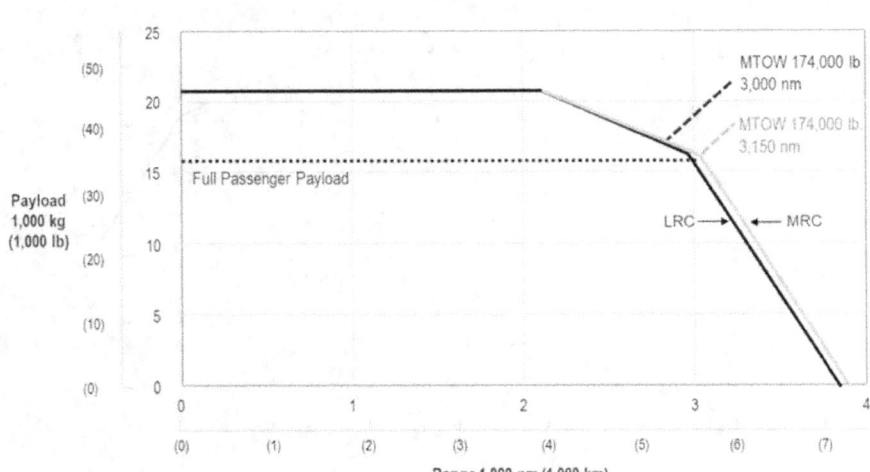

Source: Boeing. "737NG Airplane Characteristics for Airport Planning"
document, with modifications by the author [7]

Effect of Airport Regulated Takeoff Weight (RTOW) Limit

Regulated Takeoff Weight (RTOW) is a safety measure that limits an air-craft's takeoff weight in environments with short runways, high tempera-tures, or high-altitude conditions. As illustrated in **Figure 7-25**, RTOW constraints often necessitate a reduction in the maximum fuel load, directly impacting the aircraft's range. These limitations are critical in challenging airport environments where reduced runway length or diminished engine performance—caused by high temperatures or altitude—requires a lower takeoff weight for safe operations.

When RTOW constraints apply, operators must adjust either the payload or fuel load to comply with weight limits. Such adjustments can shorten the aircraft's range and necessitate careful route planning to avoid unscheduled refueling stops. These compromises may affect operational efficiency and economic performance, as airlines must balance reduced payload or fuel loads with revenue-generating opportunities and operational requirements.

Figure 7-25. Effect of airport RTOW limit

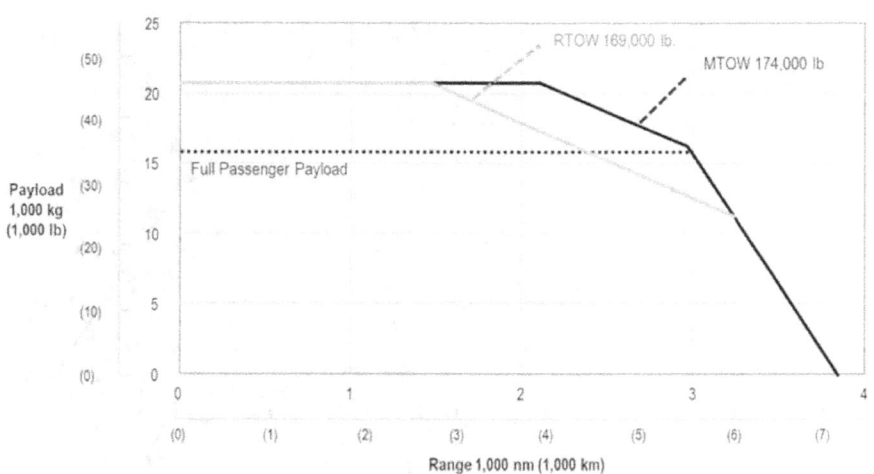

Source: Boeing. "737NG Airplane Characteristics for Airport Planning" document, with modifications by the author [7]

Effect of Optimum vs. Constant Altitude

Aircraft achieve peak efficiency within a specific altitude range, where lower air density reduces aerodynamic drag and minimizes fuel consumption. As illustrated in **Figure 7-26**, operating below this optimal altitude increases air density and drag, requiring greater engine thrust to maintain speed and altitude. This results in elevated fuel burn, reducing the aircraft's range as more fuel is consumed to overcome the additional resistance.

Maintaining optimal altitude is critical for fuel efficiency and maximizing range, especially on long-haul routes where effective fuel management is crucial. However, operational factors such as air traffic control restrictions or weather deviations may force aircraft to fly below their ideal altitude. These adjustments typically result in reduced fuel efficiency. Airlines must carefully manage these scenarios, prioritizing operations within the optimal altitude range whenever possible to balance performance, fuel costs, and operational flexibility.

Figure 7-26. Effect of optimum vs. constant altitude

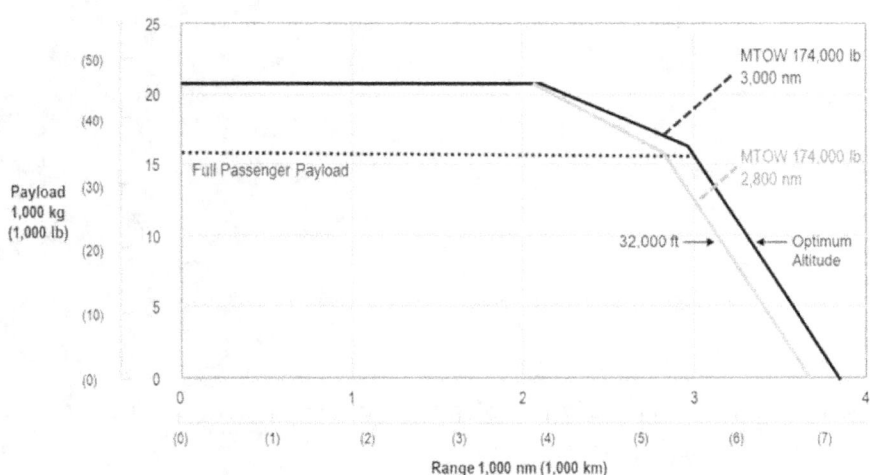

Source: Boeing. "737NG Airplane Characteristics for Airport Planning"
document, with modifications by the author [7]

Effect of Lower Contingency Fuel

Contingency fuel acts as a buffer for unexpected delays, such as weather changes or air traffic control restrictions that may extend flight time. As shown in **Figure 7-27**, reducing contingency fuel decreases the aircraft's overall weight, potentially improving fuel burn efficiency and marginally extending range.

However, adjustments to contingency fuel must be made cautiously. Regulations mandate a minimum level of contingency fuel to ensure readiness for unforeseen scenarios, and reducing this reserve below the required threshold could compromise safety and regulatory compliance. Any changes should balance operational efficiency with strict adherence to safety standards, prioritizing reliability, and preparedness in all circumstances.

Figure 7-27. Effect of lower contingency fuel

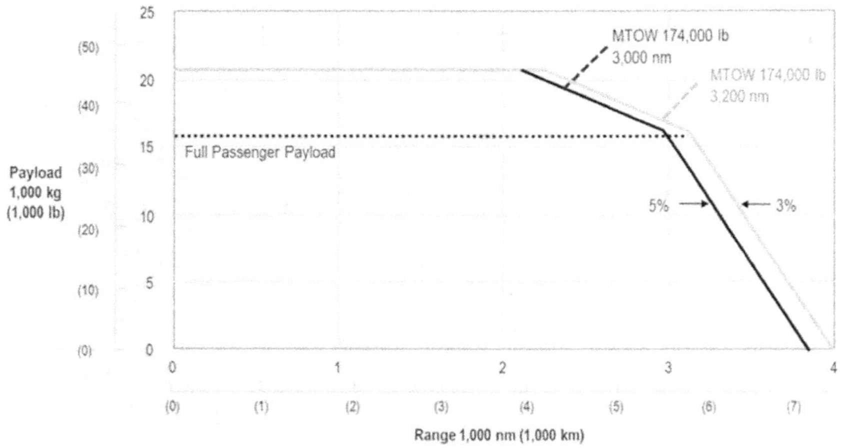

Source: Boeing. "737NG Airplane Characteristics for Airport Planning" document, with modifications by the author [7]

Effect of Longer Alternate Distance

As shown in **Figure 7-28**, planning for a more distant alternate airport requires carrying additional fuel, which increases the aircraft's total weight. This added weight results in higher fuel consumption throughout the flight, as more thrust is needed to sustain the extra load. Consequently, a portion of the fuel capacity is expended on supporting this weight rather than extending the aircraft's range.

This additional fuel requirement reduces the aircraft's effective range, as less fuel is available for covering the intended distance. Operators must carefully evaluate the trade-off between carrying extra fuel for safety and maintaining the aircraft's operational range. Strategic adjustments to payload or cruise speed may be necessary to optimize efficiency while ensuring compliance with safety requirements. Planning for a farther alternate airport highlights the need for meticulous fuel and payload management to balance safety and performance effectively.

Figure 7-28. Effect of longer alternate distance

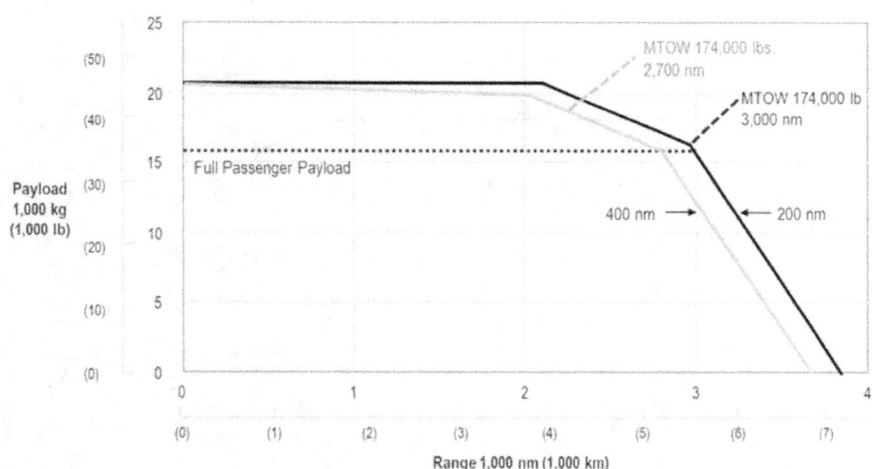

Source: Boeing. "737NG Airplane Characteristics for Airport Planning" document, with modifications by the author [7]

Effect of Increased Drag & Fuel Burn

As shown in **Figure 7-29**, the performance of an aircraft diminishes over time due to factors such as accumulated weight from structural repairs, surface wear, and modifications. These changes reduce aerodynamic efficiency by increasing drag, which necessitates greater thrust to maintain performance, leading to higher fuel consumption and shorter range.

In the payload-range chart, this increased drag appears as a downward shift in the performance curve, indicating either a reduced payload capacity for a given range or a shorter range with a full payload. This visual representation underscores the trade-off between aging-related drag and payload-range efficiency.

Additionally, engine wear affects components like the compressor and turbine, decreasing their efficiency. This decline results in higher fuel consumption to generate the same thrust, compounding the reductions in performance and range. By addressing these effects through targeted maintenance and operational adjustments, operators can mitigate aging impacts and align performance with operational goals.

Figure 7-29. Effect of increased drag & fuel burn

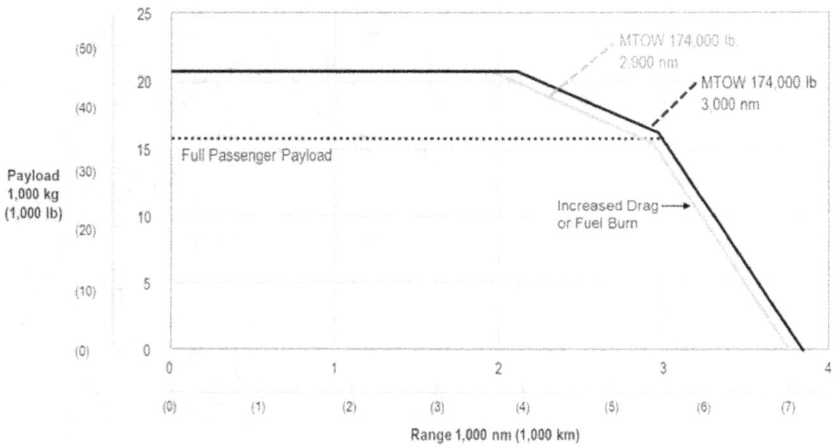

Source: Boeing. "737NG Airplane Characteristics for Airport Planning" document, with modifications by the author [7]

7.4.3 Environmental Conditions

Environmental conditions, particularly temperature variations, significantly influence an aircraft's range, fuel efficiency, and overall performance. Temperature differences across flight routes and altitudes impact both engine performance and aerodynamic efficiency, directly affecting the aircraft's operational effectiveness.

Effect of High Enroute Temperatures

As illustrated in **Figure 7-30**, elevated temperatures reduce air density, significantly affecting aircraft performance. Lower air density increases the required takeoff roll, reduces climb rates, and raises fuel consumption. Engines must work harder to generate the same thrust, leading to higher fuel burn.

These effects highlight the importance of accounting for temperature variations in flight planning, particularly on routes where high temperatures are common. Careful consideration of these factors is essential to optimize efficiency and maintain safety standards.

Figure 7-30. Effect of high enroute temperatures

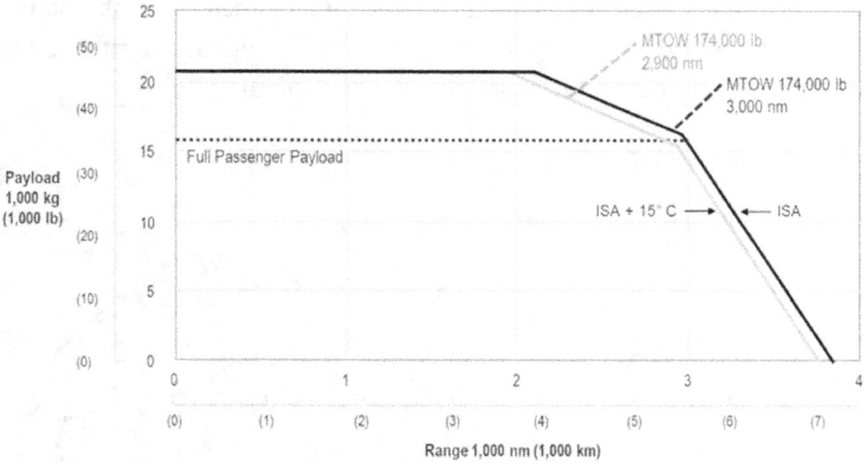

Source: Boeing. "737NG Airplane Characteristics for Airport Planning" document, with modifications by the author [7]

Summary

Accurately benchmarking airliners requires considering the complex interplay of factors that shape both economic viability and performance efficiency. These factors collectively influence an aircraft's operational capabilities. A thorough understanding of their impacts allows airlines to make informed comparisons between aircraft models, ensuring their selections align with specific operational requirements and strategic objectives.

7.5 Circle Charts

Circle Charts enhance the evaluation of an aircraft's mission capabilities by incorporating average monthly cruise wind speeds into payload-range analysis, adding a layer of realism that improves the accuracy of comparisons. Unlike traditional payload-range diagrams, Circle Charts account for wind effects, which can significantly influence range and fuel efficiency, particularly on long-haul flights. This approach provides a more precise comparison of aircraft performance in real-world scenarios.

As illustrated in **Figure 7-31**, which depicts the range performance of the 787 family, Circle Charts present a clear visual tool for analysis. Range is represented as concentric circles around payload capacity, showing how payload and range interact at various levels. The outermost circle indicates maximum range, offering a straightforward way to determine the optimal payload-range balance for specific missions while highlighting the unique design and performance characteristics of each aircraft.

Figure 7-31. 787 family circle charts

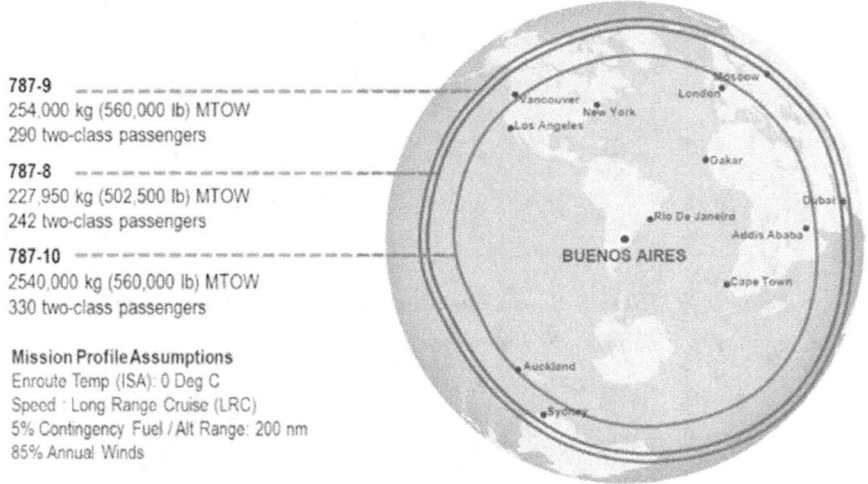

Source: Boeing, "Airplane Performance Analysis and 787 Characteristics," July 2019. [8]

In **Figure 7-32**, the Circle Chart for the A330-900 illustrates the aircraft's range capabilities at varying Maximum Takeoff Weights (MTOWs), using concentric circles centered around "Hong Kong." The inner circles represent shorter ranges achievable at lower MTOWs, while the outer circles depict the extended ranges possible with higher MTOWs. This visual format effectively demonstrates how adjustments to MTOW influence range, providing an intuitive tool for evaluating operational capabilities.

Figure 7-32. A330-900 circle charts

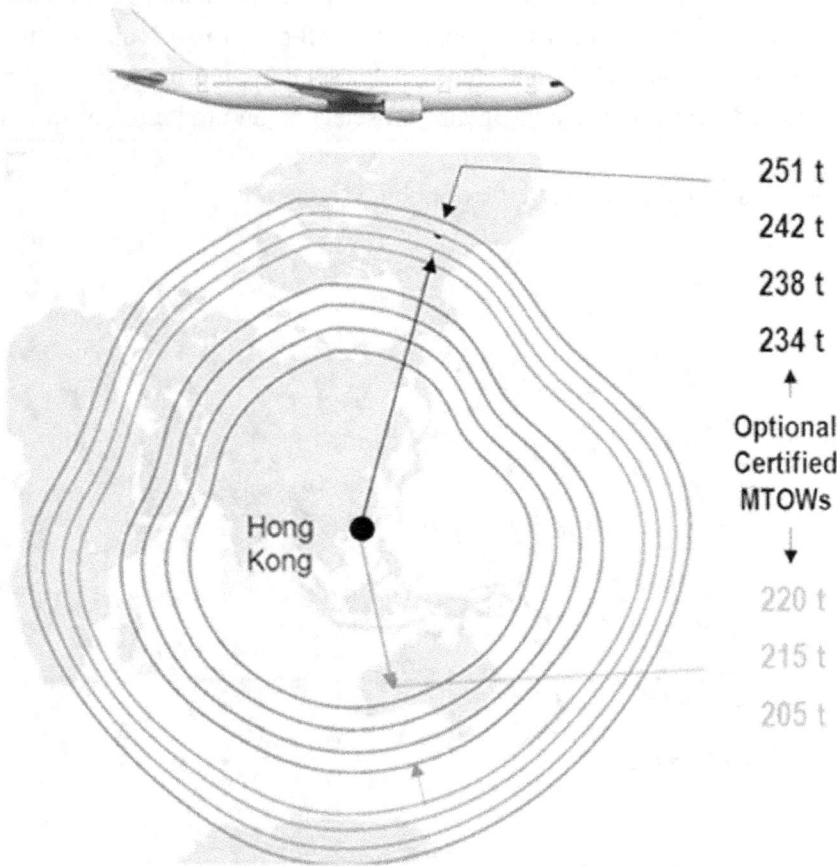

Source: Airbus, "The Leading Widebody Family," December 2019. [9]

The chart enables operators to make more informed comparisons by visually mapping the relationship between MTOW and range. This insight helps airlines optimize fleet configurations to align with diverse mission requirements, ensuring both efficiency and flexibility. By integrating such tools into strategic planning, airlines can select configurations that best meet specific payload and range needs.

When constructing Circle Charts, manufacturers incorporate statistical modeling to account for wind speed impacts on range. These models assume wind speeds follow a normal distribution, with range reliability expressed at standard levels, typically 85% and 50%, as shown in **Figure 7-33**. By factoring in monthly variations in wind speeds and temperatures, manufacturers provide a more realistic assessment of aircraft performance under actual operating conditions. This enhanced realism supports more accurate comparisons and strategic decisions in aircraft selection and route optimization.

Figure 7-33. Wind probability distribution

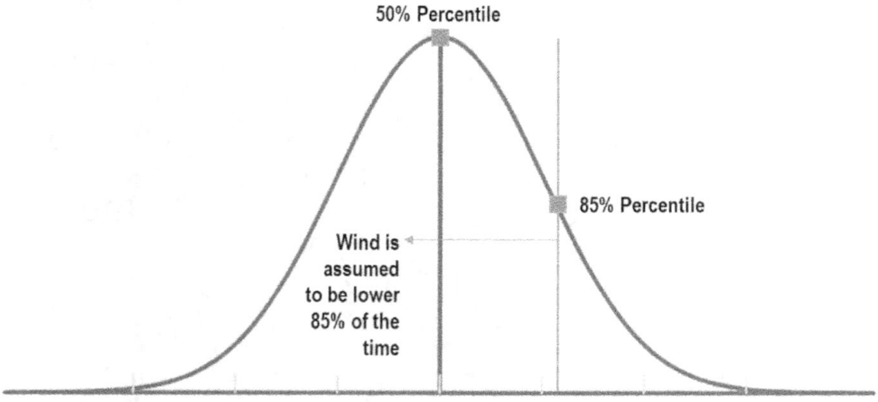

Source: Author's analysis

For example, **Table 7-2** demonstrates how manufacturers might represent enroute winds between Seattle and Narita, Japan, in January. Publicly available wind data sources, such as NOAA (National Oceanic and Atmospheric Administration) and ICAO databases, are typically used to derive these estimates. Average wind speeds might indicate -60 knots for headwinds and +18 knots for tailwinds, with a standard deviation of 17 knots.

At the 85% reliability level, most flights will encounter winds within one standard deviation of these averages, ensuring predictable performance within a typical wind range. This level of consistency aids in operational planning by accounting for wind variability in a realistic manner.

Incorporating wind data into Circle Charts enables airlines to predict fuel burn and flight times more accurately, directly influencing route planning and performance comparisons. By factoring in environmental conditions like seasonal winds, Circle Charts provide a detailed visualization of their impact on range, fuel requirements, and alternate airport planning. This makes them valuable tools for assessing an aircraft's capabilities across different routes and conditions.

Table 7-2. Implications of seasonal wind

Orig	Dest	Range (nm)	Air Speed	Month	Std. Dev	Rel.	Direct Winds	Equiv. Range	Return Winds	Equiv. Range
SEA	NRT	4,133	463	Jan	17	85	-60	4,743	+18	3,980
						50	-42	4,540	+36	3,836

Source: NOAA and ICAO wind datasets

Circle Charts Limitations

Circle charts are a valuable tool for visualizing the effects of wind on an aircraft's range, but they have notable limitations. While they provide insights into how tailwinds and headwinds impact operational range, they often exclude critical performance metrics such as takeoff performance, landing weight limitations, and operating costs. These factors are essential for a holistic assessment of an aircraft's capabilities and operational efficiency, particularly in real-world conditions.

Another limitation is that manufacturers may present circle chart data using favorable assumptions, such as idealized payloads, weather conditions, or cruise profiles, which can lead to biased comparisons across competing aircraft. As a result, while circle charts enhance understanding of wind effects and range capabilities, they should be supplemented with detailed payload-range diagrams, cost analyses, and operational performance metrics to ensure a comprehensive evaluation of an aircraft's true performance.

7.6 Seat-Range Diagrams

Seat-range diagrams, as illustrated in **Figure 7-34**, compare the seating capacity and range of various aircraft models based on typical manufacturer-provided configurations. These diagrams provide an overview of each model's standard passenger load and range capabilities, typically reflecting the aircraft's **Design Range**—the maximum distance achievable with a full passenger payload, excluding additional cargo beyond standard passenger luggage.

While useful as an initial reference, seat-range diagrams are based on standard seating layouts, which may differ significantly from the configurations adopted by individual airlines. Higher-density seating arrangements, for example, increase the aircraft's weight, potentially reducing available space for fuel and limiting its range. This variability highlights the importance of considering airline-specific configurations when evaluating range and performance.

Figure 7-34. Example seat-range diagram

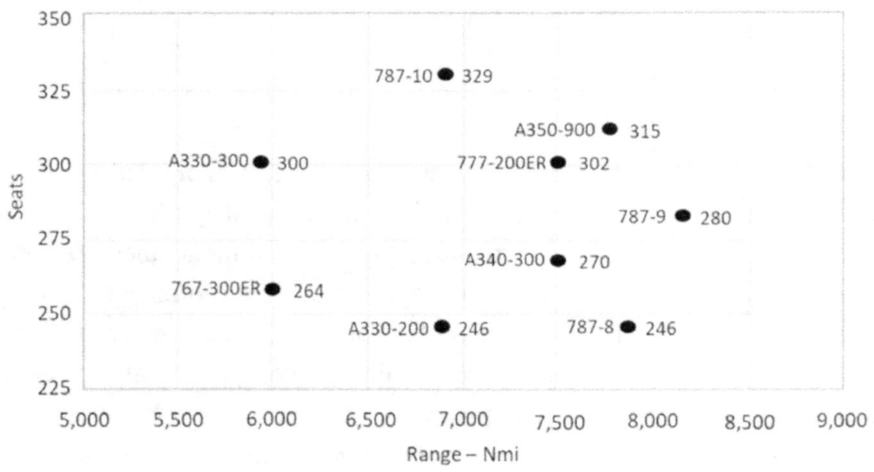

Source: Author's analysis

Seat-Range Diagram Limitations

Seat-range diagrams provide a simplified view of an aircraft's passenger-carrying capacity over various ranges but often fail to account for several critical factors that influence overall performance and profitability. For example, they exclude considerations like fuel efficiency and cost per seat mile (CASM), which are essential metrics for assessing operational costs, particularly on long-haul routes. Additionally, these diagrams focus solely on passenger capacity, overlooking the revenue potential of cargo, a significant source of profitability for many airlines operating widebody aircraft.

By ignoring operational factors such as payload-range trade-offs, runway performance, and regulatory constraints, seat-range diagrams present an incomplete picture of an aircraft's capabilities. Furthermore, they rely on standard seating configurations, which may not reflect airline-specific layouts, such as premium-heavy or low-cost configurations. While useful for visualizing passenger capacity and range, these diagrams should be complemented with more comprehensive analyses, such as payload-range diagrams and operational assessments, to better capture the full scope of an aircraft's performance and economic potential.

Key Takeaways

1. **Payload Range Diagrams:** These diagrams are essential for evaluating and comparing aircraft based on payload and range capabilities, illustrating trade-offs and operational boundaries. They highlight the relationship between fuel load, payload, and range, providing insight into how different aircraft balance these factors under varying mission profiles.

2. **Advanced Payload-Range Considerations**:
   » **MTOW and MZFW Adjustments**: Increasing MTOW allows for more payload or extended range, but incurs higher operating fees. Lower MZFW configurations prioritize range over payload, offering flexibility in optimizing aircraft for specific routes.
   » **Adaptive Payload Relationship**: The flexibility to adjust payload within a range enhances adaptability, enabling better performance alignment with diverse operational needs.
   » **MLW and Fuel-Volume Constraints**: Both Maximum Landing Weight (MLW) and fuel-volume limitations affect range, with MLW requiring careful planning to ensure safe landing weights, and fuel-volume constraints limiting maximum range, particularly on long-haul routes.

3. **Factors Impacting Payload-Range Performance**:
   » **Aircraft Specifications**: Features like MTOW, MZFW, winglets, and auxiliary fuel tanks directly impact performance, range, and payload trade-offs.
   » **Operational Factors**: Cruise speed, restricted takeoff weight (RTOW), altitude selection, contingency fuel, and alternate distances are all strategic decisions affecting range, efficiency, and safety. Adjusting these factors enables airlines to tailor performance based on operational demands.
   » **Environmental Conditions**: High enroute temperatures can reduce engine performance and lift, making temperature considerations vital for efficient and safe long-haul flights.

4. **Circle Charts:** Circle Charts integrate wind speed effects into Payload-Range analysis, presenting a more realistic assessment of an aircraft's performance under real-world conditions. These charts depict concentric range capabilities, enabling operators to benchmark aircraft under seasonal winds and environmental factors. While insightful, Circle Charts are best complemented with additional performance data for a comprehensive evaluation.

5. **Seat-Range Diagrams:** Seat-Range Diagrams provide a visual comparison of seating capacity and design range across aircraft models based on standard configurations. While useful for initial assessments, these diagrams should be supplemented with data on cargo capacity and custom configurations to fully evaluate an aircraft's operational and economic potential.

Case Study 7-1. Payload Range Evaluation

Figure 7-35. Payload range analysis

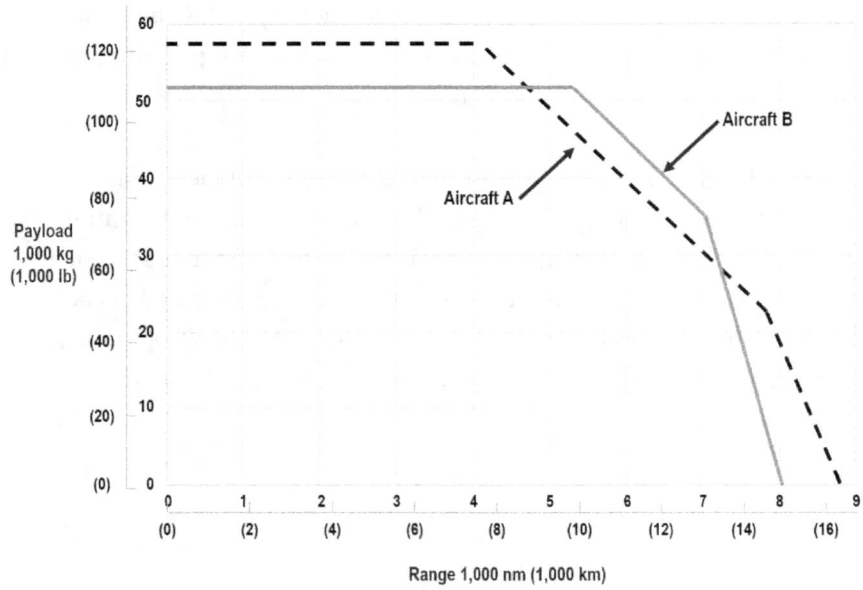

Source: Author's analysis

Questions:

1. Based on the graph, what is the maximum structural payload for each aircraft? How much cargo payload capacity does each aircraft have when operating at maximum passenger + baggage payload, assuming both aircraft are operating at a range of 4,000 nm?

2. What operational compromises must be made for Aircraft A or B to fly beyond the MTOW range or the maximum fuel capacity range? How might these compromises affect payload, efficiency, and operational suitability?

3. If reserve fuel requirements increase due to regulatory changes or unplanned diversions, how might this impact the payload and range

capabilities of Aircraft A and B? What operational adjustments would be necessary?

4. If the slope of the MTOW line (boundary) is identical for both Aircraft A and Aircraft B, what operational and design characteristics does this imply about the two aircraft? How might this influence their performance in terms of range-payload trade-offs and mission suitability?

5. If the slope of the Maximum Fuel Capacity (MFC) line (boundary) is steeper for Aircraft B compared to Aircraft A, what operational and design characteristics does this imply? How might this influence their performance and suitability for long-haul and ultra-long-haul missions?

Case Study 7-2. Restricted Performance Scenarios

Figure 7-36. 737-500 payload range analysis 1

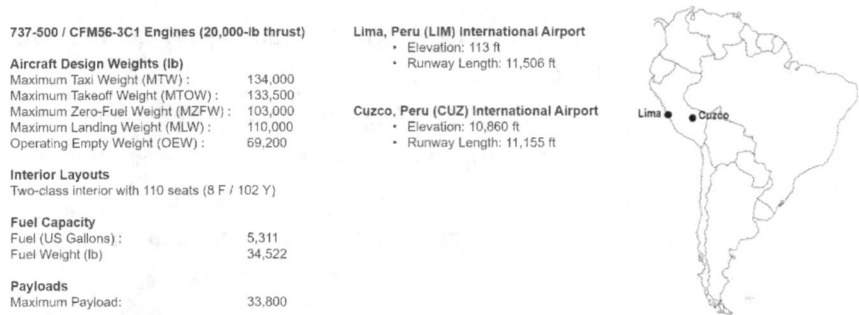

Source: Boeing."737 Airplane Characteristics for Airport Planning" document, with modifications by the author [8]

Figure 7-37. 737-500 payload range analysis 2

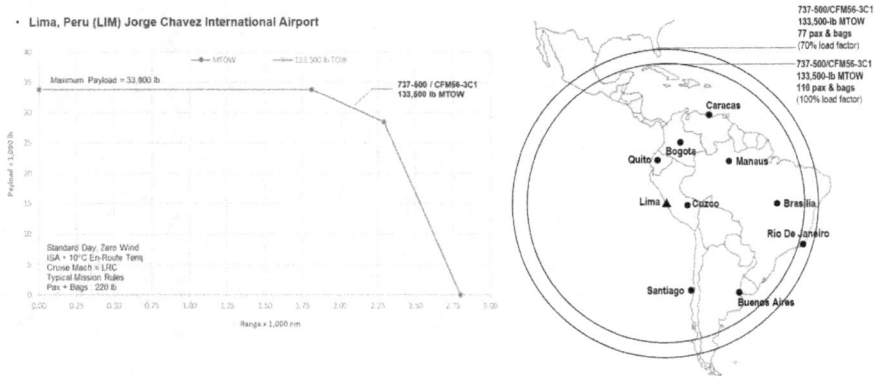

Source: Boeing."737 Airplane Characteristics for Airport Planning" document, with modifications by the author [8]

Case Study 7-2: 737-500 Payload Range Analysis

Figure 7-38. 737-500 payload range analysis 3

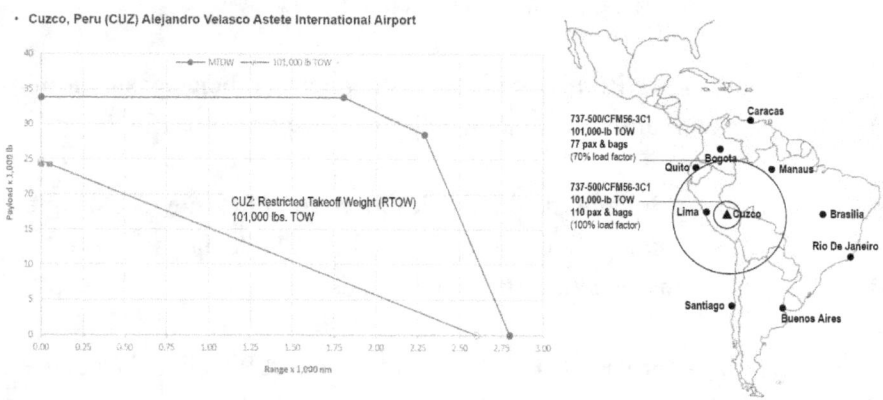

Source: Boeing. "737 Airplane Characteristics for Airport Planning" document, with modifications by the author [8]

Questions:

1. Compare the payload-range capabilities of the 737-500 when departing from Lima (LIM) versus Cuzco (CUZ). How does the higher elevation at Cuzco impact the design range at a 100% load and 70% load factor compared to Lima?

2. How do the runway length and elevation at Cuzco (10,860 ft elevation, 11,155 ft runway) limit the payload and range performance of the 737-500 compared to Lima (113 ft elevation, 11,506 ft runway)?

3. The payload-range diagrams are based on ISA + 10°C conditions. How would a further increase in temperature (e.g., ISA + 20°C) likely affect the performance of the 737-500 departing from Cuzco compared to Lima?

4. Given the performance challenges at Cuzco, what design or operational modifications could improve the viability of 737-500 operations at high-altitude airports? Discuss potential trade-offs.

References

[1] Boeing, "787 Airplane Characteristics for Airport Planning," Document D6-58333, Revision O, Feb. 2023. [Online]. Available: https://www.boeing.com/commercial/airports/plan-manuals

[2] M. Zeinali and D. Rutherford, "Trends in aircraft efficiency and design parameters," International Council on Clean Transportation (ICCT).

[3] Boeing, "777 Airplane Characteristics for Airport Planning," Document D6-58329-2, Revision F, Dec. 2022. [Online]. Available: https://www.boeing.com/commercial/airports/plan-manuals

[4] Boeing, "747 Airplane Characteristics for Airport Planning," Document D6-58326-1, Revision E, Sep. 2023. [Online]. Available: https://www.boeing.com/commercial/airports/plan-manuals

[5] Airbus, "A330 Airplane Characteristics for Airport Planning," AC A330, Jul. 2023. [Online]. Available: https://aircraft.airbus.com/en/customer-care/fleet-wide-care/airport-operations-and-aircraft-characteristics/aircraft-characteristics

[6] Boeing, "757 Airplane Characteristics for Airport Planning," Document D6-58327, Revision H, Dec. 2024. [Online]. Available: https://www.boeing.com/commercial/airports/plan-manuals

[7] Boeing, "737NG Airplane Characteristics for Airport Planning," Document D6-58325-7, Revision B, Dec. 2024. [Online]. Available: https://www.boeing.com/commercial/airports/plan-manuals

[8] Boeing, "Airplane Performance Analysis and 787 Characteristics," Presentation, Jul. 2019.

[9] Airbus, "The Leading Widebody Family," Presentation, Jul. 2019.

Chapter 8

Performance Enhancement Strategies

This Chapter is About:

8.1 Advancements in Wing Design & Aerodynamics
8.2 Aircraft Weight Optimization Strategies
8.3 Engine Technology Evolution

Aircraft performance enhancement strategies are essential for manufacturers like Airbus, Boeing, and Embraer to improve the efficiency, capabilities, and economic performance of their commercial airliners. These strategies encompass aerodynamic refinements, weight optimization, engine performance upgrades, and freighter payload enhancements. Together, these initiatives help maintain competitiveness, extend the operational longevity of existing aircraft models, and address evolving market demands.

By implementing these enhancements, manufacturers aim to achieve key performance objectives, such as reducing fuel consumption, increasing payload capacity, extending range, and meeting sustainability goals. These improvements enable airlines to remain operationally and economically viable while addressing global pressures for greener, more efficient air travel.

This chapter introduces the four main categories of enhancement strategies:

1. **Aerodynamic Enhancements:** Focus on optimizing the lift-to-drag ratio to reduce drag and improve fuel efficiency. Approaches include integrating winglets, raked wingtips, and advanced laminar flow designs to maximize aerodynamic performance.
2. **Weight Optimization Strategies:** Aim to enhance structural limit weights, such as Maximum Takeoff Weight (MTOW), to improve efficiency and operational flexibility. These adjustments enable increased payload capacity or extended range, enhancing adaptability for diverse mission requirements.
3. **Engine Performance Improvements:** Engine modifications and Product Improvement Packages (PIPs) enhance durability, fuel efficiency, and reliability. These upgrades lower operating costs, support sustainability goals by reducing emissions, and improve long-term performance.
4. **Freighter Performance Enhancements:** Focus on optimizing cargo operations by improving packing density, maximizing volume utilization, and refining payload-range trade-offs. These strategies enable freighters to handle diverse cargo requirements efficiently, ensuring they meet the growing demands of global logistics networks while enhancing operational profitability and flexibility.

Understanding these strategies is essential for benchmarking aircraft models and evaluating their performance in a competitive and environmentally conscious industry.

8.1 Advancements in Wing Design and Aerodynamics

Aircraft manufacturers are continually advancing aerodynamic efficiency to enhance the performance of both legacy and next-generation aircraft. These innovations aim to reduce drag and improve fuel efficiency, resulting in lower operating costs, extended range, and reduced emissions. A key focus of these advancements lies in optimizing the lift-to-drag (L/D) ratio, improving wing designs, and leveraging emerging technologies.

Lift-to-Drag (L/D) Ratio

The **L/D ratio** measures how effectively an aircraft generates lift relative to drag. A higher L/D ratio improves fuel efficiency and increases range, making it a critical target in aerodynamic design. Modern wing features—such as extended wingspans, winglets, and raked wingtips—enhance the L/D ratio by minimizing **induced drag** caused by wingtip vortices. **Figure 8-1** illustrates how these features improve aerodynamic performance by reducing drag.

Figure 8-1. Lift-to-Drag Ratio (L/D)

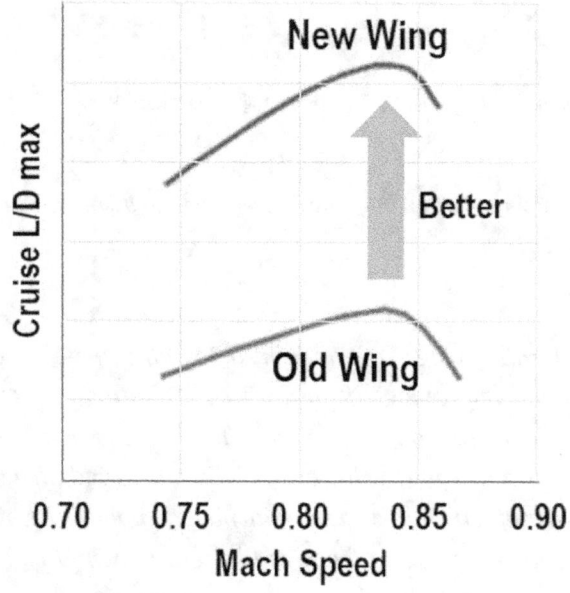

Credit: Boeing

A key factor in improving the L/D ratio is the **aspect ratio**, which is the ratio of a wing's span to its average chord. Wings with higher aspect ratios, characterized by their long and slender designs, reduce induced drag and significantly contribute to better fuel efficiency and extended range. This relationship between aspect ratio and aerodynamic performance is explored in greater detail below.

Industry Perspective 8-1. *Comparing Low and High Aspect Ratio Wings*

Figure 8-2 contrasts low and high aspect ratio wings, highlighting their distinct aerodynamic characteristics and trade-offs. Aspect ratio, defined as the ratio of a wing's span to its average chord, greatly influences aerodynamic efficiency, structural requirements, and operational capabilities.

Figure 8-2. Low and high aspect ratio wings

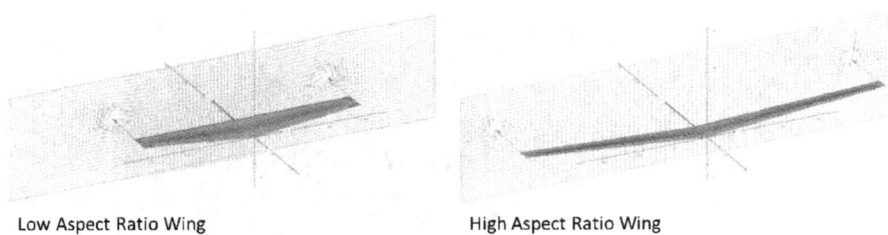

Low Aspect Ratio Wing   High Aspect Ratio Wing

Source. "The Anatomy of the Wing," by Snorri Gudmundsson, in General Aviation Aircraft Design, 2014 [1]

High aspect ratio wings are optimized for efficiency, producing lower induced drag, and improving lift-to-drag (L/D) ratios. These characteristics make them ideal for long-haul aircraft, where reduced drag enhances fuel consumption and range. However, their elongated structure presents challenges in manufacturing, cost, and airport compatibility. Advanced materials, reinforced designs, and features like folding wingtips (e.g., Boeing's 777X) are often necessary to address these challenges.

Low aspect ratio wings, with shorter spans relative to their chord, are simpler to manufacture, less costly, and offer better maneuverability, making them suitable for short-haul aircraft. However, they generate higher induced drag, reducing fuel efficiency and range, and may require robust structures to withstand higher loads during flight maneuvers.

The choice between high and low aspect ratio wings depends on the aircraft's mission. High aspect ratio designs excel in long-range efficiency but come with higher costs and structural complexities, while low aspect ratio wings prioritize cost-effectiveness, agility, and runway compatibility.

Advances in composites, such as carbon-fiber-reinforced polymers, are enabling lightweight high aspect ratio wings, while features like winglets and raked wingtips improve the efficiency of low aspect ratio designs.

Wingtip Modifications: Mitigating Induced Drag

Wingtip devices play a critical role in reducing **induced drag**, which arises from the pressure difference between the upper and lower wing surfaces. This pressure differential creates **wingtip vortices**, swirling air patterns that disrupt smooth airflow and increase resistance, as shown in **Figure 8-3**.

Figure 8-3. Motion of the air behind a lifting wing

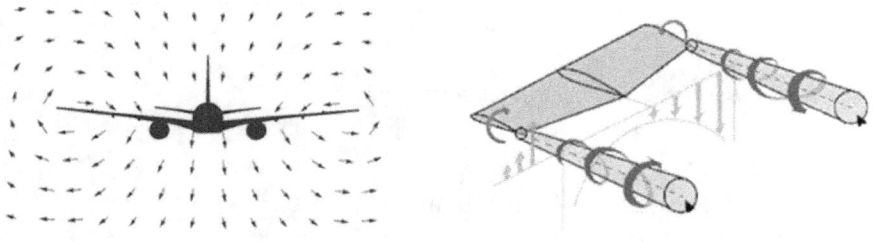

Source: Blended winglets improve performance. Boeing Aero Magazine [2]

By addressing these vortices, wingtip modifications such as **winglets** and **raked wingtips** significantly enhance aerodynamic efficiency. These devices not only reduce induced drag by optimizing airflow around the wingtips, as shown in **Figure 8-4,** but also deliver operational benefits like improved fuel efficiency, extended range, and better climb performance.

Figure 8-4. Motion of the air with & without winglets

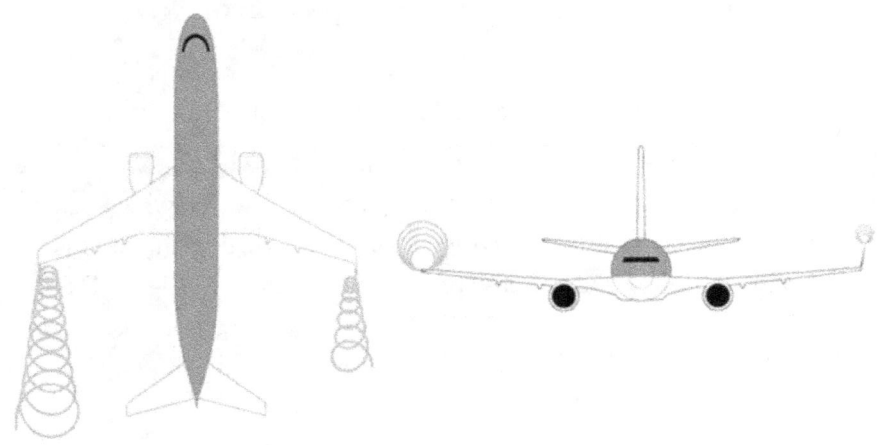

Source: Beginner's guide to aviation efficiency [3]

Winglets: A Recognized Aerodynamic Innovation

Winglets are one of the most widely adopted and impactful aerodynamic enhancements in modern aviation. By reducing induced drag, they improve fuel efficiency, extend range, and lower maintenance costs. Winglets are integrated into many Boeing, Airbus, and Embraer aircraft through **Product Improvement Packages (PIPs)** or aftermarket retrofits.

Key benefits of winglets include:

1. **Fuel Savings and Environmental Impact:** Winglets reduce fuel burn by 2.5%–4%, depending on the aircraft model and mission profile. This results in lower operating costs and reduced carbon emissions, as illustrated in **Figure 8-5**.

Figure 8-5. Typical block fuel improvement with winglets

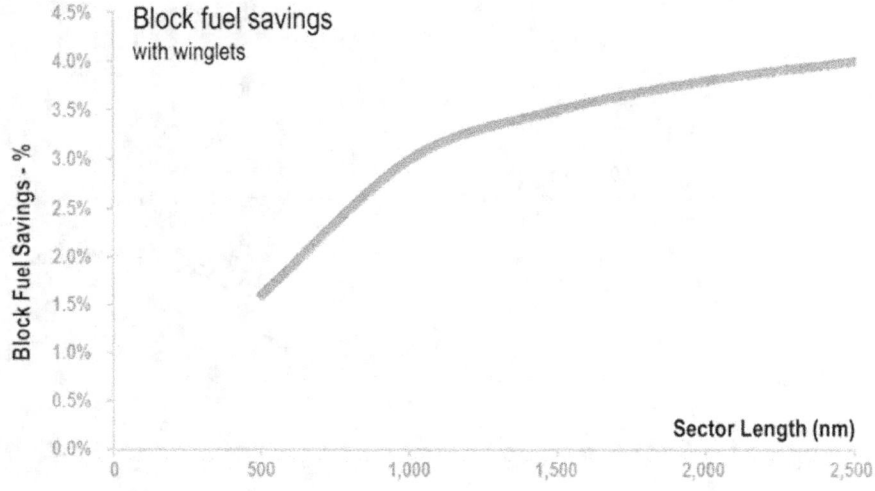

Source: Author's analysis

2. **Payload and Range Enhancements:** By reducing drag, winglets extend an aircraft's operational range and increase payload capacity. For example, a **757-200** equipped with winglets can carry an additional 10,730 pounds or fly 200 nautical miles farther than a non-equipped model when configured for a 200-passenger payload. These enhancements are depicted in **Figure 8-6**.

Figure 8-6. 757-200 payload-range performance with winglets

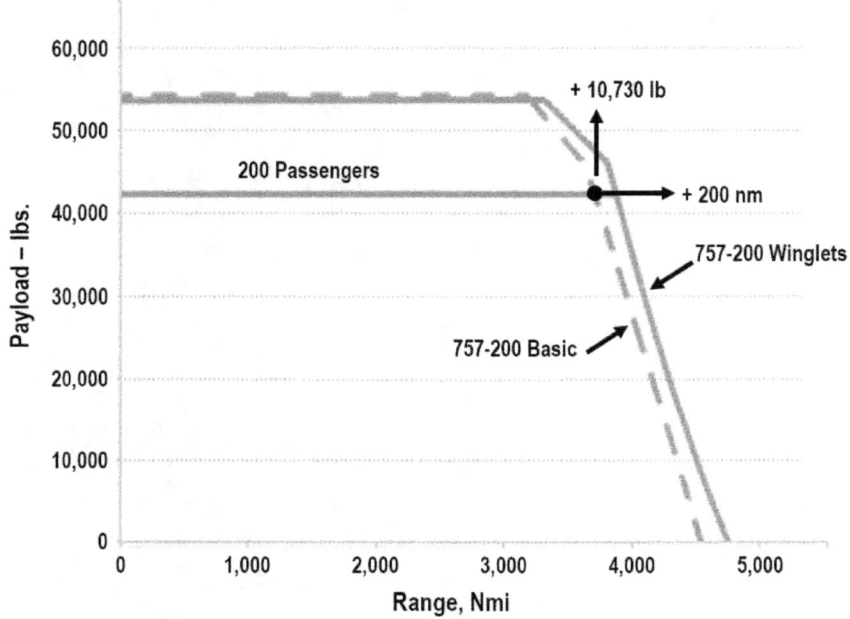

Source: Aviation Partners Boeing [4]

3. **Reduced Engine Maintenance Costs:** Winglets contribute to lower **Exhaust Gas Temperature (EGT)** deterioration by enabling reduced thrust settings during takeoff and cruise. This improvement extends engine life, reduces maintenance intervals, and lowers long-term operating expenses, as shown in **Figure 8-7**.

Figure 8-7. Impact of engine maintenance costs with winglets

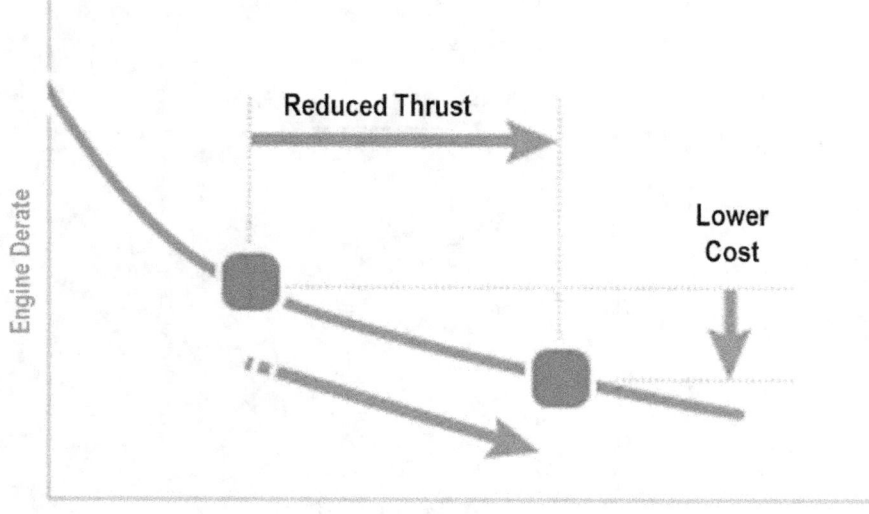

Source: Aviation Partners Boeing [4]

4. **Enhanced Takeoff Performance:** In challenging environments like high-altitude airports, winglets improve performance by increasing Maximum Takeoff Weight (MTOW). For instance, winglets enable the **767-300ER** to increase its MTOW by 4,000 kg at hot and high airports, improving climb gradients and obstacle clearance. These benefits are highlighted in **Figure 8-8**.

Figure 8-8. 767-300ER takeoff performance with winglets

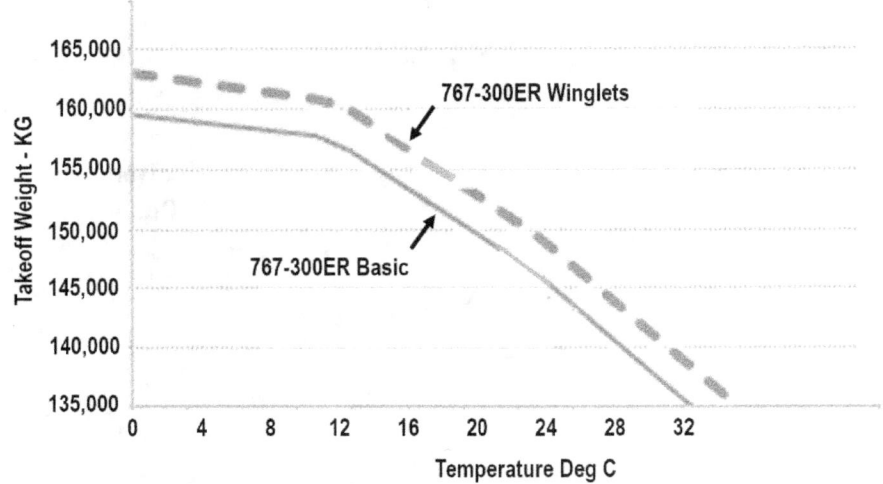

Source: Aviation Partners Boeing [4]

EXAMPLE 8-1. Boeing's Winglet Evolution on the 737NG

Boeing's advancements in winglet design illustrate the continuous pursuit of fuel efficiency and performance:

- **Basic Wingtips:** Early 737NG models had standard wingtips without drag-reducing features.
- **Blended Winglets (2001):** Upward-curving winglets reduced induced drag, achieving up to 4% fuel savings.
- **Split Scimitar Winglets (2014):** Added downward lower tips further improved lift-to-drag ratios, delivering an additional 1-2% fuel savings (**Figure 8-9**).

Figure 8-9. 737NG winglet aerodynamic enhancements

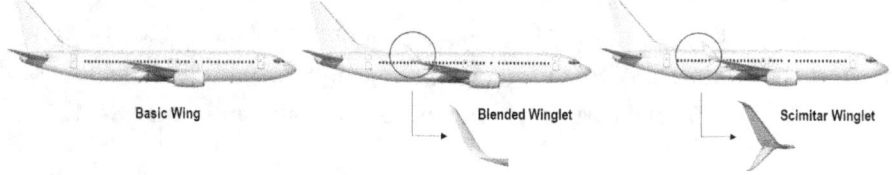

Basic Wing   Blended Winglet   Scimitar Winglet

Source: Author's analysis

Raked Wingtips: Extending the Principles of Winglets

Building on the aerodynamic benefits of winglets, **raked wingtips** represent an advancement in wing design. These devices feature a backward sweep angle that increases wingspan and **aspect ratio**, as shown in **Figure 8-10**, without significantly widening the total wingspan. This design not only reduces induced drag but also enhances lift-to-drag (L/D) efficiency, contributing to better fuel economy and extended range.

Figure 8-10. Raked wingtips

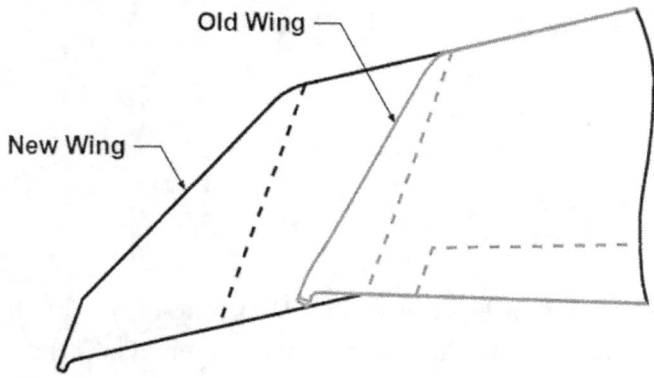

Old Wing

New Wing

Source: Boeing: Airplane Performance Analysis and 777 Characteristics [5]

Building on the principles discussed in **Industry Perspective 8-1**, **raked wingtips** represent a specific application of high aspect ratio principles aimed at reducing induced drag and improving aerodynamic efficiency. By increasing the effective aspect ratio, raked wingtips deliver better lift distribution across the wingspan, achieving lower fuel consumption and enhanced cruise performance.

For example, the Embraer E190-E2 incorporates raked wingtips that outperform the standard E190 design, achieving significant reductions in block fuel burn and improved cruise efficiency, as illustrated in **Figure 8-11**.

Figure 8-11. E190 standard vs. E190-E2 raked wingtips

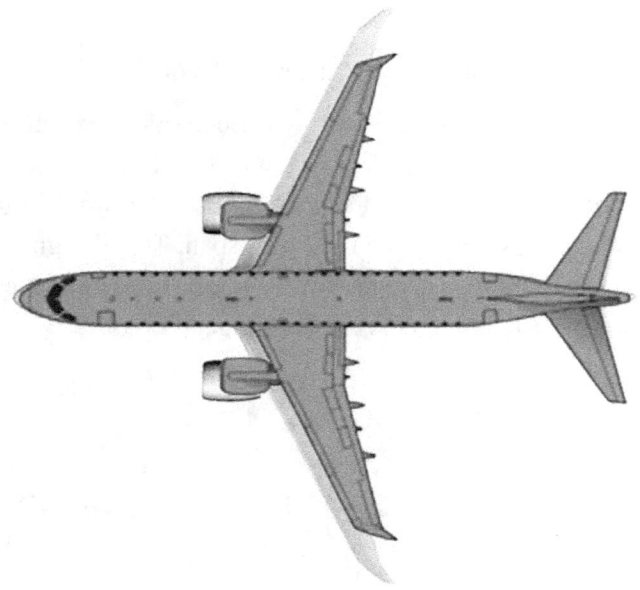

Credit: Embraer

This design has been especially valuable for long-range aircraft, where its aerodynamic benefits translate into meaningful fuel savings and operational flexibility. Boeing, a pioneer of raked wingtips, introduced this feature on the 767-400ER in 1999, incorporating it into widebody models like the 777-200LR, 787 Dreamliner, and the 747-8 (**Figure 8-12**).

Figure 8-12. Boeing widebody aircraft with raked wingtips

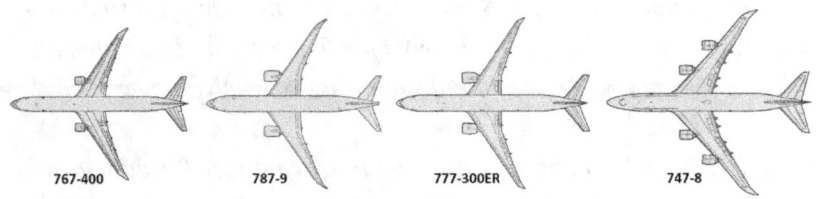

Source: Boeing Commercial Airplane Reference Guide [6]

In addition to fuel efficiency, raked wingtips enhance **operational flexibility** by supporting greater payloads or extended range. This dual functionality makes them indispensable for long-haul routes, helping airlines achieve better fuel economy, increase revenue potential, and reduce environmental impact.

***Industry Perspective 8-2.** Raked Wingtips on the P-8 Poseidon*

*Raked wingtips, renowned for their aerodynamic benefits in commercial aviation, have been adapted for military use on the Boeing P-8 Poseidon, a military variant of the 737-800. Unlike its commercial counterpart, the P-8 features raked wingtips instead of winglets to meet the U.S. Navy's operational needs (**Figure 8-13**).*

Figure 8-13. P-8 Poseidon vs. 737-800

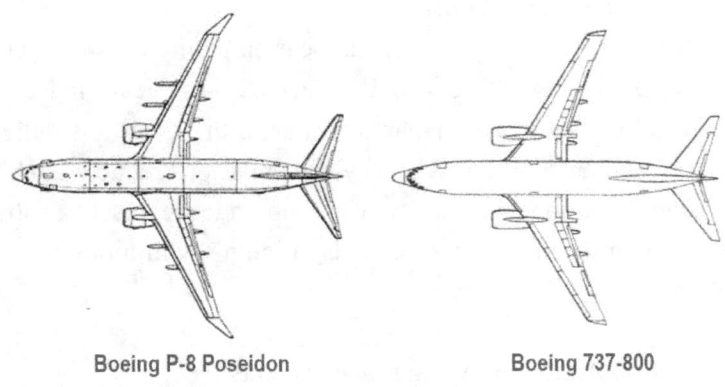

Boeing P-8 Poseidon   Boeing 737-800

Source: Boeing with modifications by the author

While winglets are optimized for fuel efficiency in commercial flight profiles, raked wingtips offer superior aerodynamic performance across a broader range of operations. On the P-8 Poseidon, they enhance lift distribution and reduce drag, making them particularly effective for missions requiring both extended endurance and operational versatility. Key advantages include:

- ***High-Speed Transit and Altitude Performance:*** *Raked wingtips improve aerodynamic efficiency at higher speeds and altitudes, enabling rapid deployment during anti-submarine warfare and surveillance missions.*
- ***Loitering at Lower Altitudes:*** *The design ensures stability and fuel efficiency during prolonged low-altitude loitering, a critical capability for patrol and reconnaissance missions.*

The adaptation of raked wingtips from commercial to military applications underscores their versatility as an aerodynamic enhancement. Designed to reduce drag, optimize lift distribution, and improve fuel efficiency, their integration into the P-8 Poseidon highlights how commercial innovations can address the specialized demands of military aviation.

Current Advancement in Wing Designs

Recent advancements in wing designs have become a cornerstone of modern aircraft performance, addressing the growing demands for fuel efficiency, sustainability, and operational flexibility. These innovations focus on optimizing aerodynamic efficiency, extending operational range, and reducing fuel consumption and emissions.

Examples of these advancements can be seen in aircraft such as the Airbus A330NEO, Boeing 777X, and Embraer E2 jets. Featuring elongated wingspans and enhanced aerodynamic features, these designs deliver significant improvements in fuel efficiency and emissions reduction while providing greater operational versatility. These upgrades represent a substantial leap forward compared to earlier models, aligning with industry goals for sustainability and performance.

EXAMPLE 8-2. A330NEO Wing Enhancements

The A330NEO demonstrates a significant evolution from the A330CEO, integrating aerodynamic innovations like reshaped slat and flap track fairings, composite sharklets, and an extended wingspan (**Figure 8-14**). These improvements, paired with optimized wing twist, deliver a 14% improvement in fuel efficiency.

Figure 8-14. A330NEO new optimized wing

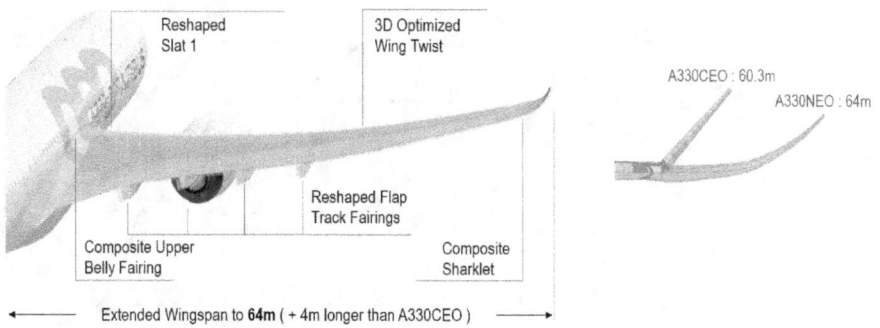

Source: https://twitter.com/AlexInAir with modifications by the author [7]

A comparison between the A330-300CEO and A330-900NEO, shown in **Figure 8-15**, highlights the impact of aerodynamic advancements and new-generation engines on payload-range performance. Equipped with Rolls-Royce Trent 7000 engines offering improved fuel efficiency and higher thrust, the A330-900's optimized wing design allows for greater payloads over longer distances. These enhancements significantly extend the aircraft's range, providing airlines with increased operational flexibility to carry more payload or expand route networks.

Figure 8-15. A330-300 (CEO) vs. A330-900 (NEO) payload range

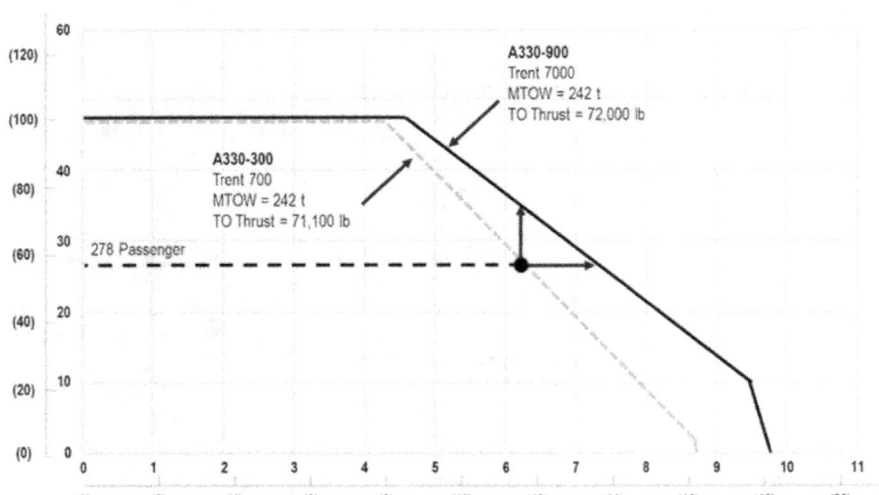

Source: Airbus. "A330 Airplane Characteristics for Airport Planning" document, with modifications by the author [8]

EXAMPLE 8-3. The Boeing 777X Wing Enhancements

The Boeing 777X highlights next-generation aerodynamic efficiency. With a 72-meter wingspan—11 feet longer per side than the 777-300ER— its high aspect ratio increases lift-to-drag efficiency by 7% (**Figure 8-16**). Composite materials reduce weight while maintaining strength, and laminar flow nacelles further minimize drag.

A standout feature is the folding wingtip, which maintains airport com- patibility while enabling in-flight aerodynamic efficiency. These innovations result in significant fuel savings and environmental benefits, cementing the 777X as a benchmark for widebody performance.

Figure 8-16. 777X new optimized wing

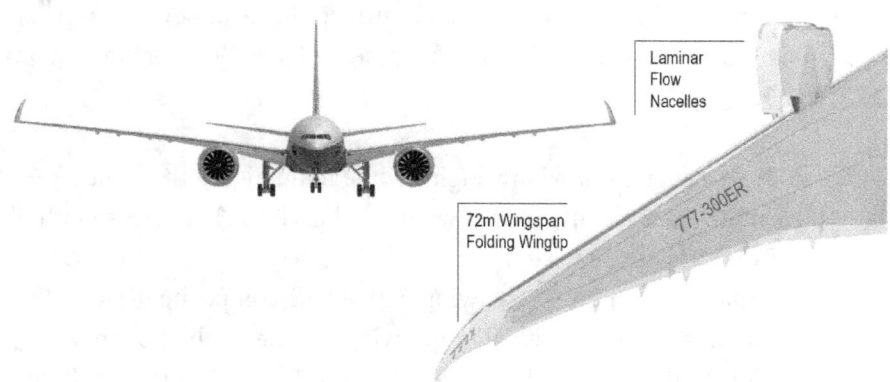

Source: Boeing. Airplane Performance Analysis and 777 Characteristics [5]

In summary, advancements in wing design, from optimizing aspect ratios to leveraging composite materials, are redefining aircraft performance. These innovations, exemplified by the A330NEO and 777X, demonstrate how manufacturers address fuel efficiency, range, and emissions in response to market demands for more sustainable and cost-effective operations.

Composite Wing Innovations

The integration of composite materials into wing structures represents a transformative shift in modern aircraft design. These materials, known for their strength and lightweight properties, enable significant advancements in aerodynamic efficiency and structural performance. The **Boeing 777X** wing, for instance, showcases an all-composite design that contributes to its extended wingspan, high aspect ratio, and folding wingtips, offering a 7% improvement in the lift-to-drag (L/D) ratio.

Composite materials allow manufacturers to achieve performance enhancements beyond the capabilities of traditional metallic wings. By reducing weight and enabling more aerodynamic wing geometries, composites support lower fuel consumption, extended range, and reduced emissions. However, the advantages of composites extend beyond weight savings, as illustrated in the following analysis of trade-offs in composite wing design.

Figure 8-17 illustrates how advanced composite materials enable significant trade-offs between weight savings and aerodynamic efficiency in modern aircraft designs. According to **Counterpoint Market Intelligence**, two scenarios provide insight into the potential benefits for an **Airbus A321NEO**:

- A 20% reduction in wing weight (while maintaining the same geometry as a metallic wing) would yield a 1.5–2% decrease in fuel burn for a typical mission.
- Alternatively, replacing the wing with an all-composite design of the same weight but with a longer wingspan and a thinner cross-section could increase the cruise L/D ratio from 18 to 19, resulting in a 5–7% decrease in fuel burn, even without weight savings.

Figure 8-17. Fuel-burn improvements using composites

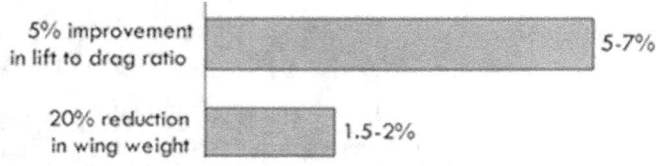

Source: CompositeWorld [9]

These examples demonstrate that aerodynamic improvements often outweigh weight savings in their contribution to fuel efficiency. Composite materials facilitate these advancements by offering the strength, stiffness, and design flexibility needed to achieve optimal wing geometries.

Industry Perspective 8-3. *Composite Materials in Design*

The Boeing 787 represents a significant milestone in the use of composite materials in commercial aircraft design. With an aerostructure comprising approximately 50% composites, it surpasses any other large commercial aircraft in reliance on these advanced materials. This innovation required substantial investment in carbon fiber manufacturing and marked a transformative shift in aircraft production methods.

While composites are often celebrated for their lightweight properties, their advantages extend well beyond weight reduction. They enable greater design flexibility, allowing for aerodynamic enhancements that boost fuel efficiency and operational performance.

*As shown in **Figure 8-18**, the 787 features a longer, thinner wing compared to the 767-300, a predominantly metallic design from the 1980s. Key features of the 787's wing include an extended span, which reduces drag and improves the lift-to-drag ratio, and a thinner profile, approximately 10% slimmer on average, further minimizing drag and enhancing efficiency.*

Figure 8-18. *787-8 vs. 767-300 wing*

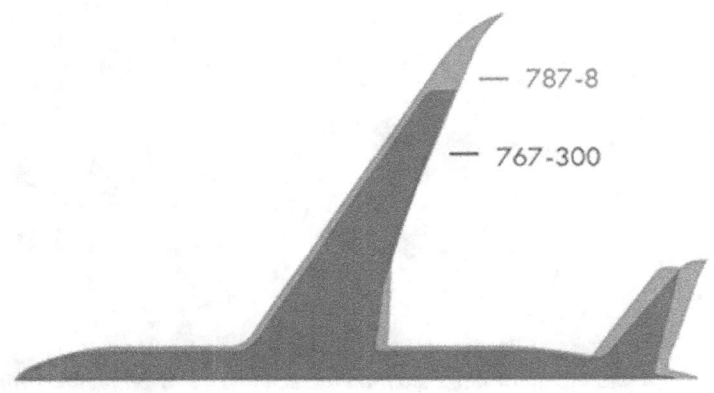

Source: The next-generation single-aisle: Implications for the composites industry. CompositeWorld [9]

These aerodynamic gains, enabled by the strength, stiffness, and lightness of composite materials, result in a more fuel-efficient geometry. Combined with advanced engines, the 787 achieves significant fuel burn reductions and nearly doubles the range of its predecessor, despite being approximately 30% heavier in empty weight (excluding engines) compared to the 767.

Active Wing Technologies

Building on advancements in wing design, **active wing technologies** represent a transformative step in optimizing aircraft performance. These systems maximize aerodynamic efficiency, improve flight performance, and reduce structural loads by dynamically adjusting wing components in response to real-time flight conditions. By adapting to turbulence, varying air pressures, and other environmental factors, active wing technologies ensure optimal performance throughout the flight. **Figure 8-19** illustrates a typical **Gust Load Alleviation (GLA)** system, showcasing the role of these adaptive components in modern aviation.

Figure 8-19. Example active wing technologies

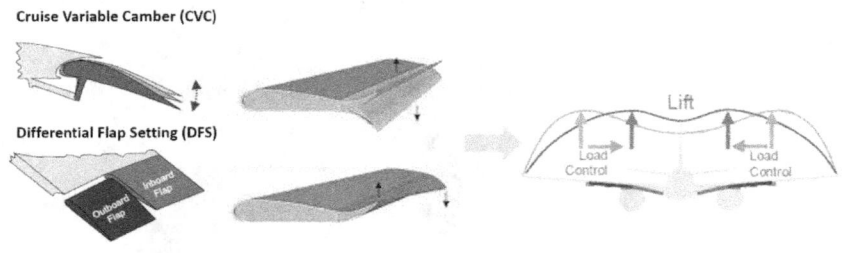

Source: Design and evaluation of distributed electric drive architectures for high-lift control systems [10]

GLA systems enhance aircraft performance by redistributing aerodynamic forces across control surfaces—such as ailerons, spoilers, and elevators—during turbulence or sudden aerodynamic changes. This dynamic adjustment reduces stress on the aircraft structure, improving safety and efficiency. Both the **Airbus A350** and **Boeing 787** feature advanced GLA systems, integrating cutting-edge technologies to improve fuel efficiency and flight stability.

Key examples include:

- **Variable Camber Wing (Airbus A350)**: The A350 incorporates a Variable Camber Wing system, also known as the **Morphing Trailing Edge**, which adjusts the curvature of the trailing edge flaps in real time. This system optimizes the lift-to-drag (L/D) ratio during cruise to enhance fuel efficiency and adjusts lift during takeoff and landing for safer, more efficient operations.

- **Variable Camber Trim Unit (VCTU) (Boeing 787)**: The 787's VCTU independently controls inboard and outboard flaps to reduce drag, improve lift distribution, and minimize wing stress during turbulent conditions. It also enhances pitch control and climb efficiency, ensuring consistent performance while reducing fuel consumption.

The integration of GLA and Variable Camber systems on the A350 and 787 marks a new era in wing technology. These systems dynamically adapt to real-time aerodynamic forces, improving structural performance, fuel efficiency, and passenger comfort. By reducing fuel burn and optimizing performance across all flight phases, active wing technologies align closely with the aviation industry's goals of sustainability and operational excellence.

Next-Generation Wing Designs

Next-generation aircraft are poised to incorporate transformative wing designs aimed at significantly improving fuel efficiency and reducing environmental impact. These innovations are central to achieving the aviation industry's ambitious goal of reducing fuel burn and carbon emissions by up to 20%.

A key advancement is the adoption of **high aspect ratio wings**, which feature longer, slender, and more flexible designs to reduce induced drag caused by wingtip vortices. By enhancing aerodynamic efficiency, these wings are expected to deliver performance improvements comparable to those of next-generation engines, making them a cornerstone of future aircraft design.

This section also examines the **Blended Wing Body (BWB)** concept, an integrated wing-fuselage configuration that, while having a lower aspect ratio than traditional high aspect ratio wings, minimizes form drag and optimizes lift distribution. The BWB's unique design maximizes efficiency across a larger surface area, positioning it as a viable long-term solution for reducing fuel consumption and emissions.

Collectively, next-generation wing technologies are projected to contribute 10-15% of the efficiency gains needed for future narrowbody aircraft.

Combined with advancements in propulsion systems and other aerodynamic innovations, these designs will play a pivotal role in achieving sustainable aviation goals.

High Aspect Ratio Wings

A key advancement in wing design is the development of **high aspect ratio wings**, which feature long, slender wings that significantly improve aerodynamic efficiency. As shown in **Figure 8-20**, these wings extend the wingspan to reduce **induced drag**, the swirling air patterns at the wingtips that increase resistance. By minimizing drag, high aspect ratio wings enhance the **lift-to-drag (L/D) ratio**, resulting in reduced fuel burn and emissions. This makes them a cornerstone of sustainable aviation technology.

Figure 8-20: Example high aspect ratio wing design

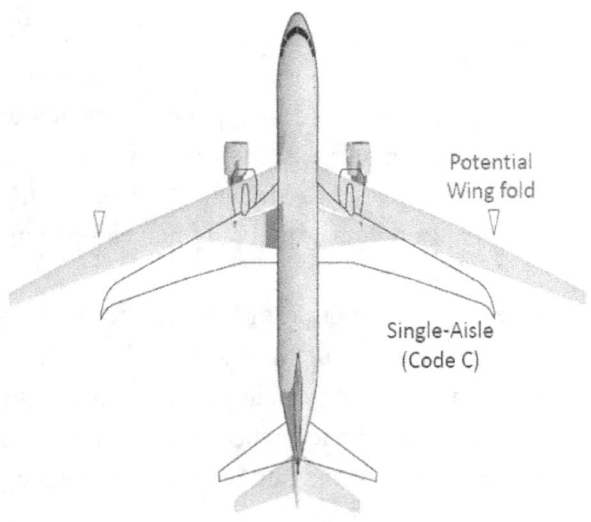

Source: Boeing. Transonic truss-braced wing maturation Conference presentation [11]

While these designs offer considerable benefits, such as better fuel efficiency, reduced emissions, and extended range, they present challenges. Extended wingspans often exceed airport infrastructure limits, like the **ICAO Code C** gate and taxiway restrictions. To address this, manufacturers have introduced folding wingtips, allowing for optimal aerodynamic performance in flight while maintaining airport compatibility.

High aspect ratio wings are expected to contribute up to 10–15% efficiency improvements in fuel burn and emissions for future aircraft. These benefits, combined with advanced materials like lightweight composites, make them critical to meeting aviation's sustainability goals.

EXAMPLE 8-4. Boeing X-66 Experimental Transonic Truss-Braced Wing (TTBW) Design

The **Boeing X-66**, developed under NASA's *Subsonic Ultra Green Aircraft Research (SUGAR)* program, illustrates high aspect ratio wing innovation. As shown in **Figure 8-21**, the X-66 features ultra-thin wings supported by truss structures, extending the wingspan to 170 feet (51 meters)—a significant increase compared to conventional single-aisle aircraft like the 737-800.

Figure 8-21. Boeing X-66 transonic truss-braced wing (TTBW) aircraft

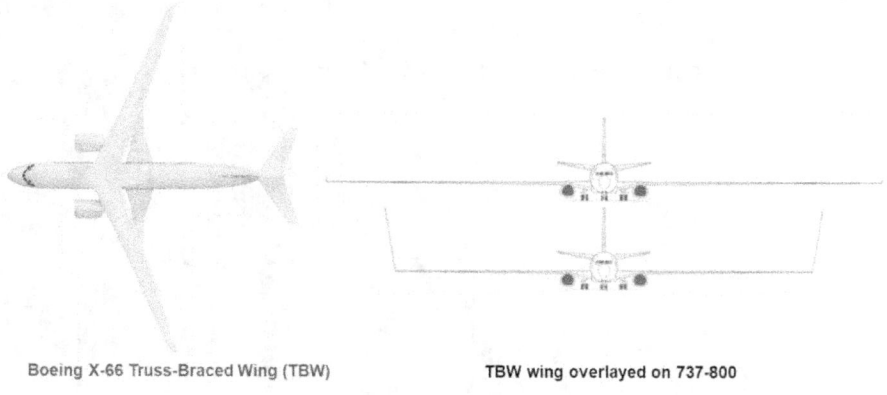

Boeing X-66 Truss-Braced Wing (TBW)   TBW wing overlayed on 737-800

Source: Subsonic Ultra Green Aircraft Research: Phase II – Volume I – Truss Braced Wing Design Exploration [12]

This design achieves up to 30% fuel burn savings on ranges up to 3,500 nautical miles by reducing drag and improving the L/D ratio. Innovations like folding wingtips ensure compatibility with existing airport infrastructure, balancing operational flexibility and aerodynamic performance.

To address structural challenges, Boeing and NASA integrated lightweight truss systems that offload wing stress, enabling the design to maintain structural integrity while achieving high efficiency. These advancements highlight the potential of high aspect ratio wings to revolutionize fuel efficiency and sustainability in future aircraft designs.

Blended Wing Body (BWB)

One of the most promising innovations in modern aircraft design is the **Blended Wing Body (BWB)** concept. Unlike conventional aircraft that employ a tube-and-wing configuration, the BWB integrates the wing and fuselage into a single, continuous lifting surface. This design minimizes parasitic drag, optimizes lift distribution, and reduces fuel burn by creating a more aerodynamically efficient airframe.

Traditional high aspect ratio wings improve efficiency by increasing lift and reducing induced drag. However, the BWB achieves comparable—and often superior—efficiency gains by distributing lift more evenly across its entire surface, as illustrated in **Figure 8-22.** This eliminates the need for separate fuselage components that contribute additional drag and structural weight.

Figure 8-22. Example blended wing body (BWB) design

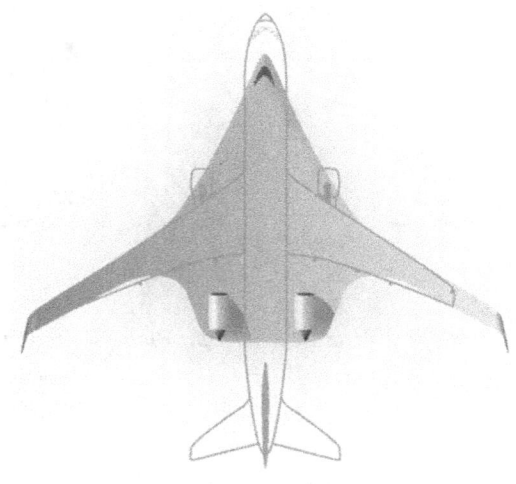

.Source: Fast Company, How JetZero aims to be the 'SpaceX of aviation [13]

Advantages of the Blended Wing Body

The BWB offers several compelling advantages over traditional aircraft configurations:

1. **Reduced Aerodynamic Drag:** The seamless integration of fuselage and wing surfaces leads to an estimated 30% reduction in drag, directly contributing to lower fuel burn and emissions.
2. **Significant Fuel Burn and Emissions Reductions:** Optimized aerodynamics and lightweight composite materials enable BWB aircraft to achieve up to 50% lower fuel consumption and carbon emissions compared to current-generation single-aisle and mid-market widebody aircraft.
3. **Increased Payload Capacity and Cabin Flexibility:** The wide interior offers greater volume for passengers or cargo, supporting innovative cabin layouts, high packing densities, and flexible freighter configurations. This opens new opportunities for both airlines and dedicated cargo operators.
4. **Noise Reduction:** Rear-mounted engines on the upper fuselage shield ground-level communities from engine noise, contributing to quieter airport operations and improved community relations.
5. **Compatibility with Existing Infrastructure:** Despite its unconventional appearance, BWB aircraft are being designed to operate within existing airport gate sizes, taxiways, and runway limits, minimizing the need for major infrastructure modifications.

Challenges in Adopting Blended Wing Body (BWB) Aircraft

The introduction of BWB aircraft in commercial aviation presents regulatory and operational challenges that must be addressed for widespread adoption.

1. **Certification Standards:** Existing certification frameworks are based on conventional tube-and-wing designs. Certifying a BWB will require new standards governing structural integrity, aerodynamics, flight safety, and passenger protection. Authorities such as the FAA and EASA will need to develop guidelines specific to BWB configurations.
2. **Passenger Safety and Evacuation:** The wide cabin layout presents challenges in meeting emergency evacuation time requirements.

Regulators will need to evaluate and approve innovative solutions for exit placement and evacuation procedures.

3. **Airport Infrastructure Compatibility:** While BWB aircraft are designed for compatibility with existing airport layouts, practical implementation may require adjustments to gates, jet bridges, and hangars to accommodate the aircraft's wider body and unique boarding configurations. Regulatory approvals and coordination with airport authorities will be essential to ensure smooth integration without disrupting operations.

4. **Operational Certification:** Airlines introducing BWB aircraft will require operational certification, including pilot training, flight operations procedures, and maintenance protocols tailored to the aircraft's novel handling and systems.

5. **Global Regulatory Harmonization:** Coordinated certification across multiple jurisdictions will be essential for international operations. Close collaboration among global aviation authorities will be needed to align certification frameworks.

Addressing these challenges will require collaboration between manufacturers, regulators, airlines, and industry stakeholders. Establishing clear certification pathways and achieving global regulatory alignment will be key to enabling the successful integration of BWB aircraft into commercial fleets.

EXAMPLE 8-5. JetZero's Blended Wing Body (BWB) Design
An example of BWB innovation is JetZero's Blended Wing Body, shown in **Figure 8-23**. JetZero's design achieves a 30% reduction in aerodynamic drag compared to conventional aircraft. With its simplified structure, composite materials, and optimized aerodynamics, JetZero anticipates delivering up to 50% reductions in fuel burn and emissions—an achievement that directly aligns with global aviation industry goals to achieve net-zero emissions by 2050.

Figure 8-23. JetZero's blended wing body (BWB) design

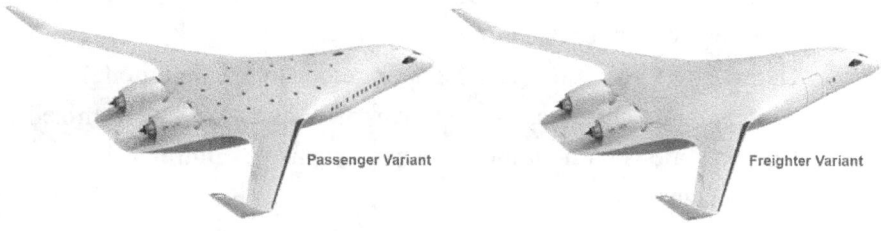

Passenger Variant

Freighter Variant

Source: Image of JetZero aircraft concept. Courtesy of JetZero, retrieved from
https://www.jetzero.aero [14]

JetZero's scalable family of Blended Wing Body (BWB) variants—designed to carry more than 250 passengers -offers flexible solutions for both short-haul, high-frequency routes and long-range operations. The aircraft's expansive interior volume also makes it well-suited for freighter applications, meeting the growing demand for increased cargo capacity and operational efficiency in the air freight sector.

JetZero's BWB platform represents a practical, near-term solution to the pressing challenges of sustainability, fuel efficiency, and fleet modernization in commercial aviation. By combining advanced aerodynamics, proven propulsion technologies, and next-generation composite structures, JetZero is positioned as a transformative force in the future of airliner design and operation.

8.2 Aircraft Weight Optimization Strategies

Aircraft manufacturers continually enhance fleet performance through targeted weight optimizations. While increasing Maximum Takeoff Weight (MTOW) has the most significant impact, adjustments to Maximum Zero Fuel Weight (MZFW) and Maximum Landing Weight (MLW), alongside reductions in Operating Empty Weight (OEW), play essential roles. These enhancements address several operational benefits:

- **Enhanced Payload:** Increasing MTOW and MZFW, combined with reductions in OEW, allows aircraft to carry more passengers or cargo, directly boosting airline revenue potential.

- **Extended Range:** Weight increases often coincide with improvements in fuel capacity and efficiency, enabling aircraft to operate over longer distances.
- **Competitive Advantage:** Weight upgrades to existing models help manufacturers stay competitive, offering airlines modernized aircraft options without incurring the expense of entirely new designs.

These weight optimizations enhance operational benchmarks, enabling aircraft to meet evolving industry demands while maintaining compliance with regulatory requirements.

The evolution of the Airbus A330-300's Maximum Takeoff Weight (MTOW) illustrates the benefits of targeted weight enhancements. As shown in **Figure 8-24**, early A330-300 models (produced between 1993 and 1998) had MTOWs of 212 to 217 tonnes, supporting operational ranges of 3,900 to 4,300 nautical miles. Airbus later introduced performance improvement packages, progressively increasing MTOW to 242 tonnes, extending the range to 6,100 nautical miles. These upgrades significantly enhanced fuel efficiency, range, and payload capacity, making the A330 series versatile and well-suited to diverse market demands.

Figure 8-24. A330-300 MTOW evolution

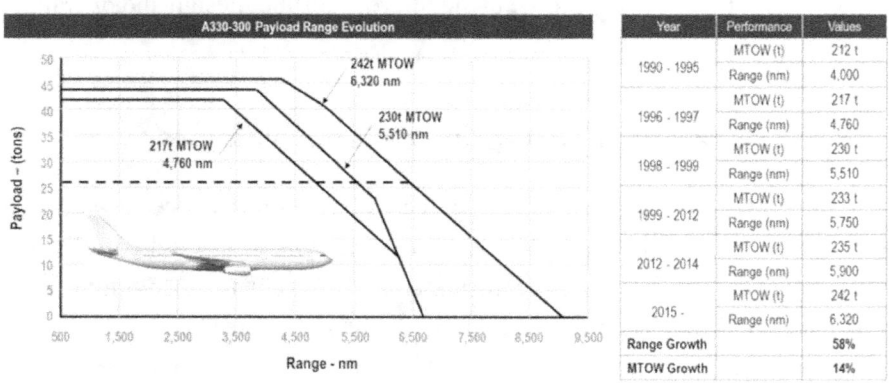

Year	Performance	Values
1990 - 1995	MTOW (t)	212 t
	Range (nm)	4,000
1996 - 1997	MTOW (t)	217 t
	Range (nm)	4,760
1998 - 1999	MTOW (t)	230 t
	Range (nm)	5,510
1999 - 2012	MTOW (t)	233 t
	Range (nm)	5,750
2012 - 2014	MTOW (t)	235 t
	Range (nm)	5,900
2015 -	MTOW (t)	242 t
	Range (nm)	6,320
Range Growth		58%
MTOW Growth		14%

Source: Airbus "A330 Airplane Characteristics for Airport Planning" document, with modifications by the author [8]

Increasing an aircraft's Maximum Takeoff Weight (MTOW) allows for greater fuel and payload capacity, extending operational range and improving economic performance. However, this often leads to higher wing loading, where the added weight is not offset by proportional wing area enlargement. Higher wing loading impacts operations by requiring longer runways for takeoff due to increased lift speeds and placing greater stress on the wings and landing gear. It also reduces climb performance, responsiveness to control inputs, and stability in turbulence, affecting overall performance and passenger comfort.

These challenges are critical considerations for airport planning and runway design to accommodate heavier aircraft. Manufacturers address these issues through innovations such as more powerful engines, advanced aerodynamic wing designs, load alleviation systems, and lightweight composite materials that enhance structural resilience without adding weight.

While increasing MTOW offers significant benefits—expanded route options, greater cargo capacity, and enhanced passenger services—these advantages must be carefully balanced against the operational challenges and costs associated with higher wing loading.

For more substantial design weight increases or improvements to fatigue resistance, significant structural modifications are often required. These adjustments, particularly to critical areas like wing boxes, fuselages, and landing gear, typically cannot be retrofitted to existing aircraft but instead necessitate a new production standard.

EXAMPLE 8-6. A330-300 MTOW Retrofits

Figure 8-25 illustrates the progressive enhancements in the A330-300's Maximum Takeoff Weight (MTOW), achieved through a combination of retrofittable adjustments and substantial structural upgrades. Retrofits typically involve structural reinforcements that enable existing aircraft to support higher MTOWs, improving payload and range capabilities without requiring extensive overhauls.

Further increases in MTOW, however, often require more extensive, non-retrofittable modifications. These include upgrades such as higher engine thrust ratings, aerodynamic refinements, and the integration of load alleviation systems to maintain performance under increased weight. Such modifications necessitate significant structural redesigns, making them available only on newer production models introduced after these enhancements were implemented.

Figure 8-25. A330-300 MTOW retrofit evolution

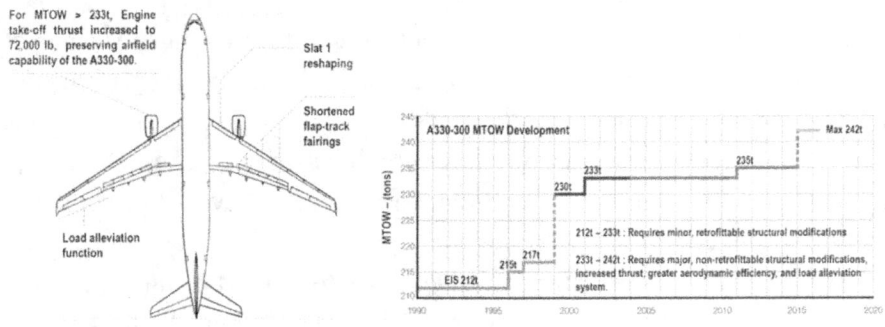

Source: Airbus FAST Magazine [15]

In addition to MTOW enhancements, reductions in Operating Empty Weight (OEW) bring critical advantages in efficiency and performance. A lighter OEW improves fuel efficiency, increases payload capacity, and extends operational range. This enables airlines to achieve fuel savings and lower operating costs while maximizing revenue potential through increased passenger or cargo capacity. For long-haul operations, reduced OEW is particularly beneficial, allowing for extended range capabilities that meet the demands of global route networks.

Through a combination of retrofittable MTOW enhancements and OEW optimizations, manufacturers provide solutions that balance economic and environmental goals, ensuring that aircraft remain competitive and adaptable to evolving industry requirements.

8.3 Engine Technology Evolution

The aviation industry continuously advances aircraft performance, efficiency, and reliability through innovations in engine technology. These advancements fall into two primary categories: complete engine upgrades and Product Improvement Packages (PIPs), each addressing specific aspects of performance and operational efficiency.

Complete engine upgrades involve extensive redesigns incorporating advanced materials and technologies. These upgrades deliver significant improvements in thrust, fuel efficiency, and environmental performance. While they often require new certification and structural adjustments to the aircraft, they provide substantial reductions in emissions and noise levels, aligning with the industry's sustainability objectives.

In contrast, Product Improvement Packages focus on incremental enhancements to existing engines, targeting specific areas such as fuel burn, emissions, and maintenance intervals. PIPs allow airlines to benefit from improved efficiency and cost savings without requiring significant modifications to the aircraft.

Both approaches play an important role in the evolution of aircraft capabilities, driving sustainability, cost-effectiveness, and competitiveness in a rapidly evolving industry.

Engine Technology Advancements

Major advancements in engine technology emphasize fuel efficiency, durability, and reliability, establishing new benchmarks in aircraft performance and operational longevity. These transformative upgrades offer the following benefits:

- **Enhanced Fuel Efficiency:** Advanced materials and optimized aerodynamics reduce fuel consumption, lowering operating costs and improving overall efficiency.
- **Improved Durability and Reliability:** Innovations such as ceramic matrix composites and 3D-printed components enable engines to withstand higher operating temperatures, reducing wear and extending engine life.
- **Environmental Gains:** By cutting emissions and noise levels, these engines support the aviation industry's sustainability goals and compliance with stricter environmental standards.

The transition from the CFM56 to the LEAP engine for the A320NEO and 737 MAX families demonstrates a significant leap in fuel-efficient engine technology. Featuring materials like ceramic matrix composites and 3D-printed parts, the LEAP engine offers a higher bypass ratio, greater thrust, and up to 15% improved fuel efficiency compared to its predecessor. Additionally, it achieves reductions in emissions and noise, aligning with contemporary sustainability targets.

This upgrade required new certification and structural adjustments, highlighting the substantial improvements over the CFM56. As illustrated in **Figure 8-26**, the LEAP-1B engine demonstrates a 15% reduction in Specific Fuel Consumption (SFC) compared to the CFM56-7BE, underscoring the transformative impact of advanced engine technology on aircraft efficiency and operational performance.

Figure 8-26. CFM56-7BE vs. LEAP-1B SFC improvement

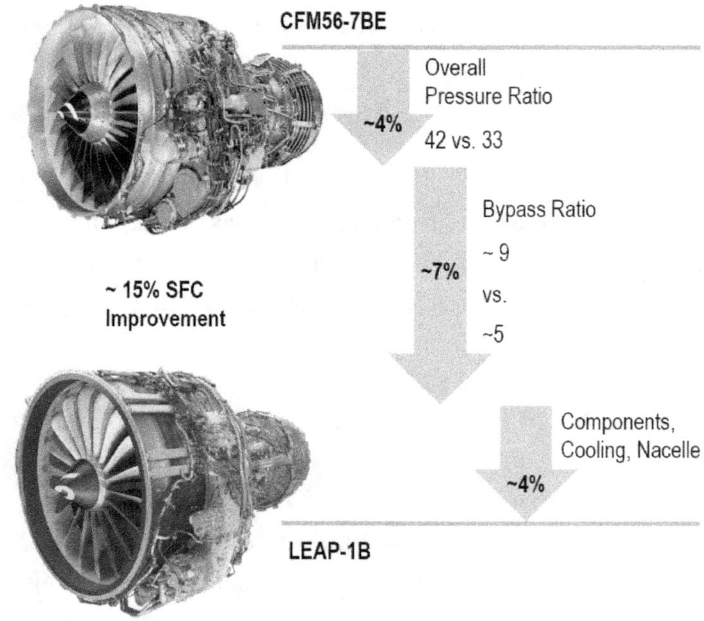

Source: CFM with analysis by the author

Building on the **LEAP** engine's advancements, the transition from the V2500-A5 to the **PW1100G (GTF)** on the A320 Family highlights the transformative impact of geared turbofan technology. The PW1100G features innovative geared architecture and advanced materials, significantly reducing fuel burn, emissions, and noise while aligning with the aviation industry's sustainability goals.

This trend continues across other major engine upgrade programs. For example, the transition from the CF34-10 to the PW1900G on the Embraer

E190/E195-E2 leverages geared turbofan technology to achieve notable gains in efficiency and environmental performance.

The Trent 7000, derived from the Trent 1000 used on the 787 Family, brings similar advancements to the A330NEO. With a higher bypass ratio, improved aerodynamics, and advanced materials, the Trent 7000 delivers up to 10% better fuel efficiency than its predecessor, the Trent 700. It also achieves reductions in emissions and noise while providing increased thrust, making it a key enabler of the A330NEO's enhanced range and payload capabilities.

Product Improvement Packages (PIPs)

Engine Product Improvement Packages (PIPs) are targeted upgrades that enhance legacy engine performance through material improvements, aerodynamic refinements, and system optimizations. These updates improve fuel efficiency, reduce emissions, and extend engine service life, while also lowering maintenance costs. Although optional, PIPs offer significant operational savings and performance gains, making them a valuable investment for operators seeking to improve efficiency and sustainability.

EXAMPLE 8-7. The CFM56-7B Tech Insertion

Illustrated in **Figure 8-27**, the CFM56-7B Tech Insertion is a PIP designed for the CFM56-7B engine used in Boeing 737 Next Generation aircraft. This upgrade includes material advancements, improved aerodynamics, and enhanced cooling systems, which collectively enhance fuel efficiency, reduce emissions, and increase engine durability. These enhancements lower maintenance costs and improve environmental performance, boosting the overall value of the engine.

Figure 8-27. CFM56-7B/3: Tech Insertion modification

High-Pressure Turbine;
Improved Blades

Combustor;
Improved Cooling

Low-Pressure Turbine ;
Stg 1 Nozzle Improved Durability

High-Pressure Compressor ;
Optimized Blades

Source: CFM with analysis by the author

While PIPs deliver clear benefits, they also present challenges. Engine upgrades create distinct sub-markets, where specific aircraft-engine combinations may face limited demand, potentially impacting asset liquidity and resale value. Additionally, some PIPs incorporate unique components incompatible with other engine variants, leading to increased maintenance costs and difficulties sourcing replacement parts, particularly for older or niche models.

For aviation stakeholders, understanding the trade-offs of PIPs is essential. These upgrades can differentiate aircraft models within a fleet and increase their operational efficiency and market appeal, but careful evaluation of investment, demand, and long-term maintenance considerations is crucial to optimize fleet performance and financial returns.

EXAMPLE 8-8. Evolution of the Trent 1000 and GEnx Engines through PIPs

As illustrated in **Figure 8-28**, the Trent 1000 and GEnx engines have undergone continuous evolution through Product Improvement Packages

(PIPs), each aimed at enhancing performance, efficiency, and reliability. These PIPs introduce critical advancements in durability, fuel burn, and thrust, culminating in engines that deliver industry-leading efficiency and reduced maintenance costs. The latest iterations align with sustainability and cost-effectiveness goals, making these engines increasingly attractive to operators.

Figure 8-28. GEnx & Trent 1000 PIP evolution

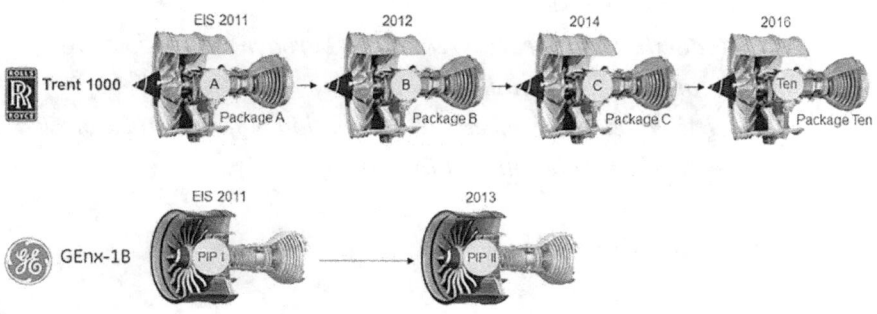

Source: Author's analysis

While these improvements provide significant operational advantages, they also present challenges for investors. Enhanced fuel efficiency and reliability drive demand for upgraded engines, but each PIP introduces market segmentation, impacting the liquidity of specific engine variants. Additionally, non-interchangeable components between PIPs complicate part sourcing and increase maintenance complexity. Careful evaluation of technological benefits versus potential resale and maintenance challenges is essential for informed investment decisions.

Industry Perspective 8-4. *Boeing 737NG PIP Advancements*

*The Boeing 737 Next Generation (NG) illustrates how systematic aerodynamic upgrades and engine Product Improvement Packages (PIPs) can substantially enhance aircraft efficiency and extend service life. As shown in **Figure 8-29**, Boeing's targeted enhancements for the 737NG have delivered significant fuel efficiency gains and operational cost reductions, highlighting the value of continuous improvement in commercial aviation.*

Between its introduction in 1998 and 2013, Boeing implemented several key upgrades to the 737NG:

- **Blended Winglets (2001):** *Reduced aerodynamic drag by mitigating wingtip vortices, improving fuel efficiency.*
- **Lighter Carbon Brakes:** *Decreased aircraft weight, further enhancing fuel consumption.*
- **CFM56-7B Engine PIP (Tech Insertion):** *Improved engine performance, fuel efficiency, and reliability, lowering both fuel use and maintenance costs.*
- **Drag Reduction Features:** *Streamlined aerodynamic efficiency through targeted drag minimization.*
- **Scimitar Winglets:** *Enhanced drag reduction with a distinct curved structure, achieving additional fuel savings.*

Figure 8-29. *737NG PIP evolution*

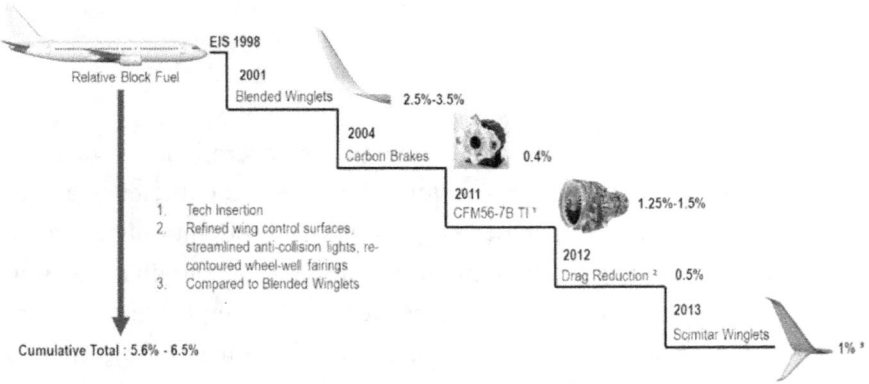

Source: Author's analysis

Collectively, these advancements reduced fuel burn by 5.6% to 6.5%, offering airlines lower operational costs and improved environmental performance. Boeing's strategy demonstrates the industry's commitment to leveraging incremental improvements to maintain competitiveness, meet sustainability goals, and deliver greater value to operators.

Next Generation Propulsion Revolution

Building on aerodynamic advancements, the next significant leap in aircraft efficiency lies in revolutionary propulsion technologies, particularly engines with higher bypass ratios that promise substantial reductions in fuel consumption and emissions. As shown in **Figure 8-30**, the CFM RISE™ (Revolutionary Innovation for Sustainable Engines) and Rolls-Royce UltraFan™ represent groundbreaking approaches to advancing propulsive efficiency.

Figure 8-30. CFM RISE & Rolls-Royce UltraFan engines

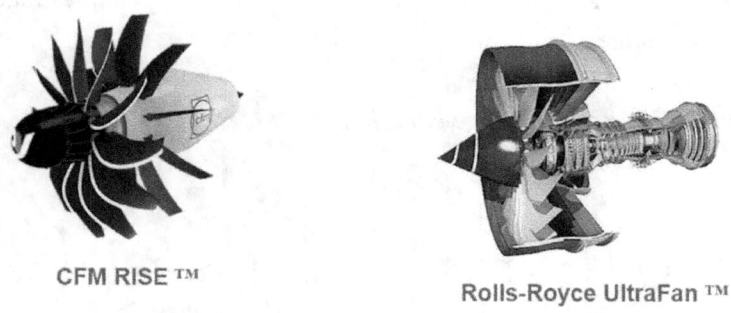

CFM RISE ™

Rolls-Royce UltraFan ™

Source: CFM and Rolls-Royce

The **CFM RISE engine** employs an open-fan architecture with an ultra-high bypass ratio of up to 70:1, significantly surpassing current turbofan engines. This unducted fan design reduces nacelle weight and drag, achieving an estimated 20% improvement in fuel burn compared to today's engines. Advanced aerodynamic features, such as pitch-adjustable fan blades, enhance adaptability across diverse flight conditions, positioning RISE as a versatile and sustainable propulsion solution.

The **Rolls-Royce UltraFan** utilizes a ducted turbofan design with a 15:1 bypass ratio, facilitated by a geared power gearbox that optimizes fan and core speeds. This architecture allows for a larger fan diameter, greater thermal efficiency, and enhanced propulsive performance. Incorporating lightweight composites and variable pitch fan blades, the UltraFan achieves up to a 25% reduction in fuel burn compared to first-generation Trent engines, making it suitable for both narrowbody and widebody aircraft.

These engines offer distinct pathways to superior fuel efficiency and environmental performance. The RISE's open-fan design emphasizes airflow and reduced weight, while the UltraFan's internal optimizations and advanced materials enhance overall efficiency. Together, they represent pivotal advancements in sustainable aviation propulsion, supporting the industry's net-zero emissions goals for 2050 and marking a transformative era in commercial aviation.

Industry Perspective 8-5: *Performance and the Breguet Equation*

*The Breguet Range Equation is a fundamental tool for analyzing aircraft performance, incorporating weight, fuel burn, and aerodynamic efficiency. As shown in **Figure 8-31**, it illustrates several core principles that drive an aircraft's range:*

Figure 8-31. *Breguet range equation*

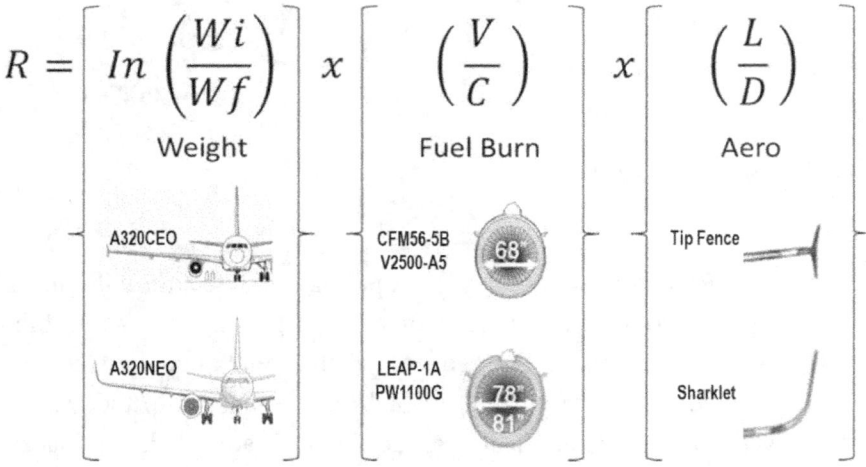

$$R = \left[\ln\left(\frac{Wi}{Wf}\right) \right] \times \left[\left(\frac{V}{C}\right) \right] \times \left[\left(\frac{L}{D}\right) \right]$$

1. ***Propulsion Efficiency:*** *A lower Specific Fuel Consumption (SFC) in the propulsion system directly increases range by improving fuel efficiency.*
2. ***Aerodynamic Efficiency (L/D):*** *A higher lift-to-drag (L/D) ratio enhances aerodynamic performance, enabling the aircraft to achieve greater range with the same fuel load.*
3. ***Weight Efficiency (Wi/Wf):*** *The Breguet Range Equation demonstrates that range depends logarithmically on the weight*

ratio (Wi/Wf), meaning small improvements in weight efficiency have a significant impact—especially on long flights. Reducing Operational Empty Weight (OEW) increases the initial-to-final weight ratio, lowering fuel burn per mile and extending range.

By quantifying these factors, the Breguet Range Equation offers a systematic framework for optimizing aircraft design and operations to maximize range and efficiency.

Key Takeaways

1. **Importance of Performance Enhancements:** Aircraft performance enhancements—including aerodynamic refinements, weight optimization, engine upgrades, and freighter-specific modifications—are critical for improving efficiency, reducing costs, and meeting sustainability targets. These strategies enable manufacturers and operators to adapt to industry demands while remaining competitive. However, trade-offs exist; for instance, increasing MTOW can raise wing loading, requiring longer runways and more powerful engines, while high aspect ratio wings may necessitate infrastructure adjustments like folding wingtips. Achieving optimal performance requires balancing these factors.

2. **Aerodynamic Enhancements**
   - **Wingtip Innovations:** Technologies like winglets and raked wingtips reduce induced drag, improve lift-to-drag (L/D) ratios, and enhance fuel efficiency.
   - **Next-Generation Designs:** High aspect ratio wings and Blended Wing Body (BWB) configurations reduce fuel burn and emissions by optimizing aerodynamic efficiency.
   - **Active Wing Technologies:** Features such as Gust Load Alleviation (GLA) dynamically adjust wing surfaces in flight, reducing structural loads and improving overall performance.

3. **Weight Optimization Strategies**
   - **Increasing Maximum Takeoff Weight (MTOW):** Structural enhancements expand payload and range capabilities but require addressing challenges like higher wing loading.
   - **Reducing Operating Empty Weight (OEW):** Employing lighter materials and eliminating non-essential components increases payload capacity and operational range.
   - **Structural Reinforcements and Certifications:** Upgrades to load-bearing components and regulatory compliance ensure safety and operational efficiency.
   - **Engine Performance Improvements**
   - **Complete Engine Upgrades:** Advanced technologies like geared turbofans and higher bypass ratios enhance thrust, fuel efficiency, and emissions performance.

- **Product Improvement Packages (PIPs):** Incremental updates to legacy engines improve fuel consumption, extend maintenance intervals, and reduce emissions.
- **Next-Generation Propulsion Technologies:** Revolutionary engines like CFM RISE and Rolls-Royce UltraFan deliver transformative fuel efficiency and emissions reductions, aligning with net-zero goals.

Case Study 8-1. Performance Enhancement Strategies

Figure 8-32. A320CEO & A320NEO payload range

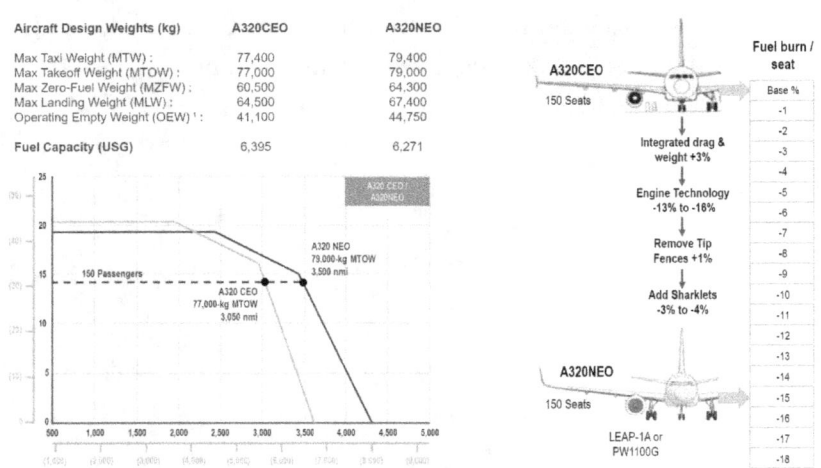

Source: Airbus. "A320 Airplane Characteristics for Airport Planning" with analysis by the author [15]

Questions:

1. Analyze the differences in MTOW, MZFW, and MLW between the A320CEO and A320NEO. How do these changes impact the payload-range performance of the A320NEO compared to the A320CEO?

2. How does the A320NEO compensate for the increased weight and aerodynamic drag compared to the A320CEO?

3. Based on the provided payload-range chart, how does the A320NEO's performance compare to the A320CEO in terms of payload capacity and range?

4. Compare the Sharklet design on the A320NEO to the original tip fences on the A320CEO. Analyze how the Sharklet's aerodynamic improvements contribute to performance benefits beyond just fuel efficiency, such as reduced takeoff distances and climb performance,

Case Study 8-2. MTOW Improvement

Figure 8-33. Payload range diagram

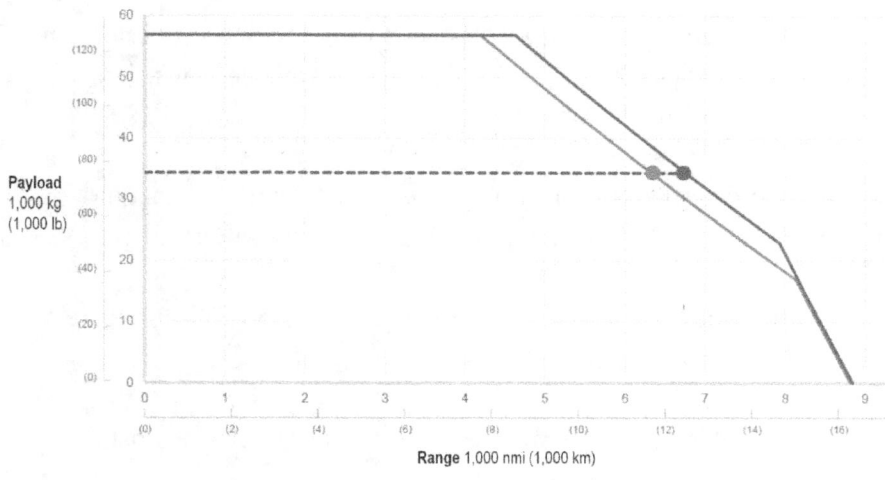

Source: Author's analysis

Questions:

1. Analyze how the increased MTOW impacts the operational flexibility of the aircraft when flying with maximum passenger payload. Based on the chart, what are the key advantages for long-haul missions?

2. Evaluate the additional payload capacity provided by the higher MTOW variant when operating on shorter routes. How might this influence revenue generation for the airline?

3. Compare the payload-range trade-offs for the standard MTOW and higher MTOW variants. How does the higher MTOW improve the aircraft's versatility across various mission profiles?

4. Given the benefits of increased MTOW, how might an airline use this capability to optimize fleet operations and route planning?

References

[1] S. Gudmundsson, "The anatomy of the wing," in *General Aviation Aircraft Design*. Elsevier, 2014.

[2] W. Freitag and E. T. Schulze, "Blended winglets improve performance," *Boeing Aero Magazine*, Q3 2009. [Online]. Available: https://www.boeing.com/commercial/aeromagazine

[3] The Air Transport Action Group, *Beginner's Guide to Aviation Efficiency*, Jun. 2009. [Online]. Available: https://www.atag.org/

[4] Aviation Partners Boeing. [Online]. Available: https://aviationpartnersboeing.com/index.php

[5] Boeing, *Airplane Performance Analysis and 777 Characteristics*, Flight Operations Engineering, May 2019.

[6] Boeing, *Commercial Airplanes Reference Guide*, 2023.

[7] A. Macheras [@AlexInAir], "A330NEO optimized wing." [Online]. Available: https://twitter.com/AlexInAir, accessed May 2024.

[8] Airbus, "A330 Airplane Characteristics for Airport Planning," AC A330, Jul. 2023. [Online]. Available: https://aircraft.airbus.com/en/customer-care/fleet-wide-care/airport-operations-and-aircraft-characteristics/aircraft-characteristics

[9] C. Heller and R. Apps, "The next-generation single-aisle: Implications for the composites industry," *CompositeWorld*, Jun. 14, 2024. [Online]. Available: https://www.compositesworld.com/

[10] T. Lampl, R. Königsberger, and M. Hornung, "Design and evaluation of distributed electric drive architectures for high-lift control systems," *Institute of Aircraft Design, Technical University of Munich*, Boltzmannstraße 15, 85748 Garching, Germany, [n.d.].

[11] N. A. Harrison, D. G. Akiyama, and G. M. Gatlin, "Transonic truss-braced wing maturation," presented at the *7th UTIAS International Workshop on Aviation and Climate Change*, Boeing Research & Technology, May 19-21, 2021.

[12] NASA, *NASA/CR-2025-218704/Volume I: Subsonic Ultra Green Aircraft Research: Phase II – Volume I – Truss Braced Wing Design Exploration*, M. K. Bradley, C. K. Droney, and T. J. Allen, Boeing Research and Technology, Huntington Beach, CA, USA, 2015. [Online]. Available: https://www.nasa.gov/

[13] S. Karlin, "How JetZero aims to be the 'SpaceX of aviation'," *Fast Company Magazine*, May 31, 2023. [Online]. Available: https://www.fastcompany.com/

[14] JetZero, "Image of Passenger & Cargo Variant." [Online]. Available: https://www.jetzero.aero/, accessed Nov. 2024.

[15] V. Lebas, "Incremental Development: Keeping the A330 Ahead of the Game," *Airbus FAST Magazine Special Edition*, Oct. 2015.

[16] Airbus, "A320 Airplane Characteristics for Airport Planning," AC A320, Dec. 2023. [Online]. Available: https://aircraft.airbus.com/en/customer-care/fleet-wide-care/airport-operations-and-aircraft-characteristics/aircraft-characteristics

Glossary

Adaptive Payload. The variable payload capacity of an aircraft that adjusts based on specific operational conditions, such as route distance, fuel requirements, environmental factors, and aircraft configuration. Adaptive payload reflects the trade-offs between payload weight and fuel load within the aircraft's Maximum Takeoff Weight (MTOW), optimizing performance for a given mission.

Aerodynamic Efficiency. A measure of how effectively an aircraft generates lift relative to the drag it produces, typically represented by the lift-to-drag ratio (L/D ratio). Higher aerodynamic efficiency indicates that the aircraft can produce more lift with less drag, improving fuel economy, range, and overall performance. Aerodynamic efficiency is influenced by factors such as wing design, aspect ratio, airfoil shape, surface smoothness, and the use of drag-reducing technologies like winglets or raked wingtips.

Airplane Characteristics for Airport Planning (ACAP) Document. A technical reference manual published by aircraft manufacturers that provides comprehensive data on an aircraft's physical, performance, and operational characteristics. The ACAP document is primarily used by airport authorities, planners, and engineers to ensure infrastructure compatibility and operational safety. Key information includes aircraft dimensions, ground clearance, runway and taxiway requirements, pavement loading, parking layouts, and environmental considerations such as noise and emissions. These details facilitate effective airport design, construction, and operations planning to accommodate specific aircraft types.

Air Density. The mass of air per unit volume, typically expressed in units such as kilograms per cubic meter (kg/m³) or pounds per cubic foot (lb/ft³). It is a direct measure of the amount of matter contained in each unit of air volume. Air density varies with altitude, temperature, pressure, and humidity, and is a critical parameter in determining aerodynamic performance, engine efficiency, and overall aircraft performance.

Aspect Ratio (AR). The ratio of a wing's span to its average chord, expressed mathematically as the wingspan squared divided by the wing area. It is a key measure of a wing's aerodynamic efficiency, with higher aspect ratios reducing induced drag and improving lift-to-drag performance, particularly in long-range and fuel-efficient aircraft designs.

Available Seat-Miles (ASM). A unit of airline capacity measurement, calculated by multiplying the total number of available seats by the distance flown in miles. Used to assess fleet utilization and operational efficiency.

Auxiliary Center Tanks (ACTs). Optional fuel tanks designed to increase an aircraft's fuel capacity, thereby extending its operational range, and enhancing route flexibility. These tanks are typically installed in the cargo hold within the aircraft without requiring significant structural modifications. ACTs are commonly employed on aircraft used for long-haul routes or missions where standard fuel capacity is insufficient.

Belly Cargo. Cargo transported in the lower hold of passenger aircraft, often complementing revenue from passenger operations.

Blended Wing Body (BWB). An advanced aircraft design that seamlessly integrates the wing and fuselage into a unified aerodynamic structure. This configuration reduces drag, optimizes lift distribution across the aircraft, and enhances fuel efficiency. The BWB design also offers increased internal volume for cargo or passengers and improved structural efficiency, making it a promising concept for future long-range and high-capacity aircraft.

Block Fuel. The total quantity of fuel loaded onto an aircraft prior to departure, encompassing all fuel required for the entire flight. This includes fuel allocated for taxiing, climb, cruise, descent, landing, and reserve requirements, such as contingency fuel for unforeseen delays and alternate fuel for potential diversions. Block fuel is a critical metric in flight planning, directly impacting payload, range, and overall operating costs, and it serves as a benchmark for fuel efficiency and operational performance evaluations.

Bypass Ratio (BPR). The ratio of the mass flow of air bypassing the engine core to the mass flow passing through it. A higher bypass ratio enhances fuel efficiency and reduces noise by increasing the proportion of thrust generated by cooler, low-velocity bypass air rather than the hotter, high-velocity exhaust from the engine core. This characteristic is a key feature of modern high-bypass turbofan engines, contributing to improved operational economy and environmental performance.

Cabin Configuration Rules. Standardized guidelines governing the interior layout of an aircraft, including the arrangement of seating, seat pitch, seat width, and the allocation of service classes such as business, premium economy, and economy. These rules ensure uniformity in cabin design, enabling consistent evaluations of aircraft performance, passenger capacity, and operational efficiency across different configurations and airline requirements.

Cabin Efficiency Enablers. Innovations designed to optimize the use of cabin space, enhancing operational efficiency and passenger capacity while maintaining comfort. Examples include slim-line seats, aft galley configurations, and Smart-Lav designs, which reduce weight and increase seating capacity. These features contribute to improved fuel efficiency, extended range, and reduced operating costs, making them valuable for airlines aiming to maximize revenue potential and performance metrics.

Cabin Exit Doors. Doors designed for passenger boarding, deplaning, and emergency evacuation. Their type and configuration determine an aircraft's maximum seating capacity by ensuring compliance with safety standards.

Cabin Layout. The arrangement and configuration of seats, galleys, lavatories, crew rests, and other interior elements within an aircraft cabin, designed to optimize passenger comfort, operational efficiency, and revenue potential. The cabin layout is influenced by factors such as seat pitch, seating density, service class distribution (e.g., economy, premium economy, business, and first class), and the placement of support facilities.

Cash Operating Cost (COC). The subset of Direct Operating Costs (DOC) that includes all cash expenses directly related to operating an aircraft. Unlike DOC, COC excludes non-cash expenses such as depreciation and amortization, focusing solely on the out-of-pocket costs incurred during operations. This metric is frequently used to evaluate an airline's liquidity and operational efficiency.

Ceiling (Service Ceiling or Maximum Operating Altitude): The maximum altitude an aircraft can maintain under specified conditions (e.g., at maximum weight), often constrained by engine performance or pressurization limits.

Certified Limit Weights. Weight limits for an aircraft that are defined by the operator and approved by regulatory authorities, based on the aircraft's structural and performance characteristics. These limits typically include Maximum Takeoff Weight (MTOW), Maximum Landing Weight (MLW), and Maximum Zero-Fuel Weight (MZFW). Operators may customize these limits within the boundaries set by the aircraft manufacturer to align with their operational needs, such as route structures or airport restrictions.

Climb Rate: The rate at which an aircraft gains altitude, typically measured in feet per minute (fpm) or meters per second (m/s), and influenced by factors such as weight, engine power, and atmospheric conditions.

Density Altitude. The altitude in the standard atmosphere corresponding to a specific value of air density. Reduced air density at high-altitude or hot-airport conditions increases density altitude, negatively impacting takeoff and climb performance as well as payload capacity. It serves as a key benchmark for understanding how temperature, pressure, and humidity deviations from standard conditions affect aircraft operations.

Direct Operating Cost (DOC). The total costs directly associated with operating an aircraft. These typically include expenses such as fuel, maintenance, crew wages, navigation fees, landing charges, and capital costs (e.g., aircraft depreciation or lease payments). DOC is a key metric for evaluating the economic performance of aircraft and for operational decision-making, fleet planning, and cost benchmarking. It excludes indirect costs such as marketing, administrative overhead, and ground services.

Emissions Trading System (ETS): A market-based framework designed to reduce greenhouse gas emissions by setting emission caps and enabling the trading of emission allowances. Programs like the **EU ETS** require entities, including airlines, to purchase allowances for their carbon emissions, creating financial incentives to adopt cleaner technologies and improve operational efficiency. These systems support global efforts to combat climate change by encouraging industries to limit emissions and invest in sustainable practices.

Equivalent Still Air Distance (ESAD): A wind-neutral metric representing the effective distance an aircraft would travel in still air, accounting for the influence of wind on the planned flight path. ESAD provides a standardized measure for comparing range capabilities and fuel consumption across varying wind conditions, ensuring consistent performance evaluations and operational planning.

Extended Twin-Engine Operations (ETOPS): Certification allowing twin-engine aircraft to operate on routes beyond 60 minutes from the nearest suitable alternate airport, typically over water or remote regions. ETOPS thresholds, such as 120 or 180 minutes, specify the maximum diversion time permitted under specific operational and safety standards.

Field Elevation: The vertical height of an airport above mean sea level (MSL), typically expressed in feet or meters. Elevation influences aircraft performance by affecting air density; higher elevations reduce air density, which can impact engine thrust, aerodynamic lift, and overall takeoff and landing performance. Airports at higher elevations often require longer runways or reduced aircraft payloads to compensate for these performance challenges.

Field Environment: The collective atmospheric conditions at an airport, encompassing altitude, temperature, and humidity. These factors directly influence aircraft performance, including engine thrust, lift generation, and takeoff and landing distances, requiring adjustments to payload, fuel loads, or thrust settings to ensure safe and efficient operations.

Field Length: The length of a runway available for takeoff and landing.

FLEX Derate: A thrust reduction technique that uses an assumed temperature higher than the actual ambient temperature to calculate reduced engine thrust during takeoff. This method minimizes engine wear, lowers maintenance costs, and improves fuel efficiency while maintaining sufficient performance for safe operations. FLEX derate is particularly useful in scenarios where the aircraft does not require full thrust, such as when operating on longer runways, in cooler weather, or with reduced takeoff weights.

Folding Wingtips: A structural feature designed to allow extended wings to fold at their tips when on the ground, ensuring compatibility with airport gate and taxiway infrastructure. This innovation enables aircraft to benefit from higher aspect ratio wings, which improve aerodynamic efficiency and fuel economy, without exceeding the maximum wingspan limits of standard airport facilities. Folding wingtips are commonly found on aircraft like the Boeing 777X, where maximizing wingspan during flight enhances performance while maintaining ground operations flexibility.

Fuel Volume Limitation. A constraint arising when an aircraft's fuel tanks do not have sufficient physical capacity to store the required fuel for a mission, even though the Maximum Takeoff Weight (MTOW) permits additional load. This limitation typically impacts long-range operations where fuel volume, rather than structural weight limits, becomes the defining factor for range capability. To address this constraint, auxiliary fuel tanks or payload reductions may be employed, though such adjustments often involve trade-offs between operational range, payload, and efficiency.

Geared Turbofan (GTF): An advanced jet engine architecture incorporating a reduction gearbox between the fan and the low-pressure turbine. This design allows the fan and turbine to operate at independently optimized rotational speeds, improving fuel efficiency, reducing noise, and lowering emissions. Geared turbofans enable larger fan diameters for higher bypass ratios without compromising engine performance, making them a key innovation in modern engine design.

Great Circle Distance (GCD): The shortest theoretical distance between two points on the Earth's surface, accounting for the planet's curvature. GCD is calculated along the circumference of a great circle, which is any circle drawn on a sphere with a center that coincides with the sphere's center. This measure is commonly used in aviation for route planning, providing a baseline for comparing actual flight paths with the most direct route. It assumes no wind or air traffic constraints and serves as a reference point for evaluating fuel consumption, flight time, and efficiency.

Gross Weight (GW): The total weight of an aircraft at any specific moment during its flight, including passengers, cargo, fuel, and all operational items. Unlike static weight measurements such as Maximum Takeoff Weight (MTOW) or Zero-Fuel Weight (ZFW), Gross Weight fluctuates dynamically during flight as fuel is consumed. It serves as a critical parameter for determining an aircraft's structural and performance limits at different flight phases, such as takeoff, climb, cruise, and landing.

Hot and High Airports: Airports located at high altitudes and/or in regions with elevated temperatures, where reduced air density significantly impacts aircraft performance. Lower air density at such airports diminishes engine thrust, reduces aerodynamic lift, and increases takeoff and climb distances. These airports often require aircraft to operate at lower weights or employ enhanced thrust capabilities to maintain safety and efficiency under challenging environmental conditions.

Humidity: The amount of water vapor present in the air, typically expressed as a percentage of the maximum possible at a given temperature. Higher humidity reduces air density, which can diminish engine performance and lift generation, particularly in hot and high conditions. This necessitates operational adjustments, such as increased runway length or reduced payload, to maintain performance and safety standards.

Induced Drag: A form of aerodynamic resistance generated as a byproduct of lift, caused by the creation of wingtip vortices. These vortices occur when high-pressure air beneath the wing spills over to the low-pressure region above the wing at the tips, creating a swirling motion that reduces overall efficiency. Induced drag is more pronounced at lower speeds and higher angles of attack, such as during takeoff and climb. Modern aerodynamic technologies, including winglets, raked wingtips, and high aspect ratio wings, are designed to mitigate induced drag by optimizing lift distribution and reducing vortex intensity, thereby enhancing fuel efficiency and overall performance.

In-Flight Shutdown (IFSD) Rate: A critical metric used to assess engine reliability, representing the frequency of unplanned engine shutdowns occurring during flight, measured per 1,000 engine flight hours. This rate is a key performance indicator for both manufacturers and operators, as it reflects the safety and dependability of an aircraft's propulsion system. A low IFSD rate is essential for meeting regulatory standards, such as those required for Extended Twin-Engine Operations (ETOPS) certification, and for maintaining operational efficiency and passenger confidence.

Lift-to-Drag Ratio (L/D Ratio). The ratio of the lift force generated by an aircraft to the drag force resisting its motion, serving as a key measure of aerodynamic efficiency. A higher L/D ratio indicates greater efficiency, allowing the aircraft to generate more lift with less drag, improving fuel consumption and range. The configuration of an airplane's wing plays a crucial role in its L/D ratio by influencing how effectively lift is generated while minimizing drag. Factors such as aspect ratio, airfoil design, wing shape, sweep angle, and wingtip devices all impact this ratio. Optimized wing designs reduce both induced and parasitic drag, enhancing aerodynamic performance and overall efficiency.

Long-Range Cruise (LRC): A cruising speed optimized to achieve a balance between fuel efficiency and reduced flight time. This speed allows an aircraft to operate economically over long distances while slightly sacrificing the maximum possible range in favor of shorter flight durations. LRC is widely used by airlines to optimize operational efficiency, aligning fuel savings with schedule requirements and passenger convenience. Compared to Maximum-Range Cruise (MRC), LRC is slightly faster but retains a high level of fuel efficiency, making it a preferred choice for many long-haul operations.

LOPA (Layout of Passenger Accommodations). The detailed configuration of an aircraft's cabin, specifying the arrangement of seats, aisles, lavatories, galleys, crew rest areas, and emergency exits. LOPA designs are tailored to meet specific operational and regulatory requirements, balancing passenger comfort, safety, and airline revenue goals. This layout directly affects cabin density, seating capacity, and operational efficiency, influencing key performance metrics such as fuel burn, range, and payload capability. LOPA is a critical tool in aircraft interior planning and optimization.

Maximum Landing Weight (MLW): The maximum weight at which an aircraft is certified to safely land, as defined by its structural design and regulatory requirements. Exceeding MLW can impose excessive stress on the landing gear, brakes, and other critical systems, potentially compromising safety and increasing maintenance needs. Airlines must manage fuel burn and payload during flight to ensure compliance with MLW upon arrival. This weight limit is a key operational parameter that influences flight planning, payload capacity, and fuel management strategies.

Maximum Packing Density: The weight-to-volume ratio of cargo that ensures optimal utilization of the available space within an aircraft's cargo hold. This metric is typically expressed in pounds per cubic foot (lb/ft³) or kilograms per cubic meter (kg/m³). Achieving maximum packing density is critical for maximizing payload efficiency, especially in freighter operations where balancing cargo weight and volume is essential for profitability. High-density cargo, such as machinery or raw materials, often approaches this limit, whereas low-density cargo, like consumer goods, may leave unused space even when the weight capacity is not fully utilized.

Maximum Range Cruise (MRC): The cruising speed that optimizes fuel efficiency to achieve the maximum possible range with a given fuel load. Operating at MRC minimizes fuel consumption per mile flown by balancing aerodynamic efficiency and engine performance. While this speed is highly fuel-efficient, it often results in longer flight times compared to other cruise settings, such as Long-Range Cruise (LRC), which slightly sacrifices efficiency for reduced flight duration. MRC is particularly relevant for long-haul operations where maximizing range is critical for mission success.

Maximum Revenue Payload: The total weight of revenue-generating cargo that an aircraft can carry, calculated by subtracting the tare weight of Unit Load Devices (ULDs) or pallets from the Maximum Structural Payload (MSP). This measure reflects the net payload capacity available for commercial cargo after accounting for the weight of containers or pallets used to secure the cargo. The Maximum Revenue Payload is a critical parameter for evaluating an aircraft's profitability, as it directly impacts revenue potential on cargo operations.

Maximum Structural Payload (MSP): The highest weight of revenue-generating cargo or passengers that an aircraft can accommodate, calculated as the difference between the Operating Empty Weight (OEW) and the Maximum Design Zero-Fuel Weight (MDZFW). This parameter represents the aircraft's payload capacity under structural and weight limitations, excluding fuel. The MSP is a key metric in assessing an aircraft's operational efficiency and suitability for specific routes, particularly in scenarios where payload capacity is prioritized over range.

Maximum Takeoff Weight (MTOW): The maximum weight at which an aircraft is certified to safely take off, including the airframe, payload, fuel, and any other onboard items. This limit is determined by the aircraft's structural design and regulatory approval, ensuring safe operation under normal and adverse conditions. MTOW is a critical factor in flight planning, directly influencing payload capacity, fuel load, and range capabilities. Exceeding MTOW can compromise safety and operational integrity, necessitating careful weight management by operators.

Maximum Zero Fuel Weight (MZFW): The maximum weight limit of an aircraft, excluding usable fuel, encompassing the airframe, payload (passengers, baggage, and cargo), and operational items. MZFW is established to ensure the structural integrity of the aircraft under load and is a key parameter for flight planning and payload optimization. Exceeding MZFW can overstress the airframe and compromise safety, making it critical for operators to manage weight distribution effectively. MZFW serves as a foundational reference for calculating fuel load, takeoff weight, and operational range.

Mission Profile Rules: Standardized guidelines used to evaluate and optimize an aircraft's performance throughout all phases of a flight, including taxi, takeoff, climb, cruise, descent, and landing. These rules ensure consistency in performance analysis by accounting for factors such as fuel consumption, weight distribution, engine thrust, and environmental conditions at each phase. Mission profile rules are critical for operational planning, allowing operators to assess efficiency, safety margins, and compliance with regulatory standards under various scenarios.

Noise and Emissions Charges: Fees imposed by airports on aircraft operators based on the level of carbon dioxide (CO_2), nitrogen oxides (NO_x) emissions, and noise generated by the aircraft. These charges are intended to incentivize the adoption of cleaner, quieter technologies and operational practices, helping to reduce the environmental impact of aviation.

Noise Certification: A regulatory process that evaluates the noise levels produced by an aircraft during various phases of flight, including takeoff, landing, and flyover. The assessment is conducted at specified points such as lateral, flyover, and approach, to ensure compliance with International Civil Aviation Organization (ICAO) noise standards. Aircraft that meet these noise limits are granted certification, helping mitigate environmental impact and supporting airport operations in noise-sensitive areas.

Operating Empty Weight (OEW). The total weight of an aircraft in its standard operational configuration, encompassing the airframe, engines, installed systems, crew, non-fuel fluids (e.g., hydraulic, and potable water), and standard operating items (e.g., galley equipment and emergency supplies). OEW excludes payload, which includes passengers, baggage, and cargo, as well as usable fuel. This weight serves as a critical baseline for calculating payload capacity, fuel requirements, and overall performance metrics, influencing operational efficiency and mission planning.

Overall Pressure Ratio (OPR): The ratio of the total air pressure at the exit of an engine's high-pressure compressor to the pressure at the engine intake. This metric serves as a key indicator of an engine's thermal efficiency and performance, as higher OPR values typically correspond to improved fuel efficiency and reduced specific fuel consumption. OPR influences the engine's ability to compress air for combustion, directly affecting thrust generation, emissions, and overall operating efficiency. Advances in materials and cooling technology have enabled modern engines to achieve higher OPRs while maintaining durability and reliability.

Payload: The combined weight of passengers, baggage, and cargo that an aircraft transports, excluding fuel. Payload represents the revenue-generating portion of an aircraft's total load and is a critical factor in determining operational efficiency, route profitability, and performance capabilities. The payload capacity of an aircraft is influenced by structural weight limits, such as Maximum Zero Fuel Weight (MZFW), and the trade-off between payload and fuel under Maximum Takeoff Weight (MTOW) constraints. Payload optimization is essential for balancing revenue potential with range, fuel efficiency, and operational requirements.

Payload Break: The point at which an aircraft's maximum payload capacity becomes limited by its Maximum Landing Weight (MLW) rather than its Maximum Takeoff Weight (MTOW) due to fuel consumption during flight. At the payload break, the aircraft can no longer carry additional payload without exceeding MLW upon landing. This operational threshold highlights the trade-off between payload and fuel, particularly on long-range flights where fuel burn reduces the total weight, shifting the limiting factor from MTOW to MLW. Understanding payload break is critical for optimizing aircraft performance and mission planning.

Payload Efficiency. A performance metric used to assess an aircraft's ability to carry payload in proportion to its Maximum Design Takeoff Weight (MDTOW). It is calculated by dividing the Maximum Structural Payload (MSP) by the MDTOW, expressed as a percentage. Higher payload efficiency indicates better optimization of the aircraft's structural and operational design for carrying revenue-generating cargo or passengers. This metric is essential for comparing the economic viability of different aircraft, particularly in evaluating operational profitability and mission suitability.

Payload-Range Diagram: A graphical tool used to depict the trade-offs between an aircraft's payload capacity and its operational range under various conditions. The diagram includes critical weight thresholds, such as Maximum Takeoff Weight (MTOW), Maximum Zero Fuel Weight (MZFW), Operating Empty Weight (OEW), and Maximum Fuel Capacity (MFC). These parameters illustrate how payload and fuel loads interact to define operational boundaries.

Payload-to-Fuel Ratio. A measure that represents the balance between an aircraft's payload weight and the fuel weight required for a given mission. This ratio is critical for optimizing operational efficiency, as it highlights the trade-offs between carrying additional payload versus additional fuel to extend range. A higher payload-to-fuel ratio indicates that the aircraft is more efficient at carrying revenue-generating payload relative to the fuel required for the flight. This metric is influenced by factors such as aircraft weight limitations (e.g., MTOW and MZFW), route distance, and flight conditions, and it is used to evaluate mission-specific performance and profitability.

Passenger-to-Freighter (P2F) Conversion: The process of transforming a passenger aircraft into a freighter by modifying its structural and operational components to accommodate cargo. Key modifications include the installation of large cargo doors, reinforcement of the main deck floor to support heavier loads, removal of passenger seats, and reconfiguration of cabin systems such as air conditioning and lighting to meet cargo-specific requirements. P2F conversions also typically involve updating weight and balance limits to optimize payload capacity and volumetric efficiency. This process allows airlines and lessors to extend the economic life of aging passenger aircraft by repurposing them for cargo operations, addressing growing demand in logistics, e-commerce, and freight industries.

Propulsive Efficiency: The measure of how effectively an engine converts the energy from fuel into thrust to propel an aircraft. It is influenced by the engine's bypass ratio, the design of its fan and turbine components, and the overall aerodynamic integration with the aircraft. Engines with higher bypass ratios, such as turbofans, achieve superior propulsive efficiency by generating a larger proportion of thrust through cooler bypass air rather than high-temperature exhaust gases. Propulsive efficiency is a critical determinant of fuel economy, operating costs, and environmental impact, with advancements in engine technology continuously improving this metric.

Product Improvement Package (PIP): Incremental updates introduced to enhance the performance, efficiency, reliability, or durability of existing aircraft engines or systems without necessitating a complete redesign. PIPs may include improvements to aerodynamics, materials, software, or mechanical components, often targeting reduced fuel consumption, extended maintenance intervals, and compliance with new regulatory standards. These updates are typically retrofitted to in-service fleets or incorporated into new production models, offering a cost-effective solution to maintain competitiveness and meet evolving operational or environmental requirements.

Raked Wingtips. Aerodynamic wingtip extensions characterized by a backward sweep angle, designed to increase wingspan and aspect ratio. Raked wingtips reduce induced drag, improve the lift-to-drag ratio, and enhance fuel efficiency, range, and overall aerodynamic performance. Commonly featured on long-haul and widebody aircraft, such as the Boeing 787 and 777X, these wingtips also contribute to smoother airflow and better lift distribution. Their integration often requires structural reinforcements and advanced materials to ensure compatibility with operational and airport constraints.

Reserve Fuel. The amount of fuel carried onboard an aircraft to comply with regulatory safety requirements. It is intended to cover contingencies such as delays, diversions, or other unforeseen events that may require additional fuel for the flight. Reserve fuel typically includes provisions for holding at an alternate airport, maintaining safe fuel levels in case of unexpected changes to the flight plan, and ensuring a safe margin for fuel consumption during the final stages of the flight.

Restricted Takeoff Weight (RTOW): A takeoff weight limitation applied to an aircraft based on specific environmental or operational factors that reduce its ability to safely achieve takeoff. These factors may include high airport elevation, short runway length, high ambient temperatures, or adverse weather conditions. RTOW ensures that the aircraft complies with performance requirements for safe acceleration, rotation, and obstacle clearance under prevailing conditions. It may be lower than the aircraft's Maximum Takeoff Weight (MTOW), necessitating adjustments to payload or fuel to remain within operational limits.

Running Load Limitation: A structural constraint that defines the maximum allowable weight distribution across specific sections of an aircraft's fuselage. This limitation ensures that the airframe can safely bear the loads imposed during ground operations, takeoff, flight, and landing. Running load limitations are typically expressed in units such as pounds per inch (lb/

in) or kilograms per centimeter (kg/cm) along the fuselage and are critical for maintaining structural integrity and balance. Adherence to these limits is particularly important for operations involving high-density cargo or uneven load distributions to prevent overstressing the aircraft's structure.

Seat Pitch: The distance between a fixed point on one seat and the same point on the seat directly in front or behind it, influencing passenger legroom and comfort. Seat pitch typically ranges from 28 to 34 inches in economy class, with larger pitches in premium cabins. It also impacts cabin density, with shorter seat pitches increasing passenger capacity and reducing cost per available seat mile (CASM). However, higher density may lead to increased aircraft weight, higher fuel burn, and reduced range.

Seats Abreast: The number of seats arranged in a single row across the width of an aircraft cabin. This parameter significantly influences cabin lay-out efficiency, passenger comfort, and operational performance. A higher number of seats abreast typically increases seating capacity, contributing to lower cost per available seat mile (CASM), but may reduce individual passenger comfort. Conversely, fewer seats abreast enhance comfort but may reduce overall cabin density and economic efficiency. The selection of seats abreast is often determined by the aircraft's fuselage design and operational mission, balancing efficiency and passenger satisfaction.

Short-Field Performance Package: A set of modifications designed to improve an aircraft's takeoff and landing capabilities on short runways. These enhancements typically include advanced high-lift devices, optimized spoiler deflection, and reinforced tail skids to reduce runway length requirements. Short-field performance packages enable aircraft to operate safely and efficiently at airports with limited runway availability, often improving operational flexibility in challenging environments. These modifications may also enhance payload capacity and operational margins in short-field conditions, supporting diverse route networks and mission profiles.

Structural Limit Weights: The maximum permissible weights for safe aircraft operation, defined by the aircraft's structural design and regulatory certification. These limits include the Maximum Takeoff Weight (MTOW), Maximum Landing Weight (MLW), and Maximum Zero Fuel Weight

(MZFW). Structural limit weights ensure the aircraft remains within its de-signed load-bearing capacity during all phases of operation, protecting struc-tural integrity and safety. These parameters are critical for payload and fuel planning, influencing range, performance, and compliance with operational regulations.

Structural Reinforcements: Modifications made to an aircraft's load-bear-ing components, such as bulkheads, floor beams, and wings, to support in-creased payload or weight capabilities. These reinforcements are often used to increase the Maximum Takeoff Weight (MTOW) and Maximum Zero Fuel Weight (MZFW), allowing the aircraft to carry more passengers, cargo, or fuel while maintaining structural integrity during flight. The reinforce-ments ensure that the aircraft can safely handle higher operational loads, improving its performance and capacity without compromising safety.

Space-Flex Configuration. An aft cabin redesign, commonly found on the Airbus A320, that repositions galleys and lavatories to optimize space, en-abling additional seating capacity or enhanced passenger comfort.

Structural Efficiency. A metric evaluating how effectively an aircraft's structure supports payload and fuel, expressed as the ratio of Operating Empty Weight (OEW) to Maximum Design Takeoff Weight (MDTOW). A lower structural efficiency ratio indicates greater capacity for payload and fuel relative to the aircraft's structural weight, translating into improved per-formance, fuel economy, and operational flexibility. This measure is critical for assessing an aircraft's design optimization and competitive viability.

Structural Limit Weights. The maximum certified weights that an aircraft can safely support during operation, determined by its design and regulatory certification. These include Maximum Design Takeoff Weight (MDTOW), Maximum Design Zero Fuel Weight (MDZFW), and Maximum Design Landing Weight (MDLW). Structural limit weights ensure the aircraft's in-tegrity under various loading conditions and are critical for operational plan-ning, payload management, and safety compliance.

Takeoff Distance: The minimum distance required for an aircraft to accel-erate to takeoff speed, lift off, and safely clear a designated obstacle under specified conditions. This distance is influenced by factors such as aircraft weight, engine thrust, runway slope, air density, and atmospheric conditions, making it a critical parameter for runway suitability and operational planning.

Takeoff Weight (TOW). The total weight of an aircraft at the moment it begins its takeoff roll, encompassing the Zero-Fuel Weight (ZFW)—which includes the Operating Empty Weight (OEW) and payload—and the fuel onboard at takeoff. TOW serves as a critical parameter for determining takeoff performance, runway requirements, and climb capability. It must remain within the aircraft's certified Maximum Takeoff Weight (MTOW) to ensure safe and efficient operation.

Taxi Weight (TW). The total weight of an aircraft while taxiing on the ground, comprising the Takeoff Weight (TOW) and the fuel expected to be consumed during the taxi-out phase. Taxi Weight accounts for all onboard payload, fuel, and operating items, representing the aircraft's condition immediately prior to takeoff. Accurate calculation of TW is essential for ensuring compliance with weight limits and optimizing performance during takeoff and climb.

Thrust Bump: A temporary increase in engine thrust output beyond the certified maximum rating, utilized under challenging operational conditions such as high-altitude airports, elevated temperatures, or short runways. Thrust bumps provide additional performance to ensure safe takeoff or climb capabilities but may increase engine wear and fuel consumption, requiring careful operational management.

Thrust Derate: A method of reducing engine thrust output during takeoff to conserve fuel, minimize engine wear, and extend engine life. Thrust derate is achieved by programming the engine to operate at a lower thrust setting than its certified maximum, based on factors such as aircraft weight, runway length, and environmental conditions. This practice is especially beneficial for routine operations where full thrust is not required, enhancing overall engine time on-wing performance, and reducing maintenance costs.

Thrust Ratings: Predefined engine power settings established to optimize engine performance during specific flight phases, such as takeoff, climb, cruise, and descent. Each rating corresponds to a specific level of thrust output, tailored to meet operational requirements while maintaining engine durability and efficiency. Examples include Maximum Takeoff Thrust (MTO) for high-power needs during takeoff and Maximum Cruise Thrust (MCrT) for sustained efficiency during cruise. Thrust ratings ensure the engine operates within safe and efficient parameters under varying operational conditions.

Thrust Specific Fuel Consumption (TSFC): A measure of an engine's fuel efficiency, expressed as the amount of fuel consumed per unit of thrust generated, typically in pounds of fuel per hour per pound of thrust (lb/hr/lb). TSFC provides a critical benchmark for evaluating engine performance, with lower values indicating higher efficiency. Cruise TSFC is particularly important as it directly influences an aircraft's fuel economy, operational range, and environmental impact during the longest phase of flight. This metric plays a central role in aircraft performance analysis and engine design optimization.

Tracked Distance: The actual flight path flown by an aircraft, accounting for deviations from the shortest theoretical route, such as air traffic control instructions, airway routings, or weather-related adjustments. Tracked distance provides a more accurate measure of an aircraft's operational performance and fuel consumption, reflecting real-world conditions rather than idealized scenarios.

Trip Fuel. The quantity of fuel consumed during the primary phases of a flight, encompassing climb, cruise, descent, and landing. Trip fuel excludes contingency, alternate, and reserve fuel but is a critical component of block fuel. It serves as a baseline for flight planning and fuel efficiency assessments, directly influencing operational costs and range capabilities. Accurate trip fuel calculations are essential for optimizing aircraft performance and ensuring regulatory compliance.

Tri-Spool Engine: An engine architecture featuring three independent rotor assemblies, each driven by its own turbine. This design enhances compression control, thermal efficiency, and overall durability by allowing more precise management of airflow through the engine. Tri-spool configurations are commonly used in Rolls-Royce engines, such as the Trent series, to optimize performance across a wide range of operating conditions.

Truss-Braced Wing (TBW): An innovative aircraft design characterized by ultra-thin wings supported by external trusses. This configuration allows for significantly higher aspect ratios, reducing induced drag and improving aerodynamic efficiency. By minimizing drag, the truss-braced wing design enhances fuel efficiency and extends operational range, making it particularly suitable for next-generation, long-range aircraft. However, the design introduces engineering challenges, such as structural complexity and weight considerations, which require advanced materials and manufacturing techniques to ensure performance and reliability.

Twin-Spool Engine: An engine architecture featuring two independent rotor assemblies, each powered by its own turbine. This configuration allows for more efficient compression and airflow management by enabling the low-pressure and high-pressure compressors to operate at optimal speeds. Twin-spool engines are widely used in modern jet engines due to their balance of efficiency, power, and reliability. This design simplifies maintenance compared to more complex architectures while maintaining robust performance across a range of operating conditions.

Type Certificate Data Sheet (TCDS): An official certification document issued by regulatory authorities, such as the FAA or EASA, that defines an aircraft's approved design, operational limits, and technical specifications. The TCDS outlines critical details, including maximum takeoff weight (MTOW), maximum seating capacity, fuel capacity, engine types, and emergency exit requirements. This document ensures compliance with safety and performance standards and serves as a reference for manufacturers, operators, and maintenance organizations to maintain conformity with certified design parameters.

Unit Load Devices (ULDs): Standardized containers or pallets designed to facilitate the efficient loading, transport, and unloading of cargo and baggage in an aircraft's cargo hold. ULDs are engineered to optimize space utilization, secure cargo during flight, and streamline ground handling processes. They are available in various sizes and configurations to accommodate different aircraft types and cargo requirements.

Useful Load. The total weight available for revenue-generating payload, including passengers, baggage, cargo, and usable fuel, beyond the aircraft's

Operating Empty Weight (OEW). It represents the weight capacity that can be utilized for operational purposes within the limits of the aircraft's Maximum Takeoff Weight (MTOW) and other certified structural weights. The useful load directly impacts an aircraft's profitability and operational flexibility by balancing fuel requirements with payload capacity for specific missions.

Volume-Limited Payload (VLP): A payload scenario in which the available cargo volume within the aircraft's cargo hold is fully utilized before reaching the aircraft's structural weight limits, such as Maximum Zero Fuel Weight (MZFW). This limitation often occurs with low-density cargo, such as e-commerce goods or consumer products, where the physical space required exceeds the weight constraints. Volume-limited payloads are a common consideration in industries that prioritize bulk transport over high-density cargo, influencing the design and operational planning of freighter and passenger aircraft.

Volumetric Payload: Cargo characterized by a low weight-to-volume ratio, requiring substantial physical space within an aircraft's cargo hold relative to its weight. Common examples include e-commerce goods, consumer products, or other bulky items with low density. Volumetric payloads often constrain the aircraft's available cargo volume before reaching structural weight limits, such as Maximum Zero Fuel Weight (MZFW).

Weight Variants (WVs): Predefined combinations of certified weight limits, such as Maximum Takeoff Weight (MTOW), Maximum Landing Weight (MLW), and Maximum Zero Fuel Weight (MZFW), offered by aircraft manufacturers to align with various operational needs. Airlines select WVs to optimize performance for specific missions, balancing payload capacity, fuel efficiency, and operational flexibility. Airbus, for example, employs WVs across its aircraft models, allowing operators to tailor certified weights to match route profiles, regulatory requirements, and airport constraints.

Wing Loading: The ratio of an aircraft's weight to its wing area, typically expressed in pounds per square foot (lb/ft²) or kilograms per square meter (kg/m²). Wing loading influences an aircraft's performance characteristics, including takeoff distance, climb rate, and maneuverability. Higher wing loading improves cruise efficiency by reducing drag but increases runway

requirements for takeoff and landing, while also decreasing climb performance and maneuverability. Lower wing loading improves lift efficiency
and performance in high-altitude or short-runway conditions.

Winglets: Aerodynamic extensions installed at the tips of an aircraft's wings,
designed to reduce induced drag by mitigating wingtip vortices. By improving the lift-to-drag ratio, winglets enhance fuel efficiency, extend range, and
contribute to reduced carbon emissions. Available in various designs, such
as blended, split-tip, and sharklet configurations, winglets are a common
feature on modern aircraft, providing operational and environmental benefits without significant structural modifications.

Zero Emissions Target: The aviation industry's commitment to achieving
net-zero carbon emissions by 2050, driven by advancements in technology, operational efficiencies, and the adoption of sustainable aviation fuels
(SAFs). This goal aligns with global climate initiatives, emphasizing the
reduction of greenhouse gas emissions through measures such as electrifica-
tion, hybrid propulsion, enhanced aerodynamics, and participation in carbon
offset programs like CORSIA (Carbon Offsetting and Reduction Scheme for
International Aviation). Achieving this target involves collaboration across
manufacturers, airlines, and regulatory bodies to ensure environmental
sustainability.

Zero Fuel Weight (ZFW): The total weight of an aircraft, including the Operating Empty Weight (OEW) and payload (passengers, baggage, and cargo),
but excluding usable fuel. ZFW is a critical operational parameter, serving
as a reference point for calculating fuel loads and ensuring compliance with
structural limits such as the Maximum Zero-Fuel Weight (MZFW). Exceeding ZFW limits can compromise structural integrity, making it essential for
flight planning and payload management.

www.ingramcontent.com/pod-product-compliance
Lightning Source LLC
Chambersburg PA
CBHW081652120626
46550CB00010B/2869